True stories of war at sea, on land, and in the air from the SEALs who lived them . . .

Ensign Erick Peterson describes the grueling process of modern BUD/S training, hell week, and what it takes to become a SEAL today.

Lieutenant Commander Wellington T. "Duke" Leonard, USN (Ret.), recalls his development from BUD/S graduation to his first operations in Vietnam and on to further operations in Grenada.

Admiral Tom Richards, USN (Ret.), talks about the bonds forged on the front lines, what it is to be part of a SEAL Team, and what it means to never leave a man behind.

Lieutenant Commander Vic Meyer remembers life as a SEAL stationed in the Persian Gulf and the beginnings of Operation Desert Storm.

Praise for the
Navy SEALs series

"A collection of oral histories knitted together with carefully researched narrative, *Navy SEALs: A History of the Early Years* traces the sea, air, and land forces' evolution from its WWII precursors to its current highly trained, high-tech incarnations."

—*Publishers Weekly*

"[An] oral history of the teams' harrowing combat duties in Vietnam. Loosely organized around the chronology of the conflict in Southeast Asia, the book at its heart is a tribute to the collective spirit exhibited here. A commitment to teamwork and excellence echoes throughout."

—*Kirkus Reviews*

Titles by Kevin Dockery

NAVY SEALS: A HISTORY OF THE EARLY YEARS

NAVY SEALS: A HISTORY—THE VIETNAM YEARS

NAVY SEALS: A HISTORY—POST-VIETNAM TO THE PRESENT

THE WEAPONS OF NAVY SEALS

NAVY SEALs
A HISTORY

POST-VIETNAM TO THE PRESENT

KEVIN DOCKERY

From interviews by Bud Brutsman

BERKLEY BOOKS, NEW YORK

A Berkley Book
Published by The Berkley Publishing Group
A division of Penguin Group (USA) Inc.
375 Hudson Street
New York, New York 10014

PRINTING HISTORY
Berkley hardcover edition / September 2003
Berkley trade paperback edition / July 2004

Berkley trade paperback ISBN: 0-425-19617-8

The Library of Congress has cataloged the Berkley hardcover edition as follows:

Dockery, Kevin.
    Navy Seals : a history : Post-Vietnam to the present / Kevin
Dockery.
        p. cm.
    Includes index.
    ISBN 0-425-19034-X
    1. United States. Navy. SEALs—History—20th century.   2. United States. Navy.
SEALs—History—21st century   I. Title.

VG87.D63 2003
359.9'84—dc21

                                                                            2003045101

DEDICATED TO THE MEMORIES OF

LIEUTENANT COMMANDER SCOTT R. LYON,
WHO SET A HIGH STANDARD FOR ANYONE TO FOLLOW,

and

COMMANDER FRANCIS DOUGLAS "DOUG" FANE,
WHO HELPED OPEN THE UNDERSEA WORLD TO THE TEAMS.

Contents

Chapter 1

THE END OF AN ERA

The Vietnam War had been a testing ground for the SEALs where they not only proved that the concept behind their creation was sound, but that it was outstanding. The SEALs had officially been incountry in South Vietnam within weeks of their commissioning, and remained there during the entire run of the U.S. involvement in the war. Direct action platoon began arriving in South Vietnam in early 1966. The Team's direct involvement with the Vietnam War ended with the last of SEAL Team One's platoons rotating back to the United States without relief in December 1971.

The date of 30 April 1975 does not hold a specific place in the history of the SEALs, but it is significant to many of them who served in Vietnam. At 10:15 A.M., 30 April 1975, South Vietnamese President Duong Van Minh, who had held the post only two days, announced that he was ready to transfer power to the North Vietnamese–backed Provisional Revolutionary Government. By noon that same day, Communist forces entered Saigon. South Vietnam had surrendered.

The almost legendary success of their combat actions in Southeast Asia did very little to spare the SEAL Teams and Naval Special Warfare as a whole from the postwar cutbacks in the U.S. military. After conducting thousands of combat operations in Southeast Asia, the Teams found themselves facing only a relatively few training operations and deployments during the year. In spite of their

A group of SEALs from Team Two move on shore in Spain as part of an exercise. The kneeling Scout-swimmer at the front left is armed with an HK MP-5N submachine gun with a flashlight-mounted fore-arm. He would have been the first man on shore. The following SEALs are armed with M4 carbines. The automatic weapons man at the back of the column is watching to the rear and is armed with an M60E3 light machine gun.

U.S. Navy

cutbacks in size and especially in funding, the Teams rose to the challenge and continued to better themselves in skills and abilities. This was to prove extremely valuable to the United States and its allies as the 1970s drew to a close and the world entered the 1980s.

Rick Woolard, Captain, USN (Ret.)

The standard deployment length for SEALs from both the east and west coasts in Vietnam was 179 days. As the platoon commander, I felt it was my job to stay around for another month or so to break in the platoon that was coming to relieve my platoon. So I had basically two seven-month tours in Vietnam.

We ran a lot of patrols during my first tour and conducted a lot of operations. The only person who was seriously wounded in my platoon was a guy named Skip Isham, who lost an eye due to a grenade. There were a few other fragmentation wounds. A guy by the name of Al McCoy took a piece of shrapnel in the gut the second time I got shot, which eventually forced him to be retired medically from the Navy. That was ten days after I was shot for the first time during an op.

The thing that sticks out in my mind about that first tour of duty in 1968 was how well John "Bubba" Brewton, my assistant platoon commander, I, and Third Platoon as a whole operated together. We really fit well together. The enlisted troops supported us completely, as we supported them. The conditions were great, and we had a good, solid, and fairly safe base from which to operate.

All the support we could have needed to run any kind of operation in our area was available. There was everything—we even had naval gunfire on call at one stage. Artillery support was available for some of the areas we went to. There were fixed-wing and helicopter gunships on call as well. And we had all the river patrol boats as well as our own boats to get us in and out again on an op. All in all, it was an ideal situation.

The first night I got shot, we needed gunfire support. Seawolves, I believe, only had one gunship up for a just a short period of time at that stage; they normally fly them in pairs. The guy who was able to fly flew for us running or air cover with only a single ship. You don't get a lot of people to do that, because it isn't safe—for good reason. But this was a man who knew us. We had eaten with him, we'd drunk with him, and we'd lived in the same place with him for months by that time. We were friends, and he wasn't going to let any SEAL get hurt if there was anything he could possibly do to prevent it.

These guys, the Seawolves, flew with us and for us all the time in Vietnam. You won't find a SEAL who was in Vietnam who won't say that those guys didn't bail our bacon out any number of times. We went places and did things that we wouldn't have dreamed of doing other-

wise, just because we knew the Seawolves would be there if we needed them.

One thing that sticks in my mind, one particular operation that I didn't see personally, but some of my troops witnessed it, didn't involve a lot of SEALs. One of the river patrol boats, a PBR, got shot up fairly badly and they needed to evacuate a man as quickly as possible. He was in the far reaches of the Rung Sat Special Zone, and it would have taken hours to get him to medical attention by boat. The quickest way to get him out was for the Seawolves to pick him up; there were no other helicopters available.

A lieutenant by the name of Al Billings was flying one of the Seawolves. As the boat with the wounded man aboard was going down the waterway, Billings steadied his Seawolf perpendicular to the direction the boat was going. That pilot set one skid on the bow of the boat, forward of the twin fifty-gun tub, which had been deflected to the side. He just hovered there as the boat was moving until they could get the wounded guy onboard the Seawolf. Then he took off and took him away to a field hospital.

They were still in enemy territory, and I don't know if they were getting shot at during the time of the rescue. But anybody who could do that from both a courage and an airmanship standpoint, deserves a lot of respect.

In Vietnam, if the SEALs heard a call that a Seawolf was shot down, they would drop whatever they were doing and get to that location as fast as they could. We didn't have any Seawolves shot down during my first tour, but we did during my second tour in 1969. A Seawolf did crash right after takeoff at Nah Beh during my first tour. We immediately dropped what we were doing, and I just ran through the platoon and shouted what had happened.

You didn't have to tell people what to do. If any SEAL thought there was any way he could help a Seawolf, that immediately became his highest priority. We went out and saw that the gunship had crashed in the water. By the time we were able to get to the site, there was no hope of saving anybody. But we dove on the downed bird and got the bodies out, doing whatever we could to help things.

After my first tour was over, I came back to Virginia Beach and volunteered to go back to Vietnam a second time. I wanted to go back; I had experiences my first time that made me absolutely certain that this (the Teams) was a group of people I wanted some more time with. A lot of people from the same platoon I had taken over the first time were going back again as well. I wanted to go back with them. So we built a new Third Platoon around the core of the original Third Platoon. I took that platoon back to Vietnam in October 1969. We came back in April 1970.

The core of the platoon was the same. Bill Garnett, Bill Burwell, Jerry Todd, and a few others had been in my first platoon. Then there were some great new guys who were on their first combat deployment, guys like Bill Beebe, Larry Rich—a really fine SEAL—and a number of other men who had gone through training after I had gone to UDT (Underwater Demolition Teams) for a while and then come to SEAL Team.

For our second tour, we were at the far end of the country, on the shores of the Gulf of Thailand at a place called Song Ong Doc. It was a mobile tactical support base, which meant that it was a series of floating barges that had been lashed together and were anchored offshore of this very small town at the far end of the Ca Mau province that had no roads leading to it. This was basically the boondocks of South Vietnam.

We ran patrols through the whole surrounding area. To the north of us was the U Minh Forest, which was a Viet Cong and North Vietnamese Army (VC and NVA) stronghold. To the south of us was a large no-go area, at the center of which was a SEAL Team One base called SEAFLOAT. We did the same thing there that we did on my first tour— we sought out the enemy and killed or captured him.

My opinion of the enemy was a good one. I felt in many ways that they were fighting for their own cause, what they considered the right

reasons, and I respected them. We did not kill or capture a single per-
son who did not conduct himself well in captivity. Most of these people
were ideologically motivated I think. Many of them had a little card
from Uncle Ho wishing them season's greetings for their new year,
their Tet.

The enemy's fighting ability varied from being very good for the NVA
type and more highly trained VC, to being just sort of locals without
much formal training. Tactically, some were good and some weren't. As
a group, you always have to respect and never underestimate your
enemy.

On both of my tours, we did not often see men from other platoons
because they were located throughout the country. For a good part of
the time SEAL Team Two was in Vietnam, there were only three pla-
toons from the Team incountry at any one time. This was ramped up to
a larger number—I think maybe six—by the end of the war.

But it's a big country, and we were scattered all over the place.
There had been other platoons incountry for four months, overlapping
my tours for that time. We were sent over at two-month intervals. I may
not have ever seen a single guy from one of the other platoons. At
most, we tended to see one other platoon at a time, and that was while
we were relieving them or they were relieving us.

On my second tour, we were basically running straight SEAL
operations. We had many interesting adventures. We were threat-
ened by everything from a cobra snake we ran into in a field one
night to the enemy. Primarily, we operated at night, just as most
SEALs did.

On one operation that sticks in my mind, we were transiting along
the Song Ong Doc River when we were ambushed by some rockets and
a little bit of small-arms fire. At the same time the fire was opening up
on us, there were about half a dozen sampans with civilian farmers or
fishermen in them all around us in the river. The Vietnamese were just
taking their goods to market, going home for the day, or whatever. We
went by them in this big boat, and when we came under fire, we turned

to go back and return fire. Our wake was enormous, and it swamped a number of the sampans.

The people were drowning in the water. Several of the other guys and I jumped into the water and rescued some of the people who were going to drown if we didn't pick them up. That event stands out in my mind, but we ran so many operations that I wouldn't care to try and pick out any particular one now.

There are several SEALs who I'd heard of as being superlative operators. One, of course, was Bob Gallagher. Mike Boynton was another superlative operator. Bob Gormly in the officer ranks along with Pete Peterson were great operators, too. But I wouldn't want to put out just those names as if they were the only good ones. Everybody did his job; it was not as if there was anybody in the Team who didn't give his all to making sure that everything went as well as possible.

On my second tour, there was one incident where we had a target that was in a very tough place to get to. We ended up patrolling through miserable terrain—lots of mud, lots of deep water, just a horrible, long slog to try and get to this particular place. To top it off, we were running late. It was starting to get to the point where we had to think about getting out of there because it was going to be daylight in the not-too-distant future.

We were patrolling along and, at the same time we were miserably slogging through this wretched terrain, we had to watch out for boobytraps. One of the Vietnamese SEALs, an LDNN (Lien Doan Nguoi Nhia), was walking point and he tripped a grenade boobytrap that went off. I was about two people behind him and we all ran up to him to see how he was. I expected this guy to be shredded.

The LDNN was lying on the ground on his side in the fetal position with his eyes closed. The guy was totally scrunched up within himself. We rolled him over to see just where he was hurt, but we couldn't find any blood on the guy anywhere.

In spite of his lack of obvious wounds, the guy was still tightly balled up on the ground. One of the other LDNNs sort of looked at him and shook him a bit, moving him around. Then the guy we thought was wounded opened his eyes and looked around. He felt himself a little bit, then smiled because he knew he wasn't hurt. That's when the other LDNN kicked the guy on the ground as hard as he could, telling him to get up and get moving again.

I don't know how he got away without a scratch. This grenade boobytrap detonated, but it must have gone off low-order. As sometimes happens with grenades, a piece that's not supposed to get you because you're out of range will get you in the worst place. Other times, you can be standing almost right next to the thing and the fragments will avoid you entirely. That LDNN just lucked out.

After I came back from my second tour in Vietnam, I wasn't thinking about a career. I had been in the Navy and commissioned less than three years at that point. In the Teams, I had already had three platoons over that time, one UDT platoon and two SEAL platoons with the two combat tours. I was assigned to the training unit on the East Coast. My experience in Vietnam, I believe, was the reason I was selected to go to the training unit and be the training officer.

As the training officer at Little Creek, I put through the last four East Coast training classes from May 1970 to September 1971. When I first left SEAL Team Two, I was not seriously considering staying in the Navy, but I knew that I had to serve out my committed time. I had extended for a year to make my second tour to Vietnam, so that still left some time for me to stay in the Navy.

What finally helped me decide to make a career of the Navy was one event with a lot of background. The background was that I had done two tours to Vietnam with the best people I'd ever met in my life up to that stage. Many of the salient and defining moments of my life took place while I was with these men. The second thing was that the man who had been my assistant platoon commander on my first tour had returned to Vietnam for his second tour with another platoon, been wounded, and died of his wounds.

The Navy named a ship after him. Even though I wasn't in SEAL Team Two at the time, I was invited to attend the launching and commissioning ceremony of the USS John C. Brewton in New Orleans, Louisiana. Attending that ceremony brought my experience into sharp focus. It was shortly after that event that I came back in and requested augmentation into the regular Navy—in other words, to go from being a reservist to a regular Navy officer. The reason I ended up augmenting into the regular Navy was that I knew there was no group of people on this earth with whom I would rather spend my life than the men of SEAL Team Two.

During my first tour in Vietnam, I was still single. I met the woman who is now my wife about a month before I left for that first tour. We lost track of each other for a bit. Her mom wasn't wild about her dating a SEAL and intercepted my letters, so she never knew where I was. We managed to find each other after my first tour, and we were married two weeks before I went back on my second tour.

The first thing you have to understand about being a SEAL is that, to me, it's an obligation. To be a SEAL means that whatever you do any time in your life reflects not just upon yourself but also upon everybody who has been, is now, or will be a SEAL. I take that very seriously. So it's an obligation to do well and be a good example in your life, not just to others, but to yourself. To be a SEAL also means having standards, high standards. You have to have very high expectations of yourself.

Going through basic SEAL training is tough. Training is very difficult from both a physical and a mental standpoint. You're subjected to a lot of adversity, and you come to learn certain fundamental truths that sound very obvious when you hear them said. But you come to really understand what these things mean during training. They're very simple things, such as it's better to be rested than to be tired, it's very much better to be fed than to be hungry, it's much, much better to be warm than to be cold, and it's much, much better to win than to lose.

Having said that, once you go through training, you develop a certain underlying confidence. In some forms it can be a bravado. In other forms, as time goes on, it matures into a kind of quiet confidence, a knowledge that you have way back in the back of your mind that you've seen some nasty times and whatever you're likely to be seeing at the moment, even though it might seem rather urgent or dire, in the perspective of what you have undergone before, it probably really doesn't make that much difference.

You end up having a certain nonchalance, a certain "don't-give-a-damn" attitude about things that some people might really consider problems. This doesn't just apply to when you're in the service or a military situation. My friend Larry Rich was a SEAL in the second platoon that I took to Vietnam and I actually work for him now. We're turning around his manufacturing company in Ohio. We have to borrow some money to do this—millions of dollars. Two weeks ago, we were talking to a banker who had the money we wanted.

We were nervous about it to a degree, but Larry handled himself superbly. I had told the banker that Larry and I had been in the Teams together. The banker asked, "What does that do for you?" Turning to Larry, the banker continued, "You seem to be a rather nonconforming specimen."

And Larry is. He does what he wants to do. So I joked and said that he had always been that way, which was true. But I also told the guy very frankly that having gone through training together and having been in combat together in a SEAL Team, there's a lot of stuff that you just don't give a damn about and don't get excited about. That's what training can do for you.

When I think of the word SEAL, I get a composite picture of the finest people I have ever known. The Trident to me doesn't mean quite what it might mean to newer SEALs. It's our badge, but I'm not too caught up in the symbolism of it. When the Trident originally came out, there was one for SEALs and one for the UDTs. The one for the UDTs did not have the eagle on it. And there was a different colored one for officers and enlisted. The officers wore a gold insignia, and the enlisted wore a silver one.

That has all been done away with, and the SEALs and UDTs, officers and enlisted, all now wear the same gold Trident. But I remember when the Trident that everybody is so proud of now first came out. A lot of people, myself included, were somewhat horrified that the thing was so damned big. There was a very strong movement after it first came out to reduce it to the size of parachutists' and aviators' wings or the submarines' dolphins. There's a more or less standard size for naval insignia, but this thing was twice as big as any of the rest of them.

So a smaller Naval Special Warfare insignia was designed, which I quite liked. But by the time that the Trident had gone through its design process and had gotten out to the Teams for evaluation, everybody had pretty much gotten used to the big one. So that's how it ended up staying as our insignia. So when you say Trident, a little history comes to my mind, not just this feeling of pride in the symbolism like Old Glory or anything. To me, it's a badge.

People often ask, "Why do people become SEALs?" Often, there's a very long, convoluted, and complex psychological reason cited. The answer is very simple in my mind: I think people become SEALs because they want to see if they can do it. There's a certain number of people in the world who just need to go to the limits. They don't necessarily choose to be that way; that's just the way they are. They need to go to the limits, and being a SEAL is one way of doing that.

The great thing about being a SEAL is that you get to go to the limits in the service of your country. It's a powerful argument for being a SEAL as far as I'm concerned.

Today, I think it's tougher to be a SEAL. I would love to be a new guy coming out of BUD/S (Basic Underwater Demolition/SEALs) right now. Being twenty-two years old and coming straight out of BUD/S and into the Teams would be the beginning of a great adventure. But I think they have a tougher road ahead of them from the moment they graduate than people did back in my time some thirty-odd years ago.

When I went through training in 1966, very few people outside the Navy and the services knew anything at all about the SEALs. Even for quite some time after that, SEALs were just not well known. I remember talking with my little English grandmother in New York at a family reunion in the mid-1980s after SEALs had been around for more than twenty years. She said, "Well, Rick, tell me, are you still with that Navy outfit? What was it? The snails?"

For a long time, a lot of people hadn't heard of the SEALs. Today, it's completely different. A guy who graduates from BUD/S automatically gets saddled with a whole load of baggage the moment he steps off the parade ground in Coronado. There's so much public knowledge about the SEALs, so much information and mis-information about them, that it's just daunting for anybody.

All these books that are out there—some of which are quite good and a lot of which are just total rubbish—give the public an image of a SEAL. The movies are even worse in giving a slanted image of a SEAL. There are impostors and wannabes all over the place. You can't help but run into them. So a guy who becomes a SEAL today has a lot more to worry about and a lot more hanging off him than did a man who was a SEAL thirty years ago. I think there's more expectations now, for better or for worse, when a guy graduates from BUD/S.

Getting back to books and the publicity that's been given to the SEALs—much of it by guys who are in the Teams—I'd like to say that generally, SEALs divide themselves into two categories. The first category—and there are many, many more of these than in the other category—are those men who love the Teams. They love what they do in the Teams, and they love to help their Teammates and their country. That's why they are SEALs. That's why they do what they do.

The second category are those guys who love the Teams for what the Teams can do for them. They love themselves more than they do the Teams, and their focus is on how the Teams and being a SEAL can help them in their lives for one reason or another. There are only a few of those, and they make a lot of noise. I think they get undue publicity in some quarters.

There are two ships in the U.S. Navy that are named after SEALs or naval Special Warfare type people. One is the guided-missile frigate Kauffman, FFG 59, named after Draper Kauffman, one of the men who helped start it all back in 1943. The other is the guided-missile destroyer McFaul, DDG 74, named after Donald L. McFaul, a man from SEAL Team Four who was killed on the Paitilla Airfield in Panama.

There was also a ship, a Knox-class Frigate, the FF 1086, the USS John C. Brewton, named after John "Bubba" Brewton, my assistant platoon commander on my first tour in Vietnam. He was a fine man and a fine SEAL. He survived his first trip with me and was extremely lucky on several occasions.

On my first tour in Vietnam, I was wounded twice. Each time, if I had not been positioned exactly where I was, the bullets or the fragments that hit me would have hit Brewton and might have killed him. He just laughed this off each time, and I'd often remind him of the situation. We'd joke about how, when we got back to the States, he would be walking down the street one day and a safe would fall on him or something like that. He never took it too seriously.

John was wounded on Thanksgiving Day, 1969, during his second tour in Vietnam. His platoon patrolled right into an enemy base camp and he was right near the front and was hit three or four times. They didn't even realize how many times he'd been hit until much later. He went to the hospital and I basically watched him die over a few weeks.

At first, he was not expected to live until Christmas. When John survived until Christmas, they said he wasn't going to make it to New Year's. He finally passed away on 11 January 1970. I was stationed in a different part of the country when John passed away. He was in the Third Field Hospital in Saigon. It had been very difficult for me to get up to see him, but I did it as often as I possibly could.

My memories of John in the hospital are poignant for me. The first few times I went to visit him, John was very lucid and able to express himself. He was in a fair amount of pain, but he knew what was going on. The doctors had to take off his leg at the knee, then they had to remove more of it higher up. The third time, they ended up taking it off at the hip. That's where they found a bullet that had been lodged in John's hip that they didn't even know was there. It was shortly after that last surgery that he died.

The thing that struck me most about the situation was where in the hospital John had been all that time. He was in the renal ward of the Third Field Hospital. I didn't realize it until I went there, but the renal ward is where they put the people who really weren't going to survive.

I just can't say enough about what fine people the Army nurses who took care of John and all the guys in the renal ward were. It must have been tough for them to serve a full tour of duty, in their case a year, in that ward just seeing these fine young men come in all shot up or blown up. I don't think more than one or two of the patients in any given year's time actually walked out of that place under their own power. Most of them died.

Every time I would go up to visit Bubba, the beds would be filled by a completely different cast of characters. I would go around and talk to them and ask them where they're from, just kind of put them at ease. These guys had been wounded badly, and many of them were draftees, although that didn't make any difference. And you could tell, without a word being said, that they weren't going to make it, and they knew it.

When the Navy ended up naming that ship, which was already scheduled to be named after another man, the Chief of Naval Operations (CNO) Admiral Zumwalt, it decided to name the ship after John Brewton. He had known John in Vietnam. I went to the commissioning ceremony. That's when I decided that I was going to stay in the Teams.

I live right in Washington, D.C., and every time I go to the Wall—I went there just a few weeks ago with Lee Barry from New Hampshire, a friend I'd gone through training with—I look up on panel 14 West and see John C. Brewton. Every time, it's tough to keep a tear back. He passed away thirty years ago.

You depend on your friends and your Teammates to keep your memory alive. My assistant platoon commander, Bubba Brewton, who I went through Ranger School, all of my pre-deployment training, and my whole first tour in SEAL Team Two with, got killed. I haven't spoken to him since 1970, and I'm sure I've forgotten things. Bubba and I had an awful lot of shared history together—things that only happened in Ranger School or SEAL Team Two or things that only the two of us really knew. I have nobody to help stir my memory of those things.

There are a couple things that SEALs are very good at right now, three things actually that I think are very essential to what SEALs are. One is being good combat swimmers. Another is being very good at cold-weather operations. And third is being excellent scout-snipers or marksmen. I'm very pleased to have been able to help develop these capabilities within the Teams.

When I commanded SEAL Team Two from 1982 to 1984, we put a lot of emphasis on combat swimming. In fact, we developed the model for the combat swimmer course that's now still in operation in the Teams. There was a training event in 1983 that illustrates just what combat swimmers can do.

It took place in Denmark and Germany in April 1983, during an exercise called FLINTLOCK. Our mission was to conduct a ship attack in Olpenitz, a heavily defended German harbor on the eastern side of the Jutland peninsula, just south of the Danish border in northern Germany.

The people who were chosen to do the mission were four Kampfschwimmers, who were the German SEALs, and four men from SEAL Team Two who we had trained to do this sort of mission. They had

Captain Rick Woolard, commanding officer of SEAL Team Two at the time, to the left, looks on with a smile as one of the new SEAL snipers is examined by a visiting foreign officer. The SEAL is wearing a ghillie suit for camouflage and is armed with a bolt-action 7.62mm rifle.

U.S. Navy

undergone the first combat swimmer course. The men from SEAL Team Two were Joe McGuire, Ron Pierce, Caleb Esmiol, and Chuck Johnson.

The operation unfolded with a warning order issued on the day they were going to attack the harbor. The harbor was heavily defended by both German National Guard and Home Guard troops standing on a full wartime defense posture. The harbor had a very narrow mouth on the eastern side and was a mile deep in an east-to-west direction, heading toward the west. The target ships that were to be attacked were at the farthest point inside the harbor.

The four SEALs and the four Kampfschwimmers parachuted from an MC-130 aircraft with their dive gear and their wetsuits and noth-

ing else. They dropped into the North Sea at a precise spot and rendezvoused with a German coastal submarine that was waiting for them there. They swam into the sub's torpedo tubes—which are barely large enough for a man to get in to—with their dive rigs on, the first man going in fins-first, the second man going in face-first. Then they could meet face-to-face and breathe from the same mouthpiece.

In a torpedo tube, it isn't a gradual lock-in, lock-out environment. Instead, you go from thirty-three feet of sea water pressure—the depth of the torpedo tubes—to atmospheric pressure in just inside of a second. So if your ears aren't nice and loose, you blow an eardrum right away.

But they all successfully locked in—that was the easy part. They spent the next twenty-four hours waiting while the submarine approached the drop-off point near the harbor. All the while, the submarine was being looked for by the exercise "enemy." The men didn't get much sleep—they didn't have any racks to sleep in and they were in their wetsuits, still wet from the insertion, for that whole twenty-four-hour period. I think they did get a salami sandwich or something like that during their wait.

The lock out of the submarine was made the same way as the lock in: just after dark a mile or so off the harbor they were meant to attack. The two pairs of SEALs and two pairs of Kampfschwimmers swam in on the surface. The Kampfschwimmers were caught up in some kind of currents, swept away, and were never able to make the attack.

The four SEALs swam to a tactical distance outside the harbor so they could visually verify where they were. Then they submerged and, using their attack boards with their underwater clocks and compasses, they worked their way to the target. The entire distance was covered underwater, and they had to change course five or six times while staying submerged. They surfaced, just barely breaking the surface so the water was still filming over their face masks, to make sure the targets were still there. Then they approached the targets, attached their limpets mines to the ships, then swam out again.

By this time, they had gone through all the oxygen in their Draeger rebreathers, or at least some of them were running on empty. They had to surface, and two of them came up under a pier where German guards were walking around looking for them. The guards knew they were coming, they just didn't know when or how.

One of the SEALs, Pierce, was getting a CO_2 hit, which made him nauseated. He had to throw up, so he put his head back into the water, vomited, then surfaced again, put his mouthpiece back in, and the pair swam a short distance away to where they could get out of the water. From there, they exfiltrated over land. They climbed the fence, got outside the harbor, made their way back to the water, and swam out to a fishing boat, a mile and a half to two miles offshore, waiting to pick them up.

This was in April, so the water temperature was thirty-nine degrees at the surface and thirty-six degrees at a depth of three meters, where they were swimming. The SEALs were in wet suits, were in the water for probably twelve to fourteen hours, and swam a total of five to six miles.

That's a world-class combat swim. The fact that these guys were able to do that caught the attention of others throughout Naval Special Warfare. Today, SEALs are trained to do that sort of thing. Not every SEAL can do it to that extreme, but there have been several operations in Panama and elsewhere that have featured this type of skill and endurance. I was happy to be the guy who was in charge of SEAL Team Two when these skills were developed.

There had been a combat swimmer course before I became involved, but it hadn't been well conducted and didn't have any cohesiveness. About two weeks after I became CO, I was supremely fortunate to have come across the quarterdeck of SEAL Team Two a young Frenchman by the name of Francois Devoux. Francois was a member of the French Navy SEAL equivalents, the Nageurs de combat, or

In front of an awestruck crowd, this night-ops clan SEAL rapidly scales the fence surrounding the UDT-SEAL Museum in Fort Pierce, Florida, as part of the Veteran's Day demonstration of Team abilities.

Kevin Dockery

French combat swimmers, based in Toulon, France. He was on exchange with SEAL Team Two and was the first French officer who had come to SEAL Team Two to be on exchange with us, although we had sent several SEALs to Toulon to be on exchange with them.

Francois came on board and quickly proved himself a wonderful man, a great SEAL, an excellent ambassador for his country, and a superlative teacher as well as being a very hard taskmaster. I put him in charge of the combat swimmer course and basically gave him carte blanc for the equipment, people, and organization he needed, and he ran one hell of a combat swimmer course for the entire time he was here.

The people who graduated from this course—and not everybody did—went on to train the people who did the attacks in Panama and other places. I have to give myself a little bit of credit because, although Francois taught the course and developed his own cadre of instructors, I did not allow any of the people who thought they already knew about combat swimming to go though the course. These were the SEALs who had been on exchange with the Germans or elsewhere and had cross-trained with those units and thought they knew about combat swimming. They were not the ones chosen for the training, in part because they generally were too senior to go through the course. What I did was take the young, hard, tough guys, who seemed numerous in SEAL Team Two at that time, and put them through the combat swimmer course instead.

Guys like Perry Bruce, Andy Tafelski, Vinnie Naple, Mike McCarthy, Clell Breining, and a dozen or two others were the ones from SEAL Team Two who went through that first combat swimmer course. The names I just mentioned are all men who have been master chiefs of various SEAL Teams or even Naval Special Warfare Commands. Andy Tafelski is the Command Master Chief of the Naval Special Warfare Command right now (1997), maybe not because he went though the combat swimmer course, although it did make him a better man, I'm sure of that.

Chapter 2

A NEW MISSION

"Terrorism" . . . premeditated, politically motivated violence perpetrated against noncombatant targets by subnational groups or clandestine agents, usually intended to influence an audience.

—United States Code, Title 22, Section 265f(d)

With the advent of the 1970s, the world entered a new decade and faced an old adversary in a new war. Terrorism had been around since the days of the Romans. With the creation of the State of Israel in 1948, a new form of terrorism began to grow in the Middle East. Political turmoil in other parts of the world, such as India, Ireland, Spain, and Europe, gave rise to regional variations of terrorists and their groups. But it was out of the Middle East that terrorism grew the most and entered the world stage.

Aircraft hijackings were almost old news by the 1970s. Along the East Coast of the United States, the hijackings of aircraft to Cuba became almost common. Soldiers returning to base from leave on the holidays spoke about having a "Cuban Extension" on their furloughs. But it was at the 1972 Olympics that Middle East terrorism really took its place on the world stage.

The 1972 Munich Olympics was the first time the West Germans had hosted the Games since the 1936 Games were held in Berlin during the days of Hitler and Nazi Germany. The Germans were particularly sensitive about not showing a hard front in the way of security guards, police, and especially the military during the Games. On September 5, terrorists from the Black September organization climbed the fence surrounding the Olympic village and took the Israeli team captive after shooting two of them during the attack.

After a seventeen-hour standoff, the terrorists and nine Israeli Olympians were taken to the Munich airport to board a plane that would take them to Cairo. Bavarian police marksmen opened fire on the Arab terrorists in poor conditions and were unable to hit their targets before the terrorists opened fire on the captives. In the end, all the terrorists, the Israeli hostages, and two German helicopter pilots were dead. This horrific spectacle took place before the cameras of the world's news agencies, which were there to film the Olympic Games.

Germany established Grenzschutzgruppe-9 (GSG-9) to see to it that the horrors of the 1972 Olympic Games would never be repeated. In a relatively short time, GSG-9 became one of the world's great antiterrorist organizations, one that was to be emulated by a number of other governments. Great Britain also established a significant counterterrorist organization when it allotted the resources necessary to establish a permanent Counter-Revolutionary Warfare (CRW) unit within the renowned ranks of the Special Air Service. France established the Groupe D'Intervention De La Gendarmerie Nationale (GIGN).

In the United States, several special counterterrorist organizations were established and in place by the end of the 1970s. The U.S. Army Special Forces established Operational Detachment Delta, commonly called Delta Force by the public, to be the primary counterterrorist organization of the U.S. military.

To counter terrorist actions in a maritime environment, SEAL Teams One and Two both created specialized platoons within their respective Teams. On the East Coast at SEAL Team Two, the counterterrorist platoon was known as MOB-Six, for Mobility Platoon Six. On the West Coast at SEAL Team One, the counterterrorist platoon was Echo Platoon.

The two specialized SEAL platoons were tasked with conducting counterterrorist actions in a maritime environment. Possible actions could range from a ship or shore facility being taken over to an ocean oil rig suffering the same fate. The SEALs trained in how to board a ship while it was underway, climbing aboard ships, structures, and buildings, and close-quarter battle, fighting from room-to-room or compartment-to-compartment within feet of the enemy or a hostage.

The SEALs on the West Coast at least used the venerable M191A1 .45 automatic as their primary handgun for such operations. The fourteen-inch barreled version of the M16 was also a favorite. On the East Coast, and later on both coasts, the stainless steel Smith & Wesson M66 .357 magnum revolver became the handgun of choice.

In the late 1970s, the Shah of Iran was overthrown and a revolutionary Islamic fundamentalist government under the iron hand of the Ayatollah Ruhollah Khomeini took his place. The diplomats and staff of the U.S. Embassy in Teheran, Iran, were taken hostage by militant Iranian students on 4 November 1979. The fifty-two American hostages were to suffer for more than a year at the hands of their captors. From 24 to 25 April 1980, the men of Delta Force conducted Operation EAGLE CLAW to rescue the American hostages and bring them home.

A number of other counterterrorist units had conducted very successful operations to rescue their captured countrymen. The Israeli Unit 269 conducted Operation THUNDERBALL on 4 July 1976, rescuing more than 100 hostages at minimum loss to the hostages or the rescue forces. Operation FIRE MAGIC was the GSG-9 rescue of the passengers and crew of a hijacked 737 at

Mogadishu, Somalia, on 18 October 1977. The eighty-six passengers and the plane's crew were rescued with the only losses being among the terrorists. In Great Britain, the men of the SAS B Squadron conducted Operation NIMROD, the retaking of the Iranian Embassy at 16 Princes Gate on 5 May 1980 after a six-day siege. These operations were all conducted successfully, with the far greater number of casualties being on the side of the terrorists. Operation EAGLE CLAW was not to see a similar fate.

On 25 April 1980, the C-130 aircraft and RH-53D naval helicopters of the rescuing forces arrived at the "Desert One" covert forward refueling base in the Iranian desert. The difficult desert conditions forced the officer in charge of the rescue forces to abort the mission when too few helicopters were functional after a sandstorm. During the return to base takeoff attempt, a helicopter collided with a tanker aircraft, killing five airmen and three soldiers. The resulting fire and disastrous withdrawal from Iran left four helicopters abandoned in the desert, along with the hopes for the mission.

The hostages in Teheran were eventually released by their captors, shortly before Ronald Reagan took office as the president of the United States. The military was smarting from the failure of EAGLE CLAW and the damage it did to the standing of the U.S. military around the world. In the aftermath, new organizations were created to prevent such a chaotic organizational mess as EAGLE CLAW from ever happening again. And the Navy decided to create a counterterrorist organization of its own as well.

The flamboyant, charismatic, and extremely creative SEAL Lieutenant Commander Richard Marcinko was tasked with creating the new Naval CT (counterterrorist) unit. Marcinko saw to it that the new organization would be a command unto itself, and instead of being a unit or detachment, it would be a stand-alone SEAL Team. To sow confusion among outsiders who would be trying to find out about the new and very classified unit, Marcinko gave the new SEAL Team the identifying number Six. SEAL Team Six would make outsiders wonder where SEAL Teams Three to Five were.

Gathering the best talent he could find from all of the special warfare community, Marcinko gathered his new SEALs at Little Creek, Virginia, in the late summer of 1980. By November 1980, SEAL Team Six was commissioned. The small number of enlisted men and officers of the new SEAL Team, about the same number of personnel who originally manned SEAL Teams One and Two, were eventually broken down into two smaller units, Gold and Blue Teams, in the Navy tradition of a nuclear submarine having two operational crews of the same name. Instead of the several years Delta Force had to get operational, the proposal for SEAL Team Six submitted by Richard Marcinko allotted only six months for the Team to reach operational capability.

The training schedule of SEAL Team Six was brutal. In his own words, Richard Marcinko was trying to fit 408 days of training into 365. He decided that his men could sleep onboard planes. The training regime was successful, and SEAL Team Six pioneered techniques for close-quarter combat, ship boarding, and other skills that are used in all the SEAL Teams today. Weapons first used by SEAL Team Six, such as the nine-millimeter Heckler and Koch MP5 submachine gun, became standard issue in all the other Teams. Eventually, a special model of the weapon was produced specifically to fit SEAL specifications.

For SEAL Team Six to conduct some of its operations, particularly undercover or infiltration ops, they had to be able to blend in with a local population. The physical fitness standards for the Team made a group of the operators standing together look like part of a professional football team. But there was nothing that could be done about their size.

One of the means Richard Marcinko used to help his Team blend in was to choose people that had skills and work experience

The upper illustration is of the left side of the MP-5N submachine gun modified to Navy SEAL specifications. The collapsing stock is slid forward and the weapon is loaded with a 30-round magazine. In front of the 30-round magazine is the more compact 15-round magazine used for concealment purposes.

The lower illustration is the right side of the MP-5N submachine gun with the collapsing stock locked in the extended position. One of the SEAL features is shown by the ambidextrous selector lever on each side of the weapon above the trigger. On the threaded muzzle of this N model is attached a stainless steel suppressor for reducing the sound of a shot.

Kevin Dockery

beyond those of a SEAL. Men who had worked on railroads, carpenters, construction workers, and heavy equipment operators were all viewed as having a plus in their ability to blend in on a dock, construction site, or other common locations.

Another aspect of the problem of blending in with a civilian population caused some friction between Team Six and the other SEAL and UDT Teams. As a practical matter, it would have been much easier to cut someone's long hair to fit a local style than it would have been to grow it out to match another style. A wig could slip at a very inopportune moment, possibly exposing an operator and putting an entire mission at risk. To eliminate this problem, SEAL Team Six adopted modified grooming standards.

Different from the Navy or military norm, or even what was accepted at MOB-Six or Echo Platoon, the modified grooming standards at Six encouraged long hair and facial growth. Ponytails, moustaches, and long sideburns were all common in the ranks at Six. This caused a little heart-

An example of the modified grooming standards in place at SEAL Team Six during the early 1980s. This SEAL is firing an M79 40mm grenade launcher. At his feet to the left is an M203 40mm grenade launcher with the barrel slide forward in the open position for loading and safety.

Dennis Chalker Collection

burn among the operators and those at Six. Not only could the men of SEAL Team Six grow their hair out, they appeared to be constantly traveling for exotic training and they had all the best toys in the way of weapons and equipment, materials they were constantly using to push the limits of their operational envelope.

Red Cell, the Navy's Own Terrorists

A new SEAL unit was established in 1984 at the direction of Vice Admiral James A. "Ace" Lyons, deputy chief of Naval Operations for

Plans, Policy, and Operations. The official designator for the new unit was OP-6D and its name was the Naval Security Coordination Team, but it was referred to simply as Red Cell.

The 23 October 1983 suicide truck bombing of the U.S. Marine barracks in Beirut, Lebanon, credited to Islamic Jihad, killed 241 Marines and others and wounded 80. A smaller truck bomb that same day killed 58 French Legionnaires at their barracks. Earlier that same year, on 18 April, a terrorist suicide truck bomb targeted the U.S. Embassy in Beirut. That blast killed 63 and injured 120.

The terrorist actions helped point out the seeming lack of security at some U.S. installations. Admiral Lyons directed the creation of a new unit capable of realistically testing and directing the improvement of security at Navy installations. For the leadership and creation of the new units, Admiral Lyons looked to Commander Richard Marcinko.

Having rotated out of his position as the commanding officer of SEAL Team Six, Marcinko was enthused about the opportunity to create another unique organization. For the primary manpower of Red Cell, Marcinko looked to the SEALs of Team Six. The final personnel roster for Red Cell consisted of eleven enlisted men and three officers—Marcinko included. The offices for OP-6D were on the E Ring of the Pentagon.

After about four months of training, Red Cell was declared operational. The men of Red Cell had learned defensive driving at a racing school. They had become even more proficient with firearms, unusual shooting situations and state-of-the-art weapons. Demolition skills were increased as the knowledge base of the operators grew in the field of IEDs (improvised explosive devices). Even State Department and Secret Service assets were included in the Red Cell training curriculum. Red Cell became a very proficient and dangerous antagonist—effectively a Navy-supported terrorist unit.

Navy bases and other specified facilities would receive a briefing and instructions on generally what to expect of a Red Cell training exercise, but they would not be told the specific time of the upcoming incident. Navy base commanders disliked having their routines and schedules disrupted by a Red Cell security exercise, and they hated it when Red Cell made their security procedures seem lax and ineffectual.

Red Cell would attack a base surreptitiously, infiltrate the facility, and secure IEDs on high-value targets. Or the men would penetrate what had been considered very secure facilities—some of the most secure in the Navy. In spite of Red Cell taking every precaution, even to the point of filming their infiltrations for later postaction briefings, commanders still looked on the Red Cell actions as something personal.

After several years of operations all over the world, Red Cell was ordered to stand down while an investigation was conducted amid accusations of corruption among some of its personnel. Finally, the unit was brought back into action under very restrictive guidelines.

Richard Marcinko, Commander, USN (Ret.)

The postwar cutbacks in the 1970s under President Carter had relatively little impact on Special Warfare, primarily because we're so small. When you cut a carrier from the Navy budget, you save a lot of money. When you take that carrier out, you also lose all the destroyers that have to escort it. You take out a squadron of planes and all of their support needs and personnel, too. If you take away one SEAL Team, you're taking away body count, but there's no support tail to it. So the money you save if you took out a Team wouldn't even be parking meter money to the Navy.

What removing or cutting back on the Teams would do is slow down research and development and maybe slow down the procurement of new buys of equipment. But Special Warfare is supposed to be a force-multiplier; it's suppose to live off the ground. So whatever you get hold of, you use to fight with, and you steal it from anywhere you find it.

Vietnam was our small-unit war. I might hear a lot from the Vietnam Vets by saying this, but the Army had problems with discipline and general leadership. I can understand their problems. Army officers in Vietnam would generally spend only six months with the troops and then six months on staff. They weren't there on the line every day. In the Teams, we were on the line together every day. We flew in together, we stayed together, we fought together, and we came home together. That makes a big difference.

Vietnam was our war. It was the first time the Navy went public that the SEALs existed and about what they did. There had been a long spell between the Korean War and Vietnam. There were little incidents along with the war—the Cuban blockade, the Dominican Republic, things like that—that were really just flash-in-the-pan, two-week jobs that didn't amount to much.

After Vietnam, the next target that showed up that was of any value to a SEAL was of course terrorism. It was everywhere in the 1970s.

For years, way back in Underwater Demolition Team days, there was an exercise called a Zulu Five Oscar. In that exercise, every ship had to repel attempted boarders from getting onboard. That became a cosmetic jerk-off.

Rules were established for the exercise that were very staged and artificial. You had to do the action between sunset and a certain hour. And if you scored a hit on a ship, they backpedaled, explaining how they had really done it and gotten us out of the water. Then we would come back with our version of what we would have done in those circumstances and we would have gotten them. It was like two kids playing a game of "I can do it, you can do it."

No one gave much credibility to the problem of repelling boarders. Then terrorism came along. Suddenly, we were doing embassies and other U.S. property instead of just ships. That was an expansion of Zulu Five Oscar. The powers-that-were said there were bad guys out there now, and we had to do something.

When the raid to rescue the Iranian hostages failed, we learned a lot. In any major conflict, every service has to get involved, otherwise there's no reason for them, there's no budget. It's a money thing. So you have to throw people at the problem to prove that what you have is worth what it costs.

When you start flying Navy helicopters across the desert, they aren't happy. When you start flying Army helicopter pilots across the water, they aren't happy. So it ended up that there were probably thirty-some options written up for the first raid that just didn't go anywhere.

The Chairman of the Joint Chiefs of Staff at the time was an Air Force general who had never commanded troops. He was one of those very bright McNamara brain kids who didn't know about war but knew about books. So we didn't get very far in all of those planned options.

In training for the operation, garbage was left all across the United States. It fell out of the sky, it got broken, or it just didn't work right together. Then, when Operation EAGLE CLAW, the raid into Iran, didn't work, it went bad big-time. At Desert One, the refueling base in Iran, it was Murphy who caused the helicopter to fly into the C-130 in the dust storm. But those helicopters that lifted off left classified materials behind them.

The situation translated to specific service standard operating procedures, which is what the guys did when the shit happened. They could practice the joint operation thing, but they fell back on what they had been doing all of their military lives when things got bad.

The white paper written up after Operation EAGLE CLAW said that the United States needed a full-time force to do counterterrorist operations and to see that such a debacle as EAGLE CLAW never happened again. That's what made counterterrorism the in-vogue thing, and the funded thing, being pushed on all the services.

And we did train together later. Army helicopter pilots took us across water, low and all while running with night-vision devices. Then there were the Air Force refueling services that could refuel us en route. There were dedicated C-130 and C-141 crews to move us and our gear. We now had a package from all the services that worked together, and we knew each other.

I'll tell you flat out that a shooter is a shooter is a shooter. And any of the shooters from any of the services can work for me, and there would be no problem. There's no difference in the cloth they are all cut from.

Harry Humphries said it very well when he said that the Vietnam era was a breeding ground for new types of fighters who might not have existed in prior wars, especially in the Pacific during WWII. But we saw a new sailor in Vietnam; we adopted a new brother during that era. That brother was the Brown Water sailor and the PBR sailor, of the inland rivers and streams, and the Seawolf pilot.

Why is that? How could we have possibly accepted somebody who hadn't gone through our training as a fellow combatant, a fellow warrior? Because when you're in trouble and there's nowhere to go—our back door has always been the water, and there's nowhere to go from there—a firefight is going down. It's an unbelievably difficult situation, and you just know you aren't going to get out.

Then, suddenly, over the horizon comes a small boat, a PBR or whatever, to support us. They came in under those conditions for us. Those guys didn't have to do that. They could have radioed back and said the gunfire was too intense or whatever. But they always came in, snatched us off the beach, and got us out of there.

The Seawolves did the same thing. How can we not accept them as brothers?

There is no question that between the Seawolf pilots, the PBR sailors, and the guys who were in our special boat support units at the time, we were snatched from the jaws of death many, many times.

I think getting us in was probably the easier part for them. When they came in to get us, we had really stirred up the hornet's nest, so they were always coming in to a lot of lead heading their way. And they were putting down fire of their own so that we could get onboard. Once onboard, we fought right alongside them to increase the fire we could throw back at the enemy.

You took those slow-moving Mike boats, or those faster plastic PBR boats, and they faced dumb odds when they had .51 calibers and RPGs coming at them. But they certainly thrived on doing that. And they never said, "Gee I don't want to." It became a new Team in terms of all of us working together.

I started off with the Chief of Naval Operations, who gave me the green light to form the Team that was SEAL Team Six. Admiral Ace Lyons was then the Ops Dep, the operations boss of the Navy in the Pentagon. He protected me in terms of his being a three-star admiral who did the Joint vote. As the commanding officer of SEAL Team Six, I had a reporting chain of command that went to the Army, who owned me. The Joint Commander was an Army general. Administratively, I reported to the Navy.

This caused problems in that the Navy paid for me, but the Army Joint Command took me to war. Every time the Navy said no to something, I could play the Army Joint Command against them. I may be a helluva brain surgeon, but I flunked bedside manner.

I did rub the commanders' noses in it. I did power play more than a little. Taking a message I had written to myself, I would take it to the Pentagon and have it come down gravity feed—everything slides downhill. The admiral found out that I was bending the chain of command, and he certainly didn't like that. But he was the key that allowed me to do that, and he remained that way after I left SEAL Team Six and created Red Cell.

I think SEAL Team Six was my military thesis. Having picked everyone there, it truly was a military mafiosa. I had psychological tests run on all of us, and we had the perfect community—we had the bell curve. We were normal. That satisfied the Navy. What they screwed up on was whether I was normal or not. I had picked those guys. And among the guys that I picked, we all looked normal. So if I was a sick *puppy, we all were. But the Navy never caught on to that one. That was giving the bureaucracy what they wanted. They wanted an answer, and I gave them one—we were normal. But they missed the real question—was I normal?*

I tried to use all the information Roy Boehm had taught me, the lessons he had learned putting together the first SEAL Team. General Wegner in Germany at GSG-9 was a friend of mine. He told me what would happen as I got bigger.

I listened to everybody who had similar units and learned about their degradation over time. That let me jump-start everything at SEAL Team Six. I used the military magic numbers to make everything at least 300 percent more. Having the Chief of Naval Operations support the development of SEAL Team Six allowed me to be creative in how I did things. That also showed me why it was good to be at the top, working out of the Pentagon versus a lesser staff position where somebody can easily nit-pick at me.

I was asked where I would get the manning numbers from. Those who are history buffs will remember that the cruiser Belknap had suffered a collision at sea. Those billets that had been on the Belknap were ashore now, because a ship hadn't been brought in to replace her.

So I borrowed those Navy billets to build SEAL Team Six until the normal programming cycle had gotten the body count we needed through Congress and all the appropriations committees and whatever. The cycle did go forward, and we had the billets we needed within five years.

When I was asked what it cost to outfit SEAL Team Six, I explained that the Navy plans on losing twelve F-14s a year. These are losses from landings on carriers, training missions, and whatever. I said that for the price of three of those F-14s, I was going to build them SEAL Team Six. I took their planned loss and gave them a planned gain.

When I had done that, I was given access to the storekeeper of the Navy, the admiral who ran all the budgets in the Navy. He sat down with me afterhours. When I told him what I thought I was going to spend, he did his magic Ouija-board work and came back with what he said I would really be spending.

He took me through the process of outfitting and budgeting, showing me what I would not have thought about, things like the out-years, for example, when you know you're going to have to replace bent and expended equipment. When you outfit a command, for example, I had learned that you buy all the parachutes at the same time. The chutes are all going to die, or reach the end of their service life, at about the same time, so you had better start incrementally building in spare parts that you can replace as you need to.

All he did was break out that Ouija board of his and his fingers flew, then the magic numbers showed up. Of course, he was the budget man of the Navy, they were his figures, and who was going to say no to him? Being at the top and seeing and doing that helped make things work. The dichotomy was that the little shooters, the chiefs I picked, chose their gear. And the Operational Boss of the Navy, and the Beancounter of the Navy, paid for it.

So I had both spectrums covered—the highest ranks in the chain of command as well as the lowest ranks. Of course, everybody else who was in the middle just got mad at me. I was considered an asshole because I cared so much about the guy who was going out there to be a shooter. But then I was going to war with those men, the other guys weren't. The mission counts.

This was my benchmark in terms of what I would take. I used secondary buildings until I got Department of Defense money to build a brand-new compound. I leased civilian airplanes, and we drove civilian cars. We got Motorola to make satellite communications gear for us.

I went out and got the best guys and bought the best toys. And at that time, terrorism was the best mission. Nothing wrong with that.

Why did we need Red Cell? Again, it was Admiral Ace Lyons, who had been a ship driver, who knew the Navy was ready to fight the Soviet bear over the horizon. But he knew that the Navy was not geared to do anything about terrorism. When was the last time a terrorist bothered anybody on a ship? So Admiral Lyons thought that there ought to be a unit like Red Flag, where they practice Soviet tactics against U.S. forces, only the new unit would do terrorism.

So Red Cell is an outgrowth of the Zulu Five Oscar exercises. Only now I had the funding to hire civilian analysts so I wasn't doing the score cards myself. I also hired a company that did video work to document our exercises. They hired ex-SEALs who could keep up with us and knew where we were going so they could keep up with us and catch us on film. Not only did we penetrate these bases, but it was all documented on film. There was no longer the "I got you before you could've gotten me" argument.

I certainly pissed off people again. Even though a four-star admiral out of the Pentagon told me to do something and a four-star CinC (Commander-in-Chief) in the area would say, "I want you to attack that base," people in command of the bases were less than happy. Those base-command positions were natural flag-builders, a step to making admiral. When I penetrated their bases and demonstrated their weakness, that ruined it for them and they didn't make flag rank. But, that was my problem, and no one was smart enough to say, "Hey admiral, you sent these guys and they ate me alive. Here's what I need."

Prior to Red Cell, the magic solution was to ask for more people and more money. When I went out to a base, I showed them how to stop us for now with what they had. It was a big change in policy and rules, and it took people to think about the terrorist as the enemy.

That was alien to the Navy back then. When you increase security, you reduce the creature comforts available to your personnel. The base people are unhappy, they can't go to the theater, the hospital is restricted, and on and on. On an exercise, we would be on the base for ten days, and for those ten days we ate them alive.

Red Cell was an embarrassment to the Navy, and the Navy as an entity, not just the people, doesn't wear embarrassment very well. If

---

you look at it from the bean-counting realm, when you're spending $2 million a year for someone to eat your socks up, somebody else asks, "Why am I paying for that pain?"

They didn't really take the negatives that Red Cell pointed out and make them positives. It was always a negative-negative situation. That was their loss. In today's world (1998), we have the same installations in terms of size, the same mission, but one-third less the people. So if I could attack a facility with ease with Red Cell in 1984 and 1985, ten years later and one-third less the people, you could drive a Mack truck through and nobody is going to know what's going on.

We are very vulnerable today to a terrorist attack here in the United States and against our bases overseas. If I had been one of the commanders of a base that Red Cell attacked, the first thing I would do after the exercise is go see the four-star admiral who sicced them on me. Then I would tell him what Red Cell had made me look like, what they say I needed to prevent such a thing from happening again, and ask for it.

An example of what happens on a base is how the hospitals report to one location while the exchange system reports to another location. These are what I call "stovepipe commands." Within a base structure, not all people report to the commanding officer.

So out in the Pacific, where Admiral Ace Lyons went to be a four-star, he made the ultimate responsibility of the bases, under terrorist event, rest with the base commander. But it was one of those things that, administratively and bureaucratically, didn't happen. If there was only one guy in charge, the powers would have eaten him alive after an incident. No one had the guts to raise their hands and say, "I'm going to break the rules under these conditions and do it this guy's way."

An oil rig, by law, is considered an island. Therefore, any terrorist action that takes place in it is in the jurisdiction of the FBI. We have some offshore oil rig pump stations that control a lot of the oil flow that's coming in. Destroying or damaging one can cause a tremendous amount of damage. So if you have a perpetrator, a terrorist, who's holding an oil rig for ransom, ultimately the prosecution of that terrorist has to go through the FBI.

But the FBI can't get out to the rig because of all of the water. So the taking down of the oil rig would fall on my men at SEAL Team Six. The feds wanted me to preserve the crime scene when my guys took down that oil rig. That way, they could come in and investigate it and build their case against the terrorists. They also wanted me to turn over the weapons from my guys who had done the operation—risked their lives, busted their asses—to see if any of our bullets had hurt a friendly or done other damage.

"Wait a minute," I said, "that doesn't go." First, as the commanding officer, I will be on the ground, I will be on the rig, and I will turn over the crime scene when I'm ready. If that meant I was going to stack bodies and make sure none of my guys were going to be caught in this BS, that's what my job is. Let the guys fight and I'll preserve their safety. I'm not going to allow someone who wants to put a feather in their cap to hang one of my guys for doing the job no one else would do.

Rules of engagement are there because of lawyers; they aren't there because of war. War says kill the bad guys.

War is another acronym that stands for We Are Ready. That's why it should be War Department, like it used to be, not Department of Defense. But that's better marketing.

Where we sit today, we have the opportunity to say how blessed we were by being in the Teams and how blessed we were for being able to go to war. We're just lucky, and there's a message there. I'm very thankful that the world's as screwed up as it is. That lets me write a lot of books now. But also it shows a need for better training. Harry Humphries and I both were doing the police training recently. It's sad that we don't train our cops enough or the right way. There are no

SWAT standards. You end up with the city bureaucracy looking at them as "goon platoons" and actually tying their hands behind their backs.

Somewhere, you have to draw the line and protect the American citizens. We have to have standard training and help out the police in policing the bad guys. There are more bad guys than good guys, and there's more money in being a bad guy than a good guy. They have better equipment, and they can throw more money at it. Thank God they don't have a centralized training program, either.

We're fortunate, Harry and I, in that we can both pass on things that we learned in war to the police today. If you look at where in the world we have sent our military for police actions—Somalia, Haiti, and Bosnia, for example. We're sending killers to do police jobs, and the cops are in the street now going to war against gangs.

As a nation, we have to take a hard look at that. Either we change the cops for the better, or we change the Posse Comitatus law and let the military help the police when they get into a heavy gang-influenced area.

Twenty-six weeks is a long time to be a trainee. And that's hard on the students. I think perhaps there ought to be a level where the students are treated more as Teammates and not as stinking trainees. However, I don't think them quitting and then trying to talk them back into the program is right. If they want to be there, then they can stay. If they don't want to be there, then let them get the hell out.

It's a society problem that comes well before they even get into the Navy. As a society, we have made quitting acceptable, if not even honorable. We have CEOs who screw up so we fire them and give them $12 million to go home. Well, how about letting me screw up for only a million dollars and I'll go home?

It used to be that if your family declared bankruptcy, you didn't even look your neighbors in the eye. Now it's considered an administrative tool and if you don't use it, people think you're dumb because it's so available. We raise kids who quit playing a sport or an instrument, then we buy them a new one. We've made quitting a way of life. It's at least acceptable, if not the norm. So when you get these young men in the Navy and into BUD/S (Basic Underwater Demolition/SEALs), it's not the first time society has to take over and correct the problem.

If the students don't have the fortitude and character to stay in training and if there aren't circumstances that warrant it, as an instructor, I shouldn't have to talk the students into staying. I mean flush them and go, we'll go get more.

We don't need people who know it's okay to call time-out in the services. I go to military bases on book signings and find it very appalling. Not only is it hard for me to talk without those four-letter adjectives, but the drill instructors can't curse at them anymore to break them out of their comfort zone.

Training has to be progressed at the pace of the slowest or the lowest. They have now even introduced a yellow card, called a stress card, that the trainee can pull out that forces the drill instructor to back up six feet until the student regroups. How do you meet the hated enemy? Time-out, sweetie, I'm not ready yet?

We're nailing guys for sexual harassment and putting more pressure on that than on proper training. So the youngsters who come into the service and want upward mobility, to be challenged, are just turned down by that. It sets a bad example.

In March 1998, I did a book signing at West Point. The plebe class, the freshmen class of the Academy, was the first class that had stress cards. They could call time-out with those cards. These are the future generals of the Army who are learning that quitting, or calling time out, is okay. However, when the news that the new Secretary of Defense found out about stress cards he had the situation changed. But that gives you an example of just how far that kind of thinking, that quitting is honorable, has permeated. We who are of the old school, and we who are special, don't have to conform.

If you want to be there, that's what they pay you for. If it was easy,

you wouldn't get paid that hard money. You need to keep BUD/S train-
ing special.

As *Harry Humphries says, there's a misconception in the civilian world about the healthy competitiveness between the militaries. That all disappears when you go into combat, when you go to war, because the guys in the air are supporting you on the ground. If you're in a combined operation and you're with some Force Recon guys, you'll find them to be excellent people and good shooters. If you're working with Special Forces A-Teams, you're going to find them to be totally dedicated and also good shooters. They're all people who you would want to have on your side, and were glad they were on your side when you needed them. There's a shooter camaraderie that exists between legitimate combatants, and the lines drawn by what branch uniform you wear disappear. When the EAGLE CLAW raid failed, we developed the Joint Special Operations Command. JSOC included what are called "trash haulers," the big Air Force transports with dedicated crews that worked with us all the time. They were specially screened and would do some nasty things with those big aircraft. And there were Army helicopter pilots, Air Force pilots, and Army Rangers who secured airfields. It was a family of shooters.*

When you get into counterterrorism and really expand it, you learn from the other units around the world. These are units you share intelligence with, and they share it with you. Our FBI used to get annoyed with me when I would arrive in a country, not check in, and be getting intelligence from that mechanism, that shooters group, when I hadn't been screened by my own government.

And the real, true intelligence came from the shooters. We would go sit and drink beer and they would tell me who they took down, what was going on, how it happened, and the lessons they had learned. That didn't usually come up in an official intelligence report.

With most intelligence that's gathered officially, the real meaningful stuff to a shooter is left on the cutting-room floor. The report writers are all trying to get the Pulitzer Prize in writing for their briefs for the president, so they do a strategic overview. The kind of stuff I worry about—who's on the pier, what kind of doorknob it is, what the lethality of the weapons they're carrying is, that kind of thing—doesn't get anyone the Pulitzer Prize, so we don't find out about it.

You can take a shooter from any of those foreign elements, any of the services or branches, cross-pollinate them, and find that they're all great guys. In fact we do that now.

The Air Force Combat Control Teams (CCTs) went and jumped in to hot targets with the SEALs. When tactical air support was coming in, those CCTs had the radio equipment to bring that tac air right to the target. I could worry about kicking ass, and the CCTs would talk to those birds up there. But they were on the ground with me, they ate the same stuff, locked out of submarines with me.

The same thing held with the Army guys with the birds. They came in more than once and saved my ass. A shooter is a shooter, and they're all USA. It doesn't matter what branch they're from, they all want to meet the challenge. And that's what's great about Special Operations. With the establishment of the Special Operations Command in Tampa, now they all even wear the same cloth. The procurement process is working for the operator more. They get the mass buys and everyone wears the same or virtually the same uniforms.

The Navy, in its tradition, somehow took the lead in funding, procuring, and developing an officer core for special operations and research programs for special operations. The other services did not at the same level. That was something that the Navy had the lead in.

The Air Force has been very good at incorporating their reserves into an active role and in special programs. The Navy still doesn't know how to use their reserves in an everyday, fold-them-right-in-and-put-them-to-war manner. Look at DESERT STORM. A lot of National Guard and Reserve units who thought they would never be going anywhere ended up on the front lines.

We have a smaller team now in the armed forces, and we have a vaster role in terms of policing the world. More and more it's going to come down to the individual. Training is going to come to the floor, and we're going to have to be good at it.

Let's look at a realistic target, Saddam Hussein.

In the United States, we send people to West Point to study history and war. They read Clausewits and study the actions of all the big wars. Then we go to a place outside Bagdad, to an operation called Desert Storm. General Patton once said something along the lines of, "Send me fuel, and in five days I'll be in Moscow." If we had stayed three more days in Desert Storm, we could have been in Bagdad and we wouldn't have the problem we have now. There's a political argument that says that we finally had our troops on Saudi Arabian soil, we would have upset the Arab brotherhood, and politically it wasn't a smart thing to do. I say that's tough. They weren't going to like us anyway.

Then there's the question that if we kill Saddam Hussein, who would be next in succession in Iraq? Saddam may be a madman, but at least we know what he is. How about Saddam's son? If we kill Saddam; is his son going to say, "Shit! I'm not going to let that happen to me!" We've never reached across the pond and punched anybody in the nose, so they're going to keep pushing us until we do.

But just how close could we get to a target like that? There's a bigger problem. I could take a team in, get close to Saddam Hussein, or anybody who looks like him, and find the right time to do it. Getting there, watching him, and setting up for a target of opportunity is a lot easier than getting the hell out of there after I got him, because once he goes down, everybody is right on my cheeks. The mission almost becomes a kamikaze.

You don't have to be crazy to be in the Teams, but it does make life easier. As a breed we are a dichotomy. You come to BUD/S as an individual, who has to be individually motivated and has the drive and ambition to be a Team member. Then you are a Teammember. The result is people who are outstanding as individuals, but who work even better as a team.

Then, because you want to go to war, you are trained to survive by yourself and go on and complete the mission by yourself. The Team is that lovely, glowing body that draws you to it. But you brought your tool-box with you, and if everybody dies en route, you're still going to finish the job. The Team is a flow point and a comfort zone for us. It's a thing we enjoy.

Bronze Bruce, the bronze statue of the World War II UDT operator in front of the UDT-SEAL Museum in Fort Pierce, Florida, like other statues, is a symbol. It's a symbol of where we came from; it's a benchmark in the history of the Teams. We have no idea of how far we're going yet in terms of the SEAL program and what kind of enemy we're going to face tomorrow.

As Harry Humphries says, we have our origins with a slate and lead line, a pair of fins and a face mask, a kabar knife, and that's it. That's the beginnings of our group, where we all came from. In fact, that's where operators our age did come from. But we lose sight of the fact that the real, real tough days were those days during the Second World War. That was when these guys were going in to the beaches, and the attrition rates of the invading forces could go into the 80 percent range of wounded and killed on the beach while executing impossible missions.

These guys had an extremely difficult job to do. These were the men who we looked to as a goal to strive for. Their story is what pulled us into the program. Where we are today with the equipment and so forth, is icing on the cake. The real individual is that guy out there in the water in swim trunks and fins.

That statue of the WWII UDT operator brings back memories for me, because what the statue is wearing is all that I was issued. We didn't have the latest and greatest toys they have in the Teams today. When I got there out of Class 26, the Plexiglas—the slate we wrote on—was taken from the salvage yards of the Naval Air Station. We went over there and took old airplane canopies and cut those slates. We poured our own lead for the weights and used colored signal flags to mark the fathoms on the line we tied to the weights.

The guns we shot were a WWII Greasegun and M3A1 submachine gun. The kabar was the only weapon we were issued. We didn't get to fire it very often. We had to qualify a thirty-eight caliber pistol. That was it in the way of our weapons in UDT.

Starting from scratch, with the basics, is what I see in that statue. That was us in those early days. We had trouble talking to the amphibious ships we could see on the horizon because of the radio gear we had. In that same era that we had trouble talking to the ships with our radio gear, we were already talking to men in space. (We should have had those radios!)

Where this program has gone in thirty years in terms of force multiplier is phenomenal. In terms of dollars, new equipment, and capabilities of the Teams, the programs have been built up a lot, yet everything goes back down to that bronze statue. That's all we started from, and that's what will make things work. If the guy is stripped down to that lowly point, he will find something on the ground to do his job.

That's what we were designed for—to live off the ground, live off the land, and make the bad guy's stuff work for us. There are no supply trains arriving in the nick of time. If you don't have it on your back, you don't have it. That's the way SEALs have to operate today, and that's the way we grew up in the Teams back then.

We call Bronze Bruce the Naked Warrior. And naked as he is, the mission will still get done. He is our root. He is our basic form. He's where it all started from. He was the warrior. As spartan as he was in terms of equipment and basic training, he did the mission of his day. And that's our bottom line, getting the mission done.

Thomas N. Tarbox, Captain, USNR (Ret.)

I left SEAL Team Two in August 1966, prior to our involvement in Vietnam, and went up to the Defense Intelligence School. From there, I went to Okinawa and other staff work assignments and never did go back to an active Team. So Team Two's part in the Dominican Republic operation in 1965 was the closest I came to action with the Team.

My involvement with the SEALs was far from over though. I was assigned to running BUD/S for a while in the early 1970s and at the very last of my service, I was the commander of the Navy Security Coordination Team, better known as Red Cell. The Navy brought me back for Red Cell after I had been retired for six years.

I didn't run the East Coast BUD/S training. It had already been consolidated by the time I was assigned. The last East Coast training class, Class 7102, graduated at Little Creek in August 1971. From that point on, all BUD/S training was conducted on the West Coast at Coronado.

The first consolidated class at Coronado, Class 62, graduated in September 1971. At that time, the West Coast was running six classes a year while the East Coast had been running only two classes a year. So the numbers were quite different.

It's not well known, but there was a period of about a year and a half during which they didn't have Hell Week in the West Coast BUD/S classes. The commander of BUD/S had arrived there and was soon told to knock off Hell Week due to the attrition of students during that single week of training. The CO at the time was being banged about the head and shoulders by the weenies back in Washington, D.C., because attrition is inefficient and they needed a lot of people for Vietnam in the West Coast Teams. So it was sometime in 1970 that Hell Week was knocked off the training schedule.

I went to Vietnam in March 1971, and Dave Schaible relieved Dave DelGudice as Naval Special Warfare Unit—Vietnam in December 1971. When I came back and took over BUD/S in March 1972, I immediately put Hell Week back into the training schedule.

At that time, BUD/S was a department of the Amphibious (Phib) School at Coronado. So should I tell them that I was going to put Hell Week back into training? If I told them I was thinking about it, I probably would have had to get their permission first, so I didn't tell them.

Hell Week is part of our training. I feel that, and I think everyone in the Teams feels it. Those kids who didn't get exposed to it were cheated, really cheated. Hell Week is one of the things that we really all have in common, and it really belongs as part of training. At that time, the Phib School was doing a lot of formal curriculum work and writing up stuff. So we did that with Hell Week and nobody ever questioned it.

There were a number of staff positions I took after leaving the command position at BUD/S. But the best thing I did during the 1970s was replacing Hell Week.

By the early 1980s, it was time for me to retire. But even that didn't last long, as the Navy had more plans for me.

The Navy Security Coordination Team, also known as Red Cell, was started in late 1984 sort of as a response to the Marine barracks being bombed in Beirut. Red Cell went everywhere there was a Navy base and conducted antiterrorism exercises and training. The unit was started by Commander Dick Marcinko, and I took over Red Cell in May 1988, well after Dick had left. I was the thirteenth commanding officer of Red Cell.

Red Cell had some problems, which is one of the reasons why I was recalled to active duty from a retired status. I was commander for two years and then Tom Mosure took it over from me in May 1990. He was the last CO before the Red Cell unit finally folded in October 1991.

The mission of Red Cell was to conduct antiterrorism training and exercises at Navy bases worldwide. We tried to increase the awareness of Navy installations to their vulnerability to terrorist attack. The first thing we would do when we went to a base was have an antiterrorism awareness seminar game. We would gather people from the FBI, Coast Guard, local law enforcement, state cops, customs, or whoever would have a role to play in law enforcement around a table and play this game.

These people should have been talking to each other all along to prepare for a possible terrorist incident, but our seminar games were often the first time these area representatives all really got together. I hoped they continued this seminar awareness game, because it was an excellent teaching tool.

After the seminar "war game," if you will, we would hold a practical exercise with events that would stress various parts of a base's defense. The base would typically have its own security people, plus they would muster the auxiliary security force. The auxiliary force was made up of sailors in other jobs who had a collateral duty to be on the auxiliary force.

The exercise would stress the bases. It had to go into a higher threat condition, which meant that all the IDs of people going into the base had to be checked. The exchanges lost sales and all kinds of complaints would come in from the support people and the families of the base personnel. Yes, the exercise was inefficient for the normal running of an installation, but at least they learned something about protecting the base.

We also had hostage barricade situations where we would take over a barracks or building and hold the people inside hostage. Then we would have negotiations between our "terrorists" and the base or law enforcement.

We found that these hostage barricade situations, if they lasted long enough, that we could start turning the people to "our" side and against the base—the old "Stockholm Syndrome." We would tell them how bad their base was because they hadn't been able to protect them and that they weren't getting food in to them or not doing this or that. The reaction of the hostages, as they would come over to our way of looking at things, was very interesting.

But the Navy didn't want to "train" terrorism victims, which is how you could look at our simulations. I still think that if Robert Stethem and the others who were on TWA Flight 847 in 1985 when it was hijacked to Beirut had gone through one of our exercises, they might have all survived that terrorist incident. But who knows.

What kind of a man is a Navy SEAL? He's an ordinary American with an ordinary background, perhaps a little smarter than the average person who comes into the Navy. He has something within him, or can be motivated, so that he can withstand a lot of pressure and a lot of physical duress, and still keep his cool.

I'd like to think that all of us who have been in the Teams, in the past or today, are pretty much the same although the Teams have changed. When I went through training with Class 19 back in 1958, very few of the enlisted men had completed high school. Most of them were high school dropouts, who then came into the Navy and got their GED. A lot of them eventually went on to college.

Fifteen years later, when I ran BUD/S, all the kids were high school graduates, and some of them had attended college. The officers had completed college and had maybe a year or so of graduate school behind them. Realize that the draft was still going on back then and the draft was a real equalizer in the ranks.

Today the kids who come in all have high school diplomas, and most have some college behind them. Quite a few even have college degrees—they remain enlisted men because it's easier to get into the SEAL program as an enlisted man rather than as an officer. Most of our officers now come from the Naval Academy, something that wasn't true twenty years ago.

Some of the enlisted men can't get in as officers with degrees because there are so few volunteers for the program taken from NROTC and OCS. But essentially, they are all the same young men, driven and hopeful to make a challenging career in the Teams.

The statue of Bronze Bruce, the Naked Warrior, is an example of a UDT operator prepared for a combat swim during World War II. He's wearing swim fins, trunks, a face mask, and little else. I think he represents all of us, but especially the WWII Frogs. The World War II generation, nationwide, was the finest generation this country has ever had, including the founding fathers. Those people who went through the depression and on to win the war are a shining example of just what an American can be. When I see that statue of the Naked Warrior, I think of them.

When we created the Teams, there wasn't a lavish amount of equipment available for us to do our jobs with. Instead, we often had to bend the rules to get what we needed. In the early days at SEAL Team Two, we had sixty people total—ten officers and fifty enlisted men. Of everything we wanted to get, we would order sixty plus 10 percent more, so we ordered in amounts of sixty-six.

We had a problem getting the jungle fatigues when they first came out. The Navy didn't have any in the supply system, but the Army had them—a lot of them—so we worked out a little cumshaw, a wonderful Navy term, with the Army down at Fort Bragg.

They always needed paint in the Army, because they had to paint all those damned rocks down there, and they liked Kabar knives. So we would give them paint and Kabars, and they would give us jungle fatigues.

The supply officer at the Naval Operations Support Group, the predecessor to Naval Special Warfare Group, took the Group credit card with him on a trip up to New England. There, he charged a set of tires on the government credit card. The FBI found out about that little purchase, and they came around to check out our supply system. Of course, they uncovered what we had been doing. But the thing that saved us was that we took the fatigues that we had traded for and put them in our stock records as we issued them out. So there wasn't anything illegal going on and no private person was making any kind of profit on our trading, we were just bending the rules to get what we needed. And the FBI guys fully understood that, so we ducked any trouble over that one.

We just wanted enough gear so everybody could be prepared and have enough clothes, weapons, and equipment to do any of the varied missions we were supposed to be able to do. Everything was new and we were learning as we went along, and the supply people were learning as well, because a lot of the things we needed just weren't normal Navy issue.

We ended up with very little at all compared to what the kids have now. We were really in the process of determining what a SEAL Team was. We didn't know, and no one else did, either. If Vietnam hadn't come along as the proving ground for the Navy SEALs, we might have turned out a little different than we did. But Vietnam did come along, and both Teams went there. And we came out pretty well.

The word I think of whenever I think of the Navy SEALs is professional. That's the key to being a good SEAL, being a professional. There are really three things that make up a good SEAL—being professional, the need to bring the youngsters along and teach them, and the need to make a difference. If you have those three things in your makeup, you're a real good SEAL.

In spite of the instructors' best efforts at BUD/S, we have a few Rambos in the Teams, but they're damned few in number. Being a Rambo isn't being a professional.

There's a photo that ran in the San Diego Union Tribune around the anniversary of Pearl Harbor some time back of the Pearl Harbor veterans who visited the USS Pearl Harbor. It showed three or four of the vets talking with maybe six sailors. Everyone was grinning in the shot; they were all just pleased to be talking to each other. They shared a history as well as a present. That photo epitomizes what I hope will always happen when the older SEALs and Frogs meet the young kids today. They share a history, a present, and probably a good future as well, and I hope they always remember that.

■ Chapter 3

BOAT SUPPORT

The long cooperation between the Boat Support Units, Brown Water Navy, and the SEALs did not end with the finale of the Vietnam War. The value of such an efficient meshing of skills, equipment, and manpower was recognized by the Navy and maintained after Vietnam ended. The Brown Water Navy had started in 1965 with little equipment and no recent unit background to build on. By the end of the Vietnam War, the Brown Water Navy had grown to a force of more than 700 small craft and 38,000 men.

In early 1967, another more specialized small-craft unit was established specifically to support the needs of the Navy SEALs. Designated Boat Support Unit One, the sailors of BSU-1 were tasked with developing, modifying, testing, evaluating, and operating small craft in support of the SEAL detachments in Vietnam. A component of the Naval Operations Support Group commanded by Captain Phil H. Bucklew, BSU-1 did outstanding service for the Teams and the Navy operating heavy, medium, and light SEAL support craft in the waterways of Southeast Asia.

Sailors in both the Brown Water Navy and the Boat Support Unit underwent an eleven-week River Assault Craft training program. During this program, the men were exposed to various aspects of riverine warfare, joint operations, counterinsurgency, small arms, and survival, evasion, resistance, and escape (SERE) training. They went on to further training in their prospective watercraft, notably the Mark I and Mark II Patrol Boat, River (PBR) for the Brown Water sailors and the various specialized SEAL support craft for the BSU-1 sailors.

After the end of the Vietnam War and the turning over of a number of river and coastal patrol craft to the South Vietnamese navy, the remaining small craft and personnel of Task Force 116 (river patrol), Task Force 117 (river assault), and Task Force 115 (coastal surveillance) were reorganized into Riverine/Coastal Divisions and Squadrons and divided between the East and West Coasts to their support of Naval Special Warfare. In May 1983, the last Boat Support Unit was redesignated a Special Boat Unit and fully integrated into a Naval Special Warfare Group.

To maintain and increase the skills and abilities of the Special Boat Units, the Special Warfare Combat Crewman training course was established at the Naval Special Warfare Training Center in Coronado, California. For eleven weeks, students in the SWCC training course are pushed to achieve a very high physical standard. In addition, they receive instruction in swimming, first aid, maritime navigation, basic seamanship, engineering, communications, combat and basic tactical skills, small arms, and special operations. As of 1995, students who completed the course and successfully served in a Special Boat Unit received the SWCC designator and its accompanying promotion points. As of October 2002, the names of the Special Boat Units and Squadrons were officially changed in order to prevent confusion with other amphibious forces with the same names. The two Special Boat Squadrons, One and Two, became Naval Special Warfare Groups Three and Four respectively. The Special Boat Units were renamed as Special Boat Teams.

On the West Coast at Coronado is stationed Naval Special Warfare Group Three, which concentrates its operations in the Pacific and Central geographical areas. Under the command of Navy Special Warfare Group Three is SEAL Delivery Vehicle Team One, based

The main armament of the PBR, its twin forward .50 caliber machine guns, are shown in this photograph. The gunner from the River Division has his two weapons aimed outboard to the port side of the boat. The large searchlight is attached to the mounting for the guns. Wherever the light is shining, that's also where the two big machine guns are aimed.

U.S. Navy

at Pearl Harbor, Hawaii. SDVT-1 conducts operations in support of Naval Special Warfare throughout the Pacific and Central commands areas of responsibility. In addition, there is Special Boat Team Twelve, which is primarily equipped with RIBs and Mark V Special Operations Craft. Special Boat Team Twelve conducts its operations throughout the Pacific and Central commands.

In addition to SDVT-1 and SBT-12, SpecWarGru Three has four of the 170-foot Cyclone-class Coastal Patrol Ships (PCs) assigned to it. These ships are designed and equipped to support a SEAL detachment on extended special operations missions throughout the world. They are commissioned naval craft with a crew of four officers and twenty-four enlisted men. The West Coast is assigned the *Hurricane* (PC 3), *Monsoon* (PC 4), *Squall* (PC 7), and *Zephyr* (PC 8).

On the East Coast at Little Creek is Special Warfare Group Four,

As part of a NATO exercise in Spain, a group of SEALs from SEAL Team Two approach the shore tactically as they disembark from their RIB insertion boat. The wetsuit-clad scout swimmer, who would have been the first man on shore to check the beach, is kneeling to the left. He is armed with an MP-5N submachine gun with a flashlight-equipped forearm. On his left ankle is strapped his combat knife. On the scabbard of the knife, secured with rubber bands, is a sealed chemical light in a plastic pouch as well as a pyrotechnic flare/smoke signal.

U.S. Navy

which concentrates its operations geographically in the Atlantic, Southern and European areas. SpecWarGru Four has under its command SEAL Delivery Vehicle Team Two. SDVT-2 concentrates on being able to support the Sixth Fleet Commander with both a SEAL Delivery Vehicle capability as well as a Dry Deck Shelter (DDS) capability. The DDS can be attached to a modified or specially built submarine to allow it to transport either an SDV or a CRRC and lock out or recover SEAL units while underwater. The DDS includes a hyperbaric chamber to treat combat swimmers for decompression after particularly long or deep dives.

SpecWarGru Four also has under its direction Special Boat Team

The Mini-Armored Troop carrier as used by the Special Boat Units.

U.S. Navy

Twenty. The primary operation part of SBT-20 is Detachment Caribbean, based in Roosevelt Road, Puerto Rico. Special Boat Team Twenty-Two is also under the command umbrella of SpecWarGru Four but is based in Mississippi at Bay Saint Louis. The Coastal Patrol craft assigned to the East Coast and SpecWarGru Four include the *Tempest* (PC 2), *Typhoon* (PC 5), *Sirocco* (PC 6), *Chinook* (PC 9), *Firebolt* (PC 10), *Whirlwind* (PC 11), *Thunderbolt* (PC 12), *Shamal* (PC 13), and *Tornado* (PC 14).

■ ■ ■

THE Special Boat Teams also operate a variety of special operations craft, including rigid inflatable boats, Mark V Special Operations Craft, High Speed Boats, the light patrol boats, Mark IV PBRs, Mark II PBRs, and the mini-armored troop carrier. All these craft are in addition to the standard Combat Rubber Raiding Craft (CRRC), the

The Mark V Special Operations Craft (SOC). The slim, fast-moving boat can be transported aboard aircraft for rapid deployment. Capable of mounting a variety of weapons, including 25mm Mark 38 cannon, miniguns, .50 and 7.62mm machine guns and 40mm grenade launchers, the Mark V can transport and support a SEAL unit in a threat environment.

latest incarnation of the rubber boat, a SEAL and UDT staple since its earliest days in World War II.

The Special Boat Teams are tasked with conducting coastal and riverine interdiction operations as well as supporting naval and joint special operations. Specific SBT missions include unconventional warfare, direct action, special reconnaissance, foreign internal defense, counterterrorism, and psychological and civil affairs operations support—all in a maritime or riverine environment. They operate on a worldwide basis, both with Naval Special Warfare assets and on their own.

The men of the Special Boat Teams have developed an illustrious reputation in the few years since their origins in the 1960s. They have and are still proving themselves a very valuable asset to Naval Special Warfare.

■ Chapter 4

THE END OF AN ERA, THE NEW BEGINNING

The Underwater Demolition Teams had performed their missions with professionalism and skill since their first days in December 1943. The operators of the UDT had blown open countless beaches during World War II, conducted demolition raids and other missions behind enemy lines in Korea, looked at nuclear missiles in Cuba, and even greeted returning space capsules during the *Mercury, Gemini,* and *Apollo* space missions.

After almost forty years of operations, the UDT had reached the end of its useful service life. The mission preformed by the UDTs— primarily that of beach and hydrographic reconnaissance and obstacle clearing—could be conducted by the SEAL Teams. The men of both the SEALs and the UDTs shared the same basic training, crawled through the same mud, and proved themselves through the same ordeals. It would be a much better use and application of manpower and resources to give the mission of the UDTs to the SEALs.

But that was not to indicate that the Teams would be made any smaller. On the contrary, while there would be no more Underwater Demolition Teams, new SEAL Teams would rise up in their place.

On 1 May 1983, the Frogmen ceased to be, but only on paper, as the Navy conducted the first major reorganization of Naval Special Warfare since the early 1960s and the commissioning of the first SEAL Teams. The Navy retired the UDTs and put SEAL units in their

A Mark VIII "Eight-Boat" approaches its holding cradle on the deck of a submerged nuclear submarine. The Eight-Boat will be secured to the cradle,
which will then be winched into the open hatch of the DDS secured to the
access hatch of the submarine. The entire launch and recovery operation can
be conducted underwater.

place. In most cases, this meant little more than a new issue of
equipment and reorganization of personnel.

UDTs Eleven and Twenty became SEAL Teams Five and Four.
UDTs Twelve and Twenty-Two became SEAL Delivery Vehicle (SDV)
Teams One and Two. The new SDV Teams would concentrate their
training and efforts to support the other SEAL Teams with longer
range underwater transportation.

The SDVs were wet-type underwater vehicles. The interior of
their fiberglass hull would be filled with water, and the occupants
needed to wear breathing equipment. With its silver-zinc batteries,
the electric motor of an SDV could drive its SEAL crew and up to
four passengers for much longer distances than even the SEALs
could swim for themselves. In addition, cargo, including heavy demolitions, could be transported by an SDV while a pair of swimmers would be hard-pressed to do more than move such a charge
into position.

The Mark VIII SDV, called the Eight-Boat, was the workhorse bus

---

A crewman in the drivers' section of a surfaced Mark IX SEAL Delivery Vehicle looks to the rear of his craft. The low, flat SDV maintains a very small cross-section, either above or below the surface. The navigator and driver of the SDV have to lie flat during normal operations.

U.S. Navy

for the underwater work by the Special Warfare community. The Eight-Boat looked like little more than a short, fat, black whale when it moved through the water. The other SDV used for a number of years had a much more sinister appearance and mission.

The Mark IX SDV was a wide, flat boat that could be used for reconnaissance operations or surgical underwater attacks. The Mark IX SDV only held a crew of two, and those operators, a pilot and a navigator, lay flat to work their craft. So no extra personnel could be moved in the Mark IX. What could be done was mount the Mark 38 Standoff Weapons System to the Mark IX. That gave the SDV two torpedoes that it could fire at a target thousands of yards away. Now the small fiberglass SDV could take on a capital ship, sink it, and move away before anyone could think to look for such a small underwater craft—if they could even find it.

So new SEAL Teams were in existence, and they now had the secondary mission of conducting beach reconnaissance and obstacle clearance. The Frogmen were not gone; they had just changed their designations. With the commissioning of two more SEAL Teams, Three and Eight, by the end of 1983, there were three SEAL Teams and an SDV Team on each coast. Each SEAL Team consisted of eight operational platoons of sixteen men—fourteen enlisted and two officers—as well as a headquarters platoon.

George R. Worthington, Rear Admiral (lower half), USN (Ret.)

In 1955, at the age of 18, I joined the Naval Reserves. For two years, I was on inactive service while I went to Brown University as a NROTC student. Following that, things got a little interesting. While at Brown, I was one of the school swimmers. My swimming coach used his contacts at the Naval Academy to help me get in there. So my next four years were spent at the Naval Academy, and those were followed with thirty-one years of active duty.

We have a second-class summer at the Naval Academy called tramid—train a midshipman. A number of us went down to Little Creek as part of this program. At the Little Creek Naval Amphibious Base, a Frogman in a nice white uniform came into the room and threw an M80 firecracker into the wastebasket.

After getting our undivided attention, this Frogman went on to tell us all about the Underwater Demolition Teams (the commissioning of the SEAL Teams still being a few years in the future). That was the first time I ever heard about the Teams. Afterward, we were told never to join the Teams, because it would be a career-killing move.

In the Navy as it was then, joining the UDT could be the end of a young officer's career. The "regular" Navy looked down on the UDTs as not really being regulation Navy. They didn't move in fleets and do combat on the high seas; instead, they swam in and blew things up. Any officers who would be willing to lead such a group of men couldn't be expected to later "drive a boat"—the normal course of a career for a Navy officer.

The next time I heard about the UDTs was in 1963, when I had rejoined the CISM, the Conseil International du Sport Militaire (International Military Sports Council), Naval Pentathlon team. When I did that, the CISM was being held out of UDT Twelve at Coronado. I believe Ted Lyon was the XO of UDT Twelve at that time and the commanding officer was Bill Robinson, who is now deceased.

During the CISM stuff, you couldn't help but meet all the guys at the Team. They were in and around the town as well. I was on a destroyer staff at the time, which kept me from being with the UDTs constantly.

The mission the UDTs performed and the job the men did at Coronado looked interesting to me. My athletic interests weren't being met by my work in the surface Navy. Besides, after a couple years as a flag officer's aide-de-camp, I was ready to do anything to get to other duties. Eating sand with the UDTs looked fine to me.

A time later, while a trainee at Underwater Demolition Team Replacement (UDTR) training, which later became BUD/S, I was down in the front learning rest position on the beach, when I remembered what I had said earlier.

Okay, Worthington, I said to myself. You wanted to eat some sand, now do it. And I happily ate the sand. It was much more pleasurable than taking brownies to the Third MATH general in Da Nang in April 1965.

I was part of UDTR Class 36, West Coast. It was a summer class, so the traditional cold wasn't as bad as it could have been. We only lost one man during Hell Week, and he came back in to UDTR later and completed training, finishing his tour in the Navy as an E-9 Master Chief.

The hardest part of training for my class was the last three weeks we spent at San Clemente. It had gotten cold and rained every day, so Neptune paid us back for the good weather and warm time we had enjoyed up to then. Although I refer to our training as an "easy day," the work was difficult. UDTR was everything I had expected and more.

You think you can get in shape for the physical demands of training, but you really can't. The course was grueling. Back then, they had an additional two-week training session for officers. As I recall, we had about thirty-five officers show up. After the two weeks were over, we were down to something like fifteen officers left.

The Hell Week we went through was a test, just as it is for all the other classes who go through it. Hell Week was an opportunity to perform, succeed, and show that you could hack it. It might sound foolish, but frankly, I felt I got stronger as the week went on. In that long week of maximum output and minimum rest, you're kind of flatlined by Tuesday.

Our Hell Week went from midnight on Sunday until noon on Saturday. But because my boat crew was the first to finish most of the evolutions—we did all the exercises as hard as we could—the instructors rewarded us by pulling my boat crew out of Hell Week about 9 o'clock Friday night.

To try to get our boat back to the base and the showers that awaited us was nothing more than a three-hour hallucination trip. We were exhausted and in a state of mind that let us see anything we could imagine out on the dark waters.

The expression in training is "It pays to be a winner." That expression means, in the parlance of the time, that they didn't put the "eeties" on you, that if you were the last boat all the time, the instructors made things worse and worse for you. It was a very difficult position to pull yourselves out of.

Being a winner didn't give you any privileges, but you did get a lot more respect from the instructors. Once you set a winning path for yourself and your teammates, the instructors expected you to win and they didn't ride you as much. And being secured from Hell Week early was a big reward on its own.

There was a time during my Hell Week that I considered quitting. Barry Enoch was one of my instructors, and we learned to dread Enoch's Time. Tuesday night, he gave us time on Enoch's swimmer line. Wearing heavy, red canvas kapok life jackets at 10 o'clock on the second full night of Hell Week, we didn't think it was too bad. We knew we could hack it.

The instructors lined us up, tied us together, and gave us our paddles from the rubber boats. In those days, training was often conducted on the bay side of Coronado. There was a nice long pier extending out into the bay that we marched along, off of, and into the waters of San Diego Bay.

We would swim out into the water in a straight line, then do wheeling movements and turns. We sang songs and treaded water for about an hour while wearing our kapok life jackets. It was fun.

Then we were ordered back in and marched out of the water and back to our barracks where we took everything off and were allowed to hit our racks. Sleep—that looked to be a really great thing.

Twenty minutes after hitting the racks—bam! An M80 firecracker was tossed into a wastebasket and we were all out of our racks and on our feet. We were out and moving again. The time in the racks had been enough for most of us to fall into a serious sleep, and now we had to get moving again. So with heavy confusion in our heads as we tried to shake off the alpha waves of sleep that we had sunken in to, we had to get dressed in our clod, wet, clammy uniforms, boondocker boots, and kapoks. That hurt.

Okay, now we sang some songs for half an hour, out into the water and back in. Then, back to the barracks, strip, and into the racks. Ten minutes after we laid down—bam—here it comes again.

We marched down to the end of the pier and held position for a moment. I thought to myself, If I have to get into that water again, I'm quitting.

Who knows if I would have actually quit or not. I don't. But as that first man hit the end of the pier, the next step was into the water. Then the instructors called an about face.

We turned and went back onto the base to Turner Field where we were run through PT for the remainder of the night.

I managed to dodge the bullet on that. I never again thought about

BUD/S trainees move across the grinder with their rubber boats on top of their heads. In spite of the uncomfortable appearance of this situation, this is the most effective way to carry the boat over any real distance—something the students learn over the long weeks of BUD/S.

quitting and got through that Hell Week and the balance of training. I have no idea what really got me through Hell Week. I can't say it was courage, because all I did was hang in there and keep on going.

The instructors exhort you to hang in and not to quit. They were very positive, which is in contrast to some recent stories and films. I don't recall the bad language you hear in the films. I cannot remember any time while I went through UDTR when an instructor used foul language—ever. They were absolute professionals, and they forced us to bring out everything we had and then some.

You have to have the desire to complete the BUD/S or UDTR course. Your heart and your brain both have to want it. Second, you hope your body holds together enough to get you through.

When I went through training, once something happened to you, whether you were seriously injured or even got a serious set of blisters, you could be turned out. Then you were sent back to the Fleet and had to go through the whole application process again to even have a chance at returning to training. Today, I think we're a little bit more sage in our handling of this kind of situation.

If a fellow is a good person—the kind of man you would like to have in the Teams—he can be rolled back to heal from an injury. Once the man has healed, he can return to training with another class. But back in the days of Class 36, it was back to the Fleet.

So your heart and mind have to be together in order for you to complete training. Having your body together and the ability to keep pushing it forward is also important. Another thing that helps you get through the training is the support of your boat crew. The leadership that's exhibited within that crew, not just the officers but also the senior petty officers, can keep a man going when he flags a bit.

We've seen in BUD/S that when an officer trainee goes by the wayside, he can take a number of the troops with him. By the same token, a petty officer can keep things together and help both the men and the officer. We had a number of first class (E-6) petty officers in my class who were tough guys. They hung in there and were a good adhesive for the rest of us, officer and enlisted alike.

The "secure from Hell Week" phrase, that line that ends that weeklong torture and test of your personal mettle, is a tremendous relief. But I've associated that sort of relief with lots of things throughout my Naval career. There's the "thank God it's open," or "survived the landing," or "passed the finals at the Naval Academy." "Secure from Hell Week" is another in a continuing series of Navy experiences that I can look back on and just think, thank God it's over and that we survived.

Both the low and high points during my UDTR training was Enoch's Swimmer Line. That was a very, very depressing period of five minutes during which we stood on the pier contemplating going back into the water. Then, when we about faced, I thought I was home free. By then, we were pretty much numb and I had faced enough things in my life up to that point that I was hopeful now of getting through the balance of training.

Other than that moment, I didn't really have a low point during my training. Even that time on the pier was relative in being a downturn because it happened so fast that I didn't have enough time to make up the excuses I would have to lay out as to just why I was quitting. At that time, I was a full lieutenant, and my leaving would have stood out.

Even though I was an officer, I didn't feel that the instructors chose us out for any kind of personal attention because of our ranks. The officers do have a little more responsibility than the enlisted men during training, though. We would have to work up the operations during training and such.

But I saw no favoritism on the part of the instructors, good or bad. It was an equal-opportunity situation; everybody got it, and we were all equally miserable.

Here I was, a Naval Academy graduate with time in the Fleet, where the officers are treated separately from the enlisted men. And at UDTR, I was right down there, crawling through the mud, sand, and surf with the lowest seaman in the class. I had no problem with that whatsoever. You would have to ask some of the other men in my class if I was a snob or not—I don't think I was.

We got into training and did what we had to do. If you're an officer, you have to show leadership and you expect the fellows to come along. The instructors told us very precisely and clearly what we were to do in each evolution, so setting out the plan for the men was a no-brainer. It was just, "Guys, here's what we have to do." And the senior instructor was always there to ask for help, if you really needed it.

Bosn's Mate Second Class Vince Olivera was my senior instructor. He was a man straight out of the backlots of Hollywood, the image of a Navy Boatswain's mate. They could not have picked a finer man to lead training than that classic character. He was the epitome of cool, of suave. His whole act of addressing the class made you almost want to throw yourself into the bay if that was what he wanted. And when Olivera told us to do something on an evolution, I had no burden of proof to give to the men. Just do it because Olly said to. It was fun sacrificing your life for Olivera. If Olivera said to do it, it had to be okay. That was leadership.

The experiences of UDTR were good, but the graduation from training held no particular excitement for me. The pain was over, but only for the time being. It would start again when I was operating in the field with a UDT. Four years of New England prep school had been kind of rigorous. Plebe year at the Naval Academy hadn't been pleasurable, and later-class years are even harder in terms of the academics. So UDTR graduation was another phase in my Naval career. The taste of completion and accomplishment is something you learn to enjoy—after all, the training has made masochists out of the bunch of us.

My first assignment after graduating UDTR was a strange one: I was made the Operations Officer of Underwater Demolition Team Eleven. As a full lieutenant, I was sent over there to relieve the lieutenant holding the position. That officer, in turn, went on to become the executive officer of the Team, taking the space John Callahan had been holding. The illustrious commanding officer of the Team was none other than Stormin' Norman Olsen. So my initiation into the active UDTs went from UDTR straight into Norman Olsen's span of control. Sure I could swim, but I was stepping into the deep end right away.

My first deployment with UDT Eleven came along rather fast. It was in April as I recall. We reported to UDT Eleven after graduating near the end of December 1965. During March and April 1966, Bill Robinson, who was a staff officer in the CTF 76 staff, worked up an operation called Operation Jackstay. That operation was to take place down in the Mekong Delta region of South Vietnam.

Our mission was to go over there, which involved fifty-two hours of flight and travel time. Once we got to town, Jim Barnes was already there with a detachment of SEALs, and some Marines were there, too.

We received our briefings on the op. The plan involved was putting four-man groups up little tributaries in the southern section of the Rung Sat Special Zone. That was just about in the Vung Tau area down there. We would go in during daylight, insert, then spend the night there in the nipa palms and tidewaters. The funny thing about the operation was to listen to Norm Olsen talk about it the next day after spending a whole night in water up to his nipples.

We went to get some information from the staff intelligence officer and were asked to bring back some incidental information about the local fauna. The intel officer had heard about a local fish that actually climbed out of the water to move on the (more or less) dry land. It was supposed to be a true amphibian, and the intel officer wanted us to bring him back a specimen.

Here we were, operating off of the Weiss where we weren't even getting showers. During our operations, we were looking for places to set up ambushes against the Viet Cong. And now this intelligence officer wanted a fish. We tried to be as kind to him as we could, because he was a commander and we were just peons. But the general opinion was that we would probably eat one of those fishes before we would ever give one to him.

The deployment for Operation JACKSTAY did involve some direct combat for the UDT in Vietnam. We did a bunch of ambushes in the Rung Sat against VC hiding in the huge swamp. This had not been my first visit to Vietnam, but it was the first time I was there squatting in the mud and brown water.

I had received my first impressions of Vietnam earlier in 1965 when I accompanied the admiral in charge of Comcrudesflot 7 (Commander Cruiser Destroyer Flotilla 7). We flew the length of the South Vietnamese coast, stopping off at various places. The staff I was with were responsible to the Seventh Fleet for developing the Operation Market Time plan.

Our first night incountry, we hit Saigon and went to the Top of the Rex, I guess it was. I made reservations for us at the Paprika Restaurant. We went out there and spent an interesting time.

I looked at the area as being the old French colonial village, a minor city. Culturally, I was kind of looking at how we could help the people *there, maybe even some of the French. Our job was to see how we could better stop the infiltration of the Communist forces coming down from the North and slipping into the area from the seacoast. The powers-that-be thought the seaborne infiltration was true due to the Bucklew report. The 1964 Bucklew report had established that the Viet Cong were using the waterways of the Mekong Delta to move personnel and smuggled supplies. It was used as part of the reason for sending direct action SEAL Platoons to Vietnam in 1966.*

Some of the Communists and their supplies came down on the Ho Chi Minh trail, with the majority of the stuff coming in to Vietnam from Sihanookville across the Cambodian border. The situation for us was kind of the blind leading the blind. The MAG Navy guy had an airplane that he flew us around in.

The SEALs' first direct combat operations in Vietnam were when Jim Barnes brought his detachment from SEAL Team One over into South Vietnam in early 1966. They conducted ops as part of Operation Jackstay. Jim didn't like Jackstay, and I don't think he participated in the operation much. But once he and the SEALs were over there, they started doing things, active combat operations and such, after that.

Barnes and company were scheduled for Jackstay, but he opted out of it, leaving the support of that operation to the men of UDT Eleven and the Marine Recon guys. On one of the missions, I had a Marine unit operating in close support of myself and a detachment of UDT.

My UDT men and myself were the Team farthest up this little river, which was almost all mud really. About 400 meters away from my UDT team was a Marine team. Mike Troy, who was an Olympic swimmer before he joined with the UDT, was there, leading his detachment. Troy's group was overrun by the Viet Cong, and we all held our breath until, thank God, we heard he was in the clear. We were operating in the jungle and mud of the Rung Sat, and that wasn't something we had been trained for.

Things became a little tight for us, doing those sorts of missions but we worked the situation and figured that we could pull off what was expected of us. Basically, we were trained to do beach recons and dives to blow up obstacles. We were very experienced in working with demolitions, not crawling through the jungle and waiting to conduct an ambush while chest-deep in muddy water.

The remainder of that tour in Vietnam consisted mostly of the more traditional UDT operations. Working with the amphibious guys while on the Dagger Thrust operations, the UDTs checked out sandbars along the coastline of South Vietnam to see if they could be eliminated or if channels could be blasted through them. Beach recons were run and the areas were charted for the national authorities in case amphibious forces had to be brought into an area quickly.

We came back from that deployment in September 1966 and found that we had a new commanding officer at UDT Eleven. At this time I was fleeted-up to the position of executive officer of the Team. The following February (1967), after only about five months back home, UDT Eleven again deployed to South Vietnam, this time with me in the position of XO.

The plan this time was to deploy the full UDT to the operational area of the deployment. There was a lot of administrative mashing about because of the plan to try and develop White Beach, Okinawa, as the headquarters area for forward-deployed UDTs.

We Teams argued that we should keep the preponderance of the guys close to the amphibious forces they worked so closely with. The amphibious forces operated out of Subic Bay in the Philippines, the closest major U.S. Naval facility to the operational theater in Southeast Asia.

So the UDT Eleven CO and his personal staff were located in Okinawa for the 1967 cruise. As the XO, I stayed back in Subic and ran things from there. We took certain officers and gave their platoons specific assignments. One officer would be told that he was the ARG (Amphibious Ready Group) platoon who would operate with the Marines, another officer would take the submarine detachment, and so on.

Some operations had to be conducted down in the IV Corps area. Surveys had never been done of the beaches in IV Corps—basically the Mekong Delta and points south in Vietnam. So the discussions went around about who should go in command of the detachment to conduct the surveys.

The first person suggested was the CO of the Team, but that was immediately denied. Then it was suggested that the XO of the UDT—myself—go as the OIC. Well, I could have gone but at the time I was in the business of training lieutenants to work in the Team.

Mike Collins, one of the officers at UDT Eleven then, was on the Weiss with his platoon. They had a pretty good CO of the boat, a former Frogman himself. So Mike was put in as the OIC, and his platoon went down and conducted those first surveys along the shore of IV Corps.

Training still didn't stop as UDT Eleven was deployed. During that summer, quite a few of us went to HALO (high altitude, low opening) school and learned military free-fall parachuting at the U.S. Army Special Forces–run school in Okinawa.

At one point, we put together some training instructions did some new training of our own. Taking a new UDT platoon, we put them through the U.S. Army jump-training syllabus, the training being run by our own UDT instructors.

Two days before UDT Eleven was to redeploy back to the United States, I was involved in a parachute accident and managed to do a number on my left ankle that basically put me in a leg cast for four months. One thing you can't do is run around and undergo SEAL training with a cast on your leg.

Only in fairly recent years has command been operating lieutenant commanders in the field, and that only with SEAL Team Six at the beginning. As a lieutenant commander by that time, with a hurt leg, the rank and injury kept me out of the active SEAL Teams during the balance of the Vietnam War.

So I left the Teams for a length of time, and went back to the Fleet to serve time aboard ship. As the ops (operations) officer on a destroyer, I participated in a Mediterranean cruise. After that, I made a career choice and told BUPERS (Bureau of Personnel) that I wanted to go back to Naval Special Warfare. My request was approved, and I was told to go back to Vietnam.

So I went over to Vietnam, first as the ops officer and later as the XO of Naval Special Warfare Group—Vietnam. Toward the end of our Vietnam involvement, things became very competitive between the Teams and the Navy. When I became the commanding officer of SEAL Team One, I had only one platoon deployed to Vietnam. Now I felt my mission was to do some interesting, if arcane, training for my Team while at the same time trying to find more work for them.

I hear people today talking about great morale problems that existed in the Teams then. I didn't see those problems, except maybe for some lieutenants who weren't able to deploy to combat. I had guys come to me and ask to be able to make some parachute jumps. These were the older operators, and I had no trouble helping make arrangements for them to go out and do what they needed. But I couldn't get a platoon for an officer who wanted to deploy. It's interesting that fifteen years later, I've heard just the opposite. What I heard from lieutenants then were things like, "I've had five platoons and I'm tired of deploying." There is a balance there that needs to be reached.

But that balance certainly wasn't reached back then in the five or six years following our drawdown from Vietnam. Opportunities to deploy, to go out and operate, were few, and the order of the day was to stand in line. That's when guys would do whatever they could to stay working, stay busy, and keep a challenge in front of them.

SEALs were intended to be men for all seasons, so they trained in skills that could prove valuable in the field. Those years following the Vietnam War were when guys were doing things like traveling the Colorado River in rubber rafts. I even sent a platoon down to get sailboat training. I set up course of ski training for the SEALs and started a little bit of winter warfare training. Anything to keep things interesting.

For the younger guys in the Teams, time goes slowly without action to keep them busy. For the older chiefs, a quarter-year could seem to go by in an instant. So the challenge was to find a training cycle that was, if not equitable for all concerned, at least something that everyone could learn from and work with. If the young kids, those SEALs on their first tour of duty, start to feel that things are dragging at the Team, they could get in trouble on their own, so we had to keep them interested.

From 1976 to 1978, I was the commanding officer of something called Inshore Undersea Warfare Group One (IUWG-1). That was a hodge-podge of expertise from electronics people, Marine Mammals and SEALs. Many SEALs loved to be involved with the Marine Mammals program, if for no other reason than they were in bathing suits most of the day and at the farthest point in the base from the "flagpole" (command). There, no one ever really bothered them.

The work was starting to get the Marine Mammals involved in amphibious operations like mine recovery. The Mammals seemed to enjoy the work. We also had a sensor group in the Inshore Warfare Group. But the Navy hadn't funded sensors for four years, so we worked with older sensor systems that were contained in these shielded Army Battle Area Surveillance System (BASS) vans.

I had an idea to take all the sensor electronics out of the BASS vans and put in communications gear and radios and make it an organic Command, Control, and Communications (C3) suite for the Group commander. That idea ultimately sold, and today it's called the Mobile Comm Teams. We used it during Desert Storm. We could talk from the Group command in Coronado all the way to the SEAL commander on site with our own equipment.

So my morale was fine in the late 1970s, and I suspect the morale of the men in the Teams wasn't bad either—at least I never got the sense that it was.

Things were changing at the IUWG. A lot of gals were starting to come over into the unit from other parts of the Navy. How to use them *and work them into the scheme of things wasn't too difficult. There wasn't any grousing about the women being here.*

Some of the women new in the unit were pregnant, and that wasn't a problem I had faced in the Teams before. But I took a little section from the personnel department, kind of a lounge area, and turned that into a nursery. That way any of the female yeomen who were nursing their kids could just bring them to work. They could type the letters and watch their kids—no problem, everyone was as happy as rain, and the situation didn't bother me.

One activity we had was something we called Monster Mashes. Two teams, blue and gold, made up of equal numbers of SEALs and Fleet sailors, would do things like negotiate the obstacle course. It was kind of fun to watch some of the women sailors negotiate the CISM obstacle course. Then they would go into the swimming pool, turn an IBS (inflatable boat, small) over, then conduct a race. All of this was done on a Friday, and a barbecue was held afterward.

There was a question about some of the women not being happy at having to wear swimsuits. So I said to watch some of the films of the Olympics and get those suits for the women to wear. If someone wanted to file a complaint, then they were free to. But no one complained, the gals all participated, and it was fun. Then by 1700 (5 o'clock), everyone got to go home. I can't speak to what it was like aboard a Navy ship at that time but we kept up the morale at the Group and all the organizations that were part of it.

By the late 1970s, I was attending the National War College from which I graduated in June 1979. Then I reported in to our OPNAV for a staff position. I moved in on 15 July 1979. Ted Lyon and Jim Barnes were there then, but Barnes was moving out because he was retiring as I remember. That meant the staff was made up of only two people, Ted and myself.

On 24 December 1979, I got the piece of paper signed that established Naval Special Warfare Unit 2 in Macrihanish, Scotland. There had been a Unit 2 earlier, but it had been put down due to some objections by a Fleet admiral. He might not have liked how the SEALs creased their pants as far as I knew.

So we had reestablished a SEAL forward-operating unit with NSW Unit 2 in Macrihanish. The following year, Ted Lyon got an opportunity to be the commodore down at Naval Special Warfare Group Two in Little Creek, Virginia. He left, and that basically left me in charge of the office for a period. There was another fellow, Maynard Wires, who came in to relieve Ted, but I held the fort on my own for four months or so. While all of this was going on, a new operations code (opcode) class, Op 09-5, was established.

This new organization was to be the honest broker for the Navy. They would look around and see if things like the sonars that were used in the Navy's aircraft were the same as those used on the surface ships and submarines. They were looking for any commonality in the technologies of the Navy that could be used by other organizations or services, such as air, surface, or subsurface. The new organization needed a SEAL in their office, so I ended up working for their amphibious desk.

While I was at Op 09-5, I was working as 09-54, strike warfare (amphibious), and created the "master plan." A master plan meant that you laid out what you wanted and then you'd fund toward it.

A bunch of people looked at my Naval Special Warfare Master Plan and said that it was daunting and that it couldn't be done. Well, in the Reagan years, if you were going to get any piece of the pie for your people, you couldn't think that just crumbs from the Surface Warfare table were going to get you where you wanted to go. So we created a master plan to encompass the entire special warfare community and asked for what we needed to really initiate the plan.

I was then sent back down to the Op-03 desk, Surface Warfare, when Wires left. So in essence, I had three back-to-back Pentagon tours.

Contrary to popular opinion, your job gets easier in the Pentagon the longer you're there. You learn the operations of the building and *how to get things done. Knowing where to get your view-graphs for briefings, your charts, and even just the phone numbers for the right people to call for a problem all come once you get some time in the building.*

I think there's a law or regulation in place that an officer cannot spend more than six years in the Pentagon at a stretch. That might be to prevent the more experienced people from staging a coup or something.

So I went from writing the Master Plan, which stated our requirements in Special Warfare and where we were and where we wanted to go, to the desk that was responsible for funding the plan. Part and parcel of this was that we got some things done, including getting SEAL Team Eight.

About that time in 1983, we had a conference in Washington of most of the Naval Special Warfare high command. At the meeting, Irish Flynn said he thought it was time that all the UDTs became SEAL Teams. As the Action Officer on the Chief of Naval Operations Staff, I said that if the Group commodores all agreed, and they were all at the table, that they should start the action. Then I would run it to ground and make sure that the name change happened.

At that time, it was rather simplistic, but I thought, Okay, we'll change the name. Of course, it wasn't just a name change. The primary and secondary missions of the SEALs and the UDTs were different. Now the SEALs had both their own and the missions of the UDTs. That meant there were equipment requirements. If you were doing beach recons, you needed flutterboards and things like that. If you were doing ambushes, you needed face paint and all the other types of things that went along with a direct combat mission.

But that's where it happened, in that meeting in Washington. The Teams changed officially in 1983, and the UDTs became SEAL Teams. In addition to that, we had to set up Swimmer (later SEAL) Delivery Vehicle Teams because operating SDVs is probably the hardest thing we do in Naval Special Warfare. The care, shepherding, and husbandry required by the SDVs are beyond the normal training of a SEAL. Keeping them moving, and the SEALs within them breathing, is a very technical and demanding specialty.

Lynn Reilander came to me and asked how we did with the growth of Special Warfare. I thought we had done fine to the extent that we were able to get things from the Surface Warfare barons, whose main mission in life was to see the *Arleigh Burke* class get commissioned.

Lynn said we were going to fix what was missing and showed me a piece of paper that outlined where he was going in terms of special ops, including Naval Special Warfare and Army Special Forces. Lynn intended to correct all the shortcomings of the special operations community in one fiscal year.

I had to tell him that it was going to be impossible to spend or accomplish everything it would take get all the spec ops community healthy. You just couldn't grow these kinds of operators overnight.

Every available engineer who could work on our problems was already working on other priority projects. The only way to get an engineer to work on our projects would mean taking him off another project and then that project would languish until someone else could come in and get it back up to speed. And it would take time to get even an experienced engineer smart in terms of what SEALs needed or even what their warfare capabilities were all about.

So a program would have to be shown that went over what was then called the Five Year Defense Plan. It would have to start in 1986 and finish in 1990. Of course, we all knew that once it started, it would never really be finished.

Lynn wrote a paper for the then Secretary for Defense. The Secretary came out with his own memo on 3 October 1983. The memo was to all the services and all the staffs in the Pentagon to fix special operations, and the action was to be completed by the end of fiscal year 1990. That made 1996 the first year to begin a new rebuilding of the Special Operations Forces for the U.S. military.

To get more SEALs, we had to look and see what we needed in the standard SEAL Team. So we redid the numbers on that. You can't get these men in just one year, but you would have to start growing them right away. In order to grow them, you had to fix the schoolhouse, the BUD/S training center.

I called a contact of mine up at BUPERS, told him we had a hot problem on our hands, and asked him to come down to a meeting. When he arrived, we told him we had to grow the schoolhouse. In order to get more students through training, we had to have a bigger facility. To make a long story short, we got the pool and other facilities, including more instructors, to increase the numbers of SEALs available for the new Teams.

The first year of the buildup was 1987, so 1986 was the planning year. With some rapid military construction, the new schoolhouse compound at BUD/S was built. In 1987, they were able to ramp up to five or six classes a year, and soon we would have the manpower we needed to build up the Teams.

Other questions came up, such as the level of readiness and whether the demographics would match the number of students we needed to come into BUD/S.

Well, the kids were nearly standing in line to try and complete BUD/S and go on to the Teams. The raw numbers were there, and we weren't going to sacrifice the quality of training just for numbers. And I don't think the increase in the numbers of students going through BUD/S lowered the final quality of the graduates.

We had some great minds working on the problems of getting quality students through the training program. It was suggested that, if we had a good man, we try harder to keep him rather than just let him go, as had been done in earlier training.

I used to talk to the classes as they graduated. I asked one graduating lieutenant, junior grade, how long he had been at BUD/S.

"Eighteen months," was his answer.

That young officer had been a UDT/SEAL trainee for a year and a half. That man wanted the program, and we would have lost him earlier *just because of a bad throw of the dice. Someone had dropped an engine or rubber boat on his leg and injured him. In earlier years, that would have sent him back to the Fleet and he would have had to reapply and try to just get to BUD/S all over again.*

But the new idea was to offer worthwhile individuals the chance to stick it out at BUD/S. If some want to call that liberal, okay, but I call it conservative because you're assuring that BUD/S is less of a crap shoot as to just who's going to make it or not due to an injury. The guy who sticks it out is the kind of guy we wanted.

We renamed the schoolhouse the Naval Special Warfare Center in 1987. We brought Phil Bucklew out to the ceremonies in a wheelchair and named the new structure after him. He had been a highly decorated veteran of the World War II Scouts and Raiders and was influential in first getting the SEALs directly involved in the Vietnam War.

At about the same time, there was also a change in the overall command structure for U.S. Special Operations Forces, a change that affected the SEALs along with all the others. An amendment to the 1986 military authorization bill ordered that the U.S. Special Operations Command (USSOCOM), a command that put all the Special Operations forces under the same umbrella, be established in Tampa, Florida.

At SOCOM, flag officers would be in charge of each of the different service's special operations forces. Chuck Lemoyne was one of the thinkers behind the idea and was the first SEAL admiral at SOCOM. This gave a command a push to make sure that what was needed to conduct special operations received the necessary priorities.

Now the Air Force could be asked why the Combat Talon aircraft was number 83 on the priority list. The small unit numbers of specialized equipment needed for spec ops support didn't make them as appealing as a new class of destroyer for the Navy or fighter plane for the Air Force. But with the establishment of USSOCOM, that situation could be better dealt with.

With the establishment of the Special Operations Command, there

The shield of the Special Operations Command, based on the spearhead patch of the World War II OSS, surrounded by its unit commands. To the upper left is the arrowhead and dagger of the Army Rangers. At the upper right is the U.S. Navy Special Warfare Command symbol. At the lower right is the Joint Special Operations Command shield. At the lower left is the Air Force Special Operations Command shield.

USSOCOM PAO

was now an infrastructure, an organization, in place that was able to monitor the health of all the special operations forces. The new organization had the knowledge and experience to know what was required to carry out these sorts of missions, what was needed in the care and feeding of the SEALs and the Special Forces. SOCOM is still evolving and growing to this day.

All the U.S. military forces are evolving and changing as the world has become such a different place after the fall of the Soviet Union. The U.S. Navy Submarine forces are an example of such changes. When the Russian subs were tied up at the docks, the Navy subs had to extend their mission parameters to keep operating. Suddenly, Navy SpecWar were the recipients of more offered submarine services after the Berlin Wall came down than we ever would have hoped to get, and the sub fleet was looking for spec ops missions.

Even the Air Force B-52 people were looking for a change of missions—not in terms of migrating away from their strategic bombing role, but to look for additional reasons for being. They were suggesting that special ops could have low-level attack missions they could do. Everyone has a vested interest in what their branch or part of the service did; that was what they had learned and what they knew. And now these skills and abilities were being applied in new ways. Everyone benefits from such a situation.

It is possible that the Special Operations Command may evolve into a separate branch of the service, standing alongside the Army, Navy, Air Force, and Marines. That possibility was argued back when the idea of something like SOCOM was being discussed. There are people in SOCOM now who say that the antecedent of the command was the OSS of World War II. That is only true when you consider the operational side of the OSS. The later CIA doing covert operations has had mixed reviews over the years. They, as the direct descendants of the OSS, have more of an intelligence-gathering mission as a holdover from the World War II days.

In my view, it would be hard to see SOCOM as a separate service today. But could it grow to something like that? I just don't know. My crystal ball is a little too foggy to make that future out, but it is certainly possible. That kind of conjecture is easy to make here in CONUS (continental United States), but out in the field, it can be harder to see.

Duplicity of missions and operations could easily be a problem. Would some future Secretary of the Navy see someone from SOCOM swimming in to their target and decide that the mission should be given to the Marines just because it was moving from water to land? And besides, the Marines probably wouldn't want the additional mission; their plate's pretty full right now.

SOCOM's present position as a central command and infrastructure for all the different service's special operations forces is probably the best situation it could be in for the foreseeable future. Whether something becomes a separate service or not ultimately depends on how that would help the man at the end of the rifle. If it would help him do his mission, then that has to be shown and justified.

That man on the ground, the operator, the eyes on the target, that man is the ultimate ground-truth guy for what is happening in a situation. That is the person who the public visualizes when they think about the special operations forces. The public image of the SEALs, and the special operations forces in general, is usually far from the truth. With the secretive nature of most special operations, the public doesn't have the information to build a correct image, and so the gap is filled with images from movies and television.

There is no Rambo in the SEALs. There cannot be. The mythical image of the SEALs is precisely that, a myth. SEALs are looked up to as military athletes, as really tough guys. But I can't see anyone taking a movie, say such as GI Jane, seriously. When the trainees stood in ranks in that movie, you saw people from different U.S. services. In my 30-some-odd years of associating with the Teams, I've never seen a Marine or an Army guy go through SEAL training. Foreign sailors or allied UDT guys, yes, they have gone through training at BUD/S. But to be a SEAL, you have to be in the Navy, period.

Only people who have gone through the rigors and testing of BUD/S and on to the Teams are entitled to wear the Naval Special Warfare breast insignia—the Trident. To me, the Trident is a symbol of respect and honor. It very much represents something to the rest of the Navy. We took a lot of jibing about it from the Fleet when it was first adopted. There were comments about how we should have had some SEALs on the selection board in order to have made it a little smaller. Truth was, SEALs would have probably made it bigger. It represents what we do; it's a symbol of all the skills held by the SEALs.

When I was going through training and for some years afterward, I had nothing on my uniform to show my association with the Teams. Those were the days when few Naval officers had distinguishing devices on their uniforms other than the Dolphins of the Submariners or the Wings of the Fliers. Then Admiral Zumwalt brought in the Surface Warfare pin and it was decided that the SEALs and the UDTs needed a uniform device.

The only unique thing worn on a SEAL's or UDT's uniform for a long while was parachute wings. Then two pins were designed, one for the UDTs and another for the SEALs. The difference between the two pins was the presence of an eagle on the SEAL pin. There were gold and silver pins respectively for officer and enlisted personnel.

But finally someone said wait a minute. Everybody took the same dose of medicine (BUD/S) to get to the Teams. Everyone, UDT and SEAL, officer and enlisted, had to do the same stuff and crawl through the same mud to graduate BUD/S. There should be only one pin, gold with the eagle, for all the Teams and all the qualified personnel, officer and enlisted alike.

One comment on the history of the Teams, past, present, and future. The misnomer that the SEALs, Underwater Demolition Teams, and the Naval Combat Demolition Units (NCDUs) somehow evolved from out of the Scouts and Raiders—which were a separate unit—is not accurate. These units did evolve one from the other, not from the Scouts or Rangers.

The reason there were NCDUs and then the Frogmen (UDTs) was that in 1942 and 1943 the Navy didn't have good charts for many of the areas the U.S. Navy would have to conduct landings on to put forward the war effort. They didn't know what the beaches were like, so recons would have to be run to supply the most up-to-the-minute intelligence. It was the men in the water—men like the Naked Warrior— who conducted these recons. They swam in and checked the bottom to see if ships and boats could get in and where any mines or other obstacles might be. If necessary, the men could then blast a pathway through the obstacles for the landing forces.

The secondary mission of the UDTs included land warfare centering around demolition raids. The UDTs did a lot of those raids behind enemy lines during the Korean War. In 1962, the SEALs were established as a separate unit from the UDTs because President John Kennedy wanted more work to be done in counter-guerrilla-type missions.

In 1983, the missions came back together. For twenty years, the SEALs' primary mission was above the high water mark, while the UDTs' primary mission was below that point. But the men who conducted the operations were the same animal.

You look at a SEAL, Marine Recon, Army SF, or Ranger, and they're all pretty much the same red-white-and-blue 98.6 guy. He might put on a different uniform or train differently perhaps, but underneath it's all the same person.

Individuals stand out in all of the services. Barry Enoch was one person I remember meeting for the first time back in 1965 when he was one of the petty officer instructors at UDT Replacement training for Class 36. There were a lot of very colorful instructors at UDTR, and Barry was one of them.

The enlisted people who went over to UDTR to train us were all very top-notch guys. In some cases, the officers weren't necessarily the equivalent of the enlisted instructors. The enlisted guys were the ones we spent the most time with, and these were some of the best people on Earth.

As I remember, Barry Enoch was a Second Class petty officer at the time, and he managed to make me question my presence at UDTR through one of his evolutions as I recounted earlier regarding Enoch's Swimmer Line. He was, and is, a great guy. Went on to the SEAL Teams and won a Navy Cross during one of his tours in Vietnam.

Another colorful guy in the Teams was Norm Olsen. He was my first commanding officer in UDT and as such made quite an impression on this very new Frogman. They call him Stormin' Norman because when you went to see him about something, you had better make sure that all of your facts were correct and the answer was right. You had to give him the answer, and it had better be a good one. Explain things to him and there was no problem. The "Stormin' " part came if you had the numbers wrong or if you had the spelling wrong on your papers. He would not abide sloppiness.

Norm Olsen was an avid skydiver, one of the original guys who was doing an awful lot of it back when everyone was still learning. I remember one day, some guys had a night jump out of UDT Eleven and some people missed the muster. Word got back to the people who were providing the airplanes that they weren't full on the jump. Norm hit the overhead on that and said "Hey, if you need space filled, you call me and I'll do a string [static line] jump." Up to that time, Norm was doing a lot of free-fall jumps. He was one of the original guys who got a parachute demonstration team going—what later became the Leap Frogs.

There are people in the Teams today keeping the community moving ahead. Admiral Ray Smith is a great guy, someone I consider to be a natural leader. His personality and drive and just the way he is with people makes you want to follow him. He is a very cordial and congenial guy as well as being a very capable man.

Admiral Tom Richards is the same kind of man. Nicknamed "the Hulk," Tom was my ops officer when I was running Group One, and he did a superb job for me. He was also an ops officer for me at SEAL Team One. He's just overall a great guy. If I was asked to write a fitness report for him, I could give him nothing less than all A's.

Chapter 5

AIRCRAFT: THE "A" IN SEAL

The SEALs used aircraft to a large extent both to insert and extract men from a target as well as to provide fire support when and where needed. In the jungles and swamps of Vietnam, the primary aircraft used by the Teams for both purposes was the rotary-winged helicopter. The Huey, the workhorse bird of the Vietnam War, could put SEALs into a target area half the size of a football field, pull out their wounded without even touching down if necessary, and place machine gun and rocket fire within yards of a beleaguered SEAL position.

The SEALs found a liking for any chopper pilot who would come in and help them when needed. But it was the Navy Seawolves who were the Teams' favorites. Close behind the Seawolves were the pilots of the fixed-wing OV-10 Broncos, the Black Ponies. Both of these units were Navy assets, and the SEALs worked with them on an almost daily basis in Vietnam.

As the SEALs downsized and changed to a nonwar footing, training became the primary activity. All forms of Navy helicopters were used for training, and several new techniques were developed. Because most of the larger Navy helicopters are fitted with an external hoist mounted above one of the side doors, capable of lifting either equipment or rescue slings, they are a ready-made securing point for a heavy line.

Rappelling from hovering choppers was, and is still, practiced by the SEALs as a viable insertion technique. But a new system called "fast roping" has developed. In fast roping, a heavy line is attached to the helicopter's rescue hoist and the SEALs simply slide down the line. Little more than a pair of leather gloves to protect the hands and a crash helmet are used in the way of special equipment, and the speed of the insertion is incredible with a practiced team. In five or six seconds, a four-man fire team can be on the ground from a single rope, the men just using their hands and legs as the braking force on the rope. Resembling the climbing rope used in school gym classes, the descender rope is a special thick, tri-weave polyester line with a tensile strength of 35,000 pounds (15,876 kilograms). The rope is used in either 50 (15.24), 90 (27.43), or 120 foot (36.58 meter) lengths.

The speed of the fast roping technique makes it a preferred method for many types of insertions, especially when boarding a possibly hostile ship at sea. Care does have to be taken by the SEALs so that they do not impact on each other as they hit the ground—a very real danger as the men are coming down at something like one-second intervals.

Once you got into an area, it was nice to have a method of extraction if things got too hot. The SEALs developed the SPIE (Special Patrol Insertion/Extraction) rig for their own use. The SPIE or Spyrig uses a single 120-foot (36.58-meter) length of 1-inch-diameter (2.54 cm) nylon line with a polyurethane core as the lifting rope. With a tensile strength of 24,000 pounds (10,886 kilograms), a single rope can lift out an entire six-man team at one time. With spaced attachment D-rings secured to the main line ahead of time, the SEALs just have to attach their personal SPIE harnesses to the D-rings for extraction. The SPIE harnesses are generally worn as part of the combat uniform.

Again made much the same as a parachute harness, the SPIE harness is made from 5,000-pound (2,268-kilogram) tensile strength nylon webbing with a single attaching point above and behind the SEALs' neck. Used in conjunction with a 12-foot safety line that would be attached to another person using the rig, the SPIE system allows the user's hands to remain free for stabilization or using weapons. The SEALs would attach to the SPIE rig in pairs, with one man on either side of the line. Attachment is quick, and a team can be removed to safety in a very short time. The SPIE rig is particularly useful in inserting or extracting a team in tight spaces such as on the deck of a ship at sea.

With the wide range of techniques available to them, the SEALs are able to operate effectively from most Navy asset helicopters. But for the best efficiency, the SEALs should be working with air crews trained in Special Warfare operations. Many of the Navy's helicopters are fitted for specific missions, and the equipment packages limit the amount of room onboard. This cuts down on the number of SEALs who could be employed from the aircraft. This situation is particularly true in those helicopters assigned to anti-submarine warfare duties.

Fleet helicopter assets today generally consist of SH-3, CH-46, SH-60, and CH-53 aircraft. With the sixteen-man size of SEAL platoons today, the CH-46 is the preferred aircraft for many Special Warfare insertions, and especially on VBSS (Visit, Board, Search, and Seizure) operations, as it can carry a fully equipped platoon along with two EOD (explosive ordnance disposal) men. However, the CH-46 is a very large aircraft and is not as suitable for clandestine insertions.

■ ■ ■

SEAL airborne capabilities received a strong upgrade with the increase of all Special Operations forces under the Reagan and later administrations. Besides increasing the strength of the SEALs with new Teams and men, several air units were created that greatly added to the overall capabilities of all the Special Operations units, including the SEALs. These new units came under the direction of the new

Special Operations Command (SOCOM), consolidating all the Service's Special Operations forces under a single umbrella organization.

The Army added the 160th Aviation Regiment, called the Night Stalkers, to the rolls of Special Operations forces. Today, equipped with MH-6F Little Birds, AH-64A Apache gunships, and other rotary-wing aircraft, the men of the 160th train heavily in night flying and all forms of special operations support. In addition to the special capabilities of the 160th Regiment, the SEALs can also rely on regular Army support in the form of AH-1G Cobra gunships for fire support and UH-60A Blackhawks for transportation. Marine air units also have the AH-1J Sea Cobra for air support, and this aircraft is also available to the SEALs.

In addition to support from the Army, SOCOM had new Air Force assets that are also available to support the SEALs. In the 23rd Air Force/Special Operations Command, MH-53J Pave Low III Enhanced helicopters are used along with fixed-wing aircraft such as the MC-130E Combat Talon and AC-130H Spectre gunship. All these craft work in close cooperation with Navy assets, including the SEALs, in conducting special operations today.

■　■　■

EARLIER transport planes, such as the famous C-47, were used as jump platforms by several generations of military parachutists. The UDT and SEALs were no exception to this and jumped from the C-47 and other craft often during tactical training. But the side-door exit point of the C-47 made it unsuitable for jumping a team and airdropping large pieces of equipment at the same time. Inserting combat swimmers by parachute would limit the equipment the swimmers could carry, or tow, through the water to their target. The distance they could swim effectively was also a limiting factor. Using the rear cargo ramp of the C-130 as an exit point, a technique unique to the Teams was developed called the "rubber duck."

A line of armed A/MH-6 "Little Bird" helicopters of the Army's 160th Aviation Regiment. The agile little helicopters are modified versions of the Hughes MD500 helicopter.

A rubber duck insertion is where a team of SEALs jumps from an aircraft along with an inflated rubber boat. Attached to a shock-absorbing platform and rigged with large cargo parachutes, the rubber duck, as the complete package is called, is pushed out ahead of the parachuting SEALs. With the inflated rubber boat immediately at hand and ready to go, the SEALs can climb aboard and move out on their mission, covering a much longer distance over water and carrying a great deal more equipment than they could if they were just inserting as combat swimmers.

■ ■ ■

THE cargo aircraft were used for considerably more than just jump platforms or airborne trucks. An idea born prior to the Vietnam War was for a cargo plane to be armed with rapid-fire machine guns aimed out of the side of the aircraft. With the plane circling over a target in what was called a pylon turn, the guns would shoot to the side

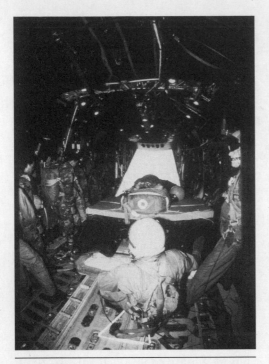

An aircraft crewman prepares to push a rubber boat out the rear of a C-130 cargo plane as the SEALs who will man the boat line up to the left. This is the rubber duck insertion and the SEALs will release the inflated rubber boat from its cardboard-padded pallet once they are in the water. The cavernous interior of the C-130 is illuminated for this training operation. In a combat jump, this procedure would be conducted under very dim light conditions.

USSOCOM PAO

and strafe the ground. The first of these aircraft was the venerable CH-47 fitted with three 7.62mm miniguns aiming out of the plane's port side. The three guns, each firing at 2,000 or 4,000 rounds a minute depending on their settings, could place a 7.62mm bullet on every four square inches of a football field in a single pass. The designation for the new flying gunship was AC-47, but it was better known by its common name— Puff the Magic Dragon.

The AC-47 aircraft suffered from the limited range of its weapons. For accuracy, the gunships would have to circle over their target at an altitude no greater than 3,500 feet, making them vulnerable to ground fire. As the Viet Cong and NVA forces became more sophisticated with their antiaircraft weapons employment, the threat to the gunships became very serious. Orbiting as they would over a target area, the rather slow-moving cargo planes were particularly vulnerable when their port (gun) side was facing away from the enemy's guns. To help relieve this situation, and utilize a more modern airframe, the C-130 Hercules was looked to as a possible gunship platform.

Initial tests were conducted with a C-130 armed with four

Flame projects out from the muzzles of two roaring M61A1 20mm Vulcan cannons as they spew their rounds out at a rate reaching 6,000 rounds per minute. The two 20mm multibarrel cannons are only part of the armament of the awesome AC-130H gunship. Other weapons include the 40mm M2A1 Bofors cannon toward the rear of the aircraft and finally, the modified M102 105mm howitzer that can launch a 33-pound high explosive shell with extreme accuracy.

M61A1 20mm Vulcans and four M134 7.62mm miniguns. The AC-130E Spectre so armed was sent to Vietnam for field testing in the late 1960s. The AC-130 quickly came online as a much heavier-armed gunship. Two 40mm Bofors cannons were installed in place of two each of the Vulcans and miniguns. The Bofors fired full automatic at a very slow rate of 100 to 120 rounds per minute. The magazine of the weapon held stacks of four-round clips, and the gun crew could top-up the magazines as the weapons were being fired.

The Bofors was a welcome addition to the firepower of the gunship, and C-130s so armed were designated AC-130H. During tests for heavier armament to be added to the gunship, the M40A1 106mm recoilless rifle was considered but then dropped due to difficulties with the weapon's backblast. Further research resulted in one of the heaviest weapons ever consistently mounted in an aircraft. A modified M102 105mm howitzer was put in place next to the 40mm Bofors. Even firing a relatively light charge, the 105mm would launch a 33-pound high-explosive projectile that could eliminate any normally encountered ground target. Even buried bunkers could be vulnerable to the incredible firepower of the AC-130H Spectre. The gunship was, and is, an awesome sight in the skies of Vietnam, Grenada, Panama, Afghanistan, and elsewhere.

Specially trained crews of the Air Force Special Operations Squadrons operate their craft with consummate skill. When absolutely necessary, the crews of the gunships could put their shells literally within yards of a SEAL position.

■ Chapter 6

GRENADA

Grenada is a small island nation in the southern Caribbean. Only about 133 square miles in size and boasting a population of about 110,000 native people, Grenada was a place little known by the average American. A small medical school on the island was the place of study for a number of American students, and the island's two major industries, tourism and spice exports, were not something to attract the attention of more than travelers and gourmets. All this changed in late October 1983.

The announcement was made on public television by President Ronald Reagan on 25 October 1983. In short, the president told the American people that the U.S military had invaded the island of Grenada. The operation, backed by a small military contingent from several Caribbean nations, was named URGENT FURY.

Under the eerie red illumination used to preserve night vision, these AC-130 gunship crewmen handle the four-round clips of high explosive 40mm cannon shells for the M2A1 Bofors cannon. Originally designed for antiaircraft use, the 40mm Bofors is seeing a new life as the medium-sized armament of the AC-130 Gunship.

Communist forces based out of Cuba had been working on Grenada for some time prior to the October action. Moscow had sent large shipments of military stores, arms and ammunition, to Grenada because an agreement had been reached between the two countries in 1980. Cuban workers were extending the island's airfield, making it suitable as a way station for bombers and cargo planes heading for Nicaragua.

The final incident for the Reagan administration was the execution of the island's prime minister, Maurice Bishop, by the hard-line Marxist Deputy Prime Minister Bernard Coard on October 19. Control of the island was seized by the Revolutionary Military Council, and a 24-hour curfew was imposed. The announcement was made that anyone violating the curfew would be shot on sight. This made things very dangerous for the nearly 1,000 Americans on Grenada, most of them at St. George's Medical College in the island's capital.

The invasion forces moved in at dawn, roughly 0530 hours Grenada time on 25 October. But there had already been losses among the incoming forces even before the invasion began.

On what was to be SEAL Team Six's first hot combat operation, a team of eight SEALs would be inserted into the waters off Grenada along with a pair of Boston Whaler fiberglass-hulled boats. Aboard a Navy destroyer well over the horizon from Grenada was a four-man Air Force Combat Controller Team (CCT).

The CCT was trained and equipped to manage forward air traffic control for the combat forces coming in to Grenada. What they would immediately do on the island would be to place radio beacons to guide in the MC-130 Combat Talon aircraft that would be carrying U.S. Army Airborne Rangers who would jump in and seize control of the Point Salines Airfield. It would be the SEALs' mission to take the CCT in to the beach and establish security for the unit.

Delays for the SEALs' jump into the waters near Grenada began almost immediately. Late on the afternoon of 23 October eight SEALs were in two C-130 aircraft along with their Boston Whalers rigged for an air drop. For security considerations, the Air Force crews of the C-130s had not been told that they would be conducting a combat operation. Instead, they thought they would be doing only a slightly unusual administrative water drop.

One plane got lost on its way to the rendezvous point with the Navy destroyer, and both planes were late arriving on site for the drop. Instead of an expected daylight drop, the lateness of their arrival, combined with errors in computing times, put the SEALs over their target in the dark.

In spite of being rigged out for a daylight drop, the SEALs decided to go ahead with their insertion. What they didn't know was that one of the aircraft was several miles off-course. The inexperienced Air Force crew knew how to operate their aircraft, but night water jumps were something new to them. But the SEALs were not going to allow their situation to cause them to fail in their

Parachutes collapse down into the water after a successful SEAL water jump. The seas are very calm in this daylight practice operation.

first hot operation. Eight SEALs—four per aircraft—and two boats—one per plane—fell into the night skies of the Caribbean.

What the SEALs had no way of knowing was that a sudden squall, common in that part of the world during that time of year, had blown in below them. Instead of relatively calm seas, the SEALs jumped into six- to eight-foot-high waves. Parachutes tangled with equipment. Boats smashed into the water, and one capsized and was lost.

Four of the SEALs disappeared into the dark ocean. Their bodies were never recovered. The rest of the SEALs struggled with their parachutes and gear in the high waves and 20-knot winds. They somehow managed to get to the one upright Boston Whaler and regrouped with the destroyer.

The first SEAL combat operation since the Vietnam War, and the first hot op for SEAL Team Six, had begun badly. Four SEALs became the first losses to the Teams on a combat operation since 1972. They were Senior Chief Engineman Rudolph Schamberger, Machinist's Mate First Class Kenneth John Butcher, Quartermaster First Class Kevin Lundberg, and Hull Technician First Class Stephen Leroy Morris. In spite of the pain of their losses, the SEALs continued with their operation. Regrouping on the destroyer, they gathered the Air Force CCT and continued with their mission.

On their way into Grenada that same night, the men spotted a Grenadian patrol boat and cut power to minimize their chance of discovery. The single Boston Whaler was overloaded with men and equipment. Water swamped over the stern of the boat, flooding out the motor. Unable to restart it, the SEALs were running out of darkness as dawn was approaching. Finally, they limped their way back to the destroyer, wet, angry, and ready to try again.

The night of 24 and 25 October, the eve of the planned invasion, the SEALs and their CCT companions tried again to get in to the beach near Point Salines. Their attempt resulted in the timetable for the invasion being changed. It was moved back several hours, but the difficult mission was never completed. On their way in to the beach, the Boston Whaler swamped again. The CCT radio equipment was lost, and the floating Whaler was swept out to sea. The first SEAL mission of Urgent Fury was a failure.

The 22nd Marine Amphibious Unit that had been on its way to Beirut before being ordered to Grenada had a detachment of SEALs as part of its normal mission complement. The SEALs from Team Four went in on a normal reconnaissance operation at 2200 hours local time on 24 October. They conducted a recon of the beaches on the north end of the island in spite of bad conditions of driving rain and poor visibility. Working first from Seafox boats and then going on to rubber boats, the SEALs conducted a hydrographic survey of the beach within hearing of a Grenadian work party on the shore.

The SEALs found the beach area and offshore waters too difficult to bring the Marines in by anything but very shallow-draft vessels. So the Marines began coming in and landing on Grenada by helicopter at 0520 hours, Tuesday, 25 October. They quickly captured Pearls Airport and took control of the nearby town of Grenville.

SEAL Team operators practice fast roping from the open doorway of a hovering SH-3G Sea King Helicopter. The very quick fast-roping insertion technique works only because of the strong grip of the leather-glove–wearing SEALs.

U.S. Navy

Two additional operations were to be conducted by SEAL Team Six while the rest of the invasion forces, including the Army Rangers and units from Delta Force, came in to the island. The SEALs would simultaneously take over the transmitting facilities of the Grenadian radio station as well as rescue the island's appointed Governor-General Sir Paul Scoon.

Being an independent nation within the British Commonwealth, the Queen of England is the titular head of State for Grenada and had appointed Sir Paul Scoon the governor-general. Scoon was being held with his staff under virtual house arrest in the governor's mansion, and his rescue had a high priority with the

U.S. government. The SEALs of Team Six assigned to the governor's rescue expected to be on the ground quickly and away with Scoon inside an hour or two. Although their mission was successful and without any casualties on the part of the SEALs or the governor-general's party, they were on the ground in Grenada for more than a full day.

Delays cost the SEALs the element of darkness for their insertion. Instead of coming in before dawn, the SEALs were over Grenada in full daylight. That allowed the Grenadian ground forces to more effectively open fire on the incoming helicopters with anti-aircraft cannon. The SEALs fast roped in to their target and almost immediately lost another helicopter to ground fire.

Limping away, one of the Blackhawk birds had the commanding officer for SEAL Team Six, Robert Gormly, onboard. The bird also had the long-range radio for the unit that had gone in with the other Blackhawk and were already on the ground. In spite of not being wounded during the insertion attempt, Gormly was never able to get back to the SEALs at the governor's mansion.

The SEALs on the ground, under the leadership of Duke Leonard, were able to rescue Scoon and maintain security for the grounds around the mansion. Several times, Grenadian troops and armored vehicles looked to be about to overrun the trapped SEALs, but their own firepower, and that of an overhead AC-130 gunship on one occasion, drove off the island forces. Eventually, the SEALs were able to link up with Marine forces and return Governor-General Scoon to safety.

The SEAL unit attempting to capture the radio station had a much worse situation on their hands. Intelligence about their target had been in error, and the SEALs captured only a transmitter site, the actual studios were some distance away in St. George. A large number of Grenadian troops and armor showed up before the SEALs were able to extract by helicopter. Using their weapons, the SEALs were able to halt the Grenadian troops and badly damage a

In flight over water is the rocket-pod armed A/MH-6 Little Bird of the 160th Army Aviation Regiment.

BTR-60PB armored personnel carrier in the process. When the Grenadian troops began to assault the site again, the SEALs saw that their firepower could not hold off the troops and abandoned the position. Using their escape and evasion training, the SEALs withdrew safely in spite of two men being wounded. Several of the escaping SEALs commandeered a small sailboat from a local marina and sailed out to sea until they were picked up by a Little Bird helicopter.

In spite of their losses, the SEALs completed the majority of their mission assignments during URGENT FURY. Several SEALs were among the crews of the Seafox boats that helped patrol the island's offshore waters after the invasion was over. The situation had been a major learning experience for both the SEALs and the U.S. military as a whole.

Robert Gormly, Captain, USN (Ret.)

Frankly, we were fighting terrorism in Vietnam. The Viet Cong were capable of doing some horrendous things that make some of the

Palestinian groups look pretty tame in comparison. To me, and to a lot of us who've been in the Vietnam conflict, terrorism was just another enemy. At the time it reared its head in the 1970s, SEALs started getting sort of tasked with "What do you do about this if this happens?"

Our big problem was not so much a lack of capability among the people; there was enough foresight to understand what had to be done against terrorism. The problem at the time (mid- to late 1970s) was that we didn't have enough money to buy equipment to do certain things.

Community-wide, I don't think we viewed the terrorists much differently than any other enemy we had to go up against. Operations were pretty much the same, and they really weren't that unique to begin with.

At the time the UDTs were decommissioned in the early 1980s, I happened to be the Chief of Staff at Special Warfare Group One in Coronado. Rear Admiral, then Captain, Irish Flynn was the Commodore of the Group, and I worked for him. We were sitting around one day batting around the notion of maybe some better ways of doing things. We took a look at what was going on operationally with the UDTs and the fact that we had an awful lot of people tied up doing a very small mission.

So we thought about what would happen if we decided to make them all SEALs. This wasn't a new idea; we'd also run this around back in the early 1970s right after Vietnam. It didn't get very far then, but we figured this would economize more the people and their use if we all became SEALs and then made the UDT mission part of the SEAL mission.

Eventually, that's what happened in 1983, and all the UDTs were decommissioned and SEAL Teams and Swimmer Delivery Vehicle Teams were formed. From what I can determine, we never missed a beat in fulfilling any of the requirements we had. It was a good idea.

The creation of SEAL Team Six was something I thought was a good idea as well because we needed to have a well-equipped, well-funded

SEAL entity to be able to do SEAL-like things. And that's what that command could do.

One thing I never expected was to receive the position of commanding officer of SEAL Team Six. That came as a big surprise to me. I'd escaped pulling duty in Washington, D.C., for about eighteen years and I figured I was due, so I was fully prepared to go to Washington after my tour as a Chief of Staff at SpecWarGru One. Instead, I ended up the CO of Team Six.

It was under my watch as the CO that Six saw its first combat operation at the island of Grenada in October 1983. Even given what I know now about what went on during that operation, I don't think there's much that could have been changed. I know you can't go back and rewrite what happened.

I inherited a command that we all—the members of the command as well as myself—learned wasn't ready to go into combat. We were lacking some training, and we certainly lacked equipment. The boats at the time were horrendous; they were in terrible shape. When I relieved Richard Marcinko, we all knew this, but there was nothing we could do about it. You can't just go out and get boats at the drop of a hat.

So we had equipment problems that I couldn't have changed, and wouldn't have had time to change anyway. Frankly, I don't know of anything that I could have changed that would have mattered.

I had no idea of where Grenada was until I was called out of my breakfast one Saturday morning to go learn something about it and to do something about it. To make a long story short, in 1983, Grenada was a British Crown Protectorate with a governor-general appointed by the Queen and a Parliament elected by the people.

During the spring and summer of 1983, the Parliament had been taken over by hook or crook—I'm not sure which, and frankly I don't think it matters—by the Communist element. The Parliament had their own internal problems, not to mention the Communists. One of their men was killed in a coup and another group of Communists took over.

While all this happening, Cubans made their way onto the island at the behest of the Parliament.

One of the things the Cubans were doing was improving an airfield on the southern end of the island. It had been a civilian airfield capable of handling small aircraft, but the Cubans were enlarging the runway and making it capable of handling bombers and fighters. Politically and strategically, that wasn't acceptable to our government, nor should it have been.

The other factor in the mix at the time was a medical school where quite a few American citizens were as students. So when the chaos developed on Grenada in early October, President Reagan was faced with a large Cuban presence on the island plus the threat to the American citizens on the island. He decided that he needed to send some forces down there to deal with that.

The joint organization, of which I was a member as the CO of SEAL Team Six, was one of the units tasked to do something about it. I first learned about the situation on 22 October 1983. Our initial mission was to put some members of an Air Force team on the beach to determine whether the airfield the Cubans had been working on was sufficient to land C-130 and C-141 aircraft on. At the time, we had no satellite coverage of the island and overhead photography apparently wasn't doing enough good. That was the task for the group that ended up losing four people.

The first part of the mission was to go to Port Salinas and check it out to see if it was capable of handling our aircraft. So we put about three guys on a plane, flew them down, and got them on a Navy ship that was at an island nearby. The plan was for the ship to drive them around, and the SEALs would then get in a rubber boat and take the Air Force guys in there to get a look at the airport.

Once the SEALs got to Grenada, my boss decided that he wanted to look at another airfield at the other end of the island. We needed more people down there to do that, and we had to conduct the missions simultaneously.

This was a pretty fast-moving train, and we had a very short time frame to operate in. It was Saturday, and they wanted to do the operation starting out at 0200 on Tuesday, 25 October. The only way to get people down there quickly enough was to fly them down and jump them in with boats.

We picked a spot well away from the island and planned to do a daylight drop, what I would call an administrative-type drop. And it would be far away from anyone who could have seen us. That was the plan as we sent them out.

They were supposed to have jumped at 1600 hours local time. The whole thing was planned on local time, not the normal military ZULU (Greenwich mean) time. But because the east coast of the United States and Grenada were both in the same time zone then, it was done that way.

At 1600, I walked into Command Center at the joint headquarters and asked how the drop went. The Air Force planned said, "Well, it didn't go. We had some problems and had to route them a different way . . . dah . . . dah . . . dah. But don't sweat it, they're time on target is 1800, and it's still daylight."

Well, it wasn't daylight. Daylight saving time had come into effect, and 1800 hours our time was 1900 hours down there. And there was no moon so it was dark. The jumpers came in on two C-130s. We had the people on the ship who had been put down there earlier and had communications with the aircraft. The aircraft came in, and in the aftermath we learned that instead of dropping in trail as they were supposed to have done, the first aircraft broke in right on the ship and the people went out of the plane. The second aircraft, for some reason, went two more miles past the ship and then turned and dropped.

To complicate matters further, anyone who has ever been in the Caribbean will understand that sudden squalls pop up down there. It can be bright and sunny and five minutes later it can be raining with thirty miles an hour blowing winds.

That's apparently what happened. A squall overcame the drop zone just before the jumpers went out. Nobody on the ship noticed it, and the jumpers went out at night, rigged for a daylight drop, in the squall. The best we can determine, four men from Team Six couldn't get out of their parachutes and probably ended up drowning. We never recovered a body or the equipment, so we don't know for sure what happened to them.

Being the commander of a Team that suffered the first combat losses since Vietnam affected me deeply. Murphy's Law certainly took over that operation—anything that could go wrong did.

I use the saying "It wasn't pretty, but we got the job done" in referring to the operations at Grenada. We did two other operations later. I will call one of them completely successful, and the other one was successful, but at the wrong place. So it wasn't pretty, but the missions were completed.

The State Department and everyone else were telling us that Grenada would be a cakewalk. Grenada had no military, but everyone underestimated the role of the Cubans there. In fact, I had a State Department gent look me in the eye and tell me that the Cubans would be in the barracks during this mission. Had I not been so sleep-deprived at the time, I probably would have said, "How do you know?"

In the aftermath of the operation I figured this out: Every place there were Cubans down there, there was pretty heavy fighting. They motivated the Grenadians into putting up a defense. We found out later that the Cubans, nearly to a man, were combat veterans from their fighting in Angola. They had brought in antiaircraft weapons and shot down a bunch of helos. In fact, one of the ones I was on was almost knocked out.

But the enemy, as it were, were a lot stiffer than anyone gave him credit for being. But where there weren't any Cubans around, like at the governor-general's house, there were only Grenadians who gave up their weapons as soon as they saw our guys. For the Grenada operation, the Cubans were the stiff resistance factor.

For the next combat operation of SEAL Team Six, we were to engage the enemy that we were originally intended for—terrorists. When the cruise ship Achille Lauro was seized by Palestinian Liberation Front terrorists, a detachment from SEAL Team Six was sent in to take back the ship. Would the plan have worked? I don't know, because it never happened.

I never heard of any aspect of the operation going down where the credit for the capture would have been given to the Italians or any other unit. That was not in my mind. In those days, supposedly everything Six did was unknown.

From my level in the command structure on down, as I remember, to give credit for the operation to another unit for political reasons was not the notion. We were just going to go and do our job. We had a good plan for taking back the ship, but unfortunately, we didn't get the opportunity to carry it out.

When I was at Six, I never felt that I was not able to go out with the men if the situation called for it. I wasn't that old, and frankly, my notion and philosophy of command was that I was going to be at the scene of the hottest action. And that's what I pretty much tried to do. Even though my job as the commanding officer is to direct the whole of an operation, my philosophy was to do that directing from the front line. I didn't believe in sitting in the back and letting others do it. So for every one of our planned missions, that's where I was going to be—and was in some cases.

If you ever lose that sort of a mentality in the SEAL business, if you ever think that you're a rear-echelon so-and-so, then you need to get out of that business. Every SEAL officer, from an admiral on down, ought to be thinking that he should be at the front. SEALs lead from the front, we don't lead from the rear.

* * *

What I would tell someone about the history and future of the Teams is that first of all, know the history of the Teams. Hopefully, this book will help a lot in that direction. Since the time I first became involved with the SEALs, the SEALs and UDTs have been excellent at never writing anything down on paper. I tell people we're like an Indian tribe: information gets passed down to the younger troops from legends being told around the fires.

That's okay, but when all your old chiefs go out, their experience goes with them. This is particularly true in the present-day SEAL Teams. I doubt there's anybody with any combat experience in Vietnam still on active duty, and I'd be very surprised if there were any more than one or two here and there.

I think I would first tell the young men of today that they need to understand their history and where they came from—the UDTs of World War II, then Vietnam, as that was the first proving ground for the SEALs, then the many other situations since then—the latest being the Persian Gulf and maybe Bosnia, but I'm not certain about what went on or is going on in Bosnia.

I would tell the troops that they need to have a sense of history, that they should understand that they're part of something that is very proud of its existence, which hasn't always been easy to maintain. They need to consider themselves professionals and not some Rambos running around with knives in their teeth. They have a job to do, and they should be committed to their Teammates, the Command, the military, their country, and all of that which, believe it or not, used to factor into a lot of our minds.

A lot of people would say that it was just flag-waving and BS, but it wasn't. A lot of us back in the old days actually thought that we were part of something bigger. We knew we were. I think the young men today need to understand that.

I'm speaking before a BUD/S graduation class on Friday, and I'm going to tell them just what I said here. They need to know where they came from and what's expected of them once they get to the Teams. And I'll tell them to never compromise their professionalism and to always maintain their honor, integrity, and just be good citizens.

I never thought SEALs were anything unique. To me a SEAL was just a guy, myself included, who just had some unique training and did a specific type of mission. That's how it is for naval aviators who fly on and off aircraft carriers, too. That scares the hell out of me and is something that I definitely wouldn't want to do.

My advice to a guy in the Teams, or someone just coming in to them, is this: You're going to be a professional and part of a professional organization, and you're going to have a lot of fun in the process.

I wouldn't use the term "bad ass" to describe the SEALs, although a Hollywood type might because SEALs are tough. We go through tough training and have a tough mission, and individually we're mentally tough, which is probably our biggest attribute. Physically, we're a lot like anybody else walking on the street. Whatever your definition of "bad ass" is, I don't know. If the connotation of that is negative, then I would definitely say it doesn't describe the SEALs. When I watch movies like Rambo, yeah, I laugh. It's funny, some of it really is.

The SEAL Teams are a team; it's the only full-time military organization that has that designation of being a team. And that's just what it is—a bunch of guys pulling together to do the job. It's inculcated into everyone who comes through our basic training course. They never lose that mentality when they leave. They aren't just individuals, they are part of a larger group that has to function like a team to get the job done.

First, JFK said "Let there be unconventional warfare forces in all the military services." The Navy leadership looked at that and said, "Well, we kind of have the UDTs who did some of these sorts of things in Korea. We'll form something out of the UDTs." And that's what happened—the SEALs formed directly out of the UDTs.

The Marines have a saying: "Once a Marine, always a Marine." I think that's even more true for the SEALs. Once you're in a Team, that's your life, and you'll do what you have to do to keep it going. The notion after Vietnam was sort of "put them back in their cages until the next war." Of course, our guys weren't going to put up with that, and we did what we had to do to keep the Commands going. I've bought my own equipment when I had to, and a lot of other guys did as well when the money wasn't there. That's just the way it was.

Frankly, there were two reasons for this. First of all, we knew that what we could offer the country and the military was something no one else could. No other unit could do the job we did. Second, I think our guys had too much pride to just throw up their hands and quit, that's about the bottom line.

If the SEALs were suddenly ordered to become a professional football team, we would probably win the NFL championship. I'm serious. I used to take a lot of ribbing from some of the regular Naval officers, the blue water types, about how the SEALs could only do one thing and could never go out and run a ship. I would tell them to give me a ship and give me my men from SEAL Team Two, and in a month, we would have the best ship in the Fleet. I fully believe that the guys can do anything. So if we had to be a professional football team, we would figure out a way to do it and win.

In my own book, Combat Swimmer: Memoirs of a Navy SEAL, *I talk about a "lock and load" mentality. Lock and load is a term everybody uses to mean be ready, but in a SEAL Team, it's a reality.*

Wellington T. "Duke" Leonard, Lieutenant Commander, USN (Ret.)

I joined the Navy in 1966. After spending a year in the Fleet, I had the opportunity to go through BUD/S training in 1967. I had a step-uncle who had been in UDT Eleven from 1959 to 1961, so when I joined the Navy, thanks to my step-uncle, I knew about the UDTs and wanted to be a part of them. The SEALs were still very classified back then, and I per-

In the surf zone at the edge of the Pacific, BUD/S students continue the most common activity they will be doing during training—push-ups.

sonally know nothing about them. The SEALs were classified even as we went through training.

My BUD/S class was 6702, Class 40 in the sequential numbering system. That was an East Coast class—a summer one, thank God—conducted at Little Creek, Virginia. I didn't have any problem getting through training, none at all. Fortunately, thank God, I stayed healthy through the course and just kept moving. Quitting wasn't a thought that ever crossed my mind.

Hell Week was just a lot of harassment and no sleep. We were cold and wet, but moving forward was all I had to keep doing. All the memories of training are kind of clumped together now. Probably the strongest memory I have is that there were only two real written tests when we went through training. There was a demolition test and a cartography test. That was about it, other than doing a lot of push-ups.

To me, it's simple. To get through training, you have to have the will to keep going. If you don't have it, you won't make it. You can be the biggest, strongest, fastest guy in the world, but if you don't have the will to complete the training, you're not going to get there.

Class 40 might have been the largest class that ever went through training. I want to say that there were 355 guys who started training, and we graduated 54. The line of helmets from the quitters went around the block. Once we got everyone thinned out, normally that was after Hell Week, we got on with the real training. That class had more retirees in it, more men who spent their career in the Navy and the Teams, than any other class that had gone before it.

When we checked in to Underwater Demolition Team Twenty-One, we started to get the word on the SEAL Team. That sounded like just what I wanted to do, so I started putting in a transfer chit once a week to get over there.

Finally, I made it over to SEAL Team Two on 11 May 1968. It was my birthday, so I remember the date exactly. My first deployment to Vietnam was with Seventh Platoon in January 1969. My first impression of Vietnam was that it was great. It was everything I hoped it could be. It was warm, the people were great, and there was all the operating you could possibly do. That's why I had gone through all the training—to be out in the field operating.

Mind you, I was just a seaman when I started my evolution into combat. Fortunately, when I came back, I had been promoted to E-5. To help break in the next SEAL platoon that had come in to relieve us, I volunteered to stay in Vietnam an extra three months when the rest of my platoon went back home. My time in Vietnam was basically spent conducting operations and taking liberty.

On my first tour, there were so many operations that picking out just a few is hard. There was Bob Thomas's op—he went down in a helo and ended up winning a Navy Cross for holding off the VC with nothing more than a couple of pistols.

My first combat mission in Vietnam was supposed to be just a "break-in" op, where the new platoon was broken in to the area of operations. We went out and I was walking point. Talk about being wired, I thought there were bad guys behind every tree and bush. Al Ashton and Paul Schwartz caught three guys walking up behind us. When they took them out the noise compromised us, so the VC now knew we were there. We extracted.

As we extracted, we started taking mortar rounds from the VC around us. The platoon officer at that time was Ron Yeaw, and he did an outstanding job zig-zagging us out of there.

The first six operations I ever went out on, we got hits—we made contact with the enemy. I think it was the third operation that I got blown out of a door by a grenade. After all this, I thought this was what was going to happen every time we went out into the field.

Unfortunately, Admiral Zumwalt thought Seventh Platoon was doing so well that we should go to the Cambodian Border for interdiction operations there. We didn't get a hit for two months—nothing, no contact. Here we were, netted a lot of action after our first six operations, then all of a sudden, dry for two months. That just destroys you.

We were a platoon operating on the border between South Vietnam and Cambodia, trying to interdict North Vietnamese coming across. And we did stop some. One time, a squad of us, Al Ashton, Dick Moran, myself, and others, were out on an op. We were sitting on the border and had intelligence that 120 North Vietnamese were going to cross. Yeah, right, we thought.

The group of us were sitting on the north side of a canal, surrounded by open terrain, nothing but low grass. Looking across to the south about thirty yards away, we could see three guys crawling on their hands and knees. We were looking through a starlight scope so we could see them clearly, but they couldn't see us. Then, about thirty yards behind the three guys, came this mass of NVA troops moving along.

Sitting there, we contemplated opening up on them. There were only seven of us. We would just hose them down and then run. And the only place we could run to was into Cambodia. So we backed off from that idea and just watched them cross by. Then we gave a sitrep (situation report) when we got back. The Intel had been good, and the report was all we could do.

It was on my second tour, with Jim Watson and Sixth Platoon beginning in April 1970. Jim and I had some great operations. One op I love telling about had Watson and I going out after an individual who had opened up the gates of Hy Yen in 1962 or 1963. With the gates open, the Viet Cong came in and killed every man, woman, and child in the place.

In 1970, I, Watson, Chuck Fellers, John Porter, Bud Thrift, and others were advisors for a Chinese company, for lack of a better description. We located our target, and Watson and I went out on the op along with five of the Chinese guys to snap this guy up.

It was a perfect op. We snatched the guy up without a shot being fired. Watson got more Intel that there were more bad guys off in another direction, and he told me that he was going to take three of the Chinese with him to check out the situation and that I was to stay where I was with the other two Chinese and the prisoner. Then he put a set of S&W handcuffs on the guy and handed me the keys, with the instructions to see to it that nothing happened to our prisoner, because he was going to be a valuable source of Intel for more ops.

So I was just sitting out there, and Watson had been gone about thirty minutes when the Chinese came up to me and told me that they wanted to talk to our prisoner. They wanted to see if there were any more of his buddies around.

My thoughts were that this guy had left the gates open to a civilian village that was wiped out by his VC buddies. Besides, I had the key and I knew they weren't going to do anything with the handcuffs on the guy. So I said they could go and talk to him.

About two minutes went by and I suddenly heard the bam . . . bam of a pair of gunshots. Oh, my God, I thought, just what's going on? Then one of the Chinese came back and handed me the handcuffs.

Not very long after that, Watson came up and asked what was going on. I said that he wasn't going to believe it anyway, so I handed him back the handcuffs. I still hear about that every once in a while.

While I was in Vietnam, I was a Stoner man. In the squad, I carried the Stoner light machine gun. We had the best and the brightest weapons and equipment at that time; the SEALs were on the forefront of all the new equipment. The Stoner was an outstanding piece of weaponry. It could put out fire at a rate of more than 1,000 rounds a minute and was loaded with a 150 round drum. Normally I would carry eight bandoleers on an operation, with 100 rounds of linked ammunition for the Stoner in each bandoleer, depending on the op. There were a few times during that tour that we would come back with less than fifty rounds in the Stoner. Things got a little tenuous on some operations, I will say that.

But, digressing to training for a second, you had to have the will to get through training. When you go out on these ops, you have to have the will to complete the operation. That's the beauty of training—it separates those who have the will from those who do not have it.

In spite of the difficulty sometimes, I was always comfortable on an op. In fact, I felt more secure out in the field, and I'm sure a lot of guys will say the same thing. We would go out and lay down in an ambush and just wait. But we felt so comfortable out there, in spite of the situation, because nothing could really get to us. We were on their territory, on bad ground, with bad guys all around, and they've got to find you. That's pretty hard.

After we pulled out of Vietnam, things changed. We came back and it was basically "lock them up, throw the key away, and we'll call you when we need you again." That was a rough period. There was a big cut in RDT&E (research, development, training and equipment) money and pay. There were a lot of exercises that we went on all over the world, but everything seemed kind of superfluous after going to Vietnam.

I left the active Navy in 1972, but stayed in the Navy Reserves. I had decided that I was going to get my college degree, become an officer, and go to OCS. My feelings were that I could accomplish more going this route than by slamming away at the promotion exams. My enlisted rate was mineman, which was really a closed rate with promotions being few and far between. After they got through with Vietnam, the Navy really shot it down.

So I spent three and a half years in the Navy Reserves and then came back in, receiving my commission in 1976. As an officer returning to the Teams, I didn't have to go through any refresher training and was able to report back without any problems.

A new enemy had developed during the 1970s, and the SEALs had to address a new kind of conflict. During the Vietnam conflict, basically, the enemy left the cities and went to the countryside where they started beating up on the farmers. That's where the VC got their resources. In the early 1970s, the enemy left the countryside and went back to the cities. There, they began pulling off their operations in the cities, hence the word urban in Urban Warfare. So that's where we had to adapt. We were good at chasing them around out there in the countryside; that was guerrilla warfare. But once they started going back into the cities, blowing up airplanes, hijacking, kidnapping, and assassinating, we had to change our warfighting skills to adapt to the city.

And it wasn't hard for us. The same principles that applied in the guerrilla theater of war also applied in urban warfare. We just had to change various tactics to operate in buildings, planes, and other vessels.

In the late 1970s, I was the operations officer at UDT Twenty-one. Lou Boink was the CO, and Tom Richards was the XO. MOB Six, the mobilization platoon tasked with the counterterrorism mission for the Teams on the East Coast, was doing its thing over at SEAL Team Two. There was going to be either an expansion of MOB-Six or there was going to be another SEAL Team created. When the decision was made to create a new SEAL Team, each East and West Coast Team was to pony up so many men to fill the ranks.

Lou Boink was a supporter of what Captain Marcinko was trying to do in developing SEAL Team Six. So he ponied up his best and brightest guys who wanted to go to the interviews. I really didn't interview or anything, they just snapped me up for the new Team. I was glad they did. I figured I was a lot older than a lot of the other guys in the new Team, plus I was a lieutenant, j. g. (junior grade) at the time.

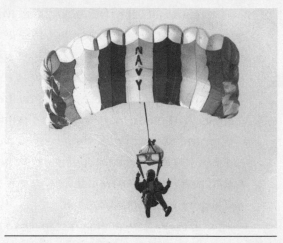

Sailing into a soft landing under the fully inflated canopy of a high performance parachute is this SEAL member of the U.S. Navy Parachute Team. His free-falling skills were gained through hard practice for a much more serious use of a parachute, the clandestine airborne insertion of SEALs to a target area.

U.S. Navy

The new assignment was something I was really excited about, simply because we were going to be on the pointy end of the spear again. I wanted to get back into combat; that's the reason I volunteered. The training they were doing was all new. It was some wild stuff and state-of-the-art operations. The Teams to this day are better for what we did because we passed on all the information we developed on the new ways of operating.

At SEAL Team Six, we really developed our insertion and extraction skills. We learned new skills, like room entry. Actually, we developed these skills, because nobody before us and including us really knew how to do it. So we just jumped in with both feet and learned it from scratch.

We learned some intensive parachuting skills. By intensive, I mean jumping out of a plane and HAHOing, which is high-altitude, high-opening, a hop-and-pop, at 32,000 feet. We would be running on oxygen and traveling thirty, thirty-five miles across the ground on a jump. It's cold up there, sixty-five degrees below zero.

So we pushed the envelope on everything. In diving, we pushed working with the Draeger to where we were doing four-and five-hour dives, because nobody really understood just how far we could go with these things. And we had the flexibility to go out there and push it.

There was a cost to this high-speed work. Yes, we had some training accidents. That's going to happen, and it's not going to stop happening. Rodney Cheuy was killed early on in a shooting accident, we lost Gary Hershey on a parachute accident, and there were follow-on accidents. The deaths had no effect on the commitment of the men in the Teams. If anything, it made them work even harder.

Our training schedule was pretty incredible. For four years, I spent roughly 300 days a year training. I'd be home 60 days a year to see my family, and I never knew just when I was going to be home. It was usually just an in-and-out situation.

It was very intense and on-step. I can remember going up to A.P. Hill in Virginia to do fire-and-maneuver problems with Blue Team. It was Hell Week all over again. In seven days, we got roughly twelve hours of sleep. We were doing around-the-clock ops.

Our first combat operation with SEAL Team Six came in October 1983 with the invasion of Grenada. I was the team leader for Governor-General Scoon's house. It was great leading all the young guys into combat for the first time, and that was due, in part, to our training.

They always told me that at twenty-five yards you had to be able to shoot two rounds into the black. I said that there were going to be a few things that are going to interface with your theory. One's going to be adrenaline, and two's going to be some bumps and scrapes. You've got to expend a lot of energy before you can fire that first round.

So we were tasked with securing Governor-General Scoon's mansion while he was under house arrest. We fast roped in from a hovering Blackhawk helicopter. I went down and went right through a tree. Fifteen guys right behind me all went through the branches of this big oak tree as well. That tree beat us up bad, and everyone had scrapes and bruises. Then we hit this retaining wall in Scoon's front yard and rolled down the hill to Luke Street.

The bad guys were all on the outside of the fence surrounding the governor-general's place, so we had to have it out down there, run back up to the retaining wall, and wait for Bob Gormly, our CO, to come in.

We were taking rounds from all over the place when I saw some movement at the mansion. I told Dennis Chalker to cover me and we crossed the driveway. Introducing myself to the man who was just coming out of a doorway, I find out that the man was Governor-General Scoon.

The governor-general handed me an AK-47 he had and we shook this other man down who was with Scoon. The other man had a pistol on him, so I took it and passed him up to Johnny Johnson. Scoon looked into the cellar door behind him, motioned, and out came eleven more people—his wife and ten of his staff. That situation had deviated from the intelligence we had received on the situation.

My guys were really pumped up with excitement. Coming in on the helicopters, we had been taking a lot of 23mm flak. Rich Hanson had been hit and he didn't even know it yet. Then we had been banged up by the tree on the insertion. The young guys' eyes were like saucers.

This was a handful, so into the house we went. I asked Scoon if the house was clear. He said that he thought so, that all the guards had run away when they saw us come in. Because we were taking rounds out in the yard, everyone was much safer in the house. So after getting everyone in the house, we started clearing it room by room. I was walking with Scoon, and I suddenly yelled out, "Everybody freeze!"

Everybody froze in place. "What do you see, Duke? What do you see?"

Their hearts had to be racing right about then. The adrenaline of combat pushes nerves to the limit. They were all excited and ready to pop.

"Now tell me about that twenty-five-yard head shot," I said. "Now go ahead and keep clearing."

Basically, we had no intelligence going into the operation on Grenada. What I was told was that on the island there were four BTR-60s, an armored vehicle armed with a 14.5mm machine gun, and only the Grenadian troops that had been trained by the Cubans to oppose us.

Under normal lighting, this crewmember of an AC-130 gunship loads a high-explosive shell into the breech of a modified M102 105mm howitzer. The cannon is the largest piece in the arsenal of the AC-series of gunships and is the biggest gun normally carried by any aircraft in the world.

When I got there, we had four BTR-60s at the front gate, two on one side of the driveway and two on the other. I thought, My God, I've got all four of them right here. Then I watched all of these trucks going up and down Luke Street. These guys might be a little more organized than we thought. Then we took an RPG rocket off the roof of the mansion, then a round came through a window.

Our Intel had been atrocious. Nobody knew really what we were going to be facing.

We had fast roped about ninety feet down to the ground from the helicopter. Each SEAL probably weighed 100 pounds more than normal with all his equipment on. We hit that retaining wall, then the tree. We were banged up pretty good coming in. In all of that crashing about, our only antitank weapon, an M72 LAW, was bent. At one point, I think Johnny Johnson told Dennis Chalker to get ready to fire the LAW. It was bent enough that I think Chalker was very glad he never had to fire it.

When we first got to the mansion, we didn't have any communications. We ended up setting up a link with Gormly's troops down at Port Salinas through our MX-360 handheld radios.

I talked to them, and they told me that they had something to take care of the armored vehicles we were facing. They had an AC-130 gunship on the horn. I thought that was great. The miniguns, vulcan cannon, 40mm cannon, and 105 howitzer of an AC-130 gunship could easily deal with everything we were facing.

The BTR-60s were coming in toward the house, and behind them were about ten or fifteen troops. The troops would then try to circle around to the backyard. They made something like four runs, and it wasn't very long until we were totally surrounded. They were conducting reconnaissance by fire and just trying to get us to crank off a round so they could figure out where we were. Everyone in my team held their fire. They did very well.

Then I got the AC-130 up online. But it wasn't a direct line. I had a three-step communications drill with the gunship. First, I had to talk to Master Chief Dennis Johnson on the hill. Then he had to relay my directions to the support personnel who had a PRC-77 radio. That radioman radioed up to the gunship, and they would start firing. Then I would tell them when to stop.

With our communications drill, I walked in the rounds to about twenty-five yards of the house. Then I had them do a 360-degree firing run around the house, then go over and hit Bishop's house some 200 meters away.

Even though we got things to work after a fashion, commo did not work well during the op. When we had first arrived at Scoon's place, we hadn't heard from anybody. We were totally surrounded, and we had four BTR-60s in front of us. The op had called for us to be at the mansion for only forty-five minutes. And I hadn't seen hide nor hair of Bob Gormly. Later we learned that he had been shot out of the sky.

Things were looking a little grim.

I got on the phone at the governor-general's mansion and called down to the airfield. I didn't want to give away anything over the phone, OPSEC (operational security) and all. When a young Army Ranger, a private, answered the phone, I spoke rather cryptically.

"Look, Private," I said, "do me a favor. Have you seen any of those long-haired guys running around down there? You know, the ones that are always wet?"

"Yeah, I did," he said. Then he did exactly what I didn't want him to do—he set down the phone and ran away.

A minute-and-a-half later—I was sweating bullets the whole time—Wally Stevens was on the phone. I started chewing him out, asking just what was going on.

"It's not pretty down here at this end," he said.

"Well, you ought to see it at this end!" I said rather sharply.

But everything worked out and we did establish communications. That was a tough situation, especially for the troops. I was very fortunate, because I had some Vietnam vets with me—Johnny Johnson, Bobby Lewis, and Timmy Prusak. I put them out on the perimeter around the house, trying to balance the situation.

When I was setting the guard around the house, I had Bob Lewis and Rich Hanson with me. As I was walking out, two guys popped over the fence and cranked off a round. This thing lands about six inches from my face, peppering me with a bit of shrapnel. All I said was "Get them."

Lewis, without any hesitation, opened up on those guys—picked them up and laid them right out on the picket fence down there. Those are the kind of reactions you want in a combat situation.

It hadn't quite been like that on the helicopter coming in. That helo ride was absolutely fantastic for me. We flew treetop level all the way into the target zone, then popped up as we approached the mansion.

The birds were crowded. I had to squat for the whole sixty-one-minute flight. Nobody could move. We had fifteen guys in the bird—all combat troops—and everybody was jammed in place. Myself and the older guys, Bobby Lewis, Timmy Prusak, and Johnny Johnson, we were just bored and only wanted to get off that flight. Everybody else was mostly just staring eyeballs.

Then we started taking flak from the ground. It was a lot of fire.

Gormly's bird ended up taking more than we did. Ours was the lead bird in and the ground gunners must have gotten a better silhouette of the bird behind us. I think Gormly's bird ended up taking forty-six rounds—heavy hits.

But we did the mission, successfully pulling out Governor-General Scoon and his people without any losses after something like twenty-six hours on the ground. The men I had to work with in Team Six were absolutely outstanding. That gets right back to that level of will needed to be in the Teams.

All the guys at Six had volunteered to be where they were, knowing they were going to be on the pointy end of the spear. The training we went through was incredibly intense. Then we had a shot at taking our training to war. That was the highlight. Those guys performed admirably, and you can expect that.

For the SEALs, the mission always comes first. But then there's always your Teammates. No one is ever left behind. Mike Thornton demonstrated that better than anyone. Mike's a good man, and what he did with Tommy Norris is just incredible. I'm glad to say that Mike's a good friend of mine; Tommy is a good friend of mine as well.

Here was Tommy in Vietnam, shot and left for dead. Mike, with complete disregard for his own personal safety, ran back to Tommy and got him. He killed three of the enemy on the spot, then he picked Tommy and ran him off the beach along with several LDNNs. They jumped into the water while gunfire from a cruiser ripped up the beach behind them. Then Mike just swam straight out to sea.

Tommy Norris was only semiconcious, bleeding from the head, and had lost his eye from the injury. But Mike saved him—a superhuman act. Mike received the Medal of Honor for his actions that day. But that kind of action, although maybe not to that degree, was pretty common among the SEALs. Mike was recognized for it, and I'm glad he was.

Bob Thomas did something very similar. Only he was in a helo that crashed in Hy Tien, near the Cambodian border. He ended up saving at least the co-pilot of the bird, also an incredible thing. Here was Bob, all banged up from the crash. And all he could find was a .45 pistol. He ended up shooting one Viet Cong at something like one-hundred yards with that .45. He received the Navy Cross for that action, and we in the Teams are all very proud of him.

There were times we saved people and times we lost them. During the first SEAL action at Grenada, the insertion was plagued with bad timing. The guys were looking to do a daylight, administrative drop from an aircraft, a "rubber duck" insertion where men jumped along with a boat. Things didn't go as planned, and somehow, something got delayed. The guys ended up jumping at 1830 hours. It was dark and they were not rigged for a night jump. The seas had picked up from around two feet to four feet to six feet, and the winds had risen from around eight knots to around twenty-two or twenty-four knots.

The SEALs mentality is, Hey, we've got to get down. We have a job to do. So they jumped. I would have done the same thing. Four men, close Teammates of mine, drowned on that insertion.

The operation at Grenada happened so fast that there wasn't any time for any real hard rehearsals or anything like that. It was more of a "let's do it" situation. I would say that the thing that hurt us most was the lack of intelligence of what was on the ground.

The development of the Special Operations Command, SOCOM, has solved many of the problems we faced back then. The Grenada problem, as far as the lack of intelligence, has been cleaned up three-fold. Panama, with the exception of Noriega taking off, went pretty well, too.

We were tasked with getting Noriega in Panama. He had run up to Colon to give a speech and just disappeared. Once he disappeared out of Colon at 4 o'clock in the afternoon, the U.S. forces basically began knocking on doors in Panama, trying to find the guy. We ended up chasing him into a Catholic church.

The bottom line was that we couldn't get Noriega because we just didn't know where he was.

He had flown up to Colon to give this speech, then got in a car and drove back to Panama City. Intel didn't know he had done this, so he just disappeared from our view.

A SEAL is your basic, normal guy. You can't tell one by looking at him; they look the same as everyone else—some are thin, some are big. The differences center on the will. These guys have the mental will to get through the training, get through the operation, and ensure mission success. That's the difference.

Quite honestly, the SEALs are so busy doing various training scenarios and exercises that they just don't have the time to go out and act like the Hollywood image of a SEAL. Basically, they don't want the visibility, the Command doesn't need it, and the personnel don't need it. They just do their job and play like everyone else.

The uniqueness of a SEAL Team centers on the camaraderie between all of its members. These guys spend more time with each other than they do with their families. I was deployed 300 days a year, so I spent a lot more time with my Teammates than I did with my own family—and I did this for ten years.

This makes all the members of the Team very close to each other. They're so close that they really don't have to verbally communicate—they can almost do it through osmosis. As a group, they tick like a Swiss watch. And that's what you want.

You put a challenge before them and everybody knows what everybody else is thinking. They should, they've practiced with each other a hundred times for every problem. Then, after the work's done, you'd think everybody would go home. No, they all go out and have a couple beers. Then they go home.

There is a tradition of going out and having a few beers for a Teammate who's been lost. I've had more than a few beers in that particular tradition, and that's unfortunate. Basically, you get a keg. Normally the family of the lost Teammate will provide that keg. After a number of SEALs were lost at Paitilla Airfield, Ross Perot came in, brought a beer truck, and parked it in the compound. We all went from the memorial service right to the beer truck. When I punch out, I hope that's what happens for me.

These guys in the Teams are self-motivating. President Kennedy formally started the SEAL Teams back in 1962. There were the underwater demolition teams back then, which were the same guys just with different names. They took the ball Kennedy handed them and ran with it. There were some creative officers, such as Bill Hamilton and Roy Boehm, who started the ball rolling and brought the idea of the Teams to fruition.

The reason why you have to expend the energy to keep training is because you know you're going to have to go back to war again. It might not be in two months, or it might not be in ten years, but it's going to happen. A conflict is going to rise up. And if it happens on your watch, you want to ensure that you're ready.

So you get very creative. You try to put up some of the slickest training exercises that you can think of. And all that time, you're still searching for the right equipment. You always want to have that edge that technology can give you.

The SEALs are a small unit. We have flexibility. We have our oversight, our commanding officers, and our staff. That's where the ability to apply our skills and our latitude to go out and try different things lies.

Back in my early days, we didn't put on the Trident because we didn't have it yet. The only unusual insignia we wore on our uniform was Navy Parachute Wings. Earning them wasn't a big deal—you had to complete ten jumps. Just going through Army Airborne training gave you five jumps right there.

Where I was, it wasn't a real big tradition. If you had ten jumps or you had fifty jumps, you just kept jumping. You had sky guys and other *guys who really didn't like jumping, but they still had to do it. It was part of the job.*

There wasn't any big moment when I knew I was a SEAL. I didn't do anything more than walk onto the quarterdeck at SEAL Team Two on 11 May 1968. Master Chief Rudy Boesch was right there on me, telling me to go get a haircut and then get ready to take over the quarterdeck. That was my first day.

Of course, when you went across the street to SEAL Team Two, the guys at UDT Twenty-One said that you were leaving them, that you were abandoning ship. And they beat the holy crap out of you. You end up looking like the ragman in off the street. Then you go across to the SEAL Team, and Rudy's standing there waiting for you. He jumps all over you with orders to get a haircut and get cleaned up and all of that so that you can assume the watch.

I ended up standing the quarterdeck watch my first thirty days at SEAL Team Two. But that's probably the best way to learn the Teams, the organization, the faces, and all that stuff. But you're so intimidated by checking in to that command that you just don't think of those things.

I was a seaman who had been hearing all these great war stories about the men over at SEAL Team Two. And here I was with Bob Gallagher and Scotty Lyon walking around. These guys have eight rows of ribbons on their chests, and here I was with my National Defense ribbon on. I just told myself that I had to get some of those ribbons myself. I just didn't know how yet.

It's a very intimidating situation for a new guy. And I pretty much stayed intimidated for a year until I came back from Vietnam. After I came back from my first combat tour, I was finally comfortable at SEAL Team Two.

The first word that comes to my mind when I think about the SEALs is aggressiveness. That goes back to what I said about training, that you have to have the will to get through training. You have to have the will to be a SEAL. Once you get into that platoon, you're with fourteen guys who have that same will. And all they're doing is waiting and watching. They want to act, to apply that will of theirs. Hopefully, something will come up.

Pride is an inherent trait in everyone, although some people have more pride than others. As far as I'm concerned, it's a quiet pride that we have in the Teams. Everyone is really proud of each other. The competitiveness of most SEALs will probably hold them back a little from showing their pride for another Teammate, but they normally love to see each other succeed, especially if that success furthers the Team's goals.

The individual SEALs in the Team are there to do one thing—complete the mission successfully. It's a Team evolution. One guy doesn't go out and do an op. It's fourteen, twenty, or a hundred guys, who pull it off. And without each and every one of those guys, the Team wouldn't be complete, it wouldn't be whole.

The guys in BUD/S right now and the UDTs from World War II are the same guy, the same faces, just different names. We've evolved since then, training's different. Plus the guys today are a little smarter. But they are all the same guy. They're just going to be introduced to some different skills then the guys from UDT Twenty-One, or UDT One for that matter.

During World War II, they needed somebody to do something hard. That's the bottom line. The Navy needed some work done, and it was hard work. They went out and found some guys who could do that hard work, and they didn't complain. Those men were the first UDTs.

I don't have any idea what the needs will be for the SEALs in the future, what their hard work is going to be exactly. What I do know is that the Teams will adapt. I can guarantee you that.

One of the SEALs I've known is Captain Bill Hamilton. Bill's a great guy, a real sweetheart, a prince of a gentleman. He's had one heck of a career. He had a career on the civilian side, and he retired from Naval Special Warfare. I had the good fortune to work with him for about three years.

Tom Richards is also great man. We call him the Hulk. Tom is one of these guys who puts his nose down and goes to work, and he doesn't quit until the work is done. Whether it's lifting weights or pushing paper or operators, he concentrates on the job at hand and gets it done. I first met Tom in 1970 in Ca Mau, Vietnam. He's a big guy—240 pounds, the Hulk just sitting there. I walked in, weighing 148 pounds, and just looked at him. Where did this guy come from? I wondered.

He was at SEAL Team One down in Ca Mau, working with Leon Rauch. He was just passing through. That was the first time I met him. The next time I ran across him, he was the XO at UDT Twenty-One. It's a small community in the Teams.

But I can't say who's the best operator I ever met. I think that they all are. Once again, to have that successful mission, you have to have all the members of a Team in sync, ticking like a Swiss watch.

I think that there are a lot of guys who have had the same experience I have. You're in your forties and all of a sudden you've got a seventeen-year-old with you. This guy is a hard-charger. He's got the hairy-chested, antimagnetic, you-can't-hurt-me type of mentality. What you have to do is basically slow him down a bit and just get him focused. That takes some time. And you might have to jerk his collar every once in a while, but he will come into line over time.

The maturation hits fast when they start getting troops under them. These guys have gone from seventeen to twenty-two or twenty-five, and now they have a seventeen-year-old to command. I got a great deal of satisfaction seeing how they handle the younger men. Dennis Chalker, Rich Hansen, Mark Stefanich, and others were my "seventeen-year-olds," if you will. Chalker was only a third class when he started under me. We grew together. Some of the great things these guys have done now makes me very proud of them.

Mark Stefanich, Signalman First Class

It was when I was just getting ready to graduate from high school when a good friend of mine, Mike Hall, had me meet his brother. Mike's brother was an Army Green Beret home on leave. I had always been intrigued by the military; I watched all the TV commercials about the Marine Corps and other services. Those images stirred something inside of me for some reason, and I was really interested in joining the service.

When Mike's brother came home, I sat around the table and talked with him about just what we were going to do with our lives. Here we were, Mike and I, about to graduate from high school in Highland, Indiana, and neither of us wanted to go into the steel mills and do all that regular midwestern thing. We wanted to do something with our lives that would be fun and interesting. So we asked Mike's brother just which would be the most elite military unit out there. We expected him to tell us the Green Berets, Army Special Forces. What he turned around and said was, "The Navy SEALs."

I'd never heard of the Navy SEALs before. So I just said, "Excuse me?"

"Yeah," he said, "the Navy SEALs. A branch of the Navy, a special operations team. They do everything—operate in the sea, air, and land. They are considered the best operators and the meanest soldiers out there."

Mike and I both thought this sounded interesting and decided to check into it. Going down to the Navy recruiter, we both got a bunch of information on the Navy SEALs. Eventually, we joined the Navy together under the buddy system for the purpose of going through BUD/S and hoping we could both make it to the same SEAL Team.

The Navy shipped us off to get qualified before we could go to BUD/S. I was trained as a signalman, and Mike became a hull technician. Mike went on to hull tech school while I was shipped off to Orlando to signalman's school. I passed the fitness test to go on to BUD/S, and later found out that Mike hadn't passed the test.

That really devastated me. I didn't want to go on to BUD/S without my friend; we had joined the Navy together just to go on to the Teams. After reflecting on the situation for a bit, I decided that I should try for BUD/S anyway. That was really something that I wanted to do.

At BUD/S, I ran into more than the usual surprises. Looking across the grinder, there he was, shaved head and running across the grinder with a green team class. Mike had made it to BUD/S. So we linked up and managed to get into the same room together. Later on, we ended up going through Hell Week together—at least part of it.

Mike ended up having really bad shin splints and, unfortunately, he finally rang out of Hell Week. I managed to hang in there and made it through, but I didn't graduate with that class.

I went through Hell Week as part of Class 97, but came down with a really bad case of dysentery during the week. The corpsman had already recommended that I not start Hell Week with Class 97. I had a really bad blister on my heel that was infected, and the infection was traveling up my leg. So I was on medication already, and he recommended that I roll back and go through Hell Week with Class 98. That would have meant staying at the base, training, and doing grunt work until the next class started.

The night of breakout, I was lying in my bunk and thinking that I didn't want to go through the workup to Hell Week all over again. What I wanted to do was go through Hell Week with my buddies, the guys I knew and who I had gone through the Green Team training with. So I looked at my boots and just said the hell with it. Cutting the heel off my boot, I put it on and thought it just might work. So here I was, wearing a boot with the heel cut off of it and pondering just what I would do now. Then all hell broke loose.

Instructors kicked the doors in with M60 machine guns blazing and flash-crash grenade simulators going off. Everything was chaotic, and I just jumped into the mess with the rest of my class. Somehow, I managed to make it through the week.

During the time in the demo pits, we had to cross this stagnant pool using two ropes hanging one above the other. Who knew just how long that stinking water lay in the bottom of that pond, or just what diseases were growing in it. And we had to wallow around in that water. We even ate our food in it a few times.

It just might have been the demo pits that did it, but I came down with a real bad case of dysentery. I lost twenty-seven pounds, and the last two days of Hell Week were a bigger mess than usual. I was running, having bad cramps and diarrhea, and just was weak. I have a picture of me, crawling under barbed wire during Hell Week, and I look like a long-term POW—my head was shaved and I weighed only 140 pounds. At six feet tall, that's not much weight, and my cheeks were sunken in.

But I had to get through; I had to make it. Just to prove a point if nothing else. Many times I thought of quitting. The reason I didn't quit was kind of strange, but kept me going. I thought of all of the people I had told that I was going to make it. What would they think if I quit? Plus, they were always stating that Team members didn't quit—ever. Teammates never quit at anything, no matter what. You just had to reach deep down inside yourself to achieve your goal.

Those were the principals I grew up with, the same ones that I continue to hold to this day. Besides, I got to hear those words that secured Class 97 from Hell Week.

At least, I think I heard the words. I was pretty much in a daze by the end of that long week. "Secure from Hell Week" is a term I don't really remember the instructors saying. All I remember is collapsing onto my bunk and being glad, very glad, that it was over and that I made it. There was also some thought about never wanting to do that week again—it had been a bit much.

Reflecting back now, I can see that completing Hell Week made me a better person. So many times I had just wanted to quit, and I saw so many friends quitting, just ringing out. I was wet, cold, tired, and miserable—and for what reason was I doing this? I had no idea what lay ahead in my years to come in the Teams. I thank God I persevered with that challenge, because it led to the most incredible time in my life. I wouldn't trade it for anything in the world.

My first cast-and-recovery during training was interesting. Luckily, we had the opportunity to watch people do it first. That allowed us to try and figure out just what not to do and what to do. When you do it your first or second time, there's always somebody or yourself, who maybe anticipates too much and screws up a little bit. Then you hook your arm into the sling and catch it in the wrong place, maybe causing a rubber friction burn along the bottom of your arm.

After you get picked up a few times, you figure out the technique that works the best for you, and you can clamber into the boat without much trouble. Cast-and-recovery was something that I've never done since BUD/S, but it was something we had to learn. It is an old UDT technique for inserting for shore reconnaissance or loading obstacles, and it's not much used anymore. That part of operations for Navy SEALs is kind of a thing of the past I believe.

The old cast-and-recovery is an incredible ride, and it connects so much to our history. For some guys, that is the time in training when they really feel like a Frogman. For me, it was the live-fire operations on San Clemente Island that made me feel that I was a SEAL for the first time—going out to the island and actually having real demolition blowing up all around you, setting off the charges, going through the woods with live ammunition in the M16s and M60s, and seeing the tracers going by at night. That was when I said to myself, Wow, I'm here now, and this is for real.

What's next? was about all I could think of at graduation, the final day of training, that and wondering about where I might be going, which Team I would be ordered to. Would it be SEAL Team One, SEAL Team Two, or the UDTs? I wanted to go to a SEAL Team. Eventually I did receive orders to SEAL Team One, but I wanted to go to the East Coast and SEAL Team Two, so I found another graduate who would trade assignments with me.

It was right after Jump School at Fort Benning that I was sent on to *my assignment at SEAL Team Two. Jump School immediately followed our graduation from BUD/S. It was a great time working with the Army there, jumping, drinking, and carrying on.*

I arrived at SEAL Team Two in September 1978. When I went to SEAL Team Two, I met people like Rudy Boesch, a legend in the Teams. Richard Marcinko was the commanding officer when I checked in. All these people around me kind of kept me in awe of them. These guys had done so much, and they had so much to teach, so much knowledge. And they enjoyed their jobs.

A lot of times as a civilian back then, you heard all the negative stuff about soldiers and their experiences in Vietnam. Most of those people hated being there, because they were drafted into the service. The people I was with wanted to be warriors; they chose to go out there and fight for our country. There was pride in just knowing that these people had gone there and fought, put their lives on the line, and enjoyed it.

Most of these guys couldn't wait to go back during Vietnam. Some of these guys had three or four tours—they just kept going back and back. They got shot, healed, and went back to war. It was their job; that was their thing in life. It was handed down to them from somewhere on high. They just found out one day that they were going to be warriors, some of the most ultimate warriors in the world, and there they were. And I was among them. It was quite an honor.

I don't remember if Rudy Boesch met me at the quarterdeck when I first arrived at SEAL Team Two, but he probably did. And what he said was probably along the lines of, "Get your UDT trunks on. We're going for an eight-mile run."

Here you had this fifty-year-old guy, built like Arnold Schwarzenegger but thinner. What, an eight-mile run? Yeah, it's going to be slow. Then he took off. Six-minute miles. Wow, I want to be like him when I grow up. But I grew up and I'm not like Rudy—it's too much work.

My first assignment at SEAL Team Two was to go to Copenhagen, where we cross-trained with the Danish Frømandskorpset, *their frog-men.* That was a great group of people. We did a lot of kayak work and a lot of running. Those Danes were really into their running, and they were very good at it. The Europeans' training was mostly running with a little bit of swimming. Then we showed up, Navy Frogmen, and we have a tendency to be jacks-of-all-trades. We like to incorporate all kinds of different types of training to our schedule so you're never completely inexperienced in one area or another.

So we introduced PT to our Danish counterparts. Boy, were they hurting. They kicked our butts big-time running—they took us on these eight-mile runs, up hill. But we figured we could get even. Let's get on the grinder and start doing 100 four-count flutter-kicks, push-ups, sit-ups, and all the other little exercises we have in our workouts. That got to our hosts. We taught them about the folly of taking us on an eight-mile run—after drinking all night.

While at SEAL Team Two, I didn't get in on the mobility platoon, MOB-Six, which had been developed to train for counterterrorist work. And I wasn't a plank owner of SEAL Team Six, which took up the job that MOB-Six had been intended to do. Instead, to my knowledge, I was the first person asked to join SEAL Team Six after the plank owners had come aboard and started training.

I had been away on a Med Cruise deployment in the Mediterranean when SEAL Team Six was created. They had commissioned the new Team in November 1980. My platoon didn't come back from deployment until January 1981. As soon as I came back, I went into a meeting and was selected for SEAL Team Six. Myself and Billy Staff never had to go through Green Team training at SEAL Team Six. Green Team training was for the new guys, and when we got there, everyone was still new guys.

When I first got to SEAL Team Six, it was an experience all over again. Just the amount of knowledge that Marcinko had mustered together in that one Team was incredible. And it wasn't just the knowledge pool that was there; the people were some real, true warriors. They might not have been the best dressed or had the best attitude, but these were the guys you wanted to go to war with.

That first group of people at SEAL Team Six was incredible. I still look back on it and know we were the best in the world at that time. I don't know how it is now; I've been out for quite a while. But those guys were something else. We volunteered to go into situations where we knew there was a small possibility of our coming back.

But Marcinko was such a great leader, and our just wanting to go and do this job made any risk seem doable. We wanted to do this job that we had been training for. Not having combat experience felt like having a sheet of paper in a typewriter and just typing away for years and years—without any ink. Then finally, you got some ink. You didn't want to just sit there, you wanted to start knocking on those keys.

We were all there with the same attitude: Who cares, let's just go do the job and not worry about it. Plan for the best and then go to kick ass and take names. And we had the men to do it.

Duke Leonard was one of the guys I met at SEAL Team Six. He was a really good leader and a lot of fun. And he had a lot of knowledge. The way he taught the younger guys, his attitude toward the right way to instruct somebody to do a certain operation or style of shooting, came across well and made you want to learn more from him. You just wanted to gain more of what he could teach you, and he didn't deliver the material in a harsh manner. A lot of people can be harsh and just tell you to do something "this way" and that's about all.

Duke wasn't like that. You could sit down and just ask him why we were doing something a certain way. If you had a point about coming across a different situation and addressing the problem in a new way, he would sit down and talk to you. And he listened. But he would also explain why something wasn't done a given way.

He always wanted us to learn the basics and learn them well. Then we could change for a different scenario and adapt to the situation as it occurred. We could do that in a split second, but only because we had studied and trained hard. The ability to adapt the training to different situations came later in our advanced training. Duke Leonard was very good at bringing that point across and explaining it to eliminate any questions you might have. Knowing him was very beneficial to me.

There were other very impressive men who had been picked by Marcinko to fill the ranks of Team Six. Mike Thornton was one of our officers, and he held the Congressional Medal of Honor. At first, I was startled to meet him. The Medal of Honor! You don't get any better than that. That's the pinnacle. I liked to sit down and listen to his stories about him and Tommy Norris, what had happened, and what it would actually take to receive a Medal of Honor. Most people who receive one aren't alive to talk about it. I was very impressed, as I am to this day.

It's not really just the Medal of Honor that makes you look up to Mike Thornton. It's what he had done for his Teammate. He had jeopardized his life for his Teammate, without question or hesitation.

A Teammate is your fellow warrior, your fellow friend, your brother. I hate to say this, but I love my Teammates more than my brothers, because I don't spend as much time with my brothers as I had with my Teammates. We bled together, we sweated together, and we froze together.

There's this bond that we created by mutual experience, suffering, and accomplishment, and I can trust them with my life in a combat situation and not have to worry about it. To me, that's a true Teammate, not having to second-guess what this person next to me is going to do if a situation becomes hazardous. All I have to do is worry about what my job is, because I know that he knows what he has to do. That leaves your mind open to be focused on the operation at hand.

Master Chief Denny Chalker is a really, really, good friend of mine, and our wives and daughters are friends. We hit it off very well together at SEAL Team Six, which works well because he was my door partner— we went through the door together on ops. We were also drinking and *workout buddies. Basically we were inseparable for about the four or five years I was at SEAL Team Six.*

Denny has done a lot. Right now, when I tell civilians about Master Chief Chalker, I say that he's probably the most experienced and highly decorated Navy SEAL of the post-Vietnam era that I know of. He's a hard-ass, but that's what it takes.

When I say that Denny is my door partner, that means he's the guy that I'm partnered up with during Close Quarters Battle (CQB). I was usually number one in going through the door, and Denny was usually number two. But we would flip-flop the order so we'd be used to either position. We were usually at each other's side, like swim partners.

Navy SEALs operate on the buddy system. It's not like the Rambo movies. Nobody is an individual—it's called SEAL Team. There aren't any individuals in a Team, and everybody works together and supports each other. Our Teams are broken down into partners. You know your partners as closely as anyone you have known in your life.

There are several instances that I remember going in to the Kill House for training, kicking the door in, and engaging multiple targets. Coming in to a second room and stepping in to the side, I would feel a muzzle blast next to my head and not worry about it. I knew that the blast was Denny right next to me, engaging targets while I was engaging others. Normally, a situation where a gun is going off just to the side of you would raise some kind of scare in you, but I knew it was Denny.

I could actually feel what he was thinking, and I think he could feel the same thing about me. You train so much together and you have to trust your partner so completely, that you just don't have to worry about him. I have all the confidence in the world that Master Chief Chalker would take care of his responsibilities and expect me to deal with mine.

Training was hard and fast, and it was dangerous. We lost a guy during training more than once. We lost Rodney Cheui when we were first training at Eglin Air Force Base while going through a door. He was shot in the kidney, I believe, and passed away. We learned a lot from that incident, but unfortunately, somebody lost their life for us to learn the principals of operating Close Quarters Battle (CQB).

Then there was Rich Horn, a great SEAL and a flawless operator. It was just one of those days; fate or whatever it was had him at the wrong place at the wrong time. A bullet went through one of the partitions and creased his vest. It went though a joint in the vest and entered his lungs. The odds of that happening were like winning the lottery twice in a row. It just shouldn't have happened, but it did. That was a really sad moment, but we had beers to him.

That was a thing about Navy SEALs when one of us passed away. We had kind of a wake for our missing Teammate. We always looked at each other and questioned just how many people could actually die doing something that they loved to do. So if we lost a Teammate, that was okay, because they went out doing the job they loved. Not too many people can say that in this world, because most people hate their jobs. But as a Navy SEAL, you love it so much that you can drink a beer to your friend and miss him for the fact that he's gone, but you know he died being happy. And if you can die being happy, then you've done something right in your life.

I was on the Grenada op, but I didn't make it to the island right away. A group of us finally got to Grenada after we treaded water for a few days. I went in ahead with the CIA, went to a nearby island, and got on the recovery ship where jumpers from Team Six were supposed to come in on a C-130. They would jump into the water and we were to pick them up afterward, plan our operation, and launch into Grenada from there. Unfortunately, things went a little off from what was planned.

We lost four of the eight jumpers, four good friends, in the high seas, winds, and darkness off Grenada. That was another very sad day.

In spite of the losses, we planned to still go in to Grenada on a modified plan. We lost several boats on the drop, and the others we had with us were barely operating. The seas were really bad, with seven-foot swells and twenty-some-knot winds. We still had our old Boston Whalers intact onboard the ship, so we packed the two boats that were left full of people, weapons, and ammunition. Our mission was to go straight in to the airstrip and continue with our job.

We got all of halfway to Grenada when the boats just died on us. They filled up with water, and we treaded water for two days until someone came by to snag us up. It was something to watch the firefights from the surface of the water.

A couple of the guys, myself included, were even thinking about swimming in to the island. But twenty miles or so of open sea is a bit much. There never was any concern that our Teammates or somebody would come along and get us, though sooner would have been better than later.

A Cuban patrol boat came by really close to us. We were sitting in the whalers, filled with water, and a lot of us were seasick. Two-cycle oil was floating on the surface from our fuel tanks, and the waves kept us moving up and down. So we were puking, wet, cold, and miserable—just like during Hell Week. All of a sudden, this Cuban patrol boat from Grenada came along and started shining its light toward us.

Oh, shit! We couldn't go anywhere, we were just sitting ducks in the water. Then somebody said, "Stefanich, get up front with the M60."

So I crawled up to the bow and sat there with my M60 machine gun and about two thousand rounds of ammunition all linked together. And all I wanted was for those guys in the Cuban boat not to shine their light on me. Then the light swept by us and they left. I like it when that happens. But we did miss the big party on Grenada.

My time in the Teams was kind of strange for me. I took a lot of it for granted. I chose to be a Navy SEAL, and I loved doing it, but I just looked at it as my job, something that I was gifted at doing. What I never did was get into the ego bit, thinking that I was a great warrior. I was around some really great people who had some very good backgrounds and a lot of training.

MOB-Six was SEAL Team Six before it became a whole Team. There were all these different names that we had for the job of countering the terrorist threat. Specifically, MOB-Six was a source of manpower when Marcinko was first commissioned with putting together the best of the Navy SEALs for counterterrorism. They were officially part of SEAL Team Two. It was an elite team that dealt more with counterterrorism than with special operations.

Eventually, SEAL Team Six was formed and we moved to behind the old wooden Cub Scout buildings on the base at Little Creek, Virginia. Most people didn't really know that SEAL Team Six even existed. A lot of people in the military would drive by our buildings and wonder what these guys with the long hair and the cigarette boats were doing. The boats were long-bodied, sharp-nosed, powerful-engined racing craft. They had gotten their name from one of the first successful open-ocean racers. The trucks full of boxes of weapons, grenades, and other odd gear also kind of stood out a bit. But they just thought it was SEAL Team Two doing their thing, or maybe an offspring of SEAL Team Two, which we were in a way.

Actually, we didn't even call ourselves SEAL Team Six for quite a while. We kept as low a profile as we could. It wasn't until probably around 1982 or so that our name even made the rounds. Very few people even knew who the Navy SEALs were, and an even smaller percentage of those knew about SEAL Team Six. We didn't go out and advertise ourselves.

The Green Berets, Army Special Forces, were like that at first. Then John Wayne did the movie The Green Berets, and they quickly became the most popular thing around. Everyone wanted to be a Green Beret, and there was a lot of press about them.

But the Navy SEALs were still relatively unknown to the public well into the 1980s. What was a Navy SEAL? Nobody really knew what we were or what we did. Even today, a lot of people still think that as a Navy SEAL, we must spend a lot of time in the water, that we must do a lot of diving. That's not true; it's only a small portion of our operational experience and capabilities.

Once you finish basic training and complete BUD/S and Jump School, you are still a long way from being a Navy SEAL. When you first go on to a Team, you're on probation. You still don't really become a Navy SEAL until you prove yourself. And you're always proving yourself. Even after you earn your Trident and are walking around like a big, hairy-chested Frogman, you can still lose it in an instant. Screw up badly once, and it's "See ya," you're back in the Fleet.

So you're really always trying to better yourself so you can continue to be a Navy SEAL, because you know it's a privilege and that privilege can go away fast, and then you become a shitbird. We always try very hard to focus on our jobs and not get a big ego. What you have to understand is that being a SEAL is a job, just as other people have jobs. This is our work, and we're good at it.

To do our job takes a lot more training than we get just at BUD/S, Jump School, and even at our Teams. Advanced training and schooling goes on indefinitely. I look at Rudy Boesch—he's the walking bible on Special Operations. Every day, you can learn something new from him, or others around him. Tactics change, and so does the world's situation. Every day of your life as a Navy SEAL, you try to better yourself through advanced training to keep up and even stay ahead of what's going on around you. You learn new things, new ways of improvising explosives, going into a room dynamically, skydiving, or getting guys together and patrolling. It never stops. You can't get to the point that you say you know everything. If you do get to that point, then it's time to say "I'm outta here."

They'll draw us together for advanced training and say they have these military schools available. Sometimes, there's cross-training available, schools conducted by another country's military forces.

That's advanced training, and it can be jungle warfare in the Philippines or Borneo, jump training with the German jump team, technical rock-climbing at Lake Tahoe, or diving practice at Key West.

We always had these schools available to us. If you were on stand-down and in your training cycle, then you could go to these schools. It would be up to the officer in charge to sit down with the executive and commanding officers to look at what was available, then he could say that he thought his platoon needed to bone up on this or this.

We also had advanced training in-house, where we had the facilities to conduct the course as needed. There was the close-quarter battle house that we could set up in different configurations. The walls could be moved around or we could have moving targets. You could even go into another room and have a screen up where different scenarios would be projected, and you could go through hostage situations or be forced to draw your secondary weapon as part of transition drills.

The training was endless. It would be up to the person in charge at the time to determine what he felt was an advanced training aid or technique that we could use. Then we would sit down, analyze it, and practice it. You would do that and might go home and just think about it. Anyone could remember something that we used, say eight months ago, and think of how it could be incorporated into what we were doing now. Then you could go back and talk about it. Even training was a joint effort, a Team effort. No one person knows everything. And in the SEALs, we would put all our heads together and make the best of a situation that we could.

Our training was so dangerous that it could kill us, absolutely. Our training had killed several of our good friends, because we train for real. And that wasn't just in SEAL Team Six; it happened in the other SEAL Teams as well. If you train as if it's a real situation, when that situation actually comes up, then you just have to work from muscle memory. You don't have to think about what to do.

You train like you fight and fight like you train. That prevents mistakes. In police training on the range, they used to reload their revolvers by opening up the cylinder and dumping the brass into their hand. Then they could just drop it in the bucket and not have to pick it up off the ground later. They used to find cops shot dead after an engagement with a handful of empty brass and an empty gun. They were so used to going to the range and shooting like that, that it became a habit, and those habits became instinctive. In a hot situation where multiple people were shooting at them, the cops reverted to muscle memory—and it got some of them killed.

Our training prevented situations like that from ever happening. When you've trained for something, you didn't have to think about what you had to do next, it was instinctual and you got it done, then you moved on to the next step. If someone was injured or killed in training, what happened was very closely looked at and studied. If a mistake had been made, it was never allowed to happen again. Lessons like that were painful and expensive, but they were never forgotten.

Navy SEALs train and operate at their peak 110 percent all the time. So when we partied, we partied at 110 percent. Everything we did in life, we did all out, 100 percent and more. That's just the way we are, because we're not afraid of the consequences. SEALs and Frogs know what they're up against, and they like being on the driving edge, a little bit more ahead of everyone else. Why? I don't know. It just seems to be something we have in us.

Nowadays, the first thing I think of when I think about the Navy SEALs are the experiences I used to have. There were things I'd done that I took for granted during the nine years that I was in. I really never gave it much thought before because I knew I was doing something I loved to do. I was good at it, and I had the best guys in the world around me.

Then I got out and became involved in the entertainment business. I haven't really looked back for going on fifteen years now. It was only within the last year that I've looked back at what I've accomplished with the Teams. Now, I'm starting to hook up with a lot of my old Team friends, and that's bringing back some very fond memories of life in the Teams and of some really excellent individuals.

Once you've gotten out into the civilian world, it's hard to have friends like the friends you had in the Teams. There's something missing. I've been out for more than fifteen years now, and I probably have only one good friend, and that's my wife Barbara. It's hard to replace the caliber of person you meet in the Teams.

The Navy Trident isn't something I've ever really put much emphasis on. It was our badge, the symbol that we earned by going through a lot of pain and a lot of hard training. We earned that badge, and some of my friends died wearing it. But it's still just a piece of metal. It's the man wearing it that really stands out.

The term "Frogman" isn't really used that much today. It's more or less a name from the past, and one that I love. I think it sounds great— "Frogman." When they first created the UDT, they mostly operated in the water environment. A lot of their time was spent underwater blowing up obstacles or placing demo charges on ships as part of sneak attacks.

Today, there are no UDTs left; they're all SEAL Teams now. We still have that beach recon and obstacle clearance job, but when I heard the term "Frogman," I think of one of the older guys, the old frog. I really never hear about the newer guys using the term to describe each other. Now, he's a SEAL, or he's in a SEAL Team.

Then there's the BullFrog. Physically, Rudy Boesch was the pinnacle of what a Navy SEAL would hope to be. Here was this guy who had been through a number of wars, was highly decorated, and had seen so much action and history—and he drinks beer with the best of us. But he'll be there at 5 or 6 o'clock in the morning, hair cut, perfect uniform, and his voice would growl out, "Let's go, guys."

Oh nooooo. I hope he's feeling a little tired today. We regretted drinking so much the night before and hoped he might feel the same way. Not a chance in hell. Rudy was out there and was what we always looked up to. Rudy was what we wanted to be as a twenty-year-old, or as a fifty-year-old. There was no difference with him. He was outrunning twenty-year-olds, nineteen-year-olds. And not just outrunning them, he was going through the obstacle course faster, or outswimming them. He was incredible, and I'm sure he still is to this day.

The thing that you would find in the Teams that you might not find anywhere else, especially in that kind of job environment, is truly loyal friends. These are people who you know, who you have something in common with. These aren't people who are trying to buddy up to you to get ahead somehow or get something from you. You're both there in the Teams on an even playing field.

To me, the best single word that describes the Teams is camaraderie. Just the friendship, the trust that was there, that's hard to find in the world these days, and I've looked very hard for it. And a lot of times I've been disappointed in my search. I think I see a quality in somebody that could come close to what I had in the Teams, and nine times out of ten, I'm eventually let down. But that's life. You live and you learn and you move on.

The saturation training program that we went through at Six was a result of the mission. Marcinko was tasked with a job that not too many people in the world probably could have accomplished. He took a group of Navy SEALs and turned them into one of the most unique counterterrorism organizations in the world—and he did it in a matter of a year.

During our first year of training at Six, we had two days off—Christmas and Thanksgiving. The rest of the time we were training fourteen or sixteen hours a day, then drinking and relaxing perhaps four hours after training while we cleaned up and prepared for the next day. That was our schedule, seven days a week. Marcinko wanted to have the best counterterrorist organization in the world, because that was the task that was given to him by Admiral Lyons. He was told, "You will not fail, Dick. This is what you have. Make it happen."

And he did that. Marcinko is an incredible leader, he did a great job and put together a phenomenal group of people. The selection process for those people was very good, too. It wasn't just him and the executive officer looking at a list of names and records. He would also get all the Teams guys together in a room, something like the Knights of the Round Table, and he would ask them about an individual candidate.

Dick wanted to know if anyone knew the man personally, what his qualifications were, and if he was wanted in the Team. Everyone had a say. That resulted in a very good group of people, because we liked and knew each other. That helped us operate that much better because there was no personal tension there. It was amazing how your operational level would go up notches just because you didn't have to worry about any bullshit, just the job at hand.

Marcinko wanted us to think like the enemy, to live like him—not to the extreme, though. We didn't become terrorists, but that let us have the mindset of what a specific terrorist or group was doing, and why. That helped us learn to hate them that much more.

I was there to protect the United States of America. I love my country. The most beautiful thing in the world to me is the American flag flapping in a stiff breeze. I was willing to give my life for my country, because we have the best one in the world. That was my level of dedication at the time. Thank God I didn't have to, but I would have made any sacrifice that was demanded of me.

What I couldn't stand was to see this country be ruined by people who hate, are greedy, or just have their own stupid little beliefs and violently try to do something about those beliefs. When they kill innocent people, there's no need for them to continue on in this world. There's only one thing to do with people like that, and that's to neutralize them.

■ Chapter 7

CENTRAL AMERICA

The SEAL losses off Grenada were their first combat losses since the Vietnam War, but earlier that year, there had been another SEAL lost to enemy fire, but not in combat. On 25 May 1984, Lieutenant Commander Albert A. Schaufelberger III was assassinated in El Salvador by what was later declared to be a unit of the FMLN (Farabundo Marti National Liberation Front).

Schaufelberger had been sitting in his armored Ford Maverick, provided to him by the U.S. Embassy. As a Navy SEAL, Schaufelberger was the senior Naval representative at the U.S. Military Group, El Salvador, at the time of his death. Faulty air conditioning had caused Schaufelberger to roll down the window of his armored car. While he was stopped to pick up his girlfriend, a Volkswagen Microbus stopped nearby. Jumping from the Microbus were a number of terrorists. One of the terrorists ran up to Schaufelberger's window and pumped four rounds from a .22 Magnum into the SEAL. Then the group escaped in their vehicle. They were never captured.

By the early 1980s, Naval Special Warfare had begun to increase its activity in Central and South America. Schaufelberger's loss had been a result of the severe unrest in not only El Salvador, but also many locations throughout Central America at the time.

Only a few SEALs—less than four at any one time—were stationed in El Salvador, supporting the Military Advisory Group's activities there. Primarily, the SEALs advised and helped train the El Salvadoran naval units on a variety of subjects from maritime operations to land combat. The SEALs worked under very strict rules of engagement and were not able to take an active part in the fighting against Communist insurgents in the country. This was a severe irritation to the SEALs on duty in El Salvador, as they were used to taking a much more active role in the surrounding situation.

SEAL operations extended through the 1980s to include missions in Honduras and along the Nicaraguan border. The situation turned into a learning experience for both the Honduran forces as well as the SEALs and Special Boat Squadron assets that were assigned to the areas.

The political defeat of the Sandinista Government in Nicaragua in the early 1990s began to settle the turmoil in the Central American area. The SEAL and U.S. military presence as a whole was reduced as the guerrilla movements lost support with the failure of communism in the Soviet Union and elsewhere in the world.

Steven Scott Helvenston, Quartermaster First Class

When I was sixteen years old and a junior in high school, I was struggling somewhat with my family life and just life in general and I looked into going into the Navy. When I went to the recruiters, I told them I was very interested in joining the Navy, and that was when I was made aware of what the SEAL Team was all about.

At that time, my SEAL recruiter basically told me that I would be a crazy man to even try out, but I went for it anyway. Later, I was part of Class 122, a winter class, with our Hell Week starting 6 December.

Because El Niño—although they didn't call it that at the time—happened to hit, the storm, surf, and cold weather that was involved with our training class stands out the most to me from those days. Sandbag PT—filling, lifting, and stacking all those bags of sand to protect the officer's quarters barracks, the Country Store, and even helping out at the Coronado Cays from water—was an exercise Class 122 did a lot of. That was a very unique element to SEAL training at that time.

Hell Week was cold and miserable. Class 122 was the next class after a no-bell Hell Week class—no one from the class before us had quit during Hell Week. The thing I remember the most about our Hell Week was that I think initially, the instructors were going to make sure that Class 122 was not going to have a no-bell Hell Week.

I remember the first six hours of Hell Week being probably a little bit more miserable than they should have been. Going through Hell Week on 6 December, at that time of the year with El Niño making it so windy and so cold, the instructors gave us field jackets when we were at Camp Swampy. I think the decision had been made that things were just too cold and we had to have some kind of covering. Shivering in the miserable cold—that's the thing I remember the most. Sure, that's probably the case with every Hell Week, but that's what I remember the most.

There were a lot of things in my life leading up to that point. I grew up in kind of a broken environment—I lost my father when I was young and I didn't really see eye-to-eye with my mom too much. So the survivor element was established in me well before I joined the Navy and decided to become a SEAL. I just knew that, no matter what, in training anyway, I wasn't going to die. These guys, the instructors, weren't going to kill me. I just wasn't going to quit, no matter what.

Sure, I thought about quitting. I thought about what it would be like to be labeled a quitter, or how negative or bad I would feel about myself because I quit. In a way, that's what inspired me not to quit. But I don't think I ever came anywhere near really quitting. That bell was nowhere near in my mind, and I wasn't going anywhere close to it if I had a choice.

It's weird, but that last day of BUD/S, graduating training, was the biggest accomplishment of my life to that point. I'd never achieved something that arduous. Now, fifteen years in the future, I look back and think how that was really just the beginning. Really, truly becoming a Navy SEAL happens after two or three pre-deployment trainings and three platoon workups. That's when you become a real Navy SEAL, when you shed all the T-shirts and get rid of all the images in your mind. You realize that becoming a Navy SEAL is a very professional job.

The training after BUD/S, at least going to Fort Benning and Army Jump School, did seem like kind of a joke. It was a lot of fun. There was one situation at Benning that I'll never forget. We were in our stick, the formation of paratroopers that line up to jump from the plane. The jump sergeant, whatever they call that guy who's in charge at that Army school, was running down the stick checking us over on a pre-jump inspection.

For some reason, I don't remember why, I failed his inspection. That sergeant dropped me down for whatever amount of push-ups he told me to do, and I started banging them out. Being a cocky young gradu-ate of BUD/S, I told him that there wasn't anything that he could do to hurt me, that there weren't enough push-ups he could have me do that would hurt me, I started banging out some more push-ups.

That sergeant kept walking down the stick to inspect the rest of the students. There were Army people and other Navy SEALs in the line. Todd French, two people away from me in the stick, was a classmate of mine. We look kind of alike, though not exactly.

Finally, I got maxed out after banging out one hundred or one hun-dred and fifty push-ups in a row. I asked Todd to help me out. So as soon as I got maxed out, I jumped back up and stood at attention while Todd dropped to the ground and started doing push-ups. He was bang-ing them out hard.

That airborne instructor came back and I peeked out at him from the side of my eye. He had an expression on his face like he had known that Navy SEALs were badasses, but he hadn't thought they were that bad. Between the two of us, Todd and I must have banged out almost five hundred push-ups in about five minutes. And I'll never forget that, because that must have been the biggest joke played on that guy ever. SEALs are in great shape, but 500 push-ups? So that's how Jump School was. It was fun.

Not everything at Jump School was quite as funny, though. There's something wrong with anyone who jumps out of a plane for the first time and isn't a jar-full of eyeballs. Of course, I was scared, but I was excited at the same time, excited and exhilarated about doing it—jumping from a plane. I really had a liking toward parachuting and sky-diving, so I became a free-fall jumpmaster and a free-fall instructor. Later, I became a parachute rigger (packer) and senior rigger for the FAA. Now I work in the civilian community, packing parachutes and teaching people how to jump.

But I won't lie to you. Jumping out of an airplane that first time makes your eyes bulge out of your head. It is a big relief looking up at that big, open canopy above you for the first time. There's no doubt about it, that's the best skirt you'll ever look up. I think you feel that way every time it opens, but there's definitely something about that first one.

Right out of BUD/S, I was given orders to UDT Eleven, which shortly thereafter became SEAL Team Five. I like calling myself an original Frog [Frogman], but the reality of it is that I checked into UDT Eleven then six days later it became SEAL Team Five. So I was a UDT Frogman for less than a week before becoming a SEAL.

The mission didn't really change that much in the beginning, but the consolidation of the UDTs into SEAL Teams was happening then, as it should have. When you look at the entry-level training in BUD/S and then where you are eventually sent, it's obvious that everybody should have been ready to do either job. All Teams should maintain something of the same responsibilities, in my opinion.

I guess I had the opportunity to experience that in the beginning. UDT Eleven/SEAL Team Five wasn't much different in the beginning except for the name change. After about a year or so, they picked up SEAL Team operations and so forth.

And I don't believe we ever really went through a plankowner process at SEAL Team Five. Basically, we were still the same command, they just changed our title. It really wasn't a new command, so I don't consider myself a plankowner of SEAL Team Five. It was definitely a different transition to the SEAL Team status than the earlier cases with SEAL Teams One and Two.

I spent roughly eleven months at SEAL Team Five and then the opportunity came up for me to transfer to the East Coast. It was very evident to me at that time that a lot of West Coast Frogs were going to hate me for this, but East Coast Teams at that time in the early 1980s, were operating quite a bit more than the West Coast Teams were. Within three weeks of checking in to SEAL Team Four, I was gone. I was in a platoon deployed to Honduras in Central America and doing real-world stuff.

Being that I sat at SEAL Team Five for eleven months and went through SERE (Survival, Escape, Resistance, and Evasion) school and one other technical school on dive maintenance, I'll be the first to say that was happy to have made that move.

While I was at SEAL Team Five, there was a list of people who would be deploying. After having been at the Team for eleven months, I was not slated to be in a platoon for another eight months. That's why I did a coast transfer. It was ridiculous to me that I was at a Team for almost a year and wasn't going to be in a platoon for another eight months. Then, I was going to do a workup that could last over a year until we went out on a deployment. So that was really my motivation for going to the East Coast. There, I was operating in the field after only a short time.

Operating in Central America was swampy. Central America was like a third-world country, and working in that environment definitely makes you appreciate being a U.S. citizen, that's for sure. I guess the thing that sticks out in my mind the most about working in Honduras and El Salvador was being involved in training kids.

Having joined the Navy at the earliest opportunity, I was young at the time. At that time, I was the youngest student to have graduated BUD/S, having completed the course at seventeen. When I was working in El Salvador and Honduras, I was eighteen to twenty years old, and the kids I was training were thirteen, fourteen, and fifteen years old.

The biggest thing I struggled with was the fact that these kids had seen more action than I had. They'd been out there and trading bullets with the bad guys, and now I was there teaching them how to do it.

At the risk of sounding like a warmonger, I think in a way I missed that opportunity to see active combat because I was training. When you train, and train intensively, to do something, I think it's just natural desire to put that training to the test. I spent tours with four different platoons, working up to putting that training to the test. I saw a little bit of combat action, but I never really had the opportunity to put my training to the test. It becomes fatiguing to practice, practice, practice, and then never really see that practice put into use.

I did once hear a bullet crack by, one that was fired in anger. I'm not going to claim to be anything like one of the Vietnam veterans or experience some of the things that happened back then. We've all heard the stories, and I have the utmost respect for the men who fought for our country in Vietnam and other wars. When I experienced combat danger, it was very minimal and just sniper fire.

My part of the combat was pretty much just covering, but I do wonder what it would be like to go out on patrol in hostile territory. To this day, I wonder what it would be like to be dealt the situation of having to enter into a firefight or a major conflict.

In Central America, the rules of engagement were definitely much more stringent and restrictive than probably what they were in Vietnam or any other previous war. It was a very frustrating experience for me. Here we were allowed to train the El Salvadorans and Hondurans, and we were even allowed to go out on patrol with them, but if we were taking enemy fire, we weren't even allowed to shoot back. That's kind of frustrating. But I'm not saying that we never shot back.

Still, it was a difficult situation. The political environment around the mission was always hard to work with. A very good friend of mine, Arthur Fusco, died in Honduras, not because of war, but because of a political agenda. At the time, I was very young, and remembering affects me now more than it did then. I'm a little bit more seasoned and mature now, so I reflect on it differently.

Arthur had been a classmate of mine. Actually, he was rolled out of the class, but he remained a very good friend. He died trying to improve Honduran relations.

Striking a pensive pose, this SEAL trainee listens intently during tactical training. This is only a small part of the almost full year of training that BUD/S students undergo to go on to the Teams as qualified SEALs.

U.S. Navy

Central America was a job, and we did it. Overall, the mission we did in Central America was a good job. It's so hard, so difficult, to get into the big, political, Washington, D.C.–Pentagon environment, to get into their heads and see what their agenda is. But when we go on a deployment like this, we're tasked to do a certain job and we do it.

As a SEAL Team, we did our job. There are certain things that we did that could have probably been done a little better, and there are other things that probably could have been done better by the Army Corps of Engineers. Certain demolition jobs we were involved with were kind of ludicrous, but we were asked to do it and we went in there and did the best job that we could.

The thing that I looked for the most in the SEALs Teams in the beginning was the challenge. I'm a very goal-oriented person, as most Navy SEALs are. Some are more goal-oriented than others. I found a lot of reward in challenging myself. The thing that I looked forward to the most in the Teams was the next challenge.

When you look at the arena of what the SEAL Teams offers a person, what comes first, the man who accomplishes SEAL Team or SEAL Team, the organization? I think it's somewhere in between. SEAL Team afforded me the opportunity to achieve a goal and to pursue something that was a criteria. Within that criteria, it allowed me to become a part of a really special organization.

I'm still a Navy SEAL. I spent twelve years in active duty, and I've been out for roughly four years now. The things I learned about myself and the things I accomplished definitely affect everything I do in my life now. The key ingredient I've learned is tenacity. There's nothing that will substitute for tenaciousness. If you feel strongly about something, passionately about something, pursue it and don't ever give up. I learned that in SEAL Team, and I learned that about myself because of the SEAL Teams.

During part of my time in the Teams, I was an instructor at BUD/S in Coronado. My focus as an instructor when training students was to push them to reach all that they were able to and more. I didn't get a lot of gratification or pleasure out of being a real mean, hard, in-your-face, critical, and insulting instructor.

What I did take a lot of pleasure in was maintaining a really high standard physically. I was a big stickler for physical standards, and I was a huge stickler for anything that was somewhat skill-related. I was a First Phase instructor from Class 157 to Class 171, then I moved on to teach free-fall, which is an advanced skill.

Free-fall is not a physical evolution. When you look at skydiving and free-fall, it's an evolution that's really an issue of teaching an individual how to compose himself in a stressful, somewhat death-defying evolution. If they mess up, they die, which is a very important element in SEAL Team. In a fire-fight—which we can never really simulate, we can simulate with paintball, paper targets, but we can never really throw live ammo at each other—you are in the ultimate, stressful, life-threatening situation.

What we can do is put an individual in a life-threatening situation such as skydiving and rock-climbing and see how he's going to respond. (I was a rock-climbing instructor as well.) What I placed a lot of value on during that training was seeing how an individual responded in those particular curriculum environments.

When I hear about some of the veterans of the Teams, the first thing that comes to my mind is respect. That's the first thing I have for those men such as Mike Thornton, Barry Enoch, and others. They performed in a wartime environment, and they performed well. There's no taking that away from them. I respect them for it big time.

At the same time, I'm very envious of those individuals. I don't want this to sound wrong; there's a fine line between envy and jealousy. Throughout my twelve years as a Frog and a SEAL, I never really had the opportunity to really put my training to the test, other than in the pentathlon, which was probably one of the most rewarding things I ever did in the Navy, competing for my country in a peacetime environment. But you get a little ridicule, a little shit run at you by some of the guys who say that you're a new-school Frog and you've never really been put to the test. That part becomes a little irritating after a while. You know that you would have tried and possibly have done just as well as the guy giving you shit, but you just didn't have the opportunity.

But again, respect is the first thing I have for anybody who fought for our country in a wartime environment. But envy and maybe a little jealousy, I'm not going to lie about that, is also in the background.

When I reflect on my training, I covered thirteen Hell Weeks as an instructor and of course went through one Hell Week myself. The fitness element kind of just comes, and it comes easier to some than to others. People who come to training not in as good shape as others have to work harder to reach the the fitness levels the others have.

The thing that probably sticks out the most in my mind about going through Navy SEAL training is the misery. There's no way you can really explain that to somebody. They have to go through it to understand it. If I have to explain it to you, you'll never really understand. I know that's cliché, but the reality is that it's true. BUD/S training is miserable.

In First Phase, which is the first eight weeks of training, the IBS, the inflatable boat, small, is glued to your head. You travel everywhere with it. There's a number of reasons for that. The main reason is for team-building. Obviously, you need to learn how to paddle the boat, but if you're not utilizing good teamwork, that boat can really work against you.

The pressure on your neck and your spine from carrying that boat around like that for eight weeks can be excruciating. But the one thing that probably influences an individual to quit more than anything is cold and lack of sleep. No sleep, and being cold, wet, sandy, and miserable, along with wondering what it would be like to just be in a dry set of clothes and living a normal life, saps your will. You have to set your mind to get through the evolution and continue on.

One night of no sleep is kind of painful. Try it three times over. And then when you're three nights into Hell Week and we give you just two hours of sleep—just two, just enough to piss you off—then we wake you up and it's "Oh my God, all those dreams I was just having . . ."

As an instructor, it's hilarious to watch students wake up after three days of no sleep. They look around in a delirium. It's kind of funny.

Because I'm a physical guy, I'm one of those CISM (Conseil International du Sport Militaire) pukes, those pentathlon guys, I've always had a lot of respect for the older guys in the Teams who, for one, achieved a lot in a wartime element but still maintained a heck of a physical standard. Rudy Boesch was one of those guys.

When I transferred to the East Coast, I went to SEAL Team Four and heard stories about Rudy Boesch at SEAL Team Two. There would be guys who would check into SEAL Team Two right out of BUD/S. You're in pretty top condition when you graduate from BUD/S. When you go to SEAL Team Two and on a conditioning run, you can't keep up with, let alone beat, Rudy Boesch, that's when the stories build up.

When I checked in at SEAL Team Four, I think Rudy was in his mid-fifties, and he was still whipping guys half his age and younger. And if they didn't beat him on a conditioning run, they were stuck on the quarterdeck for a weekend duty. I have a lot of respect for Rudy Boesch, and I hold a couple senior officers and enlisted guys in the same regard. I think Admiral Raymond C. Smith is the same way, he lives by a pretty high

In white camouflage, to include white tape on his M16A1 rifle, this SEAL from SEAL Team Two conducts winter training.

U.S. Navy

Team standard. I think it's always kind of frustrating how some Team guys let themselves go a little bit. It disappoints me, because I think we have a standard to live by. Whether you're in or out of the Navy, you have to maintain that standard.

My association with Admiral Tom Richards was through the pentathlon. He was the officer-liaison, the international office liaison with CISM. Their motto is "Substitute the playing field for the battlefield," and when you look at what that organization does, it is easy to see how Admiral Richards was such a strong supporter and proponent of the SEALs being involved with that. I hold him in high respect for that.

I wish that CISM was embraced more as a whole by the Special

The shield of the United States Special Operations Command.

USSOCOM PAO

Warfare community. Look at what it's doing—we're out there, representing our country. And no, we're not in a physical, confrontational war, but we're a part of the peacemaking process, maintaining relations with other countries and representing our country. It's just unfortunate sometimes when some people don't understand the priority of what that part of the military is all about—competing at an international level in something other than war.

I think our mission as SEAL Teams is definitely changing. It's probably going to consistently change. Whether it's a desert environment, a jungle environment, or a winter warfare environment, we will train and adapt for that arena. I think right now we're looking at a lot of counterterrorist issues that we really need to be specialized in. It's not just an issue of going out and doing fire-and-movement exercises in the woods anymore. It's a lot more complicated than that.

SEAL Team's mission is changing to meet the new threats. I've been out for four years (as of 1998), doing what I'm doing, which is still being a SEAL, only in the civilian world now, so I'm not as well versed as I would like to be to make a comment about where SEAL Teams' mission is going. But I will say that I think that it's a heck of a lot more complicated than it's ever been.

I'm not very familiar with SEAL Teams' involvement in the drug-interdiction program. I think they should play a role, because we're qualified to do so. When you look at how much involvement the Coast Guard has had with drug interdiction and where their qualifications fit in with that task, it's kind of ludicrous that we SEALS aren't doing the job. From what I hear, we are cross-training quite a bit with the Coast

Guard, but why cross-train? Why not just give the job to SEAL Team? That's what we're qualified to do.

When I think of the SEAL Teams, the first word that comes into my head is win. SEAL Team is built on a competitive environment, and it pays to be a winner. It doesn't just translate into one thing; that attitude translates into every aspect of my life. In the business world, I'm an entrepreneur now and have my own business. I'm still competitive. Even while I'm raising a family, I compete in events athletically. But the winning mentality, that stays.

■ Chapter 8

U.S. SPECIAL OPERATIONS COMMAND

The lessons learned in Iran at Desert One were not forgotten by the U.S. military or the political leaders of the country. Also remembered were the problems that cost four SEALs their lives off Grenada during URGENT FURY. The Goldwater-Nichols Department of Defense Reorganization Act of 1986 was the most significant change to the organization of the U.S. military since 1947. For the Naval Special Warfare, and special operations forces in general, the major effect of the act was the creation of a central command structure for all special operations forces in the U.S. military.

The U.S. Special Operations Command was activated on 16 April 1987 at MacDill Air Force Base in Tampa, Florida. SOCOM is commanded by a four-star flag or general officer. All the Special Operations Forces in the U.S. military are under the SOCOM command umbrella—Army Special Forces, Rangers, and the 160th Special Operations Aviation Regiment; the Naval Special Warfare Command, which includes all the SEAL and SDV Teams as well as the Special Boat Teams; and the Air Force Special Operations Command with the Special Operations Wings and Groups.

Close to 50,000 enlisted men and officers from the three different branches of the service operate under the direction of SOCOM. The different units work together on joint operations on a constant basis. This raises the skill levels of all of the units and makes their ability to conduct difficult operations much greater than before. The men who operate the aircraft know what the men on the ground or in the water need because they've worked directly with them.

Funding is less of a problem, as SOCOM manages procurement for its forces and commands. New equipment is brought online and put into the hands of the operators much more quickly than was possible earlier. Programs for the different forces can be combined where possible to give all the men the best support available.

Rudy Boesch, Command Master Chief Boatswain's Mate, USN (Ret.)

At SEAL Team Two in Little Creek, Virginia, I was the Command Master Chief forever. Actually, I was a plankowner at SEAL Team Two, which was formed in 1962, and remained at the Team until I left in 1988. I was at SEAL Team Two for a total of twenty-six years.

One of the things I enjoyed doing was physical training (PT). Once I was put in charge of it for the Team, I really enjoyed it. I knew when I was going to stop, but the men didn't. We had a good physical outfit, no doubt about it.

The men followed my lead in PT, and I led them through the exercises and the run or swim that followed. This was the order of the day for all of my time at SEAL Team Two. Once, it did cause some trouble for me and a little for the men, too.

Back in the early 1970s, after we had finished in Vietnam, we were making a two-mile swim after PT and I wasn't feeling well. We had been swimming a while, covering about a quarter-mile or so, and I had been swallowing salt water. I decided to get out of the water and walk back to the Team. There were probably about fifty people in the water following my lead, as we were all swimming together. When I got out of the water, they all followed me, and we all walked back to the Team.

When I asked them why they were following me and told them that I was sick, they just continued following me anyway. The commanding officer, Bob Gormly, got in and asked me why we had all gotten out of the water before the planned swim was over. I just told him that I had gotten sick and they had all followed me in. Why? I didn't know. He said that they could all follow me Friday afternoon at liberty call, so we had to do the swim again—and finish it this time.

In 1968, I first went to Vietnam, leaving Little Creek on Easter Sunday as I remember. It didn't matter what day you left the States, because you didn't get to Vietnam until the last day of the month. That was the way the pilots who flew the transports over there figured things out. If they did a month in Vietnam, they received combat pay. So they would plan to land a plane about 11:30 at night on the last day of the month and they would take off at 12:30 the next month—an hour later—so they got two months' combat pay. The Air Force probably doesn't want to hear that, but that's the way it was.

My first tour of duty in Vietnam was with Tenth Platoon. The second time I went over, I ended up not doing any operating in the field with a platoon. On my second tour of duty, four of us trained and went over to Vietnam late in 1970. Usually, we would report in to Saigon and they would tell you where to go. I reported in to Saigon, where Captain Schaible was in charge. I knew him, so he told me that I was going to Cam Ranh Bay, and the other three SEALs with me were going down to Solid Anchor, which was a floating base down in the swamps of the southern delta.

I asked why I couldn't go with my Teammates since we had just gotten done training together. All Schaible said was, "Shut up. You're going to Cam Rahn Bay."

So I got on the airplane and flew up to the huge navy base at Cam Ranh Bay. As we were coming in on our approach run, I looked down and it looked like we were flying over Miami Beach—big, white-sand beaches and clear water. When I finally got down to where I was supposed to be, I found out that my job was to be training LDNNs (Lien Doan Nguoi Nhia by that time in the war), Vietnamese SEALs.

We were running the LDNNs though a training course. Actually, they were running their training themselves by 1970, we just advised them on how to do things. They administered their own discipline and things like that. By this time, the Vietnam War was winding down for us. Dave Schaible had told me that if the LDNNs wanted something, such as a roll of toilet paper, they had to fill out the paperwork themselves. Earlier, we had just handed them over a roll when they asked for it.

Now, we were supposed to make them do things by the book because we were going to turn everything over to them. The LDNNs didn't like that, so they went back to using a handful of leaves just like they used to.

There were still a lot of SEALs operating incountry when I was on my second tour in Vietnam. Lieutenant Joe DiMartino was in Saigon. Where I was in Cam Rahn Bay, the Navy had the dolphins, which were trained to guard the ammunition pier. The dolphins were kept in a pen with a paddle sticking down into the water. When the dolphin sensed something in the water, like an enemy swimmer—they could sense them hundreds of yards away—the dolphins would bang their heads on the paddle. Then the person on watch would turn them loose, and the dolphins would go out and push the swimmer to the surface if he was underwater. Or they would just nudge a swimmer on the surface and push them onto the beach. Then the handlers and guards would take charge of the prisoner. That's how they would catch these enemy swimmers before they could do any damage.

Anyway, I believe Joe DiMartino was eventually assigned as the officer in charge of this dolphin program at Cam Ranh Bay. Before that, though, he came over to see me one day. I took him over to where the *dolphins were and told him all about what they did. He didn't believe it, so the people who took care of the dolphins told him to go out into the bay the next morning around 5 o'clock and start swimming in toward the ammunition piers and see what happens for himself.*

So Joe went out the next morning and started swimming in. The dolphins nailed him before he got very far. According to Joe, they hit him so hard they almost broke his ribs. But he was a believer in the program after that. That's how he got involved with that outfit.

It wasn't much longer after my tour was over and I got back to Little Creek that things really started to wind down for SEAL Team Two in Vietnam. By 1972, our last platoons had come home. Things really slowed down at the Team after that. During the war, we had ten platoons at SEAL Team Two, all coming and going all the time. With the end of the war, all that stopped.

We tried to get back to normal after our commitment to Vietnam was over. A lot of people were dissatisfied and got out of the Team or retired from the Navy. They liked the war. That's what we trained for, and they preferred the action to a peacetime Team.

At SEAL Team Two in the mid-1970s, we just participated in Med (Mediterranean) trips and started working with the British and Germans in Europe. Things finally did get busy again, but it was a different kind of busy than we had during Vietnam.

In about 1978 or 1979, MOB-Six at SEAL Team Two was formed. MOB-Six meant Mobility Group Six. They took the people for the unit from Headquarters platoon at SEAL Team Two. These people were always there. If command needed them, they could call the people of MOB-Six away in a hurry. I was part of MOB-Six.

Our mission was to conduct counterterrorist actions for the Navy and SEAL Team Two. We went to Europe, and the British commandos (SAS) taught us fast roping and stuff like that. These were new things to us, and we learned from all the different foreign national counterterrorist units.

Then, around 1980, SEAL Team Six was formed, and most of the

---

people from MOB-Six went over to the new Team. I went back to SEAL Team Two because I didn't want to go to Six. There, we went back to doing all of our conventional missions while Six continued with the new, high-speed, more unconventional stuff.

In 1988, the military formed the United States Special Operations Command (USSOCOM). They didn't have the Navy in it yet, and although the SEALs weren't part of it at the beginning, they soon became part of the new organization. A four-star Army general was put in charge of SOCOM, and he interviewed Army, Navy, and Air Force people to be his senior enlisted advisor. I was the Navy person who was put up as a SEAL for the new position.

The general was in California, so I went out there to be interviewed personally by him. Before the interview, I was briefed all morning about the kind of things he would ask me. I was told to expect questions like who was the president of Zimbabwe and things like that.

"Look," I said to my briefers, "if I don't know it by now, I'm not going to learn it this morning."

Anyway, I got in to see the general that afternoon. The first thing he asked me was how had I managed to stay in the Navy so long. At that time, I had forty-two years in the Navy, most of them with the UDTs. From 1951 and my joining up with Class 6 to 1988, I had spent thirty-seven years with the UDTs or SEAL Team Two.

So when that general asked me how I had stayed in the Navy so long, I told him that if I got the job, he was going to find out, because he would have to write the next letter to keep me in the Navy. After thirty years, the Navy wants you out, and I was already well past that.

But I got the job. Overnight, I was in charge of the enlisted men of the SEALs, the Army Special Forces, the Rangers, and the twenty-third Air Force, approximately 45,000 enlisted men. And I was the head Non-Commissioned Officer (NCO).

Not everything went smoothly during my time in the new position. I was put on the awards board at SOCOM at its new headquarters on MacDill Air Force Base in Tampa, Florida. The rest of the people on the awards board were all colonels, captains, admirals, generals, and so on. I was the only enlisted man, so I just asked them what I was supposed to do.

The officers told me that every month, they were going to give me the paperwork on the guys they were going to give the awards to. I read the first batch of papers and said that these guys weren't doing anything out of the ordinary, they were just doing their jobs, and I didn't see why they should get an award.

The Air Force general in charge of the award board didn't like it when I said that I probably wouldn't recommend the men on the list for an award. He said, "I tell you what, Chief. You might not recommend them, but I know nine people who will."

That meant that he would just tell the rest of the board to give out the awards. It didn't really matter to me very much, it just showed me how the different services worked and sometimes bumped heads. The Air Force would give medals for successfully going to certain schools and things like that. The Navy doesn't do that.

Finally, it came time for me to get my last extension for my time in the service. That last extension letter was written by General Lindsay. I had told him that if I got the job, he would have to write that letter to keep me in the Navy, and he did. About a week later, he told me that I had the extension, but that he hadn't written the letter. Instead, General Lindsay told me that he had called Frank.

So I just asked him, "Frank who?"

It turned out Frank was Admiral Frank Kelso, the Chief of Naval Operations. What the CNO told General Lindsay was that he could keep me as long as he wanted me. There was somebody a bit higher up than the CNO who signed my paperwork. On my final application for an extension, I had the signature of Ronald Reagan, the president of the United States and Commander-in-Chief of all the armed forces.

When I first started my Navy career, President Franklin D. Roosevelt was sitting in the White House. When I finally left the Service, the president was Ronald Reagan. During my Navy career I stood watch under the administrations of Roosevelt, Truman, Eisenhower, Kennedy, Johnson, Nixon, Ford, Carter, and Reagan. Nine presidents—not a bad run.

The SEALs are made up of good, dedicated men, and you know what they can do, because they've already been through it. That six months of training put the men through some hard stuff. You can depend on the men who graduate that training. They're smart enough to improvise. If they can't do the job one way, they'll come up with another way to do it. I attribute a lot of the SEALs' capabilities to their physical well-being. If you're in physical shape, you can do anything you want to do.

The guys you see in the movies, the ones who don't show their feelings and act like hard cases all the time, those aren't SEALs, they're just actors. Real SEALs have a lot of feelings. I saw a guy cry just a few days ago just at the thought that an argument that was going on among the Teams could result in his being sent out of the community. At the thought of his being cut away from the rest of us, tears came into his eyes. That's showing feeling, a lot of it.

And SEALs can be scared, just like anyone else can. Every night in Vietnam was scary. Ninety percent of the time we conducted our missions at night, and every night we went out, we were scared—excited, but scared. At least I was.

You never knew what was going to happen or what it was going to take to get you through the mission. Usually we went out on intelligence—you go to this place at this time and you can catch these guys. Most of the time, it worked because the intelligence was good. But there were a lot of times that the mission fell through and nothing happened. You were prepared for anything, but there wasn't anything there. You had just gone out for a walk in the dark.

If the SEALs hadn't been in Vietnam, I don't think things would have turned out any differently. What we did was operate like the Vietnamese did, like the Viet Cong did. They went out at night and would ambush people and then disappear. We went into the Viet Cong's backyard and did the same thing to them. Now they were afraid of us because we had become the aggressor. Instead of sitting back and waiting for them to come to us, we went out and hunted them down in their own safe areas.

The whole Navy today has come out with a lot of new equipment. The Landing Craft, Air Cushion (LCAC) doesn't even sit on the water or the land, they just go right over the beach. One day, there might not be a need for a UDT-type mission any more, but there will always be a need for a SEAL. SEALs work in the rivers, swamps, and lakes. They do a different line of work than the old UDT did, and they do it very well. And the SEALs can adapt to whatever they have to.

If you're in good physical shape, you can do anything you want to do. I'd bet my life on that, and I have. In the SEALs, we're not going to beat the New York Giants in a football game. We might not win that game, but we'll win in the end some other way. That's due to the mental attitude we guys have, and our physical abilities. We go into battle thinking that we'll win.

Right now [1997], I'm seventy years old and I exercise every day. I'd feel lost if I didn't do something every day, but there's always something new to try.

■ Chapter 9

THE IRAN-IRAQ WAR AND THE PERSIAN GULF, 1980–1988

The Persian Gulf extends inland from the Arabian Sea, northwest for more than six hundred miles. A wide, shallow body of water, the Gulf is more than two hundred and fifty miles wide at its widest point, while at its mouth in the Strait of Hormuz, it mea-

Aboard the USS *Guadalcanal*, a group of heavily armed SEALs escorts Iranian prisoners captured from the minelaying ship, the Iran *Ajr*. After treatment and interrogation, the Iranian prisoners were eventually returned to their countrymen.

U.S. Navy

sures only twenty-nine miles wide. The average depth of the Gulf is only one hundred and fifty feet, the waters reaching a maximum depth of not over three hundred feet.

The major significance of the Persian Gulf are the countries that border it. Those eight countries, most on the Arabian Peninsula, are Bahrain, Iran, Iraq, Kuwait, Oman, Qatar, Saudi Arabia, and the United Arab Emirates. All these countries are major oil producers. The area produces and ships more than half of the world's supply of oil, most of it going to the free world.

Long an area of conflict, the lands surrounding the Persian Gulf have seen wars and the ebb and flow of history for millennia. Today, anything that affects the flow of oil, and with it the energy it produces, can rock the world.

In January 1979 the Shah of Iran fell from power and a funda-

The Colt M4 carbine fitted with the M203 40mm Grenade Launcher. The sliding buttstock of the M4 is in the forward (collapsed) position, and the safety of the grenade launcher is in the On position, blocking the trigger finger of a firer from entering the trigger guard of the grenade launcher.

Kevin Dockery

mentalist militant Islamic government moved into its place. The new government was a theocracy run by mullahs, the ultimate leader of which was the Ayatollah Khomeini. The Iranian theocracy became the founders and first major leaders of militant Islamic fundamentalism, exporting their world views, enforced by terrorism, throughout the world. Iran makes up the entire northern shore of the Persian Gulf, so can exert a strong control of the Gulf waters. That put the mullahs into a very powerful position both economically and politically.

The lack of an apparently stable leadership and government in Iran caused Saddam Hussein in Iraq to seriously consider the situation. Not only was his country now facing a border shared with an Islamic fundamentalist country—and Iran made no secret of the fact that it felt it should export its form of Islam—but the country also appeared to be at its weakest level ever. Khomeini had spent fourteen years of his life in Iraq, all of it under close house arrest. He had no fond thoughts of the Iraqi people or their leader.

Saddam Hussein felt he could strike a blow for his country and not only extend his own sphere of power, but also take back some

Carefully climbing onboard the subdued Iranian minelayer Iran *Ajr*, are SEALs and EOD personnel moving under the watchful eyes of armed Teammates. The Iran *Ajr* was caught during the night by Little Bird helicopters that witnessed the Iranians laying mines. Immobilized by helicopter gunfire, the abandoned *Ajr* was boarded during the early morning hours.

U.S. Navy

lands traditionally considered Iraqi. If the government of the Ayatollah should fall in the process, that would be considered a plus by Saddam.

On 12 September 1980, Iraq launched an attack across its border with Iran. Expecting a fast and easy victory, Saddam was astonished when the fighting quickly bogged down after some quick advances by the Iraqi forces. The stalemated fighting resulted in Saddam utilizing chemical weapons to try and defeat the masses of fanatics that Iran would throw against his forces. Soon, Iraq learned how to maneuver and use chemical weapons to a greater advantage.

Now the fighting between Iran and Iraq took on global proportions, not because of Saddam's use of outlawed weapons, but because both countries tried to choke off the oil exports of the other.

Stopping the flow of oil would stop the incoming flow of money, and along with it influence, support, and weapons.

The Iranian Pasdaran Islamic Revolutionary Guard Corps ran high-speed gunboats through the Gulf waters to try and stop Iraqi tanker traffic. These attacks were against almost any tankers in the Gulf waters and increased in frequency during 1986. In December 1986, Kuwait officially asked the United States to supply aid and support in preventing the attacks on their shipping. The nature of the Kuwaiti request was to allow eleven of the countries' tankers to be registered as American ships. By 10 March 1987, President Reagan agreed with the Kuwait request and Operation EARNEST WILL was planned out.

Looking forward of the superstructure of the Iran *Ajr*, nine Soviet Mark M-08/39 contact mines stand in line on the deck. The large mines are being examined by Navy SEALs and EOD technicians.

U.S. Navy

The U.S. naval vessels patrolling the Persian Gulf did not stop the Pasdaran gunboat attacks. To increase the Navy's response flexibility in the region, assets of the Navy's Special Boat Unit Eleven along with a SEAL detachment were dispatched to the Gulf in the spring of 1987.

More deployments of Naval Special Warfare assets were continually sent to the Gulf. On 6 September 1987, two oil-servicing barges, the *Hercules* and the *Winbrown 7* were leased for six months and set up as floating Special Warfare bases in the Gulf. The

Captured intact during Desert Storm, a Chinese-manufactured Iraqi CSS-N-2 Silkworm missile is transported by a U.S. Army truck. China sold a number of the Silkworm missiles to both Iran and Iraq as well as other foreign buyers.

barges could each house ten small boats, three helicopters, more than one hundred and fifty men, and the necessary ammunition, fuel, and service support for their operations.

The U.S. Navy frigate *Stark* was struck by two Iraqi Exocet missiles on 17 May 1988. Although Iraq claimed the missiles were fired in error, that did little to make up for the thirty-seven U.S. sailors who were killed in the attack. The Persian Gulf was a dangerous place to operate in—and it was going to become more dangerous.

During the first reflagged escort mission of EARNEST WILL, the tanker *Bridgeton* struck a floating naval mine. The blast tore a fifteen-by-thirty-foot hole in the over-inch-thick steel hull of the *Bridgeton*. The ship remained afloat and there were no casualties, but the incident established that the Gulf waters were mined.

The Navy recalled six old Acme-class wooden-hulled minesweepers to duty in the Gulf. SBU (Special Boat Unit) crews would spot mines in the water and destroy them with small-arms fire. The same thing was done from the decks of larger Navy ships. SEAL

A view of the complicated deck of an Iranian oil platform, partially obscured by smoke during a SEAL takeover. The elimination of several Iranian oil platforms, used as Command and Control platforms for Pasdaran speedboat attacks in the Persian Gulf were part of Operation Praying Mantis in 1987.

U.S. Navy

marksmen also had a hand in shooting the very large reactive targets found in the Persian Gulf. On at least one occasion, a SEAL swimmer entered the water and approached a floating mine to better examine it. Within a short time, the SEALs and the Navy would get a much better look at the Iranian mines.

On 21 September, deployed helicopters from the Army's Task Force 160, the Nightstalkers, spotted an Iranian ship in the act of laying mines in the Gulf. The helicopters, as were all the U.S. forces in the Gulf, were operating under very strict rules of engagement. When they received radioed permission to open fire, the helicopters fired guns and rockets at the Iranian ship, the Iran *Ajr*. As the ship tried to flee, further firing by the helicopters drove the Iranian crew to abandon ship.

Looking back at the burning hulk of an Iranian oil platform from a boat carrying Navy SEALs away from their target. The muzzle of a SEAL's M203 40mm grenade launcher is seen in silhouette to the left.

U.S. Navy

A SEAL platoon from the amphibious assault ship *Guadalcanal* boarded the Iran *Ajr* along with a Marine force reconnaissance team and a detachment of EOD (Explosive Ordnance Disposal) technicians. They found a number of old Soviet M-08/39 moored contact mines, each containing some 253 pounds of TNT. Along with the mines, twenty-three Iranians were rescued from the Gulf waters. The Iran *Ajr* was examined closely, then taken out and sunk in deep water on 26 September.

Besides floating mines, Chinese-supplied HY-2 Silkworm anti-ship missiles became a threat when, on 16 October, an Iranian Silkworm struck the reflagged tanker *Sea Isle City* just outside Kuwait City. Seventeen crewmen and the American captain were injured by the attack. On 19 October, during Operation NIMBLE ARCHER, four destroyers shelled the two Rashadat oil platforms in the Rostam oil field. Through loudspeakers, the Navy officers had told the Iranian crews that they had twenty minutes to abandon the platforms. After the platforms were shelled, SEALs boarded them to search for intelligence materials. Demolition charges were planted and the platforms destroyed. In addition, the SEALs boarded and searched another oil platform two miles away. Documents and a radio were removed for examination.

After the U.S. frigate *Samuel B. Roberts* struck a mine on 14 April 1988, the United States responded vigorously. On 18 April, during Operation PRAYING MANTIS, U.S. forces attacked the Iranian frigate *Sabalan* and oil platforms in the Sirri and Sassan oil fields. After a naval gunfire bombardment, a SEAL platoon onboard a UH-60 helicopter tried to board the platform, but the heat of the burning oil fires prevented them from landing.

On 18 July 1988, Iran accepted the UN cease-fire offer. On 20 August 1988, the Iran-Iraq War was officially over. During Operation EARNEST WILL, the U.S. Navy had escorted 259 ships in 127 convoys over a 14-month period.

■ Chapter 10

PANAMA: JUST CAUSE

The United States had signed a treaty with Panama in 1979 to defend the Panama Canal from outside threats. By 1999, the United States was scheduled to turn over control of the strategically important Panama Canal, the most direct route for shipping between the

Atlantic and Pacific Oceans, back to Panama. Before half that time period had expired, the United States would be in Panama—in force.

General Manuel Antonio Noriega had been the de facto ruler of Panama since 1981. The military dictator was deeply involved in the lucrative drug trade from South America to the United States and elsewhere. Since February 1988, Noriega had been under U.S. federal indictment for money laundering and drug trafficking. As the 1980s drew to a close, Noriega stirred the population of Panama to greater and greater resentment of the United States. In late 1989, the situation reached the breaking point.

Democratic elections had been held in Panama on 7 May 1989. Overturning the results of that election, Noriega prepared to set himself up to be the president for life. On 15 December 1989, Panama's national People's Assembly, filled with Noriega appointees, declared a state of war between Panama and the United States. The next day, Panamanian troops shot and killed a U.S. Marine officer who had been driving around with some of his fellow officers looking for a local restaurant. Another Marine officer witnessed the shooting and was quickly arrested, along with his wife who was accompanying him.

This was the last straw as far as President George Bush was concerned. As the Panamanians were beating and torturing the wife and the young officer, long-held plans were put into play that same day. During the Reagan years, Operation BLUE SPOON had been put together as a military operations plan against Panama. Following President Bush's directives, the plan was put into motion as Operation JUST CAUSE. The objectives of the operation would be to neutralize military resistance to U.S. forces, capture Noriega, and return a stable democratic government to the people of Panama.

JUST CAUSE would have a three thousand–man airborne jump into the country to get U.S. troops on the ground. In addition, there were a number of special operations calling for a variety of units.

Rangers, Army Special Forces, and Delta Force all had assigned tasks in support of JUST CAUSE. The Navy SEALs also had a number of missions. Naval Special Warfare Group Two deployed SEAL elements to an active combat environment expected in Panama as a Naval Special Warfare Task Group (NSWTG) for the first time.

Task Force White were the SEAL units going in to Panama. Their initial base of operations would be the Rodman Naval Station on the west side of the Panama Canal. The task force had five SEAL platoons, four riverine patrol boats, and two light patrol boats (twenty-two-foot Boston Whalers) as its primary naval assets. The SEAL and Special Boat Unit forces were broken down into three task units, each with a particular objective.

At 62 men, Task Unit Papa was the largest SEAL unit, and it had the largest job. TU Papa was made up of Bravo, Delta, and Golf Platoons from SEAL Team Four. Along with additional assets, they would deny Noriega and his forces use of the Paitilla Airfield. In particular, TU Papa was to destroy Noriega's personal Lear jet stored at the airport in order to prevent the dictator from using it to escape.

Task Unit Whiskey was made up of a single reinforced platoon of twenty-one men from SEAL Team Two. The mission of TU Whiskey would be the first operation of JUST CAUSE as two swimmer pairs of SEALs would go to Pier 18 in Balboa Harbor and destroy the patrol boat *Presidente Porras*. The SEALs would be conducting a swimmer attack and place heavy demolition charges, MK 138 demolition charges each containing twenty pounds of C4 plastic explosive, underneath the hull of the target ship. Their charges would be timed to go off at exactly 0100 hours on 20 December.

Task Units Charlie and Foxtrot were to respectively secure the Atlantic and the Pacific gates to the Panama Canal. At about 2300 hours on 19 December, two rubber boats with the operational crews of TU Whiskey left the Rodman Naval Station on the first leg of their mission. Using Draeger LAR-V rebreathers, the two SEAL swimmer pairs conducted their operation without casualties. At

SEALs aboard an armed Boston Whaler conduct security patrols near the Panama Canal.

U.S. Navy

0100 hours, the *Presidente Porras* blew into the night sky, the victim of the first successful combat swimmer attack by U.S. Navy forces.

TU Whiskey would later assist in the seizure of Noriega's yacht on 20 December as well as the securing of the Balboa Yacht Club the next day. A few days later, on 23 December, TU Whiskey would help repel PDF (Panamanian Defense Force) forces who tried to take over the merchant ship *Emanuel B* in the Panama Canal. Their final mission was the seizure of Noriega's beach house at Culebra on 25 December. The men of the unit returned to the United States on 2 January 1990.

It was Task Unit Papa that went through what turned out to be the most difficult operation the SEALs conducted during JUST CAUSE. Launching from Howard AFB Beach in fifteen rubber boats at 1930 hours local time on 19 December, the SEALs traveled the eight miles to Paitilla, arriving off their target beach at 2330 hours.

Following normal procedures, TU Papa sent out a pair of scout swimmers to recon the landing site and guide the other boats in.

With the sounds of distant firing and explosions in the background, TU Papa began landing at 0045 hours on 20 December.

The element of surprise had been lost well before the SEALs reached the airfield. Forming into their platoons after penetrating the fence surrounding the airfield, the SEALs prepared to move up from the southern end of the field. Delta platoon set up a hasty ambush at the midpoint of the runway to respond to reports that Noriega was coming in on a small plane. The other two platoons continued moving up along the west side of the runway.

Arriving in front of the three targeted hangars at 0105 hours, the SEALs of Golf Platoon, which was in the lead, encountered a number of PDF troops guarding the specific hangar that held the Lear jet. Within moments, a savage firefight broke out between the SEALs and the PDF forces.

In less than a few minutes four SEALs were dead and eight more SEALs were wounded, five of them seriously. All the SEALs of TU Papa were involved in the firefight, the sharp reports and green and red tracers fire criss-crossing in the dark. By 0117 hours, the remaining PDF forces withdrew, leaving the hangar and the airfield in SEAL hands.

At 0146 hours, the SEALs were able to report that the airfield was secured. The Lear jet, in spite of last-minute order changes to save it, had been damaged in the firefight. At 0205 hours, a medevac helicopter arrived to take the wounded out for treatment. At 1400 hours on 21 December, CH-47 helicopters arrived at the airfield with the Army Ranger company that was to relieve the SEALs of Task Unit Papa.

Instead of the five hours the mission had been planned for, the SEALs had been operating for thirty-seven hours straight and suffered the worst casualties of any SEAL operation. After conducting some search-and-seizure operations, the unit was released and sent back to the United States on 1 January 1990.

Task Unit Charlie on the Caribbean end of the Canal conducted

A SEAL combat swimmer dressed for land warfare comes ashore during a daylight training operation. Normally, this kind of operation is only conducted under the cover of darkness.

U.S. Navy

patrols and prevented shipping from entering the Canal. A firefight broke out between some PDF forces who had apparently taken control of a German merchant ship, the *Asian Senator*. After a few moments of seeing the massive firepower the SEALs had brought to the occasion, the PDF troops surrendered. TU Charlie was deactivated on 26 December.

TU Foxtrot had much the same mission on the Pacific end of the Canal, but without the firefights. The SEALs stopped and searched ships, finding a cargo of looted electronic equipment aboard a Colombian vessel. The mission of TU Foxtrot ended on 2 January 1990.

Additional smaller SEAL units assisted in the search for Manuel Noriega. The Panamanian dictator was taken prisoner and removed to the United States to face trial and later imprisonment. The government of Panama that had been elected by the people in May 1989 took office in 1990.

Randy Lee Beausoleil, Warrant Officer

Back when I was about nine years old, it was my swimming coach, Coach Cunningham, who first told me about the Navy SEAL Teams. He told me he was an old Frogman from Vietnam and talked all about it. I loved swimming and swam all the way though my high school years. Coach Cunningham basically stayed with me, as he moved from the grade school that I attended to the same high school I went to.

The vision I got from his stories was one of what it was like to be in the jungle as a SEAL, as compared to what it was like to be with an Army unit, or some other large unit. From what he described to me, being with the SEALs in Vietnam sounded like the safest thing you could think of—a small unit of guys who were very well trained. They were in bad-guy territory, but they were 100 percent confident that their abilities could overcome anything in that environment. That, to me, sounded like the way that things should be done.

The one incident Coach Cunningham told me that stuck out was when he got shot in the leg. He kind of sloughed it off as no big deal. Though the particulars of that story have escaped me over time, it stuck out. Obviously, when you get hit, your own mortality kind of creeps in to the picture. You don't want to die doing this job, but that's always a possibility.

Coach Cunningham kept filling my head with stories about the SEALs. He was my mentor while I was competing, and his stories kind of stuck in my head. But when I originally joined the Navy, I didn't enlist to become a SEAL—kind of an odd twist for me. It wasn't until after three years of my enlistment passed that I started looking to volunteer for the Teams. That ended up being the path I took in my Navy career.

In August 1984, I classed up at BUD/S with Class 131, a summer into winter class but officially considered a summer class. When I got into the training, I really liked it, especially when I compared it to the other part of the Navy. In my opinion, you weren't treated like a real man when I first came into the Navy. There was a lot of pettiness, a lot of people who just didn't seem to want to treat you what your age was. When you're twenty years old, you shouldn't be treated like a ten-year-old.

When I got to BUD/S, we were off on the weekends. When we were done with training for the day, we were off-duty. That was great, and a heck of a lot better than being on a ship. I liked it.

I knew I was in trouble during training because I had never run before. That first run we went on was led by a senior chief who later ended up being the Master Chief of BUD/S. He was big and maybe a little overweight, and he took us on a two-mile run through the soft sand. I just about died during that run, so I knew I was in trouble.

But running was the only part of BUD/S I had problems with. All of the swimming events I did pretty good in, and I didn't have any problems with the other evolutions. Then there was Hell Week—that sucked pretty bad. I think that's a good way of putting it.

As a whole, Hell Week is pretty much a blur in my memories. I remember quite a bit about it. One thing I remember is that I didn't hallucinate badly like a lot of the other guys did later in the week. Extreme fatigue was very new to me, but it still didn't get me to the point that I was ready to quit and move on to something else.

Temperature extremes are something a SEAL has to get used to. I've seen some people just quit when the temperature gets extremely cold. Their body just shuts down. You can't allow your body to do that. Mentally, you have to be above that.

When I say extremely cold, it's very difficult, I think, to convey that to somebody in words. But imagine this: your core temperature, the temperature inside where all your major internal organs are, drops. Your body starts to shiver. The shivering is a way for your body to try to generate some heat. After your body shivers for so long, your hip flexors, the large muscles in your hips and the top of your legs, contract.

Now imagine having a cramp, one that runs from your mid-section all the way down to the top of your knees. All those muscles are so tight that when you stand up it's almost like you've got to have somebody straighten you out. The muscles are so cold that they're actually cold to the touch. That's how cold I've gotten in the past.

Lying on a steel pier during Hell Week makes you cold. The instructors have the old rain bird, a lawn sprinkler, running, just spitting, chiit. . . . chiit . . . chiit . . . over us. You're there all night long, in and out of the water. Your core temperature drops.

You get so cold that you can't feel your feet anymore. You can't feel your hands anymore. Your hip flexors hurt so bad that you just want to cut them out of your body. To me, that's what extreme cold is—pain.

One thing I remember about that long week was that, when it was over, when it was finally over, my feet had been cold throughout the week. Class 131 had its Hell Week in October, and I just remember my feet being cold that whole time. When we were secured late in the afternoon on Friday, I remember sticking my feet into the sand, that hot sand that had the Southern California sun beating down on it all day.

I just stood there for a while, trying to warm my feet up in the sand. Finally, Senior Chief Scarborough came by and grabbed me to tell me that I had to take my final med (medical) inspection. I was a little disappointed because my feet had finally started to warm up.

That ended the week with kind of a bang for me. I slept for eighteen hours straight and after that I was fine.

My desire to be a SEAL is what got me through Hell Week. But I never really got to that point where I really wanted to quit. I think that anyone who says that they didn't think about quitting, or how nice it would be if they did quit and go back to a normal life, is fooling themselves. You think about it at some point, but you don't quit. I never got to the point of quitting. For me, everything we did was something that was fun or new. I can't say that I enjoyed that long week, but I did definitely value the experience. That's probably the best way for me to put it.

There really isn't any specific incident that stands out in my mind from my BUD/S training. The one thing that does stand out was that first two-mile run where I realized that I was in trouble. But other than that, nothing really stands out. Everything was all so new to me. In my youth, I had been one of the kids who liked playing with GI Joes, so BUD/S to me was like playing GI Joe for real, and I loved every minute of it. I especially liked BUD/S when we got to the later phases of training, where we learned more of what being a real SEAL was all about.

So for me, BUD/S was all of that. There just wasn't any one event all though those weeks that had any more impact on me that any other event. The day I was done with training, knowing that I had accomplished that feat and was ready to move on to the Teams, was a really good one.

The weapons and demolition phase was the part of BUD/S that stood out to me with the greatest impact. The diving was nice. I had spent my life in the water, so underwater swimming wasn't really that great a change to me. They hadn't really developed a good combat swimming program at that point in BUD/S like they have now, so the diving portion didn't hold as much impact for me as it could have.

When we finally got out to San Clemente Island and started working with demolitions and getting to shoot the Army guns, that was the most fun for me. That was a great time and is something I'll never forget. Plus, I developed some pretty good friendships at BUD/S that have stayed with me over the years.

Not everything was great at San Clemente, though. I had the dubious honor of being the first guy who had to run a "flight" up to the Frog on the top of the hill at the base there. It was myself and my swim buddy, then ensign Herbert, who had to run up the hill with an eight-by-eight steel pallet on our backs, around the Frog, and back down to the starting point. That circuit was a flight, and the pallet on your back were your wings.

That very last day of training, standing on the grinder at graduation, was a tremendous relief for me. I figured the physical pain was over and we would be ready to move on to other things. I didn't realize that when I got to my Team the physical pain was only to continue.

But graduation from BUD/S still gave me a strong feeling of accomplishment. I knew I had finished something that, to me, was a monumental feat that very few people in the world will ever do. That meant a lot to me. My Dad was there at graduation and that also meant a lot. He was a World War II vet and got to see me moving forward. That definitely was a great day for me and is something that still sticks in my mind.

The Trident, the insignia of Naval Special Warfare that I wear on my uniform, signifies everything that I've accomplished. It means to me that I'm part of a small and very special unit. I am very defensive of the Trident. I get very upset when I see somebody wearing one who I feel either hasn't earned it all the way (completed BUD/S and his probationary period) or doesn't deserve to wear it and continues to do so.

My position now is one in which I have to evaluate people. I watch people who show up, and we're very strict on who actually wears a Trident. Once a man shows up at a Team, that doesn't mean he can just put it on his uniform. He has to successfully complete a six-month probationary time. And after that time is completed, we have to evaluate all the training that individual has done and we review all of his records before we put the Trident on him for the first time.

People did that to me, and it meant an awful lot to me. The day I received my Trident was a very, very big event for me. Even though there wasn't anyone there for me to share my feelings with, it meant that I had made it. Since I was nine years old, I had thought about being a Navy SEAL. I was twenty years old when I first received my Trident, so for eleven years I had thought about wearing that thing.

Every time I saw a man who was wearing a Trident, I knew that he was totally different than just about anyone else who walked the planet. Receiving the Trident was a tremendous accomplishment. BUD/S was great. And getting out of there was more of just a physical accomplishment. But receiving my Trident meant that I was recognized by all the other guys who had come before me—thousands of Team guys who had been there and some who still were—as someone who

---

was up to snuff, someone who had earned the right to wear it. And I defend that symbol to this day with a great amount of zeal, I guess you could say.

The Trident connects every Team guy with all those who have come before him. From the guys who started off in World War II in the NCDUs to the guys who are just coming out of BUD/S and the guys who we just gave Tridents to today—they are all connected, all members of the fraternity, the brotherhood, of the Teams. They all have something in common—BUD/S. Even though training has changed some, it hasn't changed all that much where it counts. Everybody can say that they are wearing their Trident because they have accomplished that major feat, completing training.

Everybody I think equates BUD/S to Hell Week. That's definitely a separator during training, but the amount and level of training that a SEAL gets is what separates him more from everybody else out there. That means a great deal.

After I graduated BUD/S and completed Jump School, my first assignment was to SEAL Team Two in Little Creek, Virginia. I arrived there on 10 April 1985, and they pretty much stuck me. There was going to be four or five months yet before I could go through my SEAL Tactical Training, which is the training that every Team gives you to indoctrinate you in the way they do business.

So they stuck me in the air operations department and threw me out of a plane a couple days later in my first free-fall. So my four months before I started my tactical training and getting into my platoon was spent jumping. That was a great experience for me.

I did feel a real connection with the old SEALs who had come before me when I arrived at SEAL Team Two. At Team Two, we had a lot of history still walking the deck. We still had Rudy Boesch as our Command Master Chief. Rudy Boesch had been at the Team since the first dinosaur went through BUD/S, and he was just a hell of a guy. He wasn't a great storyteller, but Rudy would go with you to your land warfare training up at Camp A.P. Hill. That's where he would talk to you about Vietnam and tell you stories of what Team Two did there. When he retired, he had more than forty-five years in the Navy, and he had been at Team Two for about twenty-five of those years.

When I saw Rudy Boesch for the first time, I wondered just who this old guy was. I got to the Team in 1984, and I could be mistaken, but I think he was around fifty-seven years old at the time. Here was a guy who had been in the Navy since 1945, near the end of World War II. This

A student from BUD/S Class 83 in 1975 heads for the ground after jumping from the top of an obstacle. Trainees are expected to constantly better their time in completing the BUD/S obstacle course, and continued practice under the watchful eyes of SEAL instructors helps ensure that this happens.

U.S. Navy

guy was our Command Master Chief, the senior enlisted guy at our command, and he ran the physical training program at SEAL Team Two.

Every Monday morning, you went out to quarters and you didn't have a choice. You made a right face and ran out the gate, with Rudy leading the way. We would get out and do forty-five minutes of PT— push-ups, sit-ups, pull-ups, and everything else you could think of. And after that, you would go out on a nice five-mile run.

And it wasn't a five-mile run like I'd thought about, the old Army guys singing a cadence and jogging in formation. No, this was an all-out, gut-wrenching run as fast as you could because if you didn't, you were a turd. And there was Rudy, deep in the thick of it.

Tuesdays was always a swim. When we swam, it wasn't in a pool, it *was out in the water whether it was wintertime and twenty-eight degrees or summertime and eighty degrees. And every time, there was Rudy.*

Wednesdays was always the o-course day. We did four little obstacle courses and one big obstacle course. They were just different types of o-courses. And there was Rudy, running right through the course along with everyone else.

Thursdays we kinda did our own thing. Fridays was a nice, long, ten-mile run. And there was Rudy. It amazed me. I was thinking that here was a man who was fifty-seven, he was about the age of my dad. My dad is in good health, but this guy was busting it out with all the other SEALs—and this was after nearly forty years in the military already.

Rudy was beating young guys straight out of BUD/S. It was an embarrassment if you were behind Rudy on anything. Quite Frankly, Rudy was always between the middle and the upper part of the pack. It was hard to beat him. That's just mind-boggling.

You would know when you met Rudy Boesch for the first time. Here would be a man with a kind of a tan, a flat-top haircut, and a New Jersey accent. He would be fit and in shape. But when he told you how old he was, you wouldn't think that he looked a day over forty. But he was in his late fifties. He's pretty amazing.

It's not that there's something just about an old Navy SEAL guy. There's nothing about the old guys that really separates them from the new crowd, other than maybe the way they carried themselves. But they did set a standard that you have to work at to reach.

How important is it for the new SEALs to know and remember what the old SEALs and UDT men have done before us? Talking about the old guys, I can look from my father's perspective, and I can look from the perspective of all the older Team guys who have been before me. I have been a member of the Special Operations community for a long time. My dad was Airborne in the Army so he, too, was in a special group of men.

I don't think it's fair for anyone who has not been in the military to talk or make decisions about what happens to people in the military. I come from a military background, and when I look at all the older guys the things that they have done are amazing to me. But they all did it for one reason—because they were called to do it, not because what they did was something they wanted to do. They were called to do it because it was part of their job.

The things I've done in the SEAL Team was all a part of my job. And I look at it that way. I get very defensive about our history. I think it's very important to honor the older guys because they were the ones who paved the way, not only for our country, because a major part of our history has happened in the last fifty years, but also for how I do business today.

If it wasn't for the older guys, and all the sacrifices they made, all the safety we have in training now, all the tactics we use now that have been refined more than fifty years—things that save lives today—we wouldn't have them if it wasn't for those guys who did all of that in the past. Without the older people, especially those men who came through the SEAL Teams, where would we be now? We would be starting over. We would be the old guys, because fifty years down the road the new SEALs will be saying the same things about us—which I hope they do.

We should be setting precedents now to help save lives in the future. The better we do our job, and the better that the United States does its job when it does comes to conflict, the fewer people are going to die. I don't think anybody wants to see people die, although that is part of our job. But more than that, my job is to make sure that nobody who works with me dies. I'd rather the bad guy die for his cause and my guys come back and be able to meet with the old guys.

So when I got to Team Two, we still had Rudy, and there were others—Mikey Boynton, Pierre Birtz, and quite a few of the guys who had been in Vietnam—there to give us their knowledge. They had been in the Teams or the UDTs before that. All those guys were all around us, so it was kind of hard not to be a part of the history. SEAL Team Two has a very thick and proud history to go along with it.

To this day, when people ask me where I'm from, I always mention SEAL Team Two. I'm at SEAL Team Three now (1998), but my heart's still at SEAL Team Two, and it'll always be there. I hope to get assigned back there some day.

The Vietnam vets in the Teams were guys who we always held up on a pedestal in a way. You've heard all the stories before you even meet the guys. At BUD/S, all the instructors tell all the stories about how great it was for the SEALs back then. I followed through with a habit of mine. I'm the type kind of guy who always looks into things I'm wondering about.

SEAL Team Two had a pretty good history when it came to Vietnam. They lost nine guys who were killed in action; six of those were killed in a situation that might have been preventable. That's a pretty good identifier of just how well SEAL Team Two did its business. And that carried on to the training that I got from my first platoon, for my first deployment, and all the other platoons I did after that.

All the older guys had pretty much set in stone how training was going to happen at Team Two, so you knew that you were getting trained by someone who had twenty years of background and sound tactics behind him. You knew that you were learning something that a lot of guys bled for and that a lot of guys had used many, many times in real combat. That meant a lot to me, so I didn't take anything for granted.

When somebody was talking, especially the old Vietnam vets, you listened. And I brought those men back to the Teams. I had a lot of retired Vietnam vets who I brought back to some of my later platoons when I had become senior and was the LPO (leading petty officer) and later still chief of a platoon. I brought those guys back and paid their way to come to wherever we were at just to talk to the younger guys. We had started losing a lot of those older Vietnam vets who had all that combat experience.

It means a lot to me to have those guys around. And I still draw on that vast well of knowledge. It was a tragedy when Mikey Boynton was lost a few years ago, because he was one of the guys who I brought to just about every training evolution I did.

Mikey Boynton is just one of those guys who seemed to have been around everywhere. You see the old video Men in Green Faces that was used for recruiting into the Teams, and Mikey was one of the guys getting his Silver Star out there on Turner Field. You saw this big, thick-necked guy standing there as they pinned a medal on him, and you wondered just who the heck that guy was. Then you showed up at SEAL Team Two, and there he was. I had been there a couple years before he came back to Team Two and just showed up. I knew automatically who he was.

Going right up to him, I said, "I don't know your name, but I remember you from the video."

He introduced himself and was the most likable guy you'll ever meet in your life. And he knew what he was talking about. Here was a guy who had been through some pretty wild things, which are all in the books now. So when you go through some training and Mikey said, "You'd better listen to that," or "You'd better do that," you did exactly what he said. And he would pull you aside and say, "Hey, I heard about some of the things you guys did. You might want to think about doing it this way . . ." That's a pretty weighty source of advice, so you listened.

Mikey was a great friend up to the time I left Team Two and until he died.

My first actual combat operation was as a combat swimmer attack on Noriega's boat in Panama during Operation JUST CAUSE. My platoon, Hotel Platoon at SEAL Team Two, had been gearing up for what was called a EUCON deployment, which goes to Europe. We had just formed up that July (1989) as a full platoon and had started our pre-deployment training.

For us, the two major blocks of our pre-deployment training were land warfare and combat swimmer. Combat swimmer was basically diving with the closed-circuit Draeger rigs and learning how to navigate underwater in order to get to whatever target you had to.

So those two blocks of instruction were very major, and we started with land warfare training. The officer we started with developed a medical problem so he had to be relieved. Then we got a new officer in the platoon, Lieutenant Ed Coughlin. He and I had gone through BUD/S together; he had been an ensign while I had been an E-5. We knew each other right away, and we just happened to click immediately.

Lieutenant Coughlin had come into the platoon at that time because they (the higher command) knew some things I didn't know. Command knew that the invasion of Panama was probably going to happen soon, and that our platoon was probably going to be the ready platoon at SEAL Team Two for that operation. The ready platoon is the platoon that has been through most of their pre-deployment training and is the next platoon that will head out the door on a deployment.

We were kind of the more senior platoon at the Team in relation to training, not age. We were going to become the ready platoon in December, we knew that. It was finally revealed what was going to happen down in Panama. Because SEAL Team Four's and SEAL Team Two's standard operating procedures were a little different, it was decided that because SEAL Team Two had done most of the training with a fairly major combat swimmer block, and because we had worked with a lot of foreign swimmer units and done a lot of combat swimming, we would be tasked with a special dive op in Panama.

The dive op was strictly to deny Noriega the use of his patrol boats that were going to be docked in Balboa Harbor on the southern part of the canal. Quite frankly, that's about two thousand yards across the canal from the U.S. Naval Special Warfare Unit that was based in Panama at the time.

So we were tasked with that op, and we practiced for that mission. We did a lot of dives, and combat swimming became second nature to everybody in my platoon. We dove so much that diving was as common

and natural as breathing or sleeping. That combat swimmer–type operation is something we're trained to do, that every Team is trained to do.
It just so happened that we had worked a little bit more at it.

That dive op was our task, and we knew it inside and out. We had
spent six to nine weeks just conducting combat swimmer–type attacks
for practice. It was the beginning of December, by the time we got done
with all that and we started to wind down as far as training went. Right
around 13 December, we were tasked to go down to Florida with a
bunch of other people, other units, in order to rehearse for the op we
would do in Panama. At the time, we didn't know specifically what the
op or the target was. That wasn't made clear to us until later.

During our rehearsal, we tried to keep everything pretty much the
same as we would experience on the real op. I was very strict on making sure all the guys who dove that night would be diving with the exact
equipment they would be diving with in Panama.

That was kind of hard, because the water in Florida at that time of
year was only about 50 degrees, and the water in Panama was over 90
degrees, so we had to find sort of a happy medium. In Florida we were
freezing our butts off practicing that dive. Just about all four of us got
hyped out—hypothermia—in the Florida water. It was hard to stay
warm the three days following that, but the practice paid off.

I like to train people so they're going to do exactly the same thing in
training that they will in combat. And if we have an opportunity to
rehearse the op, they're going to keep rehearsing until they are so tired
of rehearsing that they can do it in their sleep—which is what we did.

Right around 16 December, that particular exercise was over and
myself and four other guys were supposed to stay in Florida to do some
other training, some follow-on stuff. On the seventeenth, we were
recalled and had to drive to Atlanta and then fly to Norfolk, Virginia.

It was in Norfolk that we met up with the rest of our platoon, who
were already back and getting prepared. At Team Two, we had a little
cover story for what we had been doing. The exercise we had just

been on was something all the guys at Team Two knew about but not what it was for. They certainly didn't know that it was practice for a real operation.

Our CO had told the guys at the Team that our platoon had screwed up the exercise so we had to do it again. They threw us into Isolation, a secured area where we have no contact with the outside world and very little contact even with the Team. While we were in Isolation, the rest of the Team was pointing their fingers at us like we were a bunch of bad little boys.

But all the guys in the platoon knew what was going on. Plus we had some additional guys who we augmented the platoon with who were let in on what was really going on. At this point, we all knew that we were going to do the real deal.

So we flew to Panama in the middle of the night of 18 December. We climbed onboard a C-141 with all the guys from SEAL Team Four and all the live ammunition that you never get to see in training, and flew to Panama. We arrived in Panama around 8 o'clock in the morning on December 19, 1989.

Everything was supposed to happen at 0100 hours on the twentieth, so we were getting in the water that night. From 8 o'clock in the morning when we first hit the ground, we were only seventeen hours out. This fast reaction is the same kind of stuff that we train for. For the operation, we had a clock, a timer, and a firing device that nobody had ever seen before. It was real-time clock that you set with the current time and the time you wanted it to go off and it started a countdown.

We got all our charges ready. The target we were going after was an aluminum-hulled Swift boat, made in the USA. The limpet mine we normally use has magnets on it to hold it to the target, but we couldn't use it to secure the limpets to the target. There are some other things we could use, some stud drivers that secure a limpet to the target with an explosively fired nail, but we were worried that on a small craft—the Swift was only a sixty-five foot patrol boat—with the engines not running, the bad guys would hear the studs going off into the hull.

So we decided to use just a regular, standard haversack charge of high explosives. The special clock was attached with a safety and arming device, which is a device that keeps the charge from going off for at least fifteen minutes after it is set. That delay gives you some time to get away in case the clock was to malfunction and go off early.

All of that was stuffed into the haversack, which already held twenty pounds of C-4 plastic explosive. The haversacks were strapped to the swimmer backpacks that we normally carry our training limpet mines on. That's what we dove with.

Our prep work went on in the morning. There was only one target boat in the water. Originally, the platoon was told that there could be up to eight boats that would have to be targeted, but on this day, there was only one so we decided on four divers. Two guys who were picked were myself and Lieutenant Coughlin. We were the most senior guys in the platoon and had done the most diving. Then we picked our dive buddies. My dive buddy was Chris Dye, the most calm, cool, and collected cucumber you could ever find to dive with. Then we picked the other guy who became the lieutenant's swimmer pair because he could drive a compass like nobody's business.

The four of us got our rigs ready, then the wait began. This was a drill we had done a hundred times before, so there wasn't anything new to us. By about 3 or 4 in the afternoon, we were done getting ready. Although you're getting things done, you aren't thinking too much about anything but the job at hand. But after that, you have all that time to rest or get some sleep before your first contest.

All our gear was ready and we just sat. I told all my guys to get some sleep, but it wasn't easy. If you've been in combat before, the wait might have been a little easier, but none of us had. That was the most difficult part—the wait for that first dive. The anticipation was killing everybody.

I think we all were very confident about the operation. I was and I know my buddy was. But you never know just how things are going to go. You never know just what branch is going to be turned or what Murphy is going to throw at you.

In the swimming pool during training, a BUD/S student intently watches the indicator on the compass of his attack board. His swim-buddy, to the side and slightly above him, would watch out for obstacles and dangers in the water as his partner "drives" the compass.

U.S. Navy

We were supposed to get in the water that night at 11 o'clock—two hours before H-Hour. Because of all the different fears that were around at the time as far as whether or not the Panamanians knew when H-Hour was, Command didn't want us to get in the water and start diving too early. Once they put us in the water, there was no way of calling us back.

If the commanding general decided that H-Hour was going to change to, say, the next day and we were in the water, that boat was going to blow up that night. So Command had to be sure, and they backed us up a half-hour, which wasn't good for us because we had added in some crunch time on our dive.

By 10:30 the night of the nineteenth, we were across the canal from our target and put our boats in the water. Getting our dive rigs on, we were wearing exactly the same equipment we had on during rehearsal. I knew that once I got into the water, nothing was going to change for me. I would immediately be able to start diving.

Right about 11:15 or so, we decided it was time to be going. Because of the current that came down the Panama Canal when the gates were opened up north, we couldn't just get in the water and start our dive and go across the canal and hit the target. That was a little too chancy, because the current was never consistent. One minute it could be zero, and the next it could be running at five knots.

So we got into two zodiacs, one pair in each boat along with a driver, a communicator (radio operator), and M60 gunner. Driving across the canal, we hid the boats in a mangrove just north of the target. Our CO at the time, Commander Carley, decided at that point that it was time to insert us into the water. It was about 11:30 at night.

At that point, we started motoring over to the insert point, where we were going to get off and enter the water. We started breathing on our rigs before we ever got into the water to make sure we weren't going to have any problems with them.

The boat I was in was having some problems, and the motor wasn't idling all that well. It had been tuned pretty much for the fifty degree water back around Florida. We hadn't had an opportunity to lean them out for the warmer water around Panama. So our boat conked out.

They went ahead with the other boat and inserted the first swimmer pair into the water. Then they came back and took the bow line on our boat and motored us out to where we were going to get into the water, just outside of the mangrove. Myself and Chris just slipped over the side of the boat and immediately went under the water and started diving. There was no wait for us.

At that point, both Chris and I felt very normal. This was something that we were very familiar with. All the anticipation and anxiety immediately went away for me because I was doing exactly what I knew how to do.

We hadn't swum more than a minute or two before we hit a tree that was under the water. It had obviously fallen down at some point and become waterlogged. Chris and I had dove so much together that *we knew exactly what to do. Chris climbed up on my back and we drove right through the obstacle, got to the other side, and kept on diving. It was nothing new to us.*

That tree was something that might have thrown us off earlier on in our training. We would have been down there wrestling around in the quagmire of branches. But it didn't really affect us because of the amount of training that we had. As we kept on diving, we hit the first big pier that was our first reset point.

Without going into all the sordid details, because of the little things that did happen, Chris and I had decided at that point that diving underneath the pier was the better option for us. What worried us was the large current that would flow through the open area when the gates were opened.

Driving with the compass out in the open water probably wasn't the best way to go for that op, but it was something that we had trained for so Chris and I followed the long pier that led down to our target using the available light to guide us on our way.

The boat was docked on a floating cement pier that had two halves, about seventy-five yards each half. The floating pier was big enough that a six-by (2½ ton) truck could have driven along it. The pier had a big old awning over it, and there were a lot of fluorescent lights underneath it.

All the water within fifty yards of that pier was just like daylight to us, so as we were diving up to the target, we could see it coming. There was a ship parked on the outside of the pier, so we were still diving along the outside of that ship. As soon as the water grew light, we knew we were within about fifty yards of the pier.

We cut in at a forty-five and drove on until we hit that floating cement pier. Once there, we got down underneath it to maintain our concealment and started diving down to where the target was.

Remember, we were running into a time-crunch. When you're driving around a pier underwater, it's not as fast as swimming in the open. We were backed up about a half-hour on our schedule, so that fudge factor we had in our schedule wasn't there any more and now we were worried about time.

Because of the clock on the charge and everything else, we had to arm that thing thirty minutes prior to when we wanted it to go off, which was 1 o'clock in the morning on the twentieth.

We were starting to come up on the time that we really had to get that thing up on the boat. As we continued on, I could hear something that sounded like somebody on top of the pier dropping fifty-five-gallon drums on the cement. I didn't know what it was; it just sounded like somebody was up there working. They were going to be dead in a few minutes anyway.

But we kept on going and got to where the boat was. We could tell we had gotten to the boat because there was a nice big shadow in the water to our right side where the boat was docked, butt-end in against the pier.

Immediately, we went underneath the boat. Chris got all the way underneath the target. I stuck one hand on the boat and one on the pier and kind of let myself up a bit so I could make sure the number on the boat was the proper one.

My head just broke the surface and I could see the number, "P202." It was the right one. It was at that point that I figured out what was going on up on the pier. Somebody was up there, one foot on the boat and one foot on the pier, and he was definitely a bad guy. He had a gun in his hand, and he was frantic about something.

All I did was go right back underneath the boat, and I don't think Chris and I spent more than a minute there. All we did was take off the backpack and clip it onto the boat around a propeller shaft. Then we prepared the clock and armed it. I checked everything, then Chris and I went back under the pier and we started on our way out.

It turned out that the other swimmer pair had gotten into the water about five minutes before we did. But we just happened to get to the target before they did, I think because of the route we selected. They were only maybe a minute behind us. They got to the target and put their charge on, connected the two, and were on their way out. During the whole dive, I don't think we were more than a hundred yards apart, even though we never saw each other.

On the way out I was pretty much straightforward in the route we chose. Because of the time crunch and because of the way the piers were constructed and our fears about that big current when the gates were opened, we stuck close to the pier on the way out. So it was slow-going again.

Chris and I were maybe five hundred yards down when it came time that the charge would be going off. At that point, he and I got as far back up underneath the piers as we could. You could say we broke a tactic at that point because we surfaced, put our rigs offline, and just sat there. The water was so hot at that point. It was over ninety degrees, and we had been practicing in fifty-degree water, and we were overheating. That made it a good time for us to stop and get something to drink from our canteens and listen for that charge to go off.

The only problem was that everything had started early and it would be hard to hear the shot. With any kind of detonation that goes off in the water, the sound is pretty muffled. Because I had been the one who set the clocks by my watch, I was counting down to the firing time. There was so much stuff going on at that point that I never did hear the shot go off.

Not hearing the shot made me pretty worried. Something was wrong. But what are you going to do? The only thing we could do now was extract, get back, and continue on with the next mission.

It was at that point that my mind started working against me. I started thinking that because that guy on the pier had been so frantic, the other pair of swimmers could have been compromised. If they were, could they have found the charges? That might have been why they didn't go off.

It turned out that I was all wrong. The charges went off exactly on time. There had been some people across the way that had set their watches to mine. They counted it down, and the charge went right off.

The boat actually came out of the water and then settled back down. A piece of it landed next to a friend of mine who gave it to me almost three months later. He came back and gave me this piece of the hull and said, "Hey, this is from your boat. It blew up and then this piece landed next to me." I still have it. You keep that kind of stuff.

So Chris and I were stopped underneath the pier. It was a good time to get some water and cool down because we were really hot. Part of our tasking was that we were supposed to have made it farther on and actually called back on a radio to our higher-ups and tell them that the charges were on the boat. But because of the time crunch, that wasn't going to happen. We were still so close to the boat after we had set the charge that we just didn't get far enough away with enough time allowed to call back and let them know the charges were on.

Once we were done and all cooled off, we decided to get going again. We got our rigs back on and started diving back out. When a boat blows up in the water and there are other boats docked near it that might be of questionable origin, boat crews worry about guys like us. There had been some large ships docked along that pier and they started jacking their screws—they started turning their propellers while they were still next to the pier to potentially blow a diver off the bottom of the boat.

I know of one boat that felt like it was doing that to me. But after that, the dive out along that pier was pretty much like standard training. When we got past the end of the pier, we were supposed to dive out and box around an area that had some additional piers where some larger ships were docked in a dry dock area. So we were going to box out around it, make ninety-degree turns to our heading, and go around the area rather than trying to run past underwater lines and whatever else might have been there. We were worried about getting sucked up into the suction intakes underneath one of the boats.

Diving out away from the boats was all part of our plan. It was pretty simple. But the gates must have been finally opened and a good current was heading down the canal at that point. What was supposed to be a twelve-minute leg out that should have put us a few hundred yards out, ended up putting us a lot farther out into the bay.

Both dive pairs, us and the other pair, ended up right in the middle of the canal, because as the current came it pushed us a little bit faster than we had figured. So as we started our westbound leg to get out of that op area, I started hearing a large ship moving through the water.

When you're underwater, ship sounds carry pretty far. When you have a large ship coming, it can get bad. And I've been under some big ships before, aircraft carriers and the like, and I knew that whatever was coming at us was big, so I started going deeper in the water. When you're diving a pure-oxygen rig like we were, the deeper you go, the more toxic oxygen becomes to your system.

We were still within the depth limits of the training that we had done before, so I was very confident that nothing was going to happen to us—but I could still hear that ship coming.

The approaching ship was getting louder and louder. It was dark in that water. There was a lot of bioluminescence in the water when all the little microorganisms glow like little fireflies when you move through them, but I wasn't worried about that showing us up. We were far enough away from the piers for that. But it was still really dark in the water.

We hit about thirty-five feet of depth, and I was thinking to myself that I had no idea of just how deep in the water a big freighter drives, so I wanted to go a little bit deeper. I don't think Chris wanted to go that deep because he was pulling me the other way as I pulled him down deeper. We ended up down around forty-five feet, and that ship above us was extremely loud.

There's a strap that goes around the breathing rig's mouthpiece that's there just in case you go underneath a ship. The noise vibrates you so much that your teeth can't hold the mouthpiece in your mouth. So you cinch that strap down so that the mouthpiece won't come out.

When we were down there at forty-five feet and I heard that boat coming, I reached up to tighten up my straps. Just as I did that, I heard the zip-zip sound of Chris tightening his straps. He tightened them at the same time I was planning to. He had been thinking exactly the same thing that I had been thinking. We definitely were in sync with each other.

It was dark, but when that ship went over the top of us, the water got even darker. It was unbelievably loud and passed right over our heads. We probably were only at that depth for five minutes or so. As soon as that freighter went over the top of us, both Chris and I swayed back and forth a little bit—that meant the screw was over and had already passed. We both were thinking the same thing and headed straight for the surface.

We were not thinking about the bad guys at that point, whether or not there was somebody on the back of that freighter looking for a diver in the wake. I went to the surface so I could take a bearing and figure out which way I wanted to go. What I wanted to do was extract and get picked up by my guys because there was now a war going on around us.

After taking a compass bearing on the extract pier, I went back down, and Chris and I dove as fast as we could to the pier. We ended up getting back to the pier and because all of the work we had done getting there, we decided to stop again, vent ourselves a little bit, and take on some water. That put us a little behind the other swim pair. They had decided not to stop and had just gone on to the extract.

At the end of the pier we were under was another pier. It was at the end of that second pier that our boats were supposed to have been sitting and picked us up.

Because of everything that was going on, that spot was pretty much out in the open. The boats moved to the pier before the planned op, staying away from the bad guys and doing what they were supposed to do.

We got to that point and I was just going to go up and radio that we were late but we were coming. As I ascended, I was still in between the pilings, and I popped out of the water right between two zodiacs.

Like a knucklehead, I went right back down, wondering what the Panamanians were doing underneath the pier in black zodiacs. Then it dawned on me that they probably didn't have black zodiacs and that those had probably been our guys. So I went back up and took a look at the engine without exposing myself above the water. Sure enough, there was a big blue "H" painted on the side of the engine. I surfaced and obviously it was our guys.

I had to splash a little bit in order to let them know I was there. Then we took our rigs off, they pulled us into the boat, and we headed back over to the good guy's side, down by the naval facility across the canal.

All in all, the operation probably took us about five hours, in and out. It was a long op, but it was standard. There was nothing we did that any other SEAL Team couldn't have done. We were just lucky enough that our platoon was there. And I feel that we were the most prepared for that particular job.

The dive went flawlessly. It went just as it should have and exactly as we had planned except maybe for the stops to prevent us from over-heating. It turned out to have been a great op for us. And we were rewarded nicely for it.

There aren't any SEALs that I know of who'll pat themselves on the back, because you get humbled every day in SEAL Team. Every day you go to work and although you might think you're the hot thing on the block that day, there's always somebody that's better than you in something. That has a humbling effect.

I go and I work with these guys, and I might think that I'm the greatest at this inside. Then, I meet somebody who's better at it or there's somebody who can teach me something I don't know. So it's kind of hard to feel at all superior when you're in a group of what I perceive to be amazing people. I not saying that there's not a lot of amazing people outside the Teams, but SEALs, in my opinion, are the most amazing people on the planet because of what they do and how they do it. And they go home at the end of the day to the wife and kids, and it's like nothing ever happened that day.

And you also get humbled by the older guys. Some of the stuff we do today, the stuff we think is great, that we did this monumental feat—Hey, I did this great and wonderful thing. Then you hear stories from an old guy that make what you did seem like just eating breakfast. That's pretty humbling. It has a humbling effect to just be around people of the caliber that SEALs are.

I feel gratified that I'm a SEAL. I don't feel lucky, because there was nothing about luck that got me to where I was. It was putting forth effort that got me here. But I do feel gratified that I am here, because every day I get to come to work with people who there isn't a match for anywhere else on the planet. You just can't find people of this caliber. I hear it all the time from guys who retire, get out of the Navy, and go on to other work places. They just say that it's not the same.

That's why we get so many people back at our reunions. That's why we have so many guys get out of the Navy and soon come back in. They go out into what I call the real world and see that there's nothing like what we do every day.

There's a camaraderie there, because when you go to work in the Teams every day, you banter back and forth, call each other names, and do whatever. That doesn't happen anywhere else like it does here. And with us, it's all in fun. Hopefully you don't see all the back-biting and that kind of thing in the SEAL Team as you do in the real world, although I'm not saying that it doesn't happen, but it's at a minimum. It's nothing like what's out there in the rest of the world.

One thing I don't want to see in the future is the core basics of training that everyone has gone through in the past change all that much. I think most of the changes need to be at the Team level. That's what bonds SEALs together, training. Every SEAL, no matter where he's been or what he's done, can always talk about BUD/S.

There's one thing that a SEAL will never forget, and that's his class number. You can always talk about BUD/S. I might have a guy who went through Class 1 and a guy who went through Class 217, and they can both talk about their experiences at BUD/S. What's amazing is, if you're outside the conversation, how a lot of the stories are the same as what you could tell.

The one word I can use to describe what I do and what we do as a group is amazing. I am always astonished at what new thing can come up, and how we will accomplish that new mission or reach that new goal. I think we would be grossly neglecting ourselves or our training if we didn't keep up with the pace of the world around us. Of course, the world is always changing, and the SEALs have to change right along with it.

I don't want to say technology is the wave of the future, but it is something that we will have to use to do our job better. And we have to be on the leading edge of that technology. We need the money and the backing and everything else to make sure that the SEAL of the future is equipped with what he needs to properly go out and do his job.

There's always going to be the basic equipment—knife, gun, explosives, that kind of thing—but there's a lot of technology, a lot of electronics, that we need to have, too. So the SEAL of the future not only has to be a physical specimen in order to go out and do the things we do in and out of the water, but he also has to be smart and educated. We're constantly upgrading our training to keep pace with the technology and all the other things that are happening out there in the world.

If we sit on our laurels and rest, the world's going to pass us by. And just how effective is a group of SEALs going to be if they go out on a mission ill-prepared? They aren't going to be effective at all.

The Hollywood version of a SEAL is this good-looking guy. He's big, buff, and carries a lot of guns that he uses to kill a lot of people. But that's such a small part of our job. I might be six-foot-one and 210 pounds, but I work with guys every day who are five-foot-five and 150, and they're doing exactly the same job I'm doing, they're swimming *though the same surf I am. And there are guys in the Teams who are bigger than I am. I've got guys who are six foot six and 260.*

The stereotypical SEAL you get in the movies comes nothing close to the guys I work with every day. We've got guys who are single and guys who have five, six, or seven kids. They go home every day to their families and have a normal life, then they come to work and perform on an unbelievable level. It's this diversity that I find intriguing every day I go to work.

You've got guys who have families that they go home to. They can't be in the same mind-set at home as they are at work. They can't be that way with their kids. But when you are at work, you have to be focused. If you're not focused on the task at hand in our job, you're going to die. And you can die any day. That's what's so weird about being a SEAL.

You come to work, but you might not go home the next day. It's the same as it is with police officers, firemen, and other guys who are out there on the edge. One day in the Teams, you might be jumping out of airplanes. The next day, you're diving under water. Any one of the things you do on a daily basis could do you in, so you have to be focused, and you have to be hard. But it's nice to be able to see that guys can differentiate between the two. That's something you probably don't see in the movies.

The other thing you don't see in the movies is how one minute, a SEAL can be sitting at his home base, and the next minute he can be overseas killing bad guys. One thing Hollywood doesn't show you is the hours and hours of packing, palletizing, flying, and waiting at airports for airplanes—the military's airplanes break down just like anybody else's. The negative side of traveling to get to where we have to go to do our job is not something Hollywood will show you.

Chapter 11

DESERT SHIELD/DESERT STORM

The end of the Iran-Iraq War allowed shipping to return to relatively normal in the Persian Gulf region. The aftermath of the war left the Iraqi economy in a shambles. The infrastructure of the country was damaged, primary Iraqi port facilities on the Gulf were choked with wreckage and unexploded ordnance, goods were difficult to move, and exports of oil were equally hard to get out of the country.

The Iran-Iraq War resulted in Iraq being deeply in debt to much of the world, especially its neighboring Arab states. The other major result of the war was a militarily weakened Iran and a militarily very powerful Iraq. Saddam Hussein was now in control of military assets that added up to Iraq having the fourth largest standing army in the world after the United States, China, and the Soviet Union. And Saddam's was a bloodied, combat-experienced military with 955,000 troops under arms, 5,500 armored vehicles and tanks, 3,500 pieces of artillery, and 665 combat aircraft. It was by far the largest, fully equipped, modern army in the Middle East.

On 2 August 1990, at 2 A.M. local time (1100 Zulu, 1 August) Saddam Hussein ordered 100,000 troops and tanks across his southeastern border and into Kuwait. There was little prior warning of the invasion detected by the United States or the other countries in the Gulf region. There was even less effective resistance put forward by the limited Kuwaiti forces. The small country was over-

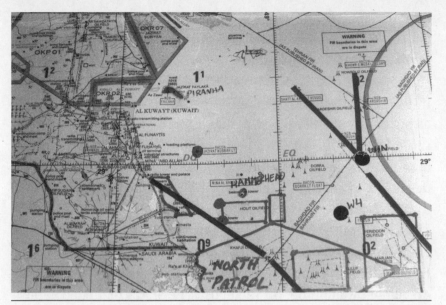

A close-up view of a map of the Kuwaiti shore in the Persian Gulf during Desert Storm. The map was hanging in the ready room of Fighter Squadron 41 (VF-41) aboard the nuclear-powered aircraft carrier USS *Theodore Roosevelt* (CVN-71). At the center of the shoreline on the left side of the map is Kuwait City.

whelmed and conquered in less than half a day. Within a week, Hussein declared Kuwait the Nineteenth Province of Iraq.

Under orders from the Commander-in-Chief, President George Bush, the U.S. military immediately put standing plans into effect to reinforce the Saudi Arabian border with Iraq and Occupied Kuwait. The U.S. Central Command (CENTCOM) held the primary U.S. military responsibility for the region. As CENTCOM finalized preparations to send U.S. forces into the area, the special operations component of CENTCOM made ready to put special operations forces into the area as soon as possible.

Within a few days of the invasion, a five-ship amphibious group left Norfolk, Virginia, en route to the Mediterranean. A detachment of SEALs were onboard the ships as part of a normal component of a deployed amphibious group. A stop in North Carolina brought 2,100 Marines onto the amphibious group, which then continued on across the Atlantic. Originally scheduled to go into the Mediterranean for maneuvers, the group now was being deployed to the Persian Gulf and Saudi Arabia.

On the West Coast, a 105-man Naval Special Warfare Task Group (NSWTG-1) assembled from Navy Special Warfare Group One assets in Coronado, arrived in Saudi Arabia on 10 August 1990. A second group of NSWTG-1 personnel arrived incountry almost a month later on 9 September. Operation DESERT SHIELD, the defense of Saudi Arabia, had begun immediately with the first of the U.S. forces being deployed to the Middle East in August.

To establish a "tripwire" warning system, as well as to direct close air support if needed and gather intelligence on Iraqi deployments and movements, SEAL elements were deployed to the Saudi Arabian–Kuwait border on 19 August. The SEALs remained in position, maintaining listening and observation posts dangerously close to the border, until the SEALs began to be gradually relieved by assets from the 5th Special Forces Group beginning on 5 September. The SEALs had been the first U.S. combat forces to directly face Iraqi troops. They had the ability to call in air strikes from the limited U.S. forces available. But if the Iraqis had decided to invade Saudi Arabia, the SEALs could expect to do little more than raise the alarm and attempt to withdraw.

Within days of the Iraqi invasion, the second of many UN resolutions against the situation in Kuwait was made. UN Resolution 661 of 6 August imposed trade sanctions against Iraq and Kuwait. By 25 August, teeth were put into the trade sanctions when UN Resolution 665 went into effect. Resolution 665 allowed the use of limited Naval force to ensure compliance with the embargo of goods to Iraq. The SEALs became a close part of that "limited" naval force.

Visit, Board, Search, and Seizure (VBSS) operations were conducted by various naval elements of the Coalition forces. One of the more common landing parties were Navy SEALs moving in to a stopped ship by small boat, or fast roping down and seizing a ship

Aboard the USNS *Joshua Humphries*, SEALs from SEAL Team Eight practice Visit, Board, Search, and Seizure (VBSS) operations in a safe environment. This was an almost constant mission for the SEALs as part of the Maritime Interception Force during Desert Shield.

U.S. Navy

that refused to stop for inspection. SEALs conducted these VBSS operations at all times and in all kinds of weather. Airborne SEAL snipers in helicopters would circle stopped ships to provide precision fire support to their Teammates aboard the ship. Many of the techniques used were developed or directly adapted from those of SEAL Team Six. The VBSS mission has since become a standard part of the SEAL training and mission parameter.

Missions continued to be conducted by the SEALs task group in support of DESERT SHIELD and in the buildup of native coalition naval special operations units. A few Saudi naval personnel had completed BUD/S in Coronado the years prior to 1990 under the allied personnel exchange program. The Saudi commander had worked with the Navy SEALs during Operation EARNEST WILL in the 1980s. With this as a nucleus, the SEALs initiated the further training of their Saudi counterparts and produced three Saudi SEAL

Teams. Special Boat Unit operators instructed Saudi navy personnel in the operation of high-speed boats. Additional Saudi personnel were taught how to conduct general water-borne operations.

In September, NSWTG-1 undertook the assistance of the Kuwaiti navy in the reconstitution of the limited navy assets that had escaped occupied Kuwait. Two Kuwaiti fast-attack craft missiles, the TNC 45 Type Al Sanbouk and the FPB 57 Type Istiqlal along with the motorized coast guard barge *Sawahil*, joined a handful of small patrol craft to make up the Kuwaiti navy in exile. The SEALs trained thirty-five Kuwaiti sailors in seamanship, naval engineering, and small arms. Further training was conducted by instructors from the U.S. Fleet Navy. Kuwaiti naval assets were eventually able to take successful part in combat search-and-rescue exercises. In addition, the *Sawahil* acted as an operational platform for NSWTG-1 assets during DESERT STORM.

It has been reported that assets from SEAL Team Six arrived in the Persian Gulf theater with the intent of performing a water-borne rescue of U.S. Ambassador Nathaniel Howell and his staff who had been held under virtual house arrest at the U.S. Embassy in Kuwait City since shortly after the invasion. The fact that the U.S. Embassy in Kuwait City was only across a street and a few hundred yards from the waters of the Persian Gulf made the possible rescue operation a SEAL responsibility. The sudden release of all foreign hostages by Saddam Hussein in December 1990 eliminated the need for a rescue operation.

Naval Special Warfare Task Group assets included four SEAL platoons, a SEAL fast-attack vehicle (FAV) detachment, a high-speed boat unit, a SEAL delivery vehicle detachment, and a joint communications support element. This gave the task group a great deal of flexibility in carrying out various assignments and tasks during both DESERT SHIELD and DESERT STORM.

Kuwaiti military personnel had been receiving specialized training in unconventional operations by SOCCENT (Special Opera-

The Fast-Attack Vehicle used by the SEALs in Desert Storm. The modified racing dune buggies were fast-moving gun platforms and transportation in the desert sand. The SEAL at the rear of the FAV is manning a .50 Caliber M2 heavy machine gun.

tions Command-Control) instructors. The intent was for the Kuwaitis to infiltrate across the border to transmit out information and support the Kuwaiti resistance forces. The beginning of the Air War and Operation DESERT STORM on 16 January 1991 changed the plans to infiltrate across the border.

On 18 January, SEALs helped in the attack and capture of Iraqi-held oil platforms in the Durra oil field that had fired shoulder-launched missiles at Coalition aircraft. After an aerial attack by Army OH-58D helicopters, SEALs moved in and landed on the Iraqi installations. Guns, communications gear, and intelligence documents were captured along with twenty-three Iraqis. A number of small islands were searched and captured on 24 January with the specific mission being to capture maps of the Iraqi Gulf mine fields. The results were much the same as they had been on the oil platforms—intelligence materials and Iraqi personnel were collected up by the SEALs with no casualties on their part.

SEALs supplied swimmers for combat search-and-rescue (CSAR)

An HH-60H Sea Hawk helicopter on a Search and Rescue training flight in California. These helicopters are Navy versions of the Blackhawk.

operations prior to the beginning of the air campaign and DESERT STORM. SEALs would join Navy helicopter crews aboard patrolling Navy ships in the Gulf waters. If a call came in for the rescue of a downed pilot, the helicopters would be launched. Special CSAR crews would normally do the entire operation, but rescue swimmers were in such short supply that the addition of SEAL combat swimmers helped increase the measure of safety and rescue that could be offered pilots going down in the water.

On 23 January, the SEAL/CSAR mission was put to the test when a USAF F-16 pilot was shot and had to bail out into the Gulf. A Navy SH-60B helicopter along with a pair of SEAL swimmers, launched from the USS *Nicholas* immediately on hearing the distress call. The CSAR helicopter crew located the downed pilot quickly, and the SEALs jumped into the water only six miles from the Kuwaiti coast. All three men were quickly retrieved from the water, and the helicopter returned to the *Nicholas*. The whole operation, from launch to landing, had only taken thirty-five minutes.

The blasted remnants of an Iraqi concrete aircraft hangar. Targets such as these were destroyed by precision-guided munitions dropped by Coalition aircraft during Desert Storm. Many of the precision bombs were guided by laser lights that illuminated the target invisibly. Some of those laser designators were aimed by special operations troops on the ground.

U.S. Navy

With the beginning of the air war campaign and DESERT STORM, the Iraqi forces further sealed the Kuwait–Saudi Arabian border to infiltration. On some of the first bombing operations of the air campaign, high-value targets in Iraq and Kuwait were illuminated by compact laser designator devices intended to guide in high-tech bombs. The lasers were operated by SOCCENT assets, including Navy SEALs.

The only viable infiltration routes left to the Coalition forces were by air—a very dangerous option for Kuwaiti operators with limited training—and along the shoreline. The SEALs had already established that they could effectively operate along the shoreline of Kuwait, so they were given the task of getting the Kuwaiti operators into their country.

The SEALs trained thirteen Kuwaitis in maritime infiltration techniques from 14 to 20 February with a dress rehearsal conducted on 21 February. The target beach was south of Kuwait City. The infiltration operation was given the green light and launched on 22 February.

Five Kuwaitis followed SEAL swimmer-scouts into the shoreline of Occupied Kuwait. The specific target of the operation was a pier where the Kuwaitis would rendezvous with local resistance contacts. The meeting with the locals never took place. After waiting on the pier, the Kuwaitis signaled for extraction. The incoming SEALs met the Kuwaitis, who were swimming out to sea, about five hundred meters from shore.

Later reconnaissance of the beach area after the war was over showed that there had been a much greater concentration of Iraqi troops in the area than had first been estimated. The density of beach fortifications indicated that the Kuwaiti resistance forces might not have been able to ever reach the pier for the planned rendezvous.

SEALs also conducted a great number of hydrographic surveys and other traditional UDT operations off the shores of Kuwait during DESERT SHIELD and up to the beginning of the ground campaign of DESERT STORM. Many of those recons were in support of U.S. Marine and Coalition amphibious forces. The very large Marine presence off-shore of Kuwait—more than 17,000 men and their equipment—made the threat of an amphibious landing in Kuwait a very real one.

Operation SEA SOLDIER I took place on the shores of Saudi Arabia 1 through 5 October 1990. A further exercise, Sea Soldier II, was conducted on 30 October to 8 November. The same forces of Amphibious Ready Group 2 and the 4th Marine Expeditionary Brigade took part in both exercises. Deployed SEALs, a normal component of the amphibious group, conducted their usual recons in support of the exercises.

From 15 to 21 November, Coalition forces conducted IMMI-

Some of the barbed wire and steel hedgehog beach obstacles along the shore of the Persian Gulf south of Kuwait City during Desert Shield/Desert Storm. Interspersed among the obstacles are mines.

Kevin Dockery

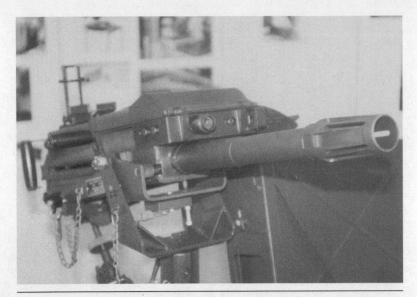

The Mark 19 Mod 3 40m grenade launcher. The MK 19 has been in Navy hands since the Vietnam War and can throw its half-pound high explosive grenades for more than two kilometers. It can be mounted on any facility that can accept a .50 caliber machine gun.

Kevin Dockery

NENT THUNDER, a massive amphibious landing exercise. The U.S. Marines as well as Saudi Arabian and other Coalition forces also took part in the exercise. Landings took place only one hundred miles from the Saudi Arabian–Kuwait border, near al-Jubail. IMMINENT THUNDER was a very obvious show of force and intent to the Iraqis. To be certain that they received the message, a number of news services were allowed to observe and broadcast the exercise. It was known that Saddam regularly watched the Western news services.

Continuing reconnaissance missions were conducted by the SEALs along the Kuwaiti shore. Ordered by CENTCOM as part of a deception plan, fifteen separate close-in recon operations were conducted by NSWTG-1 SEALs between 30 January and 15 February 1991. The missions ended with a single, large-scale operation conducted on the night of 23 and 24 February, the eve of the beginning of the ground war to liberate Kuwait.

A floating antiship mine in the Persian Gulf. During both the Iran–Iraq war and Desert Shield/Desert Storm, these mines caused tremendous difficulties for shipping in the Gulf. A large amount of Navy resources went into trying to chart, clear, and defeat these old weapons of war. The lead horns sticking up from the mine can easily bend on contact with a ship's hull, breaking a vial of acid within the horn. Electrical current generated by the acid detonates a huge charge of high explosive, more than 250 pounds of TNT in a Soviet M-08/39 model.

U.S. Navy

Foxtrot Platoon of SEAL Team One went in to the Kuwaiti beaches south of Kuwait City aboard two high-speed boats. The SEALs switched to rubber boats for the final paddle in to shore. For the last part of the approach, the SEALs slipped into the water to conduct a classic UDT demolition swim. Each SEAL of the eight-man squad was towing a twenty-pound haversack of C4 explosives. The clocks of the explosive firing trains had been set to a specific time. After placing their charges and arming them right under the noses of the Iraqi troops on the beach, the SEALs withdrew to their boats.

When the explosives detonated, the SEALs swept the beaches with automatic weapons fire from 7.62mm and .50 caliber as well as 40mm grenades from Mark 19 grenade launchers. With the massed groups of Marines afloat offshore, backed up by an armada of ships that included battleships complete with their sixteen-inch guns, the Iraqi command was convinced that an invasion was following the SEALs' demolition swim.

Elements of several Iraqi divisions were diverted from their positions to reinforce the beach defenses. That left fewer Iraqi forces to face the real incoming Coalition ground forces, thrusting in from overland.

From 30 January to 15 February, the SEALs and the SDV detachment from SDVT-1 conducted the first operations of their kind. Using the Mark IX SDV and its integral sonar system, SEAL operators conducted six searches for moored sea mines in the Northern Persian Gulf area. The Kuwaiti coast guard barge *Sawahil* acted as a transport and service craft for the SEALs and their SDV. The crane on the barge could move the SDV for launchings and recoveries. This was reportedly the first combat use of the Mark IX SDV, a flat, two-man craft.

Although the SEALs and their SDVs did not locate any mines, the search area was considered a particularly vital one. Searching an area of twenty-seven square miles, the SEALs examined the offshore areas and channels surrounding a number of islands that could be scheduled for future invasion. In addition, the SEALs helped establish cleared channels for Naval assets, including the battleships *Missouri* and *Wisconsin*.

Throughout DESERT SHIELD and DESERT STORM, SEALs assisted in mine clearing and protection operations. SEAL sharpshooters aided in destroying floating mines with precision rifle fire. SEAL and EOD swimmers entered the Gulf waters to approach floating and moored mines. After examining the mines, the swimmers would place demolition charges to safely destroy the floating menaces that could even threaten the thick armor of a battleship.

One of the last SEAL combat missions of the ground war took place on 27 February. Even though the Iraqis had effectively abandoned Kuwait City, precautionary measures had to be taken against

This floating contact mine has been prepped for destruction by the demolition charge attached to it. The charge is in the rectangular bag strapped to the right side of the mine. Both the SEALs and the Explosive Ordnance Disposal divers (one is shown here in the photograph) dealt with a number of Iraqi mines in the Gulf using the same methods.

possible "stay-behind" forces. When the special operations forces planned a takedown of the U.S Embassy in Kuwait City, the SEALs joined in the operation. Adding the SEAL fast-attack vehicles to the ground convoy, the Embassy compound was quickly encircled. A search of the buildings by troops fast roping down from helicopters showed there to be no danger from boobytraps or Iraqi soldiers. The U.S. Embassy in a free Kuwait was once more in American hands.

Raymond C. Smith, Rear Admiral, USN (Ret.)

My position as of about one month ago (November 1998) was the Director of Navy Assessment for the Chief of Naval Operations. I joined the Navy on 12 February 1962. Enlisting with a buddy, I joined because

I decided I would be able to take advantage of the Service, in terms of what it offered. I wasn't doing well in college at the time, so I enlisted.

The first time I heard about the Underwater Demolition Teams was while I was on a midshipman's cruise. After joining the Navy, I went on to the Naval Academy after receiving an appointment. So I finished my first year at Annapolis, Maryland, and we went on a summer cruise, part of which was to Coronado, California. While there, I was able to see a demonstration by the ten underwater demolition teams. It was in 1964, and that was the first time I had ever heard of them.

In 1964, there wasn't very much spoken about the SEALs. I suspect that at that time, they were still a classified unit. The UDTs were really the "front-office" units, so to speak, for the Navy Special Operations. At that time, Frogmen were the officers and enlisted men who had worked so hard during World War II to clear the beaches of Normandy and in the Pacific, so they were a common term among the military for the men of the Underwater Demolition Teams.

What attracted me to these Teams was not so much the fact that they were clearing beaches, but the camaraderie that went on in the units. That's the kind of thing I had looked for and was the kind of military unit I wanted to be involved with.

What was unique to the UDTs, and what built such a great bond in the units that existed then, and still today, was the fact that the officers and the enlisted men went through training together. That's really rather unique, and it's a wonderful gift that we in Naval Special Warfare have because we're small enough to get away with it. And it's recognized that, if you can do it, you set yourself up for a community that has great bonding between the men and the officers. So it really was something that attracted me. I also wanted to be involved physically in things. Normally, as a commissioned officer, you don't do that. So those were the kinds of things that attracted me to Naval Special Warfare.

The payoff is that when you graduate from BUD/S training and you go across the street to report to your unit, every one of the enlisted men in that Team know you've done everything they did. Simply put,

A long area view taken of the beach obstacles at Normandy during World War II. The scale of the obstacles can be seen against the size of the running figures to the left of center in the photo. It was because of obstacles like this that the Naval Combat Demolition Units were founded. Through the NCDUs came the UDTs and then the SEALs.

National Archives

that's it. You've proven yourself in exactly the same manner as each and every other man in the Teams. There's a great respect for the officers in the Teams for that reason.

Basic Underwater Demolition/SEAL (BUD/S) training is a course for Naval Special Warfare forces that enables the Navy to look at, screen, and grow young men who, as the product of that course, will normally wind up a young man who has proven to be fearless, in the sense that for twenty-five weeks he has been forced to do things he's never done before, he doesn't like to do, and he's afraid of doing. You can't go through the course without confronting those things.

So the product of the BUD/S course is a young man who now has learned that there's almost no limit to what he can do. The only way you can achieve that is by putting a man through stress that constantly upgrades his level of awareness of himself. Coming out of today's society, young men lead a very relaxed life in the sense that there's not a *lot of extreme stress. In BUD/S, we train them to be ready to go to combat. The only way you can do that is to push them beyond the limits they expect to be pushed to. That is the gift and the beauty of BUD/S training—it enables us to draw from within, out of the young man's soul. That is the key. I've always said that BUD/S training manifests itself in things physical, but it's all about a man's soul.*

If you can capture his soul and make him realize that there's nothing that can prevent him from doing his job, then you got him. The kids who go through training recognize that. Some don't see it until the last day of training, and some see it the first day they're there. But during that twenty-five weeks, all of those who stay the course get it. And once they got it, you have a product that you can depend upon.

The use of the word Teams *probably comes from a couple places, one of which is that in BUD/S training, nobody goes through there by themselves. Even on swims, you're with a swim buddy. In almost all cases, those who try to go by themselves don't make it through the course. It's not a course for young men who are individualists, and we inculcate this idea of teamwork throughout BUD/S.*

The students hear the word teamwork *probably every day for twenty-five weeks. Team, team, team. And so it becomes part of their very being. Combined with the fact that our units are named Teams— whether it was Underwater Demolition Teams or SEAL Teams, the word* Teams *has become synonymous with what we are. They aren't SEAL people, they're SEAL* Teams. *I think that underpins the very philosophy SEALs go by.*

Naval Special Warfare is synonymous with the name SEAL Teams. Just as a more common term, the SEAL Teams themselves embody what we call maritime special operations. Special operations, by definition, are a host of small unit operations that are not done by conventional forces, whether it be gathering intelligence, conducting raids on small targets, doing counterterrorism work, or any of the things assigned to a special operations force.

The kind of people who make up that force have to have certain kinds of characteristics. First of all, they have to have gone through a vetting process, in our particular case, BUD/S training; in the case of the Green Berets, Army Special Forces school. But in any case, there has to be a vetting where you look at the young man and decide that he's physically capable of doing the job, that he's mentally capable of doing the job, and that he has a great heart and soul. They have to have all three things.

Physical work is easy to see in BUD/S training. For the intellectual part, we do a lot of work in terms of their ability to do diving and conduct diving operations. And finally, we test them for their mettle every day for twenty-five weeks. Every day they finish, they feel they've reached a plateau, but the next day is always harder. The students are constantly reassessing where they are in their life. All of a sudden, they realize that, no matter how hard it gets, it can always be tougher. So what you get is a young man who is totally capable and totally confident of his own abilities. That's the kind of person who has to be in a SEAL Team.

There's no way that you can call time out in combat. As is known in the terms of the Navy SEALs, we have never left a man on the field in combat. That is synonymous with the kind of person we breed, so to speak, in BUD/S training. So the term Team just underscores the whole idea that we are not a "Rambo" organization. When a SEAL platoon is formed, those men become as close as brothers—in fact probably closer than most brothers are, because they rely upon each other for their very lives.

All officers and enlisted men who want to become a Navy SEAL, or in the past a Frogman, have to volunteer. It's a voluntary force. You volunteer in, and you can volunteer out.

I don't know that one looks at a life in the Teams as being fun. I always explain it according to the fact that young men and young women in today's society approach their careers in a lot of different ways. One psychologist named Maslow, in the late 1960s, developed what is called Maslow's Hierarchy of Needs. It explains why people do things in their lives.

In most cases, most people approach careers and life in the sense of gathering security, having friends, and succeeding financially. But at the top of Maslow's pyramid is the term self-actualization. Self-actualization is a term that means doing something for the sake of doing it for the individual himself and for whatever higher authority the individual believes in. That holds true for the men who accept the challenge of the Teams. They do it for themselves.

There were a lot of instructors when I went through BUD/S training who "inspired" me—and I use that term loosely here. They were all remarkable people, the kind of men I wanted to try to be. They were certainly models for me. In the Teams themselves, I thought one man who personified what I thought was a great SEAL was a guy named Frank Perry. He was legendary in our community as a quiet, extraordinarily intense, and extraordinarily competent man. I always put him on a higher level than most. There are several others also, but certainly Frank Perry is one. Most of the men know him. If you knew him, you knew what a great role model Frank was for junior officers and junior enlisted men.

I think the thing that makes SEALs, SEALs is that they're—and I use the term cautiously—humble. They are very content with who they are; they don't need to tell people who they are. I don't really call that humility per se. What I do call it is a human being who is totally at ease and confident with himself, what he's doing in life, and what he's capable of doing. I think that really personifies what makes SEALs so unique. They are very self-satisfied people in terms of they've accounted for something already in their lives, and they don't feel the need to have to advertise about that.

In terms of how young men go through BUD/S training and the

transformation that takes place, I do believe that the vast majority of young men who get through that course, are the kind of young men who were just mentioned. That is, solid physically; solid mentally; very, very intense in terms of their ability to focus on things; but also quiet people. There's very few young men who get through BUD/S with the habit of talking about themselves.

The young man who gets through BUD/S training is the kind of man who helps his Teammates and who stays focused on what he's doing. Normally, that's not the kid who's talking about how good he is. Those aren't the kind of people who make it through to graduation. I think what we find is that those kind of young men, and they might be very good, lack the capacity to be team players. That might be because they've always been very successful at, say, a sport or something like that. If they can't subjugate themselves to a higher organization, a Team, then they aren't successful.

So what you get out of that training program is the kind of person who has been talked about, the kind of man who's self-satisfied with what he is doing, but who has also subjugated his own ego to a higher part of society, his Navy SEAL Team.

Between 1981 and 1983, I served as the commander of the BUD/S training course. It was the first time I had returned to BUD/S training since I was a student and now I was a Commander in the Navy. Something struck me shortly after I arrived, was that in the interviews all the students had to write, all their answers about why they were coming to BUD/S training and what they hoped to accomplish all had a common theme that sort of transcended all the young men who showed up here. I think it personified the kind of young men that we have coming in to SEAL training, even today. It's a young man who's looking for goals in his life, who wants to be part of an organization that he knows is successful because he has read about it and appreciates it. So he's coming in with the idea that he wants to be part of this, and he wants to know what it takes to do it, what the rules are, and *how to get there. He wants a black-and-white world. He wants to see what it takes and have a shot at it himself.*

When I saw that time after time on these papers of students who were not taking these interviews together, it became clear that these young men of America were looking for this kind of thing. I think this underscores some of the things that we have in society today in terms of what our young men and women are looking for in all walks of life. In our particular case, the goal was to become a Navy SEAL, but it was clear that these young people wanted to know how to succeed. They wanted us to show them what needed to be done, and they were going to go after it. That was very reassuring to me.

What I didn't see in those interview answers, almost without exception, were statements like "I want to go out and kill the enemy" or do things like that. That is an understood part of what we do when these young men come to us, but that's not the reason they come. The reasons are organizational and the betterment of their own lives. That knowledge is very satisfying to me.

When I graduated from BUD/S with Class 52, I was married and had two little kids, and that's what was going through my mind at the time. But I was very proud of what I had done. I had been serving on a destroyer for two years after graduating Annapolis, which I did enjoy. I wanted to try something different, so off I went to BUD/S training. Graduation was something that gave me a tremendous feeling of accomplishment and pride. It was one of the great achievements of my life.

I felt the same thing when I first had the Trident, the Naval Special Warfare insignia, pinned to my chest. That established that I had accomplished my goal and had become part of a community as elite as the Navy SEALs. It was certainly another high point of my life.

In terms of our evolution in warfare and the history of our military, the Navy SEALs have grown from 1962 to today. We moved from Vietnam and the very great success we enjoyed there in doing what we could do in a very limited war. As the world moved on, the United States took a different role in being the only superpower in the world and shouldered its burden to have to provide leadership across the world to all the nations, enemies and friends.

The Navy SEAL has evolved with that change. What we see now is definitely changed what we saw ten or twenty years ago, and is most certainly different from the operators of World War II. The young Navy SEAL now is very much akin to the Army Green Berets in the sense that they are much more culturally skilled—many more SEALs have second-language qualifications today. And all these young men are out and about in the world today, doing our nation's work conducting peacetime operations in one hundred and thirty to one hundred and forty nations a year.

We have a State Department that believes in the use of the military to conduct certain parts of its foreign policy. Special Operations, and SEALs in particular, do that—we do those operations for the maritime forces. So what you see are language-qualified young men who are going out, doing operations in small countries, in groups of two, three, five, ten, fifteen, or twenty, on their own, very mature and very capable.

In many cases, these SEALs are working with a U.S. ambassador directly in a nation or the deputy chief of mission. In any case, they are working to help support and progress our foreign policy. That is a much more sophisticated mission than we had, say, thirty or forty years ago.

Accomplishing the new missions requires a young man of extreme maturity, who is very good on his feet, and who is able to understand the politics of the given nation, vis-à-vis America. And so it is a much more complicated environment that our SEALs live in today than they lived in thirty or forty years ago.

Operations DESERT SHIELD and DESERT STORM are both typical examples of what I mean when I say that the role of special operations forces, and SEALs in particular, has expanded. When we were deployed to Saudi Arabia in August 1990, we were sent there basically without a mission per se. We were just told to get to Saudi Arabia and be prepared for follow-on operations.

Within nine days of arriving in Saudi Arabia, I had a platoon of

A SEAL in the early (chocolate chip) pattern of desert camouflage aims his M4 carbine fitted with an M203 40mm grenade launcher. This arrangement is a favorite of the SEALs as it combines the range of the 5.56mm round from the M4 with the high explosive fragmentation of the 40mm grenade.

U.S. Navy

SEALs forty kilometers below the border of Kuwait, teaching the Saudi army close-air support. Within another five days, I had more SEALs in the harbor of Jubail conducting harbor patrol operations as the U.S. Marines off-loaded their equipment. Inside of another two weeks—less than a month since we arrived in Saudi Arabia—we had met with the Kuwait navy in exile and began a three-month course to train the Kuwait navy to take back their nation.

It is easy to see the breadth of operations we were confronted with early on in the campaign, not even including the combat operations during DESERT STORM, which is another matter altogether. Throughout DESERT SHIELD we worked training foreign military forces. There were coalition support teams from many of the coalition nations that we assisted. Training was conducted with the Saudi military, and we lived and worked with the Saudis. We had actually planned to work operations with the Saudis.

All these things were done before the war even started, which is *really an expansion of what we do. When DESERT STORM came, we were prepared to do combat search-and-rescue. Our primary mission, in fact our only assigned mission, at that time was to rescue downed pilots. General Schwarzkopf believed that we probably would take some pretty good losses and that the SEALs would be in charge of conducting maritime search-and-rescue, but we only did one of those. Only one pilot was shot down over water and we picked him up.*

In the scope of DESERT STORM, we conducted more than two hundred and seventy operations—everything from the famous diversion operation that Lieutenant Commander Deitz ran, to scaling oil platforms and capturing the first Iraqis of the war, to conducting intelligence operations and photographing the Iraqis off the stern of one of their now-famous mine-laying vessels. We trained Kuwaiti resistance forces to go in and set up communications in Kuwait City. SEALs captured right away the first piece of territory in Kuwait, Quruh Island, which was held by the Iraqis. We ran the gamut of operations.

The main thing to take away is that those special operations were not conducted in and of themselves for themselves. They were conducted to contribute to the campaign. What I found out shortly after getting to DESERT SHIELD/DESERT STORM was that this was not going to be a special operations campaign—this was going to be a war. And unless special operations forces, i.e., the SEALs or the Army Special Forces, could adapt what they do to support the higher objective of the war, we were going to be left out.

We turned around our entire conduct of operations and went to the Marine Corps and Army and asked them what we could do for them to support their campaign. That was the genesis of the deception operation and all the reconnaissance work we did on the beaches of Kuwait. That was to help the larger-scale forces. That's what I think is the beauty of special forces today. We can adapt to conduct very singular operations or work operations that support the general purpose forces in a large-scale operation.

DESERT SHIELD/DESERT STORM was a campaign. It was a campaign first to come up with a plan to defend Saudi Arabia. And then, the ultimate aim was not only to defend Saudi Arabia, but to return Kuwait to its rightful owners. It was a large-scale campaign with large infusions of conventional forces. That was really what DESERT STORM was all about. The special operations forces (SOF) had very specific and focused missions to support the campaign, and they needed to support it at the operational level, i.e., the level that would affect and benefit the large-scale forces.

General Schwarzkopf did not need us to do very precise tactical operations; he needed us to do operational things. That's what I tried to do in DESERT STORM, to get our forces involved in operations that would benefit the entire campaign. We were very successful in doing that only because the general purpose forces recognized the value of the SOF. They recognized that we could do more than just very singular operations, that we had more to bring to the table than being able to just swim in and take out a small target, for instance.

We could do other things that would benefit the campaign. We were able to do many operations that led to a number of breakthroughs for the campaign. Certainly the capture of two hundred Iraqis early in January 1991, with no opposition, indicated to General Schwarzkopf that this was probably how the war was going to go.

In and of themselves, they were great operations that took courage on the part of our young men. The fact is, when we took it all back and looked at those operations, we very easily deduced that there was more to it than just capturing those men. The fact that they didn't fight—none of them—led us to believe and recommend to General Schwarzkopf that maybe, just maybe, this was what we were going to see when the land assault started. In fact, that is what we saw.

So those kinds of benefits that you can give to a large scale conventional force have great value to the conventional force commanders. And I think it underscores SOFs value in a new era where not only are we able to do small-scale operations, but we can bring benefit with small insertions of forces that we couldn't do in the old days.

There are a number of notable individuals who have served and are serving in the Teams today. I'll never forget the first day I met Rear Admiral Tom Richards. He was an ensign, and he stood out in this field in BUD/S training. He weighed about 240 pounds, most of it in his chest. I looked at this guy and asked to myself, This is the kind of guy I have to train with?

Tom and I are very close friends. He's enormously strong physically and intellectually in all matters. There ought to be a law against somebody that strong. He's fearless and aggressive. He's taken all the hard jobs in our community and has led our community very well.

One of the things that underscores the kind of person Tom Richards is that he's an extraordinary competitor. Tom was the biggest guy in our class, and as most would say, the slowest runner, because he carried so much weight and was such a physically strong guy. I watched him go though that class, and I saw the determination of this guy who really could not deal with the running at BUD/S training.

In order to go through BUD/S, much running is required. Tom was enormously strong in everything we did, and was especially a great swimmer. When we got on the beach, though, it was another matter altogether. Tom took much grief from his instructors, but he would not give up. That just highlights the kind of person he was. To this day, he still runs and he's still a big guy, but his intense focus on what he does drives him to always be better.

The only thing Tom really was not very good at is boxing. Although he was a great wrestler and a great weight-lifter, he was not very skillful with his fists. In those days, we had to box in BUD/S training, and I drew the enviable task of having to box Tom. Having boxed at the Naval Academy, I was a little better at it than he was, so I avoided his swings with great skill and managed to put a few on him, but I could not move him.

I've already mentioned the kind of young man who comes into the SEALs. I think it's a surprise to many people when they meet a young SEAL to see the kind of professional the young man is. Normally, he's a quiet, very competent individual, and I think that underscores the kind of jobs our Navy SEALs are doing now. They're not in the limelight very much and you don't read a lot about them, but every day, throughout the world in fifty, sixty, eighty, one hundred countries, there are groups of SEALs doing things.

There is a definite benefit that accrues just from having a special operations force like the SEALs in the military. Several years ago, we had an operation in the Ivory Coast. The Ivory Coast Navy was having a problem with poaching. They had bought a number of the kind of swamp craft we see in America, the air boats with large fans in the back, but they did not know how to operate them, maintain them, or surveil or approach poachers with them. We sent a platoon of SEALs— a couple of lieutenants and about fourteen enlisted men—over to help deal with this problem.

The SEALs spent three weeks working with the Ivory Coast Navy and Coast Guard. When they left there, after teaching them how to do what they needed, the defense minister of that nation came out himself to wish the best to that platoon. That was just two officers and Navy sailors. What that does for the United States, our embassy, and our relations with the Ivory Coast cannot be quantified. That's the value of a special operations force.

We've had SEALs on the border between Peru and Ecuador for the last four years. Peru and Ecuador have been fighting over that border for more than one hundred years. Who do you put on that kind of border to handle the sensitivity of two nations grappling over this undefined border? You put out Army Special Forces and Navy SEALs. You send men who are language-qualified and understand the culture and the history of the nations and who can deal with the people there.

That's the kind of thing you don't hear much about, but it's happening all the time around the world.

Our Navy SEALs are involved heavily in counternarcotics operations throughout Latin America, working with the nation's navies and marine corps to train them to conduct their operations. This is also something you don't see very often in the papers, but they are the kind of forces that have to be able to do that. They have the wisdom, intellect, language, and cultural acclimatization they need so they can talk to these nations' navies and marine corps about how to deal with their problems.

Those are the kind of things we see going on today and that are heavily supportive of the idea of special operations forces and SEALs in particular. There is a need to have a very sophisticated force of small numbers that can deal with small interruptions in our foreign policy around the world. That is the beauty and the value of the Navy SEALs.

As we look at our nation's role in foreign policy today and look at adapting that foreign policy to the world, I think that it's apparent to everyone involved that our nation is the preeminent world power. We have taken it upon ourselves to use that strength and our example to help placate the problems that exist around our world. There's no other nation that can do the things we do in this world. And if we're not involved, if we're not engaged, then the other nations that can support us won't be engaged, either.

Accomplishing that task requires a lot of things. It requires a foreign policy and a foreign service that can do the negotiations and the deliberations. It requires a military that can back us up when we really, really carry through with the threat. Between those two, there's the special operations force.

The SOF stands between the foreign service of our State Department and the large, conventional forces that we use to go to war. They are the scalpel to the hammer of our conventional military. Of the military special operations forces, the Army Special Forces and the Navy SEALs are the preeminent members of those forces, although there are many other ones as well. I believe those two forces probably do the most to deal with supporting our foreign policy around the world.

The Navy SEALs and the Army Special Forces accomplish their support of our foreign policies in part by professionalizing the third-world nations' militaries. That is a very important role in the third world. Their militaries have a preeminent role in their society; in many cases, they run the country. In our particular case, we work very hard, both the SEALs and the Special Forces, to train the militaries that their role as the military force of a nation is to be subservient to the political leadership and the people it represents. That's a very hard concept to bring across in many nations and an even harder one to bring some people to believe in.

Our military, in this case our SEALs, can do that kind of stuff. That is a very sophisticated operation, but it has a big payoff in terms of our foreign policy and the acceptance of our leadership around the world. We see that every day with the reception our SEALs receive all around the world.

Shortly after our nation failed at DESERT ONE in Iran, our military went through a whole reassessing of our special operations forces. That culminated in 1986 in the Goldwater-Nichols Defense Reorganization Act. That act instituted a new organization for special operations forces in our military.

The act decreed that we would create a U.S. Special Operations Command (USSOCOM), commanded by a four-star general or flag officer who would have budgetary authority. He would be able to buy equipment, train his people, and deploy them around the world. And his people would be made up of all the services' special operations forces. That has been a stunning success for special operations forces in our military.

Our Navy SEALs are a key component of USSOCOM. Although while

---

they now wear the Navy uniform and serve proudly in the U.S. Navy, the SEALs are funded and equipped by Special Operations money. It's a totally different approach to how special forces had been handled for thirty or forty years—as a small part of each conventional military force. It has been a great success and has allowed U.S. special operations forces, and SEALs in particular, to actually grow over the last ten years.

Though our conventional military has decreased by almost 40 percent in the last ten years, the Navy SEALs have almost doubled in size. That isn't because we're just nice guys. Our military and political leadership as well as our congress have looked and asked, "What are the kind of forces we need for this nation?"

Well, there are many kinds that we have to have, but certainly special operations forces and the Navy SEALs are the kind of forces that we have to have in today's world and the world of the future. I think that, all things considered, the Navy SEALs are in a great position. They are highly needed around the world, they have been consistently successful during the last ten years in all the operations that they have run, and they have a great record of success. Recruiting is good, and funding is as well. The SEALs are really a military success story today.

To help meet the personnel needs of the SEALs' success, I think every Navy SEAL is a recruiter at heart. We're always out looking for great young men who are willing to take up the challenge the Teams offer. I have done it a hundred times over myself and would do it again in a second if I felt a young man needed guidance and was interested in the program. You have to look at them and get them focused, but I would do that without hesitation, as most SEALs would.

Wearing the Naval Special Warfare insignia, the Trident, is something you don't think about every day when you get up in the morning. But when you stop and think about it, and think about the people you have met in your career, the people who have come and gone, and the young men still coming in, you realize that you are part of a very special group of people. That fills me with a great deal of pride, just to be one of those guys, regardless of rank. I don't care who you are, a young seaman or a four-star admiral, the very fact that you're a part of this, of Naval Special Warfare, the Teams, transcends rank. I am as close to some of my enlisted men as I am to many of the officers. The rank, although it has a great deal of importance to our military society, in the Navy SEALs, the friendships and brotherhood you form transcends rank. So when I wake up in the morning, if I think about it, I tell myself that I'm a lucky guy.

Besides just being in the Teams, I'm also very fortunate to have two sons who have followed me in my career as a Navy SEAL. I'm very proud of that. When most fathers who are SEALs deal with their sons, they always want to know their son's answer to the question, "Why are you doing this?" I can tell you that the PT grinder at BUD/S is littered with the bodies of sons whose fathers were SEALs and who were there for the wrong reason. I didn't want my sons to do the same thing.

Of course I was particularly interested because of my rank. My sons would not be singled out; they would be held to the same standard everyone would be expected to meet. So I quizzed both my sons on their motivations for volunteering for BUD/S. If they were doing it for me or for anyone else, they weren't going to get through the course. They assured me that they weren't, that they joined for their own reasons. They are in the Teams today.

The BUD/S graduations of both of my two sons were unique events. I can't think of too many things in my life where I could be as proud of two young men as I was of my two sons, and of my nephew, who also served as a SEAL. I guess the thing that struck me was the fact that it didn't seem that long ago that I had graduated from BUD/S myself. When my sons graduated, I had to stop and contemplate that twenty-five years had gone by in a flash, which I guess underscores the whole idea that if you do something in your life, have fun doing it. When you're having fun, time goes by fast—it certainly has passed quickly for me.

The value of making sure all the young men coming in to the SEALs today recognize the past warriors who have preceded them, I think, is the same principle that we should apply to our nation as a whole. We should never lose sight of the people who have preceded us in this great nation. If we don't study our history, we're liable to make the same mistakes that have been made in the past. The same thing applies with the SEALs.

Although we all think we know more than our parents and our other predecessors did, the fact is that they were a lot smarter than we give them credit for. I think it's very important that we don't lose sight of the fact that heroism has no hold on any particular generation. Heroism can happen any time at any place, in most cases when you least expect it. So for young men who watch the event horizon, with the amount of time they look ahead, it's very difficult for them to look back and really ponder the heroism of the great men who came before them.

There's great wisdom that comes from studying the past. Our junior officer course brings in retired enlisted and officers to talk to our young officers and make them understand that many of them had been through the same things that the young officers were about to go through. They can give the young men some things to live by that will help them be successful.

I think most of the kind of guys who come into the SEALs are sensitive to the fact that our strength is in the people who have gone before us, so I don't find it surprising at all that the young men coming in to the Teams today believe that they need to really respect the great men who have come before them. They feel that they need to elicit from those men the wisdom that they developed from their experiences.

The young men coming into the SEALs today are very, very smart. If you were to give them college boards exam, I think they all would do very well. We're looking for smart young men, and we're looking for a lot more than just book smarts. I think we're finding that more of the enlisted volunteers today have had some college, many of them, in fact, have college degrees.

Does that matter or not? It only matters in the maturation process. There is a big difference between an eighteen-year-old young man and a twenty-one-year-old man. Having three sons, I can tell you that. So when a kid goes off to college for a couple years, he matures. He grows intellectually and emotionally. That makes him better able to handle the kind of things he's going to be exposed to on his way to becoming a Navy SEAL.

I think that it's great that we're getting this kind of young man to volunteer for the Teams. It is a challenge for us, because young men with a lot of college, and especially those with degrees who are sailors, are certainly looking for upward mobility. So how do we get these young men commissioned if that's what they decide to do? That makes it sort of a good news–bad news story.

It's great to have these bright young guys. But how do we motivate them to stay in? How do we keep upward mobility for them and make sure they stay in the Teams for a career? Answering those questions is a challenge for us, but it's better to have that challenge than not to have it.

The Navy SEALs are very blessed today because we have great equipment. We have the money to buy good equipment, and we have the talent available to be able to use that equipment. But that's not what we do in the Navy SEALs. We don't man the equipment, we equip the man. That's the key thing to realize here. The man is, in fact, the weapon system. The things that adorn his being are all the manifestations of technology. The real factor is the human being underneath all that. That's what really counts.

Some have mentioned that when they went to BUD/S training, they didn't see a lot of big guys there—guys with eighteen-inch biceps and twenty-two-inch necks. The fact is that you will see a few of those, but you'll also see a bunch of guys who aren't very big, aren't very physically impressive—on the outside anyway. But that's not what BUD/S training is all about. It's not about having big guys; it's about having men with soul.

Unfortunately, there's no way we can look into a man's soul when he arrives at BUD/S. You learn of the strength of a man's soul, his com-

mitment to himself and to excellence, only when he goes through the course. At some point in time during that course, his soul will bare itself, and you'll find out what kind of person he is.

Once you see what kind of person he is, you'll see that the kind of man he is has nothing to do with his biceps or how fast he runs, or swims, or completes the o-course. It's the inner strength that comes to some people that we're looking for. That inner strength is what a man's soul is built of.

When you graduate from BUD/S training, that's a great event. That's the good news. The bad news is that you haven't earned your Special Warfare insignia yet. Even after twenty-five weeks of vetting so to speak, that young man reports to a Team after having gone to Jump School at Fort Benning and earning his parachute jump wings. There he begins to prove that, after all those push-ups he did, after as cold as he got in BUD/S training, above all of that, he can still think.

We ask those young men, over the next six months to a year, to go through a thirteen-week course of advanced training. We watch and observe these young men for their maturity, their military behavior, their appearance, and how well they integrate themselves into the Teams. At the end of six months to a year, he earns his Trident. Then he can start to become a SEAL operator.

Many people ask me that now we've left our roots as Frogmen, where pretty much the young Frogman swam in with a pair of swim fins, a knife, and a haversack full of explosives, how do those men relate to the warrior of today? You'll notice that in BUD/S training, the students spend a lot of time doing the same very thing that those Frogmen did. We start with the roots from which we came. There are a lot of long-distance ocean swims with very little on other than maybe a wetsuit, a Kabar knife, and a lifejacket. The whole idea is to start at the very basic level of training—that is starting at the level of a Navy Frog, just as he was in World War II, so they never lose that link between our history and tradition of old to where we are at today.

On top of a parade float after the successful conclusion of Desert Storm, this SEAL in full desert combat camouflage and armed with an M60E3 light machine gun shows the American public just who was among the troops that helped liberate Kuwait.

U.S. Navy

To give an example of the irony of history, after all the years of the Teams going through World War II, to Korea and Vietnam, through the Mayaguez incident, Grenada, and Panama, we wound up in DESERT STORM with many of our SEALs embarked on U.S. Navy ships. From those ships, they were prepared to go in and swim in to the beaches and do a combat demolition, just as we did during World War II, to enable the Marines to cross the beach.

General Schwarzkopf decided not to do that. But the fact was that after all these years, after all this time had passed and compared to all the sophisticated things we do in the SEALs, doctrinally, our young men are basically Frogmen. We had four to six SEAL platoons sitting out on those ships ready to conduct the same operations as their forefathers did in World War II.

Vic Meyer, Lieutenant Commander

Presently, I serve as the Executive Officer of SEAL Team One. My start with the Teams was fairly conventional. I first heard about the Teams while at the Naval Academy. In a lot of ways, I was sort of an underachiever at the Naval Academy. The one thing I was interested in was the physical aspect of the Teams.

There were only five billets offered the year I went through the Naval Academy. My choice was to be a pilot, which appealed to me, but not as much as being a Frogman. My other option was to go into Surface Warfare for two years and qualify for my surface warfare pin. Then I could try and do a lateral transfer into Naval Special Warfare. Ultimately, I chose the Surface Warfare route and went to a destroyer for two years, three months. Finally, I received orders to BUD/S and then on to SEAL Team One after graduation.

I don't really remember when I first heard about the SEAL Teams. My dad was a Naval officer, a submariner. So I was always aware, sometimes on the periphery, sometimes a little more directly, of the Teams. We lived in Virginia Beach and saw guys running up and down the beach all the time. They were SEALs or UDT Frogmen. There was no seminal moment, no epiphany, where all of a sudden I decided the Teams was where I wanted to be.

My decision was made while I was at the Naval Academy. I think, though, that it was more that the Teams sort of found me rather than me finding the Teams. Fortunately, there were some instructors at the Naval Academy who were from the Teams, and they helped get me even more interested in the SEALs. I sort of fit in more with those guys than I did anywhere else and felt very at ease with them.

I was in BUD/S Class 156, a summer class, a very, very warm summer class. In fact, Hell Week was balmy. The water temperature seemed to be around seventy-two degrees, which frustrated the instructors. They really couldn't hammer us by throwing us into the water, so they just ran us back and forth between Imperial Beach and the base all week with rubber boats on our heads.

BUD/S wasn't that difficult for me, in spite of my having been in the surface fleet for several years. As an officer, there was still an inherent degree of professional distance I was able to maintain because I was the class leader. However, I was very comfortable for the line between officers and enlisted men to become blurred during training. There was always that measure of respect for my position, and I think that was

Constantly on the move at BUD/S, these students move away from the surf zone carrying the rubber boat that has been their constant companion since the beginning of training. While his classmates carry the boat, at the rear of the group is a single student carrying a large outboard motor on his back.

U.S. Navy

accorded me because I showed a great deal of respect for the guys with me.

No where else in the military do you maintain those enduring friendships developed in training, as you do with the guys who go through BUD/S with you. You continue to work with those same people throughout your career in Naval Special Warfare—at least I've certainly found that to be the case.

The closeness between the officers and the enlisted men in the Teams is one of its strengths. It's much easier to demonstrate your good faith to your Teammates, and the enlisted men know you inside and out. Your reputation as an operator and your reputation as a human being, sort of precedes you wherever you go in the community. The men know your strengths and weaknesses, and the enlisted guys are very demanding and tough. They do not tolerate weaknesses easily. But they are also pretty forgiving and will forgive an officer a mistake if they see a redeeming quality in him.

The officer-students do make a number of mistakes going through

BUD/S. That's one of the things that's sort of important. You go through the good times together, and you get hammered together when a mistake is made. That's all just part of being a SEAL.

I found that instructors take a particularly personal interest in the officers going through training—and with good reason. Someday, they could easily have to follow that same officer they're pushing through the mud at BUD/S. It is in their own best interest to make certain that each man who goes through training makes the grade completely, and that goes even more so for the officers.

The things that stand out for me in my experience in training, are somewhat difficult to admit. I found that hate is a very powerful motivator. You get into the dark side of your character, that dark part of you, and pull out what you need to get you through the most difficult parts in BUD/S. That was the single most important quality I noticed. To be able to use that dark side to overcome pain and adversity, extraordinary fatigue, and everything else, and then put it back in its place when it was no longer required, that was probably the thing that helped me the most.

I think we search for those kind of guys in the Teams. We search for guys who thrive on hardship. We search for guys who thrive on chaos. And those men have to be able to manage that chaos, that pain, and overcome it through whatever part of their character they use. I think a lot of those qualities are found in the dark side of the soul.

Hell Week, I will admit, was very physical. But I think the cold is the most debilitating thing about every Hell Week. My class certainly experienced cold out at San Clemente Island. Our Hell Week was so warm the instructors had to hammer us another way. Their technique of running us back and forth until we started to hallucinate worked out for us. Once you start to hallucinate, the hard part's gone. You really just cease to be aware of your surroundings.

I had an advantage in that I had come to BUD/S directly from the fleet. I was not physically broken down and I classed up and went through in one class. When I came out of Hell Week, sure, my feet were swollen and bleeding, and I had difficulty walking around, but I wasn't in the physical shape that some of the other guys were—bleeding from their crotches, swollen testicles, just some extraordinarily painful situations. Some of the new doctors who were at the training center and hadn't worked with Special Warfare before had rarely seen stuff like this. It was pretty incredible.

What got me through Hell Week was creating sort of an image in my mind, almost a mental photo. When everything else sort of closes in on you, and that picture gets real small, you focus on that image and see yourself on the other side of Hell Week.

There's also a great amount of peer pressure to keep going in the class. I was the class leader, and if I quit, I could have taken a number of the other students with me. There was a case where a class leader quit and almost the entire class followed him out of BUD/S. I had an enormous amount of pressure on me to finish the class, and I'd like to think that I rose to the occasion. That might not have been the case, though, because I think I was surrounded by extremely capable, confident, and dedicated people, and we just helped each other succeed. That's one of the things I think makes BUD/S so significant.

I had come from the Surface Fleet. I don't want to cast disparaging remarks on the Surface Fleet, but I never thought of quitting BUD/S. They were going to have to take me out of BUD/S in a body bag before I would quit and go back to the Fleet.

Other than my platoon in the Gulf, the most significant, and rewarding, event of my life, and that includes my diploma from the Naval Academy, is graduating BUD/S and entering the Teams. I place more value on my Trident than I do on my diploma. It really defines who you are to a large extent.

Standing there on the grinder that last day was a little weird. Because the instructors played so many mental games on us, I still refused to believe that training was really over, even at graduation. It wasn't until I had gotten home, grabbed something to eat, and taken the phone off the hook, that I finally didn't expect to see an instructor show up at the front door and send me back to the surf zone. I was always looking over my shoulder for the instructor I knew had to be there. After graduation, I got in the car as quickly as possible and had my girlfriend drive me home.

The Trident on my chest is, most important, representative of a commitment to a legacy and a commitment to those who have gone before. Guys from the Teams in Vietnam, such as Barry Enoch, Mike Thornton, and Don Crawford, had sacrificed a lot. And other guys left their lives back in Vietnam. Guys in the Teams take that very seriously. At SEAL Team One, we have those guys come back and talk to the Teams. They let us know where we came from.

I also think that there's a legacy of leadership in the men who went before us. You have only to look around you to see guys in and out of the Teams who have continued to be leaders, officer and enlisted alike, in civilian life. They continue to be extraordinary men. So it's not only a leadership role to be in the Teams, to be a SEAL is also a leadership role for the community, the culture at large, and the nation.

BUD/S training creates a guy who is capable of thinking on his feet and acting individually to the maximum of his capacity. But he also knows that he is part of a team effort. In a singular, visceral manner, a BUD/S graduate is able to concentrate on the mission at hand to the exclusion of everything else. It doesn't matter how cold he is, how painful his situation, or how tired or beat up the guy is, he is able to concentrate on the mission. And he is able to do that in part because he knows he is acting in concert with one, six, seven, eight, or sixteen other guys to accomplish that mission.

I don't think there is such a thing as a loner in the Teams. There are guys who are eccentric, guys who are quite different from even the average SEAL, but they all work as part of the Team, part of a platoon. I've had a couple such men in my own platoons. Each platoon has its own dynamic, and each platoon integrates all its parts and brings out the best in those guys. They would not have made it through training if they did not have the raw materials to make it in the Teams. And the most important of those raw materials is the ability to work as a team.

So the teamwork attitude is there. It's innate in every SEAL, but it might not be as obvious in some people as it is in others. So when each platoon develops its own dynamic, it brings out the best in those people, in all its parts, and uses them to its greatest advantage.

It's always been sort of a dichotomy that there's a great deal of individualism in each member of a SEAL platoon. But they all sort of subjugate that individuality and concentrate to develop the dynamic that allows the team to work best together. I think that's an incredibly powerful message about what they are able to do in BUD/S, and it's a very powerful message about what a SEAL platoon can accomplish, to be able to transcend those differences and individuality between its members and become a very effective, functioning team.

My first assignment after BUD/S graduation was to SEAL Team One. Since then, I've moved around a lot, but my operational career has been centered on the West Coast, primarily at SEAL Team One. I was fortunate enough to have two platoons at SEAL Team One, one of which I went to the Gulf War with.

In the Persian Gulf during DESERT SHIELD/DESERT STORM, we were doing primarily reconnaissance missions. We did a reconnaissance and surveillance mission on the border between Kuwait and Saudi Arabia, north of Khafji—which was attacked by the Iraqis on 16 January 1991.

We were tasked with seeing if there were any mine-laying activities, troop movements, or anything of consequence going on up there. We saw quite a few things going on, and we were there on the border the night when the air war was launched and the war actually started. By the time the ground war was launched, we had abandoned our observation post, as the area was no longer tenable.

Until Khafji, we conducted ground operations as our primary mission. After the Iraqi attack on Khafji, Admiral Ray Smith, the SEAL commander in the Gulf, decided that we could best serve the CinC

(Commander-in-Chiefs pronounced sinks) by conducting maritime reconnaissance missions into Kuwait. These were missions conducted well behind Iraqi lines to see if there was a good point for an amphibious landing.

Our operations off the coast of Kuwait were very much like those conducted by the UDTs on enemy-held beaches in the Pacific during World War II. I'd like to think that we were doing the operations as our forefathers had. I have always admired those early Frogmen. The degree of courage it took to go in at daybreak, search for obstacles, place demolitions on them, then blow the demolition—all while under enemy fire—took and extraordinary amount of courage, especially with the losses the NCDU (Naval Combat Demolition Units) took in Normandy.

I'd like to think that the mission we did in the Persian Gulf was still a viable mission. Tom Deitz's platoon succeeded in distracting and diverting a large number of the Iraqis into a coastal area we had no intention of invading. That was a very successful operation. I have since found out that the diversion operation was very much like the those run by the UDT during World War II and even Vietnam.

The thing that sticks out in my mind about DESERT STORM is the extraordinary character of the guys I worked with, the guys in my platoon. Their sense of humor was great. We still laugh about some of the things that happened today.

It is right around Christmas now (1998), so I think a lot about the season and being there in the Gulf at that time of year. My platoon chief, Randy Palladium, had just missed being in Vietnam, and here he was in the Gulf. He loved that movie Platoon, which had only been released for a couple years then. He had a copy of the soundtrack with us. He would often play that very poignant passage by Samuel Barber, the adagio for strings. Then he would say to us, "If I ever don't come back, you guys know what to do. Give my wife the flag . . ."

It was so melodramatic that we would all laugh about it. "Randy, you're not going to die," we would say. And of course he didn't. We

UDT operators in the Pacific during WWII prepare explosive charges prior to an operation. They are cutting the blocks from M1 tetrytol chains apart to make smaller individual charges. The blocks are further wrapped with a length of cord to secure them to a target. This procedure made the equivalent of a Hagensen pack for use in the hot environment of the Pacific Islands. The men are very comfortable working with this quantity of explosives. So much so that several of the men are sitting on loaded haversacks.

U.S. Navy

laughed at him then, and we sort of laugh at him now. He is a great operator, but that was a very funny moment to us.

There was another op that we were on in the Gulf. We were about a kilometer from the beach, about twenty kilometers north of the border, and it was pitch black. There were A-6s (intruder strike aircraft) running air strikes into the area where we were inserting for a beach reconnaissance. Three swimmers were to be inserted—myself and Jimmy and Jerry, two members of my platoon. My communicator, Lafe, was on the radio, and he also had the GPS (global positioning system) receiver, so he knew exactly at what point we would put the swimmers in the water.

It was very cold, and the boat was advancing slowly at an idle. It took us quite a while to get from the 2-kilometer point in to the 1,000-meter point where we were going to launch the swimmers. We were still about two kilometers off the beach when Lafe leaned over to Jimmy and nodded his head. Then Jimmy went into the water. Lafe started laughing hysterically because Jimmy was now wet, cold, and miserable—and we were still about an hour from the insert point.

We did see the oil wells in Kuwait, but we didn't see them when they were on fire. We were at a place called Ras al-Mishab, the base from where we launched the high-speed boats, when they were burning. It was very eerie, almost like the movie Bladerunner. There was no day and no night, and it just rained a thick, black oil that accumulated in puddles on the ground. It was almost apocalyptic in the appearance. It was just black and there was nothing but oily water coming out of the sky. It really made you think of Armageddon. That fact wasn't lost on the guys, and they laughed pretty hard about that.

We were extremely busy during the whole of DESERT SHIELD/DESERT STORM. A lot of our staff were involved with the early days of the conflict. Some had been working all through September, October, November, and December. During the air war in January, we were very involved as well. When the ground war finally started in February, it was almost anticlimactic to us.

To a certain extent, that was due to Admiral Raymond Smith. He realized that once there were troops moving in on the ground, advanced force ops were no longer relevant, and our job was basically done. There wasn't anything to be added to the CinC's objectives once the ground war had occurred.

The mission we did have, that we ultimately weren't successful in, was to go and interdict elements of the Iraqi police force that was escaping from Kuwait City on to Bubiyan Island. We were just a little too late and didn't encounter any Iraqis, but we like to think that we were the first ones into Kuwait City proper. We had fast-attack vehicles with the Marines at the airport, but my platoon was actually sitting in the boat basin in Kuwait City when they were fighting it out on the runway. There just wasn't anyone there at that point for us to engage.

One thing we were very concerned with prior to and during the war was the mine threat in the Persian Gulf. We had been listening to the news reports and no one really knew just how capable the Iraqis were in laying sea mines. We had heard reports that the Iraqis had laid the mines but never armed them. Mines, for a Frogman, can be a very pronounced deterrent effect.

We were very worried, it was so pitch black when we were swimming into the beach that I figured that since I couldn't see the Iraqis, I knew they couldn't see me. Or at least I contented myself with that fact. But there was a good degree of apprehension as we went in on our first combat operation. At the same time, there was a high degree of exhilaration. Missions like that, classic SEAL water ops, are very few and far between. And here I was, swimming in on an enemy beach to go do one.

We ran into some problems just moving offshore in our boats after Saddam had ordered the valves opened up in Kuwait, creating the oil spills in the Gulf. Our high-speed boats, the equivalent of cigarette boats, would leave Ras al-Mishab and quickly run into trouble. Oil on top of the water would be so thick that our boat engines would overheat because they were not able to draw in cooling water.

About eight months after the war, I went back to Ras al-Mishab as the platoon commander of another SEAL platoon. I was amazed at how the environment had rebounded from the effects of the oil spills and fires. But I'm sure a lot of the oil just sank to the bottom and caused untold environmental damage that just didn't show on the surface.

Although I did not see the actual oil well fires while they were burning, I experienced some of the results. Black, oily rain falling down on you twenty-four hours a day made the duration of the war no fun.

We're losing some guys on the Teams now. The economy is really good on the outside and private industry does a great job of marketing, so men leave the Teams for the civilian sector. There are still a lot of guys who are staying on, and I think that speaks well of their character. They're just extraordinary guys. I think one of the reasons that guys stay around is that the Teams attract purists. There's no "just in time delivery" or "just good enough to get by" attention on the profit margin.

The men in the Teams are purists doing a very dangerous job to absolute perfection—because there is no margin of error in our line of work. Our mission demands nothing less.

Last night, I went to the airport to greet one of the platoons coming in from the Persian Gulf. The leading petty officer of that platoon was at Khafji. He was one of the three guys who had been able to escape the Iraqi advance and let us know they were coming. We, my platoon, had just left the border about fifteen minutes before that happened, so we had a only fire team in Khafji at the time.

When I greeted him, that man was coming back from his third or fourth Gulf deployment since then. These guys all sort of remind me of Horatio Hornblower at the bridge. They're just extraordinary guys doing an extraordinarily difficult job, and for not too much pay. They're largely underappreciated and forgotten in peacetime. They are men of incredible character, and their degree of self-sacrifice is too high to be measured.

Even if they can't express it very eloquently, I think they all realize that happiness is not achieved through any pursuit of self-indulgence or self-fulfillment. It's really achieved through assiduously pursuing a just cause.

And I think they believe in the cause, as they believe in their Teammates. That's what makes Naval Special warfare so successful—the bond that develops between us. The bond between myself and the guys that I got to work with during the Gulf War remains very strong. I talk to those men on an almost daily basis, and I have served with the few of them who are with SEAL Team One right now. That fact was not lost on me last night when that man came back from the Gulf after a six-month deployment.

A SEAL is someone who is almost perfectly adapted to the aquatic environment and is extremely adept in transitioning from the water to the land. SEALs operate mostly in the littoral area, that area relating to the shore and coastal regions, to accomplish a variety of missions.

The thing that sets us apart from other Special Operations forces is our ability to operate seamlessly in that area. It is the most demanding area that Special Operations is tasked to work in.

The reason we can do that work starts at the Naval Special Warfare Center with the instructors at BUD/S. When I think of the instructors, I'm reminded of a quote from Goethe in which he said something along the lines of, "If you treat a man as he is, he will remain as he is. But if you treat him as he should be, he will become who he should be."

The instructors at BUD/S create an image of themselves, an image of a SEAL as a SEAL should be. I think that is what is so extraordinary about BUD/S and why SEALs come out of BUD/s without necessarily thinking that they have done anything particularly extraordinary. They're proud of their accomplishment, to be sure. But after graduation, it's time to move on, do other things, and get into the work of being a SEAL and actually get into the work where they can utilize the skills they spent so long acquiring.

The road to being a SEAL doesn't end with BUD/S. That's really only just the beginning of training. After graduation, you're qualified to take part in the platoon training cycle—which is extremely demanding. In the Teams, I've been colder than I was in BUD/S, and I've done harder stuff than I did while in BUD/S. But BUD/S is the psychological training that lets you know you can do it. The rule of thumb is that your body can do ten times more than your mind thinks it can do. I didn't believe that before I went to BUD/S, but now I do believe it.

There were runs at BUD/S where I thought my heart was going to come out of my mouth and I was going to turn inside out and die on the beach. But there was always something that got me through it. One of the instructors' favorite things was to do the run, say a four-mile run, and then, just as you thought you were back at the Team, they would continue running down the beach.

The lesson learned was that the op is never over. You never can relax until you are actually back home and the gear is cleaned up. You can never say, "Well, the way the op is planned, we'll be home in four hours."

There is no "four hours", there is no time limit. That's what they try to instill in training, to not get demoralized when the rules change. If you do get demoralized when the rules change, that's the mark of an amateur. The mark of a true professional is to be able to persevere through that, and anything else. That's what they create at BUD/S, the raw material of the professional.

Our last war of consequence was DESERT STORM. In spite of that, I think it's important not to dwell too much on the Gulf War as a milestone in Naval Special Warfare. It certainly taught us some very valuable lessons about boats, our mobility, and our ability to operate in a maritime environment. We also leaned how to better conduct those seamless transitions from the water to the land that are so important to our operations. But as a seminal event in Naval Special Warfare, we're not going to have a compliant enemy like we did in the Gulf ever again.

We're going to have to be able to think on our feet and to deploy much faster with a much more adaptable force package, than we deployed with for DESERT SHIELD/DESERT STORM. We won't have six months to built up and train for the missions we'll have to do. The actions will be now and with what we brought with us.

That's the lesson that might have been learned in the Gulf. We were very well led and very fortunate not to have any casualties. The missions we did supported the CinC but were very justifiable in the amount of risk that was assumed. Those were important factors that were laid out in the beginning by Admiral Smith. He did not take missions that we were not suited to do, and he did not take missions for the SEALs that did not support the CinC's objectives.

That was very clear to us. We knew that lives were not going to be put in danger unnecessarily. SEALs will put their lives at risk, they'll do a mission regardless of the risk—if they know it's not a frivolous mission and if they know that the mission supports the national, or at least the CinC's, objectives.

To concentrate on the Gulf would be a mistake. We need to look toward the future. There were lessons learned during DESERT SHIELD and DESERT STORM, and we need to continue to integrate those lessons into the way we do business now.

I think Vietnam was the crucible in which modern Naval Special Warfare, the SEALs, were formed. We owe an extraordinary debt of gratitude to those guys from Vietnam.

The SEALs who served in Vietnam are very magnanimous about their service in that war. They did what they did for the right reasons. They did it for their country, and they did it for their Teammates.

President Ronald Reagan said that there's no limit to what you can do if you don't care who gets the credit. SEALs are like that. Good SEAL officers realize that it's not their leadership, it's their ability to bring out the best in their men. It's the men who are responsible for all our successes in the Teams. As officers, we provide a minimal amount of guidance and direction, and the guys just exceed themselves at every opportunity. It's very gratifying to watch that. It's also very, very humbling to be around men of that caliber.

I think that's why you find that SEALs—especially those SEALs from Vietnam—don't go around patting themselves on the back. They've faced fire and seen friends die. To walk around and puff themselves up, to pat themselves on the back, would be to desecrate the memory of their fallen comrades.

They should be justifiably proud of what they do. But I think it's also quite understandable why they don't show it. Barry Enoch wrote a great book called Teammates that explains it much better than I ever could.

The guys from Vietnam created a legend. Their stories were around at the Naval Academy. The stories circulate around the Navy, even on my ship. Guys like Mike Thornton are in the community. You run into a guy in the commissary who has ribbons that go from his pocket, over the top of his shoulder, and down his back. You can figure that he has been there and done that.

You see Mike Thornton someplace and you just go, Man, just who is that guy? I want to be like him. When I was younger, I saw the way SEALs were confident and how they carried themselves—poised, articulate, no-nonsense, and no-compromise kind of guys—and that made me want to be with them. They have principles, and they adhere to them. They get a mission, and they do it. That's what appealed to me about the SEALs before I even joined the Teams.

When I did join the Teams, I wasn't surprised at the people I met and worked with. I had found exactly what I was looking for. Working with guys who exude confidence from every pore of their body and are the ultimate professionals at what they do is more than a pleasure. They are purists who won't rest until the job is 100 percent complete—not just "good enough," but 100 percent complete, because they know there's no margin for error in their world.

I think the Hollywood image of the SEALs is excessive. I think the best thing that could happen to Naval Special Warfare is to put up a big, black fence around every SEAL Team with a big sign that says "DO NOT ENTER UNDER PENALTY OF DEADLY FORCE."

That would be our best recruiting poster, too, because we would attract the right kind of guys to the Teams. It's not that we don't now, but there are guys who are attracted to the SEALs because of the

Rambo image. They rarely make it through BUD/S. If they are guys who show up that way, but have the character, the innate skills, and most important, the psychological makeup to make it through BUD/S, they will. It was always there in them, they just came for the wrong reasons—but they stayed for the right ones.

What I hope people learn from this is that being a SEAL is very, very hard work. The guys work extremely hard. They spend a lot of time away from home and make extraordinary sacrifices for their chosen jobs. And they do a job that's absolutely essential to our national security. It's very often forgotten around Thanksgiving and Christmas, but those guys are always there, on the edge. They are always vigilant, and they're always downrange and doing that job.

When the rest of us are sleeping or worried about how our stocks are doing, when we're tucking our kids in at night or taking them to child-care in the morning, and when we're just sitting down to eat, there are always those guys who are downrange, doing the job. They have to leave their families far behind. And they do their jobs for not much pay, because they're professionals and they're proud of what they do.

The first word that comes to mind when I think of the SEALs is competence. That word speaks for itself. The level of competence SEALs are able to demonstrate in three different environments—sea, air, and land—is governed by a document that lists the skills we're required to maintain.

The quantum leap in technology that has occurred between Vietnam and today demands a smarter guy. That is to take nothing away from the men who worked in the swamps and rice paddies of Vietnam, but the guys who come into the Teams now are technically proficient. They're brilliant. A full third of the enlisted men who graduate from BUD/S have college degrees.

At SEAL Team One right now, there's a Rhodes Scholar. Another lettered scholar just left a few months ago to study in Paris. These are exceptional people, with exceptional educations and diverse backgrounds. It's been healthy for the Teams to take in that kind of guy. Conversely, those guys who are so talented are also highly sought outside the Navy. Some of them succumb to the temptation and leave, that's sort of the nature of the beast. But the guys in the SEALs are, by and large, extremely competent.

It's so gratifying to work with guys who have achieved the levels of skill, competence, professionalism, and most of all the self-discipline to make the most of their skills. It makes being an officer in the Teams a privilege and a pleasure.

It's trite to say that the world is not becoming any safer. I think it's difficult to realize that unless you go to some other countries. I had the opportunity to live in France for two and a half years. In 1995, on almost a weekly basis, there were bombs going off in Paris subways, killing scores of people. We have not had anything like that, to that degree, here in the United States yet. [Note: This interview took place several years prior to September 11, 2001.]

But the schism between the haves and the have-nots, and the mass migrations of refugees and people seeking a better way of life in the more developed countries, is going to create a great deal of friction. That friction is going to create instability.

SEALs, and special operators in general, thrive in that chaos. There are missions that require us to go to those regions and to monitor that instability, to perhaps aid refugees and decrease that instability. And in some cases, to manage violence for U.S. national objectives.

I mentioned that SEALs thrive in a chaotic environment. They are language-trained, they are operationally savvy, and they're street smart. They are strong, mentally tough, and self-disciplined. They are mature, and they know how to fade in and out of situations in complete silence. The world is not becoming a safer place; instability is going to continue to grow. For that, we have the Teams. As Plato said, "Only the dead have seen the end of war."

Tom Deitz, Commander

When I was deployed to the Persian Gulf, I had to have a mini history lesson on Saddam Hussein. When I first heard that Iraq had invaded Kuwait, my first question was, "Where's Kuwait?" Then we did an intelligence study on Saddam Hussein. Really his persistence was impressive—ten years in the Iran-Iraq War, which resulted in sort of a stalemate, yet he was still in charge.

Special Operations is a group of military personnel from all services who focus in small number on certain missions. Our missions as SEALs are primarily direct action, special reconnaissance, psychological warfare, guerrilla warfare, and foreign internal defense.

The role of Special Operations during DESERT SHIELD was to get in place and to find out exactly what we needed to do in case a war broke out. We did that by working with the Saudi Arabian special forces and doing some training missions with them. While we were doing that, we were also able to look at the coastal bases the Saudi Arabians had, to see if we could possibly use them later in a wartime situation as a forward staging base.

The Saudi Arabian navy special warfare forces at the time were very determined. They were fearful for the fate of their country, therefore they were training harder in case they had to be deployed. They were defending their country, so they were very proud. I've worked with them since, and their equipment and tactics have increased dramatically over time.

I only know of a few, about three, Saudi Arabian naval personnel who went through the full BUD/S course. I don't think we've had any go through since DESERT SHIELD/DESERT STORM, but there are others who would know that much better than I.

A force multiplier is really what Special Operations brings to the table. We are small in number, yet the missions we can conduct have a dramatic impact on the military as a whole.

The biggest advantage the United States had during the Gulf War was our determination. We knew why we were there. We saw the atrocities committed by the Iraqis on the Kuwaiti people. There was really a purpose for us to be there.

The devastation of Kuwait by the Iraqis was horrendous. There really cannot be a reason for a country to do that to another country, much less a neighbor with the same ethnic and religious backgrounds. The atrocities committed by Iraq were truly uncalled for.

On 2 August 1990, it was really a total surprise when the Iraqis came across their border with Kuwait in strength. Looking back, yes, there was some intelligence, and the Iraqis had been gathering near the border. But they had done that many times before. The idea of them actually attacking Kuwait had never been a realistic thought. But they did. They just stormed in.

Militarily, it was a great operation. But the way they treated the Kuwaiti population was excessive. They drove them out of their country. I got to see some of Kuwait City after the cease-fire and the war had ended. It was just devastated.

The Iraqi troops I encountered during my reconnaissance and direct-action mission either weren't paying attention, or we really were as sneaky as we claim to be. We saw a lot of their patrol boats and some personnel back off the beach a little bit, yet they never saw us.

When I was looking at how we would conduct DESERT STORM, if we did move to that phase, I was very confident that America would do it the right way, from President Bush, a World War II veteran, to Generals Schwarzkopf and Powell, both Vietnam-era Army captains. They saw firsthand on the ground in Vietnam what a poorly fought and poorly directed war can do to a country. From my perspective, I was confident that they would not let that happen in DESERT STORM.

My platoon was SEAL Team Five, Foxtrot Platoon, and our mission focus was coastal reconnaissance. We did reconnaissance missions, gathering intelligence all along the Kuwaiti coast. Our missions were not just on the beach itself, but we also looked at what type of patrol boats were being used, what type of navigation aids were out there in

One of the Soviet-made Iraqi S-60 57mm antiaircraft guns. The weapon is emplaced so that it could sweep the beach and offshore waters with its full-automatic fire of high explosive shells. A number of the four-round clips of ammunition to the gun are stacked along the left side of the weapon.

Kevin Dockery

the water, and how the Iraqis were manning the water and the coastline.

Looking at the missions we conducted, they were very similar to what the Navy Combat Demolition Teams and Underwater Demolition Teams did in World War II both in the European theater and in the Pacific. We swam in to beaches with explosive charges, then we placed those charges on and near obstacles. Other than the PowerPoint briefings that we had to give via computers, our missions were probably very similar to the missions conducted in World War II.

Part of getting the intelligence from a beach is determining the trafficability. By that I mean determining if the sand is strong enough to hold the vehicles that would be crossing the beach. We were told that we would be going in and doing a deception operation; therefore, getting sand samples really wasn't in our mission area. It was planned to be a deception from the very beginning. I was the platoon commander in charge of the deception operation on the Kuwaiti coast.

The threat of an amphibious invasion by U.S. forces was very clear. I think the Iraqis realized it was a definite option for the U.S. Navy and Marine Corps, and we played along with that idea. There were rehearsal landings in the southern Gulf conducted by the amphibious ships and the Marine Corps.

So the Iraqis were looking at history, and they were looking at CNN. They really thought that there was going to be an amphibious invasion. In addition to the reconnaissance missions, my platoon was tasked with scouting out a beach where it would be feasible to support an amphibious landing.

Even though we were going to be doing it as a deception, we still had to find a beach that was suitable. If you try to deceive someone on a small beach that couldn't handle a landing, they wouldn't take it seriously. The idea behind the deception was really to hold the Iraqi troops on the coast and not have them move inland to try and stop the ground forces from coming in.

The Iraqis in Kuwait had been bombed for upward of forty days and were a little shell-shocked at the time of our deception operation. Twenty-four hours prior to when we were going to blow up the beach, we ceased any air strikes and any naval gunfire in the area of our target beach. We wanted it to be quiet.

We left our base in northern Saudi Arabia in four forty-foot high-speed boats. When we were seven miles off the coast of our target beach, we took to our eighteen-foot rubber zodiac boats, which held my fifteen-man SEAL platoon. The zodiacs then moved in to about a thousand yards offshore. That's where six of us got out and swam in to the beach. We left the boats probably around 2215 hours (10:15 in the evening), and swam in so we could be on the beach and pull the pins at 2300 hours (11 P.M.).

Myself and five other SEALs swam in off the zodiacs, each of us

---

towing a twenty-pound haversack of explosives. We spread out to cover two hundred and fifty yards of beach. The timing clocks on the charges we set to go off at 0100 hours; the ground war was scheduled to commence three hours later at 0400 hours. We wanted to give the Iraqis about three hours to react to our deception.

We swam in, placed the charges on the beach, pulled the timers, and came back out and rendezvoused with our boats. The firing runs we were going to make along the beach were to start at 12:30, thirty minutes prior to our explosives going off.

If you had been an Iraqi on the Kuwaiti shore, you hadn't been bombed for about twenty-four hours and you thought the U.S. Marines were going to be coming in to your beach. Then, all of a sudden, in the middle of the night, you were being shot at. You would know it wasn't an airplane, and you would know it wasn't a battleship firing shells at you. If you peeked your head up, you'd see small boats about five hundred yards offshore just hammering your position.

All kinds of fire would be coming in—.50 caliber and 7.62mm machine guns as well as 40mm grenade launchers. An Iraqi on the beach would keep his head up a little bit, but not too much because all our fire would have been coming in strong.

Our boats shot at the beach for about ten minutes. Following that, we threw four pounds of C4 plastic explosive wrapped in plastic over the side of the boat with delay fuses attached. They exploded sporadically over the next fifteen minutes. Again, the Iraqis would be seeing and hearing explosions very close to the beach. Five minutes after that, the six charges went off. Twenty pounds of C4 makes a heck of a noise. We had six charges that size going off in a span of about thirty seconds.

That was the picture the Iraqis would have seen. That was what our deception consisted of, and it worked. The Iraqi forces along the coast stayed there. Additionally, elements of two separate Iraqi armored divisions that had been facing south and waiting for the ground forces to come in began to move toward the coastline in reaction to our deception.

This was the fifth time we had gone north. The first four times had been reconnaissance missions. The adrenaline, especially that first night we went north, was definitely peaked. I think the adrenaline probably pushed down any nervousness we might have been feeling. When we got to the actual mission of swimming in and placing the charges on the beach, knowing the ground war was starting three hours later, the professional side of being a Navy SEAL took over. You become very focused on your mission, and you don't let any outside forces come in on your thoughts. You conduct your mission, pull back out, and they never see you.

The fear of being captured really did not come into play on our ops. Certain Special Operations missions put you more into harm's way. We were in the water or we were in our boats. Yes, there were Iraqi patrol boats out there, but in a small zodiac boat going pretty slow. It was very doubtful that anyone was going to see us. We also had communications directly to the airborne controller. If we needed close-air support, we could call in a plane to help us.

Usually, we would take our own boats and go north on an op. The third night we went, the seas were brutal. The Persian Gulf is usually a picture of calm waters. In the winter, though, it gets very rough. The winds that night were about thirty-five knots, and the seas were running six to seven feet. Our boats just couldn't make it.

That night, we got dropped in by two MH53 Pave Low's from Air Force Special Operations and MH60s from the Army's 160th SOAR (Special Operations Aviation Regiment) flew in as gunship cover. That was a great night because it was true joint special operations mission—an Air Force special operations helicopter dropping in Navy SEALs with Army special operations helicopters flying cover.

The 160th Special Operations Aviation Regiment, better known as the Nightstalkers, are, I would say, the premier combat helicopter pilots in the world. Whenever we can work with them, we will.

Obtaining ground truth is having a real person in an area who can come back and debrief the exact intelligence that's there. Satellite cov-

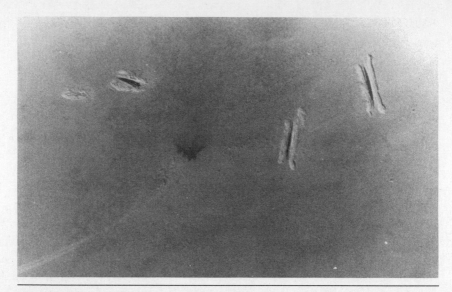

The faint markings of Iraqi Scud missile launcher emplacements in the sands of the desert. The small raised sand berms are for the protection of the missile crews when the weapons are launched. The long black scorch marks in the sand are the only remaining evidence that the long-gone Scud missiles were ever actually there.

U.S. Navy

erage can get really tricky, especially in the Gulf with the oil fires creating cloud cover. When someone swims into a beach and comes back and tells you that there are these types of mines, these types of concertina wire, and this amount of personnel activity, there's no doubt that it is exactly what's there.

Today's technology allows detailed satellite coverage—yes, you can read a license plate from space. But when a cloud comes in, a storm rolls in, or there are fires and smoke covers the target, a satellite cannot get through that, so you need people on the ground.

The smoke from the oil fires made working in the Gulf area very eerie. Cloud cover, actually smoke cover, maybe a hundred feet off the deck of the Persian Gulf, acted as almost a sound barrier for some of the explosions that would happen inland, reverberate off the smoke, come down to bounce off the water, then come up to us on the boat. It was a pretty good show.

A direct-action mission is just what the name says: You go in and conduct an action. Special reconnaissance is when you're going in to collect intelligence, and a lot of time that leads to a direct-action mission. Scud hunting is another kind of reconnaissance and was possibly a direct-action mission in the Gulf.

The Naval Special Warfare forces in the Gulf were on search-and-rescue alert twenty-four/seven. We had one SEAL platoon that was out and divided among three ships in the northern Gulf on CSAR (combat search-and-rescue) alert with a helicopter element. We were pier-side with our boats. At any one time we had four personnel with CSAR equipment and ready to go.

There was one Air Force pilot who was shot down and bailed out into the water. Our boats were under way in under five minutes, and the helicopter from the ship with the SEALs onboard was off the deck in under five minutes. From the time the pilot ejected to the time he was back onboard a ship, healthy and recovered, was only thirty-five minutes total.

The importance of recovering pilots is crucial, and it's the American way. You never want to leave anyone behind, you never want to have anyone captured. In reality, some people are going to get captured. But we need to be able to stand by and prevent that from happening whenever possible.

A classmate of mine from the Naval Academy at Annapolis, Lieutenant Jeff Zaun, was in the Gulf. I came down to our office one morning and looked at the list of pilots who had been shot down and saw his name. Three days later, his face was on the cover of Newsweek. That really hit home. The treatment the Iraqis were giving our warriors was uncalled for.

We did no rescue operations on land. That was the job of the PJs, the Air Force Pararescuemen. They were the guys who picked up an F-14 pilot who was shot down over land.

The commander for Naval Special Warfare in the Gulf was Captain Ray Smith, who just retired as a rear admiral. When we went over there, he was discussing our employment with his superiors. He came back and told the SEAL platoon that we were going to keep one foot in the water. By that, he meant that we would be doing work along the coast, on the coast, and maybe a little bit inland from the coast. But we weren't going to get out of our sphere. The water is where SEALs come from. The water is where SEALs go back to. And there's no one who does that better than us.

For a Navy SEAL, water is our element. If we get in trouble, we look for the nearest way to get back to the water. Once we're there, we feel safe.

Everything we do in training and in real-world missions comes from the water. We'll have sixty to seventy pounds of gear we'll take in the water. You look at the normal person and ask him to carry that amount of gear on land, and it will be difficult for him. You tell him to swim three miles with that gear, and that's a much greater level of difficulty. But that's what SEALs do every day.

A psychological operation, psyop, is a method of getting into the mind of the enemy. We were able to do that with CNN showing the Marines and the amphibious forces doing landings in the southern part of the Gulf as rehearsals. Then Newsweek wrote an article saying that the ground war had actually started because Navy SEALs had been swimming in to the beaches. All that built up in the Iraqi mind-set that "Hey, these guys are coming in!" Then our deception operation was one final psychological aspect to help make the Iraqis think that yes, we were going to conduct a major landing.

Doug Waller, who wrote that Newsweek article, also wrote a book called The Commandos. When I told him I read his article, he started laughing. He really thought that we were swimming in. That article had been written some time earlier. I came back the first night I had done a reconnaissance, debriefed, and went out to a Saudi store and bought that Newsweek. There it was written up. I said, "I did the first one, and it hasn't happened yet." But the media were pitching the idea. It was great for us.

The media have a lot of ex-military and a lot of very intelligent analysts, so they can sort of get a good picture of what we might be doing. If that convinces the enemy that yes, we are doing it, so much the better for us.

The deception operation and the rehearsals that helped make it so believable worked. The only people on our side who were unhappy with it were the Marines. When there's a war, the Marines want to go ashore. When they don't get to, they are not happy. The rehearsals were good, but the Marines and the amphibious forces really wanted to do that mission.

The world knew that when the SEALs go in to a beach to blow up obstacle, a landing force isn't far behind. Later, in Somalia in late 1992, the guys who swam in to the beach and faced all the cameras were Marine Force Recon swimmers. The SEALs were a quarter-mile down the beach. They had told the Marines that there was a bunch of press where they wanted to land, and that they didn't want to go in there. The Marines decided to go ahead with their landing reconnaissance anyway and were filmed for the whole world to see.

The deception operation was really what we were focused on, and that was a kind of psyop. The leaflet campaign conducted by Air Force Special Operations was fantastic. Millions of leaflets, designed to help convince the Iraqi soldier to surrender, were dropped over enemy areas. I think it's a tribute to that operation that a lot of Iraqis were holding those pamphlets when they surrendered to U.S. forces.

Psychological operations are not always meant to deceive. They're also meant to tell the truth to people who are not receiving the whole picture. The Iraqis were not being told the truth by their chain of command. When we dropped leaflets saying that we would bomb this area tonight and you need to leave and go to this other area and then actually bomb that area, the soldier on the ground believes us and not his chain of command. That undermines what the enemy is trying to do while we are still telling them the truth.

On a whole, the performance of Special Operations in DESERT

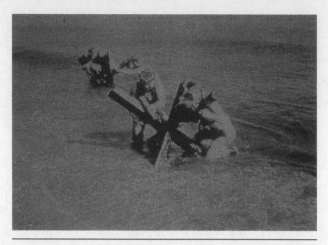

Navy frogmen emplace demolition charges on beach obstacles. This classic
UDT operation was carried forward and assigned to the Navy SEALs today.

STORM was a true success. We went in there and there were Army, Air
Force, and Navy Special Operations units. Each of us had our own task
to do, and we weren't stepping on each other. Naval Special Warfare
went over there with 275 personnel, and we returned with 275 personnel. When everybody comes back and the task is accomplished, it
is a success by every measure of the word.

The platoon that was out on the three ships also conducted some
hot operations besides CSAR duty. U.S. helicopters came under fire on
18 January from several Iraqi-held oil platforms in the Gulf. SEALs
counterattacked and boarded the platforms, capturing weapons and
gathering valuable intelligence documents. The Iraqis basically surrendered by the time the SEALs got there, so it wasn't as hostile a takedown as it could have been. The Iraqis had been beaten up pretty good
by the surface Navy before the SEALs went in. In some respects, it was
a preview of what the ground war would be.

We left for the States soon after the war was over. We were the first
West Coast platoon to return to CONUS. The reaction of the Kuwaiti

Examples of some of the psychological warfare leaflets dropped over Iraqi positions during Desert Storm. Just holding the colorful leaflet overhead was supposed to signal the peaceful surrender of an Iraqi soldier.

people to our liberation of their country was phenomenal. I was able to go into Kuwait City after the cease-fire, and they were having spontaneous parades thanking not only the United States, but all the Coalition forces. It was a great feeling to see the American flag being held up and Kuwaitis looking up and being very proud of that.

I don't think Saddam Hussein really expected us to come in the way we did. He probably thought he could wait us out. What President Bush, General Schwarzkopf, and General Powell did was make sure that we had the exact forces needed to do the mission in a timely manner, succeed in the mission, then leave the area.

Probably the best lessons we came away from Desert Storm with was not to underestimate an enemy, and not to move until we were firmly sure in our military and political minds that it is the right thing to do.

Our expectations when we landed in Saudi Arabia on 12 August were really, "Okay, how can we get out of here if the Iraqis come south?" They had the fourth-largest standing army in the world. If they wanted to come south at that time, there would have been nothing to

---

Iraqi troops surrendering in a group. The man in the front is holding a surrender leaflet dropped by psyops forces.

USSOCOM PAO

stop them. With the possible nuclear, chemical, and biological weapons they were purported to have, that was a something we really couldn't worry about much. If it happened, there wasn't much we could do.

As DESERT SHIELD went on, it became pretty obvious that the Iraqis weren't going to come south. If the U.S. and Coalition forces continued to build up as we did, then our fear, our anxiety about the Iraqis, lessened.

As with U.S. intelligence, the Kuwaitis looked at the buildup of the Iraqi troops in the beginning of August 1990 as just another ruse. This was just another bully tactic from Saddam Hussein. The Kuwaiti military forces were taken by surprise as much as we were, and the conquest of Kuwait was relatively easy for the Iraqis. Granted, with the size of the Iraqi army, even if it wasn't by surprise, they would have still been able to take Kuwait. It would have just been a little more difficult and costly for them.

Victory is the only acceptable outcome. Commanding officers are supposed to put together a command philosophy. Some guys write it out as narratives; I made mine "SEAL TEAM FIVE." For every letter I *wrote a sentence. When I got to the V in FIVE, I wrote "Victory is the only acceptable outcome."*

There's no substitute for real-world operations. Timing is such that a SEAL can go his entire career and never do a real-world mission. The fact that timing was on my side, and we were prepared for it at the time, definitely helps me when I have the young SEALs coming in now. They know that when I was a lieutenant, I was in real-world missions. That gives me a little bit of credibility, but nothing much. If I don't build on that myself, then all it is is history.

All the various units in Special Operations have their purpose, their mission. The Rangers, coming in with the size they have (it's relatively small compared to the Army, but relatively large compared to a SEAL platoon or Special Forces Operational Detachment), come in hard and hit you hard. The Army Special Forces, better known as the Green Berets, are small units like us. Their cultural and language skills allow them to work with almost any nation in the entire world, and they do a great job at it.

■ Chapter 12

SOMALIA

Somalia is a long, slender country on the east coast of Africa. Roughly bent in the shape of the numeral 7, Somalia makes up the point of what is called the Horn of Africa. If the continent of Africa was a face looking east, Somalia would be the nose.

A national rebellion overthrew the twenty-one-year-old dictatorial Somali government of Siad Barre in early 1991. The elimination of the Barre regime was not replaced by a central government, and the control of Somalia was split up among various groups of feuding military strongmen who proposed themselves as warlords of the country. The warlords took over the extended family clans that made up the clan system that had managed Somalia for decades. The warlords pillaged the country to build up their own power bases and obtain funds, food, and supplies for their men. In the wake of this situation, hundreds of thousands of Somalis faced famine and death by starvation.

Somali warlord fighters destroyed farms and stole foodstuffs sent in by the world's relief organizations. The death by starvation of 100,000 Somalis cause the United Nations to dispatch a humanitarian peacekeeping mission to protect the relief efforts and help stop the severe famine.

In support of the UN relief effort, President George Bush ordered Operation PROVIDE RELIEF initiated. In August, men from the 2nd Battalion, 5th Special Forces Group, deployed to Kenya to provide security for Somalia-bound relief flights. These relief efforts were expanded, and Operation RESTORE HOPE was begun with the intent to secure transportation facilities at Mogadishu, Somalia.

Ordered in by Chairman of the Joint Chiefs of Staff, General Colin Powell, Operation RESTORE HOPE began on 2 December 1992. An amphibious squadron of three ships, the USSs *Tripoli,* *Juneau,* and *Rushmore* were off the coast of Somalia in December to secure the Mogadishu airport by means of Marine amphibious landings. Onboard the squadron was a Marine Expeditionary Unit, a Special Boat Unit (SBU) detachment, and a platoon of Navy SEALs from SEAL Team One.

Initial operations by the SEALs were dictated by the needs of the intended amphibious landing. No up-to-date charts of the beaches off Mogadishu were available, so the first operation of the SEALs was to be a throwback to the earliest days of the UDT in World War II.

A classic UDT beach recon was conducted by the SEALs, supported by the boats and men of the SBU. The night of 6 December 1992 had twelve SEALs of the deployed platoon conducting a swimmer beach recon, measuring the water's depth with lead lines, a method first developed by Draper Kauffman during World War II. In spite of the passage of almost fifty years, the technique was sufficient for the needs of the SEALs and the cartographers back aboard the *Juneau.*

As the bulk of the SEAL platoon measured and noted the depth of the offshore waters, the balance of the platoon swam ashore and examined the beach proper. Obstacles, the shore gradient, the composition of the beach itself, and the measurements of the beach berm were all taken down for inclusion into charts for the Marine planners. Returning to the *Juneau,* charts were compiled from the SEALs information and the Marine commanders were briefed.

On the night of 7 December, the SEALs swam into Mogadishu Harbor to examine the waters and facilities. The SEALs' mission included locating satisfactory landing sites, assessing any existing threat from warlord or other armed forces, and determing if the port facilities could support the offloading of maritime prepositioned supply ships.

In spite of the relatively simple mission requirements, the conduct of the SEALs recon swim on 7 December was anything but easy. The warm waters of Mogadishu Harbor combined with a strong opposing current exhausted and overheated the SEALs as they conducted their operation.

Another threat, one not foreseen by the SEALs or their planners, were the waters of the harbor itself. Instead of facing enemy fire, the SEALs found themselves facing the heavily contaminated waters of the harbor. Raw sewage filled many areas of the harbor, making even the worst days of BUD/S training and the mud pits pale in comparison. A number of SEALs became sick from the mission.

Sliding through the mud—backward. Students at BUD/S receive extensive familiarization with how to move through mud. It is during evolutions like this one during Hell Week that they also learn even more about the importance of working as a team. Only if the boat crews shown here work together can they move as a unit and not receive further incentive from their ever-present instructors.

U.S. Navy

It was on the night of 8 December, during the actual landing of the Marine forces, that the SEALs faced a very modern threat to special operations forces, one that they had not been trained for. To increase the beach coverage for the amphibious landings, both the SEALs and elements of the Force Recon units from the Marine Expeditionary Unit went in as scout-swimmers ahead of the landing forces. On the beach were a number of media and press corps reporters, complete with cameramen and bright lights. Caught full on film were a number of the Marine Force Recon operators. The SEALs conducted their part of the pre-landing scout about a quarter-mile away from the reporters.

On television screens across the United States and other parts of the world were live pictures of some very confused and unhappy Force Recon swimmers. When the actual landing force of U.S. Marines started coming in some minutes later, the attention of the media went to them, leaving the Force Recon operators and SEALs to continue with their operations in relative peace.

The SEAL detachment conducted a survey of the port of Kismaayo, operating from the French frigate *Dupleix*. It was during this operation that the SEALs came under fire from Somali snipers. In spite of the sporadic fire, no SEALs were hit and they completed their mission without further incident.

The SEALs provided additional sniper support to the Marines who were coming under fire from warlord forces. Addition-

A SEAL sniper adjusts the Aimpoint sight on his modified M14 rifle. The SEAL sniper will provide precision fire support for his Teammates as they conduct training in VBSS operations for Desert Storm. The vertical front handgrip on the rifle is a personal modification of the weapon by the user.

U.S. Navy

ally, the SEALs gave personal security to their commander-in-chief when President George Bush visited Somalia to see the difficulties firsthand. The SEALs also conducted joint training operations with further UN forces in Somalia, a unit of Indian naval commandos.

The SEALs of the first platoon in Somalia were relieved by a platoon from SEAL Team Two who came in as part of the Wasp Amphibious Ready Group when they arrived in February 1993. The men from SEAL Team Two also faced a new threat when they conducted their first operation in Somalia, a more active one than their compatriots had found in the harbor waters of Mogadishu.

To gather intelligence on gun-smuggling operations, the SEALs conducted a reconnaissance of the Jubba River in the southern part of Somalia. While gathering their intel, the SEALs found that they had to dodge the crocodiles that infested parts of the river. Natural obstacles aside, U.S. Marine forces were able to conduct two raids on towns along the river based on SEALs intelligence.

A number of operations were conducted by the SEALs during April and May, including further reconnaissance swims of Kismaayo; the clearing of a potential beach landing site south of Mogadishu; recon missions of the Three Rivers region south of Kismaayo, relatively close to the border between Kenya and Somalia; recons of Koyaama Island; and a reconnaissance of Daanai Beach, conducted in very bad conditions and rough seas.

In addition to the SEALs deployed with the Marine Ready Groups, further operators from SEAL Team Six were deployed to Somalia to assist the U.S. special operations forces there. SEAL snipers conducted a number of supporting operations for both Marine and SOCOM units.

U.S. commanders determined that the chaotic situation in Mogadishu could be brought under control if the local warlord leader of the Habr Gedir subclan of the Hawiye clan, Mohamed Aideed, was eliminated as a functional threat. Orders were put out to either capture or kill the elusive and troublesome Aideed. This action served to increase the number of attacks on UN forces, especially those of the U.S. contingent.

In one reported incident, a SEAL sniper with an M88 .50-caliber sniper rifle prevented a number of Marines from becoming possible casualties. The SEAL sniper had seen a Somali gunman duck down behind a rock wall to prepare his RPG-7 for firing. RPGs proved to be a very popular weapon among warlord forces for attacking the heavily armed U.S. units.

As the Somali gunner prepared his weapon, the SEAL noted his location and the amount of damage he could do to the Marines

A SEAL sniper, posed for the photograph, takes aim with his McMillan M88 .50-caliber sniper rifle. The massive clamshell muzzle break visible on the end of the barrel helps reduce the recoil of the huge cartridge fired by the weapon. If this was an actual firing position, the sniper would be much more concealed and difficult to locate.

USSOCOM PAO

before they could be given a warning. The power of the .50-caliber rifle was ably demonstrated when the SEAL sniper punched a 700-grain bullet through the intervening rock wall and dropped the probably astonished Somali gunman.

It was in October 1993 that the U.S. forces in Somalia were involved in the worst and most costly urban firefight since the 1968 Tet Offensive during the Vietnam War. On 3 October 1993, a joint unit of Rangers, specialized Army assets, and SEALs were to conduct an assault on a targeted building on Hawlwadig Road near the Olympic Hotel in Mogadishu.

During the insertion by vehicle to the target area, a SEAL chief was struck by a Somali bullet. The SEAL heard the shot and felt it strike him on the left hip where he sat in the rear of a Humvee. Amazingly enough, the bullet was stopped by the knife the SEAL was wearing on his right hip. The bullet shattered the blade, driving several pieces into the SEAL's hip, but the blade prevented the wound from being life-threatening. After having several blade fragments pulled out of the wound and his leg quickly bandaged, the SEAL continued with the operation.

Later in the op, a Blackhawk helicopter was shot down by a Somali gunner with an RPG-7. During the ensuing battle to rescue the downed crew and passengers of the Blackhawk, the streets of Mogadishu were filled with armed gunmen, U.S. forces, and Somalis caught in the middle of the raging firestorm. When it all was over the next day, eighteen Americans were dead, seventy badly injured, and an estimated one thousand Somalis killed or wounded.

After the incident on 3–4 October, reinforcements to the U.S. military forces in the area were made both in Somalia and neighboring Kenya. AC-130 gunships, starting now in Kenya, flew patrols over Mogadishu. Additional USSOCOM assets were deployed to the area, including a platoon from SEAL Team Two and a platoon from SEAL Team Eight. The SEALs helped raise the general level of security for all the U.S. forces as well as the UN contingent in Somalia.

Operation UNITED SHIELD, the pullout of all U.S. forces in Somalia, was the final result of the actions that took place in Mogadishu on 3–4 October. SEALs helped maintain security on the beaches of Mogadishu, the same beaches that they had to conduct reconnaissance on to determine their suitability for use by the Marine landing craft and vehicles. By 3 March 1995, the U.S. withdrawal from Somalia was complete.

Chapter 13

HAITI: OPERATION SUPPORT DEMOCRACY/ OPERATION UPHOLD DEMOCRACY

Occupying the western half of the Island of Hispaniola, an island it shares with the Dominican Republic to the east, the country of Haiti has had a turbulent past. Periods of military governments put in place by coups were spaced by times of no government whatsoever where simple anarchy ruled. In 1956, a military coup put François Duvalier in charge of the country, ostensibly as an elected president. Any pretensions of democracy were eliminated when in 1964 Duvalier proclaimed himself president for life.

"Papa Doc" Duvalier, previously a medical doctor, ruled with a strange mixture of military force and voodoo rites until his death in 1971. Succeeded by his son, Jean Claude "Baby Doc" Duvalier, the situation remained one of grinding poverty for much of the population. In 1986, Baby Doc was overthrown in a military coup.

The situation was little improved for the Haitian population as a whole as they remained in poverty with little chance for escape. A bright point for the country were the democratic elections held in 1990. The election results put Jean-Bertrand Aristide in the president's office. On 30 September 1991, a military coup removed Aristide from office.

To replace Aristide into office, the United Nations placed economic sanctions in place against Haiti, establishing an embargo against most shipping, on 23 June 1993. The situation went from bad to worse for the people of Haiti, who were leaving the island in droves, mostly traveling on very poor boats to the United States as economic refugees. On 15 October 1993, President William Clinton ordered the U.S. Navy to help enforce the economic embargo against Haiti in an attempt to break the power of the military regime in place.

The combined joint task force (CJTF) 120 was established to plan, lead, and execute Operation SUPPORT DEMOCRACY, a multinational action against Haiti. The more than six hundred U.S. and allied warships of CJTF 120 conducted more than six hundred shipboardings against smugglers and shipping during the first five months of the operation. To escape the reach of the large Navy ships, smugglers turned to smaller craft that could use the shallower waters close to the coast to move embargoed goods between Haiti and the Dominican Republic.

The shallow-water tactics of the smugglers directed the U.S. Navy to put the new Cyclone class patrol boat into action off Haiti. Very new to the fleet and assigned to Naval Special Warfare Group Two in Little Creek, the two first Cyclone-class patrol craft were ordered to CJTF 120 after their crew training and ship certifications were completed. On 24 May, the *Cyclone* (PC-1) and the *Tempest* (PC-2) left Guantanamo Bay, Cuba, for Haiti. Arriving on-station on 27 May, the ships came under the operational control of CJTF 120, and they began active operations three days later.

The patrol craft went into action quickly, under the escort of the Peary-class guided missile frigate USS *Simpson* (FFG 56). The *Simpson* was to familiarize the *Cyclone* with the standard shipboarding practices of the task force. On the first voyage, a smuggler was encountered who at first refused to stop under the orders of the *Cyclone*. Flares fired over the fleeing boat and the launching of a rigid-hull inflatable boat (RIB) with a crew of SEALs onboard caused the smugglers' ship to try and wait out the larger craft as it came to rest in shallow waters.

The USS *Tempest* at dockside. The rubber boats that support SEAL operations can be seen at the stern, next to the rear deck that allows the easy recovery of SEALs in the water.

U.S. Navy

The next day, a combined party of SEALs from the *Cyclone* and six Canadian sailors from HMCS *Terra Nova,* a CJTF craft that had come onto the scene, conducted a board-and-search operation very close to those VBSS ops conducted during DESERT SHIELD/DESERT STORM. Contraband (embargoed) goods were found aboard the smuggler's ship, and it was impounded and towed to Guantanamo Bay.

The economic situation on Haiti continued to deteriorate, and more refugees tried to come into U.S. waters. The Clinton administration sought for and received approval on 31 July 1994 from the UN Security Council to lead a military invasion of Haiti to reinstate Aristide. Fifteen thousand multinational forces would conduct the invasion, the bulk of them being from the United States.

The threat of Operation UPHOLD DEMOCRACY was first established with the orders given to General Shalikashvili, the Chairman of the Joint Chiefs of Staff, to execute the invasion within ten days of 10 September 1994. Navy SEALs conducted a hydrographic sur-

A Rigid Inflatable Boat (RIB) bounces up into the air as it rides the waves with SEALs and crewmen from the Special Boat Teams aboard.

vey of the invasion site along Cap Haitien during the night of 16–17 September. The invasion was prepared and planned to go ahead within days.

On 21 September 1994, a last-minute deal brokered by American politicians and the military rulers of Haiti changed the format of the invasion. The troops landed unopposed and relatively peacefully the morning of 19 September 1994. The patrol craft *Monsoon* (PC-4) became the first U.S. ship to enter the harbor of Port-au-Prince on 19 September. The new patrol craft had proven their worth off the waters of Haiti as both effective military craft and operational SEAL-launching platforms. The patrol craft and deployed SEALs remained off the shores of Haiti for some time after the landings.

On 31 March 1995, Operation UPHOLD DEMOCRACY became RESTORE DEMOCRACY as the UN mission took over in Haiti.

Chapter 14

BOSNIA: OPERATION JOINT ENDEAVOR/ OPERATION JOINT GUARD

Yugoslavia and the Balkans area in general has suffered through centuries of fragmentation, occupation, and unrest that stretch back to the days of the Roman Empire. In the post–World War II world, Yugoslavia, which had only been named as a country in 1929, was held together and controlled by one man. After the defeat of Nazi Germany and the ousting of its occupying forces from Yugoslavia in 1945, elections were held that WWII leader Joseph Tito won easily with 90 percent of the vote. Very quickly, Tito transformed Yugoslavia into a Communist republic under his solid control.

Tito's death in 1980 caused some serious unrest in Yugoslavia, but it continued to be governed as a Soviet state. The harsh system of Tito's government did continue to be relaxed during the 1980s, with nationalistic tendencies continuing to rise among the separate ethnic peoples of the country. With the general fall of communism and the breaking of the Iron Curtain starting in the late 1980s, Yugoslavia began a final breakup as a country. On 3 March 1992, the Muslim and Serbian population of Bosnia-Herzegovinia declared themselves an independent country.

The Bosnian-Serbs soon began an internal armed struggle for control of the newly independent state. The term *ethnic cleansing* took on meaning as the Bosnian-Serbs raised an army and seized more than 70 percent of Bosnia. The resistance of the Muslim-Croatian coalition soon changed the situation in Bosnia to one that was considered an international humanitarian crisis.

A UN protection force was deployed to Bosnia to ensure that aid to the civilian population and the estimated five million displaced persons in the area was not interfered with. Attempts to force a peace settlement on the strife-torn area failed within a year.

U.S. forces airlifted and dropped in supplies to cut-off groups of civilian populations during Operation PROVIDE PROMISE, which ran from 3 July 1992 to 1 October 1994. After thousands of civilian Serbs and Muslims had been killed in the fighting, a formal peace agreement, developed in Dayton, Ohio, in November 1995 and signed in Paris, France, on 14 December that same year, was established. Operation JOINT ENDEAVOR was put forward to implement the terms of the Dayton Peace Accords.

The U.S. Special Operations Command Europe (SOCEUR) had been involved with the peace efforts in Bosnia since February 1993. At that time, the Joint Special Operations Task Force 2 (JSOTF2) was established. The general mission assignments of JSOTF2 included combat search-and-rescue, fire support, air drops, and the VBSS operations necessary to enforce a UN blockade of former Yugoslavian waters to unauthorized ships. The blockade had been conducted as Operation MARITIME GUARD from 1 November 1992 to 14 June 1993 and then as Operation SHARP GUARD from 15 June 1993 to 18 June 1996.

Rumored and unofficially reported SEAL actions in Bosnia included a wide range of missions. Verified SEAL missions include the hydrographic survey of the Sava River in Croatia in December 1995. The operation was conducted by SEALs from Delta and Hotel Platoons of SEAL Team Two, part of SEAL Team Two Task Unit Alpha. The fast-moving river was at the border of Croatia and Bosnia, and U.S. Army engineers wanted to put a pontoon bridge across the fast-moving, very cold waters.

The SEAL detachment conducted the operation in water that gave them zero visibility. The normal dangers of the operation from the cold, muddy, fast-moving waters were increased by the situation in the area and the aftermath of the war. The SEALs remained in body armor and were armed when on the surface and shoreline. That did little to protect them from floating debris in the water, though, including a dead cow that floated by.

The missions of the SEALs at the river included the hydrographic survey as well as taking bottom samples of the riverbed. The three hundred-meter-wide river had a current of three to five knots. The severe current in the river sapped even the SEALs' strength in swimming.

A later repeat of the SEALs' mission to include a search for lost weapons was conducted in late January with the intent being the erection of a permanent causeway. Two M16 rifles had been lost by U.S. forces in the rapidly moving river. Although the SEALs searched, they were unable to find the weapons. The SEALs also later surveyed a partially destroyed bridge at Brcko in Bosnia-Herzegovinia. The SEALs' assistance in providing a gift to the people of Bosnia included an open road in Croatia, and a soon-to-be-in-place bridge courtesy of the U.S. Army.

Other missions were conducted by the SEALs in Bosnia but have yet to be declassified—some of the operations may never be reported to the public at large.

■ Chapter 15

AFGHANISTAN: OPERATION ENDURING FREEDOM/OPERATION ANACONDA

In the mid-morning hours of 11 September 2001, the people of downtown New York City witnessed what they at first thought was the most horrendous air crash in modern U.S. history. In stunned disbelief, at 8:45 A.M., the normally unshakable New Yorkers watched the Boeing 767 of American Airlines Flight 11 smash into the upper floors of the 1,300-foot-tall North Tower of the World Trade Center.

Such a crash of a large aircraft into a skyscraper hadn't happened since 28 July 1945, when a B-25 bomber plowed into the seventy-eighth floor of the Empire State Building. That accident happened during wartime, and the casualties were relatively light. What the New Yorkers watching the smoke billow out from the North Tower didn't know was that they were seeing the first major attack of a new war.

Eleven minutes after the first plane struck, those same New York people knew that what they had seen was no accident. A second plane, Flight 175, a United Airlines Boeing 767, flying from Boston Airport, smashed into the South Tower of the World Trade Center.

Thousands of pounds of fuel from the two jet aircraft, both filled for a cross-country flight, ignited and burned. The tall towers of the World Trade Center were breached and acted as chimneys, feeding air to the massive fire. Rather than face death by the flames, many individuals who had been trapped above the impact floors chose to jump to their deaths on the concrete hundreds of feet below. A lasting image of one such jumper, who might have been a skydiver, was captured on film. The camera tracked the individual as he maintained perfect form while he hurtled to the ground, smoke trailing from the clothes burning on his back.

The bodies on the cold ground did not have long to wait in the open. At 9:50 A.M., the South Tower collapsed, killing and injuring thousands. A huge billow of smoke and dust roared through the streets of New York, a sight of such magnitude that it had never been seen before outside of Hollywood special effects in a disaster film. Only this was no movie.

The South Tower collapsed almost straight down as its structure gave in to the massive damage and steel-softening fire. At 10:29 A.M., the North Tower collapsed. The steel, glass, and concrete of the upper floors drove down through the building, causing the lower floors to explode outward in their collapse. The tall radio spire on top of the tower remained pointing up as it fell until it descended into the roiling cloud of smoke, dust, and ash.

Earlier, at 9:38 A.M., prior to the collapse of the towers, the Boeing 757 of American Airlines Flight 77 plowed into the northwest side of the Pentagon near Washington, D.C. A fourth plane, the Boeing 757 of United Airlines Flight 93 bound for San Francisco, crashed into the ground near Shanksville, Pennsylvania.

All the flights had been hijacked by terrorist members of al-Qaeda and followers of Osama bin Laden. The passengers of Flight 93 learned about the fate of the other hijacked planes through the cell phones some of the passengers had. They made the fateful decision to try to take back the plane—an action that cost them all their lives but may have saved thousands on the ground.

The people of the United States wanted vengeance. They wanted the leader of al-Qaeda, Osama bin Laden, brought to justice and punished for his crimes. The Taliban government of

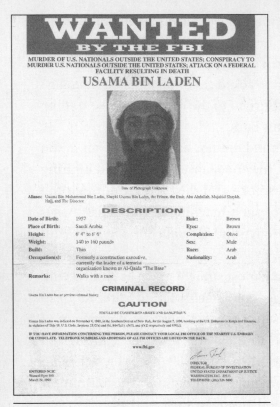

WANTED
BY THE FBI

MURDER OF U.S. NATIONALS OUTSIDE THE UNITED STATES; CONSPIRACY TO
MURDER U.S. NATIONALS OUTSIDE THE UNITED STATES; ATTACK ON A FEDERAL
FACILITY RESULTING IN DEATH

USAMA BIN LADEN

Date of Photograph Unknown

Aliases: Usama Bin Muhammad Bin Ladin, Shaykh Usama Bin Ladin, the Prince, the Emir, Abu Abdallah, Mujahid Shaykh, Hajj, and The Director

DESCRIPTION

Date of Birth:	1957	Hair:	Brown
Place of Birth:	Saudi Arabia	Eyes:	Brown
Height:	6' 4" to 6' 6"	Complexion:	Olive
Weight:	140 to 160 pounds	Sex:	Male
Build:	Thin	Race:	Arab
Occupation(s):	Formerly a construction executive, currently the leader of a terrorist organization known as Al-Qaida "The Base"	Nationality:	Arab
Remarks:	Walks with a cane		

CRIMINAL RECORD

Usama Bin Laden has no previous criminal history.

CAUTION

SHOULD BE CONSIDERED ARMED AND DANGEROUS

Usama Bin Laden was indicted on November 4, 1998, in the Southern District of New York, for the August 7, 1998, bombing of the U.S. Embassies in Kenya and Tanzania, in violation of Title 18, U.S. Code, Sections 2332(a) and (b), 844(f)(1), (f)(3), and (f)(2) respectively and 930(a).

IF YOU HAVE INFORMATION CONCERNING THIS PERSON, PLEASE CONTACT YOUR LOCAL FBI OFFICE OR THE NEAREST U.S. EMBASSY OR CONSULATE. TELEPHONE NUMBERS AND ADDRESSES OF ALL FBI OFFICES ARE LISTED ON THE BACK.

www.fbi.gov

DIRECTOR
FEDERAL BUREAU OF INVESTIGATION
UNITED STATES DEPARTMENT OF JUSTICE
WASHINGTON, D.C. 20535
TELEPHONE: (202) 324-3000

ENTERED NCIC
Wanted Flyer 589
March 29, 1999

The official Wanted poster issued by U.S. Department of Justice for Osama bin Laden. This poster was sent out by the FBI several years before the events of 9-11 made bin Laden the most wanted man in the world.

Federal Bureau of Investigation

Afghanistan was harboring bin Laden and refused to surrender him. The Islamic Fundamentalist Talibans had long been known to harbor terrorists and allow them safe haven in the mountains, passes, and caves of Afghanistan. Terrorism was nothing new to them, and its use against non-Muslims was not only allowed, it was sanctified by the Taliban mullahs.

After repeated warnings to give up bin Laden, and the Talibans continual refusal to do so, President George W. Bush initiated Operation ENDURING FREEDOM, the American War on Terrorism in Afghanistan. On 7 October 2001, military targets in Afghanistan began to receive the first of many strikes against them by U.S. aircraft. By 19 October, more than one hundred Rangers landed in Afghanistan for a raid near Kandahar. The campaign against the Taliban and al-Qaeda in Afghanistan had fully begun.

The war in Afghanistan quickly turned into a ground campaign by Special Operations soldiers. The visible military targets of the Taliban and al-Qaeda were quickly eliminated by air strikes, but the majority of the terrorists were hiding in caves and tunnels under the rocky mountains of Afghanistan. The Soviet Union had finally called it quits when they invaded Afghanistan in the 1980s. The

United States had no intention of remaining in Afghanistan after the elimination of the Taliban and al-Qaeda as functioning units. That made the people of Afghanistan generally look to the U.S. forces as liberators.

The U.S. Special Operations forces in Afghanistan included elements from the Army, Navy, and Air Force. Navy SEALs were on the ground in the fighting regardless of Afghanistan being a land-locked country and even drinkable water being sometimes hard to find. A twelve-hour mission was planned in January to put special operations forces, led by a SEAL platoon, into the Zawar Kili cave complex to search out the area. On 6 January, the units went in. They didn't come back out until January 14.

The SOCOM operators and SEALs, part of Task Force K-Bar, scoured more than seventy caves during the operation, which covered a three-mile-long ravine near the Pakistani border. They found caches of weapons, ammunition, supplies, and a treasure trove of intelligence information. The intel materials included planning documents, New York City tourist posters, and other landmarks around the United States.

In spite of the success of the operation, the strain on the SEALs and other SOCOM operators was severe. They had been running light in terms of food, water, and shelter equipment. The twelve-hour mission becoming one eight days long forced the operators to face dehydration, hunger, and subfreezing temperatures for two days before additional supplies could be flown in.

To survive as the sleet and snow started coming down in the thin air of their encampment at 6,500 feet, the SOCOM operators moved into three abandoned villages in the ravines around Zawar Kili. Inside the simple mud huts, they found clothes and blankets they were able to use to keep warm. Al-Qaeda supplies were used as a last resort when the food started to run out, but as the SEAL commander suggested, the goat meat they were able to locate was "not good."

The SEALs were in a "boots on the ground" mission, which meant that they would face the Taliban and al-Qaeda forces face-to-face. The SOCOM operators used all the means at their disposal to fight the al-Qaeda forces, including air strikes with heavy bombs that were called in dangerously close to the SOCOM positions. In the words of the SEAL platoon commander, "We were able to surprise them. They did not surprise us." There were daily firefights, though no SOCOM personnel were hit or wounded. More than a dozen enemy forces were killed with an additional eight subjects detained for further questioning.

SOCOM operators also conducted a ninety-minute raid on a five-building complex at Yaya Kehyl in Paktika Province. There, the intelligence finds included sophisticated satellite phones, operational computers filled with al-Qaeda data, stockpiles of weapons, and two pounds of unrefined opium. At almost every target hit by the SOCOM forces, they found what were being called "terrorist escape kits." The kits were suitcases filled with clothes, small arms, Pakistani currency, passports, and work visas. The materials were packed and ready to be grabbed up by a terrorist operative trying to flee Afghanistan.

In spite of the hardships and danger of their operations, the morale of the SEALs and the special operations forces in general was very good. They were fighting "the good fight," taking the terror to the terrorists and denying them a safe haven. But the situation was anything but safe for the men of the Teams and SOCOM. Casualties were taken by SOCOM and the SEALs.

One of the biggest ground attacks of the Afghan campaign was Operation ANACONDA. Delayed from beginning for twenty-four hours while B-52 heavy bombers and other aircraft strafed and attacked Taliban and al-Qaeda positions, as many as two hundred Taliban and al-Qaeda followers were killed in the first four days of ANACONDA.

The first Navy SEAL killed in action since the Paitilla Airfield action during Operation JUST CAUSE was Aviation Boatswains Mate (Handling) (SEAL) 1st Class Neil Roberts, who was killed on 4 March in eastern Afghanistan. The MH-47E Chinook helicopter Roberts was riding in was operating in support of Operation ANACONDA. At around 3 A.M. on Monday, 4 March 2002, the helicopter that Roberts was riding in was struck by a rocket-propelled grenade just as it touched down.

The helicopter and a second bird in the flight immediately took off from the hot landing zone to fly off and check for damage. What wasn't known was that Neil Roberts had fallen from the MH-47E when the rocket hit and the bird took off.

An unmanned Predator gave the commanders real-time access to a video of the SEAL being captured by al-Qaeda forces. Roberts did not go down without a fight, and his death is being investigated for a possible Congressional Medal of Honor. At least one report has Roberts single-handedly attacking a machine gun nest to prevent it from hitting the helicopters as they escaped.

A large number of SOCOM troops immediately boarded helicopters to go in and rescue Roberts or at least recover his body. The Teams do not leave anyone behind—ever. The resulting twelve-hour battle cost the lives of seven U.S. servicemen and eleven more were wounded before the helicopters could evacuate the SOCOM forces. Circling AC-130 gunships poured down a hail of steel and high explosives at the approaching al-Qaeda forces as the SOCOM unit extracted.

Roberts had been last seen from the overhead Predator being dragged off by al-Qaeda men. His body was recovered later. Roberts was apparently shot at the hands of his captors.

Later in the month, on 28 March, SEAL Chief Hospital Corpsman Matthew Bourgeois was killed while conducting small-unit training near Kandahar. There was no enemy fire involved, and Bourgeois was killed after apparently stepping on a mine or other piece of unexploded ordnance. The lands of Afghanistan are littered with mines and other ordnance left over from the years of Soviet occupation and fighting and the years of near civil warfare that followed.

In August 2002, two SEALs from the West Coast teams were wounded by enemy gunfire during intelligence gathering operations in the Oruzgan Province of southern Afghanistan. Both SEALs were shot in the legs during the early morning hours. They were able to be medevaced out to a field hospital and later moved on to more permanent medical facilities.

■ Chapter 16

TRAINING: THE BUILDING OF AN OPERATOR

There is no single item that ties the Teams together like the basic training that all operators have to go through to enter the UDTs or the SEALs. No matter what era a SEAL or a Frogman was in, he can share training stories that each man can understand. Whether they went through Underwater Demolition Team Replacement training or Basic Underwater Demolition/SEAL training from the early 1970s to today, every operator in the Teams has shared the common experience of training.

Each training class is known by a number. It isn't any exotic code, simply the consecutive number of the class in the history of training. Classes used to be run on both the East and West Coasts, and Teams would supply instructors for their own replacements training. But with the graduation of the last East Coast class in August 1971, all BUD/S training is done on the West Coast at Coronado, California.

An operator's class number is something that no man will consciously forget. It would take a disease or injury to make a Teammate forget that number that indicated to him the men he first trained with. Along with the number, the names of his Teammates are something a SEAL or Frogman expects to take to the grave with him. And the number of a student's class is not classified by the Navy. It doesn't matter to the Navy who attended BUD/S or UDTR, only if they graduated and where they served afterward. The class numbers are effectively a matter of public record, although the Teams make sure the numbers aren't *that* available to the public at large.

BUD/S is conducted a number of times each year at the Naval Special Warfare Training Command in Coronado. The "Schoolhouse," as it is known in the Teams, is located in sunny, pleasant, Southern California, close to the U.S. border with Mexico with the waters of the Pacific to the West and the protected waters of San Diego Bay a short distance to the east.

The sunny weather the San Diego area is known for does little to warm the Pacific waters off the SEAL Training compound. The California current running close offshore maintains itself with water from Alaska, water that remains close to 55° F throughout the year. The California current waters mix with the warmer waters of the Pacific off California, but the warmth of the water is only relative. BUD/S instructors maintain a close watch on their students as they force them to sit in the cold water. A time chart, stopwatch, and thermometer readings of the water add up to a safety measure against hypothermia—although the miserable, shivering, cold students wouldn't know that or care if they did.

Training has gotten more sophisticated over the years, and the course has grown longer—it's twenty-six weeks long at the time of this writing (2002). Exercises have changed, as has equipment. As older gear became worn and unavailable, it was replaced with modern components. In some cases, the newer gear, boats, life

A line of BUD/S students struggle up the sand berms in Coronado, carrying their rubber boats along with them.

U.S. Navy

jackets, etc. are lighter and stronger. Exercises that were found to cause more physical damage than good have been dropped or modified. But one thing has not changed at BUD/S—it hasn't gotten any easier.

The one thing that is easy at BUD/S is quitting. It is intentionally made that way. The basic philosophy is that anyone who is in fairly good shape could get through a week or so of BUD/S. But when the course is twenty-six weeks long, and each week makes even more physical demands on the individual than the week before, it takes a special mental discipline, a drive, to go the distance. This drive is especially important because it is so easy to quit.

A student can DOR, drop on request, at any time during the training. Once he has quit, the ex-student is gone from the training usually within the day. Students wear painted helmet liners during their training, and the color of the liner indicates the phase of training they are in. During the earlier years of UDTR, a student taking off his helmet liner was enough to signify that he was quitting.

Today, there is a brass ship's bell hanging at the northeast corner of the training compound. Ringing that bell three times is the signal that the individual is quitting. Given that some of the individuals at BUD/S have never failed at any real challenge in their young lives before, the walk to that bell can be the longest one they've ever taken.

The individual attitude of a student and their personal resolve to complete the course mean the most toward an individual getting through the training than any other single attribute. Tremendous high school and college athletes, excellent physical specimens, have attended BUD/S and they have failed because they didn't have the drive to complete the course. Any student who completes the physical screening tests to enter BUD/S has the physical necessities to complete the course—if they have the heart and the drive.

There is no single physical type that is an example of a SEAL. The men of the Teams are tall, short, stocky, slender, muscular, and slight. They are never fat, but they can be big. What all the graduates of BUD/S share is a very positive mental attitude. They are fit and in shape, and they are supremely confident that they can do the job, no matter what the job is. If they don't know how to complete a specific task, they will either learn, or find a Teammate who knows how to do it. It is as a Team that the SEALs accomplish their missions. The learning of just what it means to be a Team begins at BUD/S.

Arriving at BUD/S is a bit of a shock to newcomers. The center court of the main building at the training center is a large, square expanse of packed and leveled asphalt. Painted on the surface of the asphalt and facing north are sets of swim fins. These are where the students will stand as they face the small podium at the northern wall. On that podium, an instructor will stand and run them through calisthenic exercises—lots of exercises. The big square is known as the grinder. On its rough surface, thousands of strong young men have been ground down. What finally stood on the grinder were men on their way to the Teams—SEALs.

A SEAL demonstrates an unusual rope skill during a demonstration at the UDT-SEAL Museum in Fort Pierce, Florida.

Kevin Dockery

There are three phases of training and an introductory or beginning time period. The first weeks of training are referred to as the indoctrination period, the time before a class formally "classes up" and begins training. Now sometimes referred to as Fourth Phase, the initial time gives the students a chance to learn the basic exercises, skills they will need, and procedures that they will be expected to follow while at BUD/S. More important, it is a time that allows the students who were not sure of why they were at BUD/S, or were insufficiently prepared physically, to drop out of training without being officially counted in the class totals.

There is a large dropout rate at BUD/S. The instructors simply say that the course is not for everyone. Sixty percent of a class dropping out is not unusual. Between one hundred and twenty and one hundred and forty students might start training as a class, and only twenty to thirty will be expected to eventually finish. At one point, an entire class disappeared. No one graduated.

After Fourth Phase is completed, the students will have learned their basic combat swimming strokes, the side stroke and the breast stroke. These are used because they expose the absolute minimum parts of a swimmer above the water. The side stroke is also a very useful, maximum-efficiency long-distance stroke—and the students will be doing a lot of long-distance swimming.

About every two to three months, a new BUD/S class begins training at First Phase. Their helmets are painted green with each student's name and their class number stenciled on in white. As the days go on during training, the helmets of the students who dropped out will be lined up next to the bell at the corner of the grinder—mute testimony of those who couldn't make it and a motivation booster for those who remain in training. More than one BUD/S student has heard the bell ring and knew a classmate was gone but that he was still there.

And the students will need every bit of motivation they can get for the rigors of First Phase. Exercises will be conducted several times every day. The physical training, PT, seems more like a constant thing to the harried students. And they are chased, harassed, and needled by their instructors, each one a very qualified SEAL who is trying to make sure that only the best will go on to graduate and join the Teams.

Instructors for BUD/S are more than just impressive; they are very imposing figures, especially those instructors in First Phase. These SEALs are volunteers from the Special Warfare community, all the combined Teams. Only the very top percent of the SEALs qualify to be instructors. They have to be proven operators to begin with. On top of the skills that the instructors bring with them from their experience in the Teams, they are given further training to make certain that they can develop a good, high-quality BUD/S product and that what they do and know how to do is as safe as it can be made. They are consummate professionals at their jobs.

The Teams operate in a very dangerous environment. Just their operations in the open sea are conducted in an environment that can easily kill you if you make a mistake. Meticulous attention to detail prevents accidents. And when an accident does happen, careful and complete analysis of the situation helps prevent that accident from ever happening again. But the SEALs do operate in a dangerous world. If the students get scared of what they are told to do, that's fine with the instructors. You can be scared, that's a normal human reaction to danger. But it is how you act even though you are scared that matters.

And the students can be very scared, or at least apprehensive, of one part of First Phase: Hell Week. That is the fifth week of training, originally officially called Indoctrination Week during the World War II days at Fort Pierce. Listed on the official training schedules as Motivation Week, this time period has been named from almost its very inception as Hell Week.

During the first years of training in World War II, Hell Week was the first week of training. The Team had no time to waste on someone who couldn't cut it as an operator. So Hell Week became the fastest way of getting rid of the dead wood.

Draper Kauffman, the individual who founded the original Naval Combat Demolition Unit training at Fort Pierce and who is considered the father of the UDTs, looked to the most physically demanding course of training in the Navy at that time in 1943. Training at Fort Pierce were the Scouts and Raiders. They had a very demanding course of PT, put together by the best individuals available at that time. Kauffman and his staff took the weeks-long training schedule of the Scouts and Raiders and condensed it to a single week. That was Hell Week.

The concept behind that demanding time is multifold. First, it was Kauffman's opinion that an individual was capable of ten times the physical output that they thought possible. All an individual had to do was learn that the mind could drive the body past what had been considered possible. Second, Hell Week brought out the motivation in the individual, the "won't quit" attitude. Individuals who went through that week would not stop when the going got tough, they proved that. Third, Hell Week exposed an individual to explosions, noise, fear, lack of sleep, and physical exhaustion. It was as close as training could come to simulating the combat environment, especially what it was like on an invasion beach. If a person couldn't hack Hell Week,

A fully equipped SEAL demonstrating the equipment and weapons he would carry during an operation. This is a far cry from the "naked warrior" of the UDT during World War II, but underneath all of the modern gear is the same warrior.

Kevin Dockery

it was better to find out right at the start rather than later when it could cost men their lives.

Hell Week is a full week, from Sunday night to Saturday, of constant, nonstop activity. Students are scheduled to receive four hours of sleep total for the entire week. Sometimes the students regret even getting that small amount of sleep. It isn't that they aren't exhausted; it's that they have to get up afterward and keep going.

From that first night, the students are wet, cold, and confused. Men who cannot face the cold cannot operate in the water. The value of the rigors of Hell Week have been proven time and time

In spite of the constant reminder that Teamwork is the essence of being a SEAL, students are also asked to put out the maximum possible effort from the individual. Here, a single BUD/S student carries a massive outboard motor over the sand.

U.S. Navy

again in combat. Men who have passed Hell Week know they can make it, no matter what obstacles rise up in their way. They know this fact simply because they have completed Hell Week. Very little can compare to it.

The Teams demand the maximum effort an individual can give—and more. But it is as a Team that a class completes Hell Week and BUD/S. Students learn to depend on each other unlike they have ever depended on anyone in their lives. This is one of the reasons that no one ever forgets their Hell Week or the men they survived it with.

Crawling through the mud, exposed to the cold and wet, rocked by explosions and noise, and forced to complete evolutions that look impossible, are all part of Hell Week. An evolution in training is a event. It can be a simple as a period of exercise, a boat drill, or the completion of the obstacle course. Hell Week is considered the biggest single evolution of training, although completing it hardly means that an individual will get though BUD/S.

Valuable students who are injured, but who the instructors consider worthwhile material, can be "rolled back." They are held back to the next class and allowed to heal as needed. If the student who is rolled back has completed Hell Week, he will join the next class after they have completed that evolution. If he hasn't completed Hell Week, or if he only went through part of it before he was injured, the rolled-back student gets to do the whole thing again.

After First Phase comes Second Phase, where the students paint their helmets red and go on to learn diving operations. This is the phase where students must be able to learn complicated dive physics and physiology to continue training. They must be able to operate underwater with very dangerous equipment. The breathing equipment is as safe as it can be made, but without knowing the rules and limitations of the human body underwater, a swimmer can be killed before he ever knows it. Even excellent physical students who could get through First Phase as leaders, bringing their classmates along with them, have failed training because of the academic side of Second Phase.

Third Phase is land warfare, where the students wear a blue helmet and learn the tools of their trade. Basic weapons, explosives, demolitions, tactics, and operations are taught in this phase. At the end of the course, the student will be standing on the grinder one last time to receive his graduation certificate from BUD/S. That is when each man will ring the bell to indicate he is leaving and going on to the Teams. Actually, they will be going on to more training.

After BUD/S graduation, the students will be sent to Fort Benning, Georgia, where they will complete the basic three-week Army Airborne course that will qualify the students as basic paratroopers.

Instead of going on to an assignment to a Team and a six-month probationary period after Fort Benning, students go back to Coronado and complete the SEAL qualification program. The fifteen-week-long program instructs the students in the more advanced skills used in the Teams. They learn combat swimming, further demolitions, and advanced patrolling. After they complete the program successfully, the students receive their Tridents, the Naval Special Warfare insignia, the outward uniform symbol of a Navy SEAL.

Joseph Valderrama, Engineman First Class

I was first exposed to the Teams as a trainee in 1976 until I finally graduated in 1979. Then I went to SEAL Team One. The SEALs were something I first heard about while I was in boot camp when a friend of mine, Mark Scolari, had a buddy in the SEAL Teams. He started to talk to me about his buddy who was a BUD/S trainee, what a crazy man he was, and how he fit in well with the persona of a Navy SEAL.

At the time, being a SEAL wasn't something I wanted to do. While I was standing in the classification line in boot camp, I thought I was going to be a photographer's mate. It ended up that my interest was in photography and I didn't have an A-school. My brothers had told me that if you didn't have an A-school rating in the Navy, you were going to be chipping paint. Through my friend Mark, I found out that if you pass the BUD/S screening test, they'll give you an A-school.

So right there in the classification line, I decided to let the chief behind the counter know that I wanted to be a Navy SEAL. He was asking for my Form 509 or whatever it was, to say that I was qualified for BUD/S. I didn't have any form at all, so I ended up taking the BUD/S screening test right there at boot camp. Out of eighteen people, I was the only one to make it through the screening test.

The screening test gave me a taste of what I would be facing at BUD/S, but it was a small taste. When I finally arrived in Coronado, I was very apprehensive. I knew there were some things to be afraid of, and I knew that there were some things in training that I probably would enjoy. Basically, that information had come from the men who had given me the screening test.

The tester's conversation was with a friend of his while I was taking the test. He was talking about something I wasn't used to hearing as a nineteen-year-old. These things they were talking about let me know that I was going to be getting into something different.

The physical end of training was something I enjoyed. My attitude was that this was something I was going to do for the rest of my life. I fully enjoyed it. There were times when the instructors put us into the surf zone and I was having a good time and the officer in charge came up and told me to knock it off—I was having too much fun and it might project the wrong impression on the instructors.

Hell Week, the first time, was tough, but this was something I wanted to do. So I never thought about quitting. I had been on the ocean my entire life, and I loved it. The instructors who put me through training were men I would do anything for. And Hell Week was just something I had to do to be one of them.

The first incident that really stands out in my mind about that Hell Week was a very valuable lesson. It had to do with an insertion point. When you insert somewhere, you have to make sure that it is the exact spot you were supposed to go in at. The incident had to do with myself and my swim buddy. It was the third day of Hell Week, and everybody was cold. We were all cold and I thought we would swim in to the beach, just turn around, and signal the rest of the guys in without doing a recon of the beach area or anything. We would just get them in because it was cold.

We got to the beach and there was an instructor up on the berm. I figured he was just observing us. Not seeing any reaction from the instructor, we didn't do the recon, spun around, and signaled the boat in. When I turned around, my swim partner was gone. I figured he was maybe scouting the beach, so I didn't really think much about his being missing and kept signaling the boat in.

The boat came in about fifty yards south of where my swim buddy and I had landed. When I turned back around to get my swim buddy so we could rejoin the boat crew, he had reappeared. I was calling his name, but he wouldn't respond. So I picked up some small rocks and threw them at him while saying, "Come on, let's go."

When I turned to go, I was immediately tackled to the sand, spun around, and two hands grabbed my throat. The instructor on top of me said I was dead. Then he proceeded to go down to the boat and kill everybody in my boat crew. After it was all said and done, the instructors took us for a little extracurricular activity. Then we were told about an operation in Vietnam that entailed a whole company of Marines who had been helicoptered in to the wrong insertion point and slaughtered. That wasn't something I have ever forgotten, and insertion points were very important after that.

By the end of Hell Week, things were all kind of a blur when they secured us. We were at Gator Beach, and back then they had beer there. We had a couple beers and I was thinking about getting back to the barracks and crawling in that rack. It was probably the first thought that came to me after I heard those words, "Hell Week is secured." Sleep, that was a good thought right about then.

I had difficulty graduating my first class. I failed the diving physics portion of the diving phase. I was given the opportunity to take a makeup test, took that, and failed it as well. Then, the instructors did something that they normally don't do and gave me a third try. But I failed that one as well and was academically dis-enrolled.

BUD/S training isn't all physical. The most important aspect about going through training, as far as the physical, heart, or mental aspect, I think is the determination. It is your heart, but also, because of the structure of BUD/S, the mental aspect is heavy also. The psychological portion of the training is tough. As far as the instructors go, you have to be mentally strong to overcome the adversity they throw your way.

We did a run on San Clemente Island. It was a long, hard, run as it stood, and the instructor asked, "Who wants to go another two miles?" Well, you're not going to say you don't want to go another two miles. What you're going to say is, "Yes, let's go another two miles."

That's the way I look at training as far as the mental aspect goes. You have to be prepared for that. I guess your heart will follow.

It took two months, but I did get back into a class. Going through BUD/S the second time was harder in that I knew what was coming and I started thinking ahead. The worst thing you can do is to start anticipating. You're wet, cold, and sandy now, and you know you're going to be wet, cold, and sandy tomorrow. Once you start doing that, you've more or less lost the "bubble," the insulated world you withdraw yourself into and just do things as they come. That's when you'll break down.

Diving was the Third Phase when I went through the first class. The time period between my first and second BUD/S class was two months. The time between my second BUD/S class and when I finally graduated was two years. When I was thinking ahead in my second class, that wet, cold, and sandy day after day just caused me to hit the wall and say enough. I DOR'd, dropped on request.

For two years, I was in the Fleet Navy, serving on an LST (Landing Ship, Tank). I knew I wanted to go back when my ship was in Subic in the Philippines and I ran into all the friends I had back in Class 90. I saw what they were doing, which was laying around the pool getting suntans while I was working in the scullery onboard a ship. I was willing to go back and endure another six months of BUD/S so I could lay out by the pool and get a suntan.

I don't know if going through BUD/S three times is an unusual situation, I think there are a lot of guys who have gone through multiple times. Mr. Todd, who was a mustang officer, pulled some strings for me and got me orders back two months later that first return. That was unusual.

By the time I got to the third BUD/S class I attended, I had refocused and had found that same spark I had the first time I went through. I was going to make it. This time through, I was married and I told my wife, "Sorry, but graduating from this training is my number-one priority right now." I ended up graduating with Class 104 in 1979.

I honestly don't remember much of the last Hell Week I went through. I remember more of the Class 90 Hell Week than I do of Class 104's. What I do remember is that during that last try, I never thought about quitting. Finally, it was instilled in me to make sure I studied a lot harder and different than I had the first time.

The center of the BUD/S compound is the grinder, the exercise and parade ground. The SEAL grinder is a big, square piece of asphalt that gets very hot during the summertime. You can burn your hands on its surface. I never really thought about why they called it the grinder before right now. I think it's because we're put into the grinder so to speak, and that's where we conducted most of our physical evolutions, the calisthenics. It ground you up and spit you out, because it's also the last place you stand when you graduate.

Standing on the grinder that last day, we had Admiral Lyons as a guest speaker. (He went on to become the mayor of Oceanside, California.) Standing up there for graduation that beautiful California morning, shaking hands with the admiral, getting my diploma, and having a look around the grinder at all the people there—there were even other BUD/S classes that sang to us—it was a swelling feeling, and it was a relief. Finally, finally, I had made it.

The first place I was assigned was SEAL Team One. Like everyone else, I was in a probationary period for my first six months. I wasn't immediately in a platoon until about four months after my arrival in September. All of us new arrivals were officially on probation as far as our abilities to accomplish the basic skills of a SEAL.

After successfully completing our probation, we were awarded the NEC, Naval Enlisted Code, that says you're a SEAL, and you get your Trident. Pinning the Trident on my uniform added some height and weight to me. It was something I feel was in my blood, and it definitely reflects who I am. It's a nice, big, piece of gold on my uniform that tells everybody that I just completed the toughest training in the world. Receiving it was one of the proudest moments of my life.

My first years in the Teams were spent at SEAL Team One. Then, I was transferred over to the new SEAL Team Three, where I held plankowner status. I didn't look back on the history of the UDTs when they were turned into SEAL Teams in 1983. I had been a SEAL my whole time in the community. There was always that playful animosity between the UDTs and the SEAL Teams. The old saying was that you were just UDT, and we were only a SEAL Team.

What I think about now when I see a Underwater Demolition sticker on a vehicle with Freddie the Frog on it, if it's a young guy behind the wheel, I wonder if he really knows the significance of that emblem. The UDT mission was a lot different from the SEAL mission. It's a shame these young guys don't know more about the UDT.

The connection between myself as a SEAL and that Naked Warrior, the UDT man of World War II, is a tough one to make. I think those World War II guys were just hard as nails. They were absolutely a special breed, the forerunners to the elite unit known as the SEAL Teams. I think that's a legacy that should definitely always be in the present. It's where I came from as a SEAL.

Thinking of the Naked Warrior, I think of a man by the name of Tom Winters, who's one of the toughest men I've ever met in my life. He never wore a wet suit while we were in Korea. He had been a Naked Warrior, an Underwater Demolition Team member. That's no small example to follow.

Even though you leave the Teams, you will never not be a SEAL. There's one thing in common that we all have, and that's the blood and tears that were shed at BUD/S. We've all done it. The only difference are those who have gone on to combat and other accomplishments in the SEAL Teams. That's the only difference between us. But we've all gone through BUD/S. That's the common factor that will be between us forever.

It's funny to think of, but any SEAL who forgets his class number is not a SEAL. I don't know if any class numbers are classified, I've never heard of that. But any SEAL who forgets his class number, isn't a SEAL, and never was.

When I think of the word SEAL, I think of closeness, tight-knit, cohesive, intelligent. The Teams to me are a core group of men who impart the rule that it takes a Team to be successful.

Tom Richards, Rear Admiral, USN (Ret.)

I first showed up at BUD/S training fresh out of Villanova University where I had placed third in the National Collegiate Weightlifting Championships as a heavyweight—that's more than 242 pounds. Afterward, I thought I had trimmed down nicely to about 233 to 235 pounds. But what did I know about going through BUD/S training?

That first day, I was standing out there on "the line," as it's referred to. One of the instructors had seen me at 235 pounds, which was arranged a little bit differently about my person back then. I was standing out there with the rest of the student officers when the instructor asked for the muster report.

The muster report was that we had eight officers and forty-seven enlisted men. But that wasn't what the instructor felt. What he said was that we had seven officers, one gorilla, and the enlisted. Things kind of went downhill from there.

That instructor was Vince Olivera. He said he felt I could go out bear hunting armed with just a switch [stick]. Once he said that, I had an image to maintain at BUD/S.

My Navy career had started without my first thought being to go out for BUD/S. Back in 1964, my father said, "Tom, why don't you go up to the high school and take this Navy ROTC scholarship exam?"

We had discussed my taking up a career in the Navy, where my father had been a petty officer during World War II. My father thought a career as a Naval officer would be a pretty good thing. His impression of an officer in the Navy, and my mother's as well, was that one was not necessarily always down there in the bilges. They used the phrase "three squares and clean sheets."

Well, when I joined the Navy and ended up in Naval Special Warfare, my mother could not exactly understand what it was that her son was doing out in the mud and the blood, getting shot at and all that kind of thing. So although I might have originally gone into the Navy looking for the three squares and clean sheets, that's not exactly what I ended up with.

I first learned about the SEALs while I was still in high school. What I heard about them came from an early article in Reader's Digest. What they said those men did sounded like the kind of thing I wanted to do. Growing up on the southern shore of Long Island, New York, I spent all of my time on the water. If I wasn't on the water—water skiing, boating, or fishing—I was in the water bodysurfing, surfing, or so on. Being in the Navy, small boats and that type of thing is what I thought I was going to be getting in to. So the SEALs sounded about like what I wanted to do.

There's an old expression, "When opportunity knocks, you answer the door." I volunteered for the SEAL Teams because that's what I thought I wanted to do. To be honest, I recognized that I had a different outlook on life. You'll find that everybody in Naval Special Warfare is a risk-taker and an achiever, probably even an overachiever. And that's what I wanted to do—live life to the absolute edge—and so I have.

Whether I was in a summer BUD/S class or a winter one, who cares? The point is that I graduated training. Having been both a student and, later, an instructor, I can tell you that the instructor staff has a way of leveling the pain across the summer and the winter months. I specifically started in the fall (1969) and graduated in the spring (April 1970).

There isn't enough time to talk all about my BUD/S training. It was a great experience. The friendships, the associations that I made during that period of my life, as I overcame some of the most difficult challenges that will ever be presented to me in my life, those associations are the strongest I have had in my life since then.

Training is something that a lot of people know only from what they've seen in the media. There, they talk about how physically challenging SEAL training, specifically Basic Underwater Demolition/SEAL training. They're missing the boat. It isn't about the physical.

Every individual who shows up at BUD/S training today has proven that they have the basic physical skills needed for the course. Everyone who stands tall on the line, day one, week one, has the physical skills to graduate from training. Day one, week one, all that physical stuff is out the door. Now, the question is what do you have between the ears? What kind of guts do you have? What kind of focus do you have? What kind of self-discipline do you have? How far are you willing to go to achieve your goal?

That's not physical, that's all mental. Let me give you a few examples. In my training class, we had a kid who started who had been a junior college runner. He had run a four-minute, fifteen-second mile. By anybody's standard, that's greased lightning. As I remember, they timed my runs using a sun dial; today, they've shifted to a calendar. But I was there at the end, and it didn't matter to me that I was cold, wet, tired, hungry, and miserable. Those are just the facts of life. That's the environment you live in while you go through training. Getting through that is a given that you just have to accept.

This guy, instead of running in his Adidas or his nice little running shorts and a tank top, was running in boots, long pants, and probably a heavy military blouse. And by the way, he's wet.

Have you ever gone running down the beach with a pair of wet boots on? They weigh about five pounds each, so it becomes a given that you're going to run slower. The point is that you're going to run, you're going to keep going and be there at the end. That's what we're looking for in training. We don't need the guy who is the fastest runner or the fastest swimmer. We need the guy who's going to keep swimming, no matter what it takes, to get to where he needs to be.

Mike Thornton was a man in the Teams who is a Medal of Honor recipient. He received that medal because he took the body of Tommy Norris offshore in Vietnam. He was swimming on his E&E (escape and evasion) route, as they had briefed for the mission. He was going to swim until he couldn't swim any longer—and he was going to keep Tommy Norris with him—and that's just what he did. That's the kind of guy we're looking for.

When I went through training, I started with Class 54 and graduated with Class 55. The reason I graduated with Class 55 has been taken care of since then. That is, at the time when I went through training, if you had an injury, you were sort of pushed off to the side—we don't care about this, we don't want to hear about this, and so on. I ended up with a 104-degree temperature from a major infection and was in surgery the day after they admitted me to the hospital. So I wasn't exactly whining.

As a result of my illness, I had to be rolled back from one class to another. So I started with 54, ended with 55, and I have a lot of close friends from both classes.

Just trying to speak about one incident of my Hell Week sort of sells the week short. But one incident I can relate involved an all-night paddle. I believe it was Wednesday night of Hell Week, and I say I believe that was the night because sometime after Monday night of Hell Week, you're no longer completely sure of what day it is.

So there we were that Wednesday night, paddling down the ocean parallel to the Silver Strand south of the training base. We were doing pretty well. "It always pays to be a winner," as they say at BUD/S, so if you're the first boat crew to finish that particular paddle, you get a chance to rest while the other crews are still paddling. Then, when they come in, they'll do push-ups or sit-ups, whatever the instructors feel is necessary to remind them that it pays to be a winner.

My boat crew was paddling along, making pretty good time, and we were out ahead of (now) Admiral Ray Smith's boat crew. It was usually his boat crew and mine that tagged for one and two on most of the evolutions. On this paddle, I was having a certain amount of difficulty staying awake. Granted, I'd only been awake for three days, and this situation wasn't unusual among the trainees.

The boat crew officer's job is to steer, so his position was in the rear of the boat as the coxswain, so I was steering as we were going. I noticed myself starting to nod off a bit. One way to stay awake is to engage in a bit of banter with the boys in the crew, so I spoke up and said, "You guys are probably not going to find this funny, but your nice, slow, steady paddling is lulling me to sleep."

I was right, they didn't find any humor in that.

But what I did just to make sure we would be winners, was to move things around. "Okay guys," I said. "What we're going to do is rotate through the coxswain's position. I'm not going to sit back here and rest and try to stay awake. We're going to make sure we come in first."

It might not have been a great idea. Smith beat us on that paddle.

What got me through Hell Week was all between my ears. When I was at Villanova University, I met a corpsman who had served with the Teams. He was working out at the YMCA, and we talked about a lot of things. As a result of our discussions, I decided that there was nothing that another human being had done that I couldn't do.

As instructors, every one of us have done what the students were about to do or about to be asked to do. So I said to myself, if another human being could do it, I could as well. And I'd be damned if I wasn't going to do it. That attitude—and you have to have an attitude, you need to be positive about everything you do in training—got me through.

Breaking training down from one event to another helped get me through training. You just can't look at a six-month program that has a fourteen-mile run in boots, a five-mile ocean swim, and Hell Week—with a maximum of six or eight hours of sleep in the course of five days of constantly going—in one piece. You can't look at that elephant and expect to swallow it whole. You take it a bite at a time.

The way I did it was that I said that we had a run, we had a swim, and we had a PT evolution. There's a start and a finish to every one of those evolutions. I was obviously there at the start, and I intended to be there at the finish. Breaking it into manageable chunks like that helped me make my way through it all.

I had been a weight-lifter before going to BUD/S, so I sort of like food. At the end of the morning's evolutions was lunch. At the end of the afternoon's evolution was dinner. And during Hell Week, we got to eat four times a day. I sort of looked forward to those meal times, a self-reward if you will.

After graduation from BUD/S came the assignment to the Teams. With Vietnam still being very active then, the time came for me to go into my first combat. My wife still has the letter I wrote to her following that.

Combat was what I was trained to do. That's something about the Teams. Throughout the years, there have been a number of movies about Vietnam—how screwed up it was, how unfair this was, and how miserable that was. I knew it was going to be miserable. That's why I raised my hand and volunteered, that's why I wanted to do it. I knew I could do it, and I knew the people with me could do it, too.

We were all trained and prepared for what we saw. Okay, this is the environment, these are the conditions, this is the job. Let's go do that. In the Teams we wanted to do that, and we were good at what we did. We took pride in doing what we did well. We took the war to the enemy in his own backyard.

During my first combat tour in Vietnam, we had a couple operations where there was no real contact with the enemy. The first contact we had, being shot at and missed or hit as the situation might be, I had no difficulty with. Several of the people who fell during the course of the engagement fell as a result of my marksmanship. I did my job and did it well. It wasn't that Tom Richards or SEAL Team One said "Hey, let's go fight a war." We were fighting in a conflict that our government was engaged in. You can debate whether you feel the war was right or wrong, but we went over there and did our jobs well.

My first impression of Vietnam came as I stepped off the airplane at

Tan Son Nhut air field. It was the hottest place I had ever been in my life. The weather was hot, muggy, and sticky, but there's nothing you can do about that. What I was a bit concerned about was how lax things seemed to be. There was a lack of attention to security in and around the area the base where we were. My impression was that I had gone into a third-world country, and I wasn't exactly sure what to expect next. I was damned sure not going to be walking around as relaxed as some of the folks were nearby.

Again, going back to our training, for the entire time I was there, and most of the other SEALs who were incountry, we would not lose that focus on our environment. Today, we talk about force protection in the military, the protection of our personnel and equipment in all locations and situations. We were doing force protection back then.

Vietnam gave a lot of other impressions than just the weather. My platoon was assigned down to the very southern tip of IV Corps at the southern end of South Vietnam. When we moved ashore, we actually had some ground water available and set up some showers. That ground water was always at 110 degrees and smelled like sulfur. I don't think Vietnam itself has a different smell than say Barbados or Florida or Hawaii. I didn't pick up anything that really separated it. Yes, Vietnam was primarily an agricultural country at the time, and there were water buffalo in the rice paddies and the farmers used waste products as fertilizer. But once you were there a couple days, you didn't smell anything much any more.

My first tour was with Zulu Platoon, SEAL Team One. We went over were in August 1970 and came back in January 1971. The platoon commander for Zulu Platoon was Lieutenant Grant Telfer, who was later the commanding officer of SEAL Team One [30 March 1974 to 3 April 1976] as was I [7 August 1986 to 1 September 1988].

Vietnam was the experience I trained for. On the many operations we went out on, I did things well. A most memorable one would probably be the prisoner-of-war rescue mission that we executed.

We had intelligence that there were three American pilots being held about fifteen or twenty miles as the crow flies from where we were. Getting to that spot was a different matter.

Taking two platoons, we went out on the operations. Lieutenant Dick Couch was the commander of one platoon, and his platoon had the primary responsibility for the operation. I went in with my squad as his assistant. Unfortunately, we arrived at the POW camp a day late and a dollar short as the saying goes, and didn't find any American prisoners of war. But we freed twenty-one Vietnamese prisoners of war who were being held in cages that you wouldn't keep your dog in.

Just to see how happy those people were to see us Americans and to release those twenty-one prisoners of war was the most rewarding operation I did during the entire period I was over there.

There were two SEALs who influenced me the most during my first tour. One was a guy we referred to as Uncle Dave Schaible. If Uncle Dave hadn't retired before we had our first flag officer selected from the Teams, there's no doubt in my mind that Dave Schaible would have been that man.

Commander Schaible was the commanding officer of SEAL Team One, my first CO. He was an impressive man who believed in leadership by example and could talk to the troops or up the chain of command with equal ease.

The other individual was Leon Rauch. Chief Rauch taught me a lot about operating. He also taught me about dealing with the chain of command. There are some people out there who haven't got a clue about what's going on, who couldn't find first base if they were standing on it. Leon told me that there was a way to deal with those people—you can say no.

There I was, a lieutenant, junior grade, sitting with Leon Rauch and then Lieutenant Grant Telfer, getting a briefing on the mission we had coming up. The target was in the middle of nowhere, no fire support was available to us, and we had no E&E support in case things went to hell in a handbasket. And this Navy captain wanted us to go in to his target and do something.

Leon looked at me, then he looked at Grant, and he said, "We're not going to do this."

"Sounds good to me, Grant," I said. And we didn't do that operation. It would have been absolutely foolhardy to go in under the conditions that had been set up for that operation. Leon taught me a lot about taking a good look at a situation and making the right decision.

Probably a tougher question about the SEALs in Vietnam would be who the most unusual operator I knew there was. The answer to that would just follow the roster for SEAL Team One. That would be a list of the most unusual SEALs. Every SEAL is unique. Every SEAL is an achiever and a risk-taker. We all went out and did such difficult things that people would not believe other human beings could do.

Names come to mind as I think about the question of unusual SEAL. Frank Bomar was a huge E-6 petty officer who carried more ammunition on an op than you could store in an ammo dump. Frank was unusual because, like everyone else in the Teams, there was no "can't do" in his vocabulary.

Leon Rauch would also fit the bill. There was no operation he couldn't figure out a way to carry out. If it was worth doing, if there was a valid mission concept, a reason, and a justification for going after a target, Leon could figure out how to do it.

Mike Thornton is a SEAL who I don't know personally very well, but I do know the operation Mike participated in that resulted in his receiving the Medal of Honor. As I had said earlier, Mike Thornton received his medal for swimming Lieutenant Norris away from an enemy beach. Mike didn't know if he was dead or alive at one point, but he was not going to leave the body behind.

What Mike did personifies the attitude of the SEALs. We, that is the Navy SEALs, have never left anybody behind. We didn't do that—it was a creed of ours. Mike's swimming out to sea for hours, not knowing if Tom was going to survive, but not going to let him go—that tells you an awful lot about Mike Thornton. I don't know Mike well enough other than to say that he was a fantastic SEAL, a hell of a hard worker, and had an attitude that was indomitable. Those are characteristics you will find in every other SEAL.

We recently had a building dedication to Lieutenant Tom Norris, the individual who Mike earned his Medal of Honor for saving. Tom had actually been on an operation that he later received the Medal of Honor for himself. That operation had taken place well before his long swim with Mike Thornton. In Norfolk, Virginia, we dedicated a building to Tom—a highly unusual occurrence given that the honoree was still alive and attended the ceremony.

As Tom made his remarks, one of the things he said was that he had been in the right place at the right time to conduct the action that resulted in his earning the Medal of Honor. Tom looked at the formation of troops made up of today's young SEALs, doing the things he did during his time, and said to them that he had no doubt that any one of those SEALs would have done the same thing given the same situation. That's the kind of people we have in the organization.

Other SEALs have gone farther, literally, than anyone else in the Teams. There ought to be a law about people being as smart as Bill Shepherd is. He's quite an individual. Bill is in the astronaut program, and he worked on the project that we have between the United States and the Russians. He has the mental focus and drive that gets a man through Naval Special Warfare training, and that's exactly the thing that got him into the astronaut program. Bill did not get accepted the first time he applied to the astronaut program, but that was okay for the first time. He figured out what he needed to do to fix that situation, and he reapplied and made it.

Bill was on a training operation back off the Virginia coast during his Team days. A limpet mine, a live limpet mine, did not attach itself solidly to the side of the ship that Bill and his Teammates were attacking. The mine fell away from the side of the target ship before it detonated.

There was now a live, armed piece of explosive ordnance somewhere out there in the Chesapeake. Bill probably has several degrees, but I know that one of them is in naval architecture. He went back to the Team compound and examined the situation. He knew the location of the target ship, what the tide was, its direction, and its speed. He took the shape of the limpet mine, sort of an inverted bowl but not as smooth, and made some calculations.

Shepherd decided that, given the weight of the mine, it would fall at a given rate through the 150 feet or so of water at the target site. That would mean that the mine would be in the water column for a certain amount of time. The current and directions were known, and he determined how far the mine would travel before it reached the bottom. It wasn't a very big mine, and the situation was very much like looking for a needle in a haystack. After just a few dives, the search party found the mine where Bill said it should come to rest— an absolutely incredible demonstration of knowledge and ability.

There is no difference between the SEALs who went through training back in my day and the young men who are going through training today—they are the same. We have exactly the same kind of individual coming into the Teams today as have been coming to the Teams since the days of World War II. These are people looking to accept the challenge we offer, to see what they are made of, among other things. That is absolutely the same for every man ever in the Teams. It's the same focus, the same drive, and the same self-discipline that has always been needed to get through training.

How are these young men today different? When I graduated from Villanova University, Mendel Hall, a science building, was next to John Barry Hall, the Naval ROTC building. The entire basement of Mendel Hall was the computer system at Villanova University. Today, I carry a laptop computer that probably has as much or more capability as that computer in the basement of Mendel Hall.

Our kids coming in to Naval Special Warfare today take things like that for granted. I didn't know anything about computers when I came into the service. I didn't know anything about the technology that we have today. Cars and that kind of thing were what I knew about as a young man. Computers and those types of things are what the youth of today play with when they socialize. That's the difference between the people joining today, their level of experience with technology.

Our missions are changing in the Teams today as well. Instead of trying to find a courier moving along a jungle trail as we did, the couriers of today can be a fiber-optic cable. That's what has to be found and attacked. The vulnerable points of a fiber-optic cable and how it can be attacked and penetrated is something that the young SEALs of today know.

The people who conduct the operations are the same as they have always been. The experiences they have now, that developed them into the individuals in the Teams, are slightly different.

There was an operation we did in Vietnam where we were set up to conduct an ambush against a VC supply route. There was a trail about twelve or fifteen yards in from the river bank we learned about during the op. The VC didn't come down the river in a sampan as we expected, they came down along the trail. We were set up for our ambush facing the river, between the river and the trail.

There was no way we could get up and turn around to reorient the ambush when we heard them start coming down the trail. The VC would have heard us moving about, and we would have been in a particularly vulnerable position. So we had to sit there while the enemy walked by, carrying their mortars and everything, chatting away to each other. They ended up launching a few mortar rounds on our base camp nearby, but there was nothing we could do. We just had to sit there and be quiet. We never did get them.

Trying to rate the three things that get you though training—the heart, the mind, and the body—will give you some consistent answers from all the SEALs you talk to. The priority might be a bit different for individuals, but what gets you through training is drive and focus. Everybody who shows up to start training has proven that they have the basic physical skills to get through training. That's a given. What's next?

What is not only next, but foremost, is that mental drive, that absolute and total focus on the task at hand. Monday morning of a training week through that Friday evening, you are totally focused on going through the training. There's nothing else in the world but that task. As soon as you relax, as soon as you let yourself think about your dog, your car, or whatever, you're done. You have to maintain that total focus.

So I'm going to rate the body as third in importance. The total focus is first. Second, I would put the risk-taking and challenge aspect of the training and the Teams. If you want to get something done, you go in and tell a SEAL Platoon; "You know, I really don't know if this operation can be done, so don't spend too much time on this. If you don't think we can do it, just let me know."

Two hours later, that platoon commander and his men will come in, and they will have a plan. If you want something done, you challenge a SEAL.

The Trident stands for our capabilities. SEAL stands for SEa, Air, and Land. The flintlock pistol on the symbol is for the land activity we do. The sea is the anchor and the Trident. The air is the wings of the eagle. Every SEAL is an excellent marksman, every SEAL is diving-qualified, every SEAL has differing levels of training in demolitions, and every SEAL is jump-qualified. That's what we do.

What does the Trident mean to me? That one's hard to explain. The level of pride I have in wearing the Trident is really difficult to express. What is even more difficult to express is the honor I have to lead a community of 5,000 Naval Special Warfare people. It's mind-boggling. The responsibility I hold, and the faith and trust they have placed in me . . . I just can't put the feelings I have for that in words. I just can't tell you.

In order to get through Naval Special Warfare training, BUD/S, you have to be totally focused on one goal—getting through training.

Everything else just goes along with that. There's an expression that we use in the Teams, "Mind over matter—you don't mind, and it don't matter."

Pain is another of those four-letter words. Navy, Boat, SEAL—there's a bunch of four-letter words I live with. Pain is a frame of mind. It's something you're can either accept, or you can blank it out. It is something you're going to have to put up with.

Here's an example of pain. We're cold. I can't tell you how cold. There's no concept of this kind of cold that can be told in terms of degrees. That doesn't matter. We're standing there in line, my class, and I'm vibrating like you would picture a jackhammer operator. You know those guys you see on the street, bouncing about as they handle the heavy jackhammer? They're not even moving in comparison to how badly we're all shaking in that line.

That's a degree of pain. There are more definitions of pain, here's one: We were out on a particular operation in Vietnam where I was shot in the hand, for which I received my Purple Heart. How do I describe the sensation? Well, take your hand and put it on an anvil. Then take one of these, say, four- or five-pound sledgehammers, wind up as hard as you can, and just smack your hand. See what it feels like? That's pain.

That was my definition of pain, and I took it just a little bit further. We've all been to the movies, and some of us have seen John Wayne in Green Berets or his cowboy movies. There he is, standing there with this arrow sticking out of his chest. What does Wayne do? He pulls it out and keeps going.

Heck, I told myself I could do that. I looked down at my hand after I was shot. It kind of looked like some bloody hamburger down there. But I could see the bullet sticking out of the back of my hand. This is a piece of cake, I thought. John Wayne did it, and so could I. So I lifted up my hand, clamped my teeth down on the bullet, and got ready to pull it out of my hand.

Minor complication. My vision at the time wasn't what it could have been. That wasn't a bullet; it was a bone sticking out of the back of my hand. Unfortunately, it was still attached.

I grabbed it, I pulled—and my toes curled.

I told myself I'd worry about that later. That's pain. You can put it out of your mind. I loaded three guys who were shot much worse than I, two in the lungs and one in both legs, into a helicopter with that hand. It was somewhat painful. But pain is something you can accept, deal with, and put out of your mind when you have to.

When you report to a Team, you have to let the rest of the guys know who you are and what you're going to bring to that Team. We SEALs tend to be pretty low-key and don't brag about what we do, especially not to outsiders, but when you arrive at a Team, you're already 90 percent known to those guys. Somewhere between six to nine months or maybe a year later after starting your training, you go before a board. There you get the authority to wear the Special Warfare Insignia, the Trident. Once you're a member of that club, what else do you need? You've been through the hardest military training there is.

When I say that BUD/S is the hardest military training there is, it's because of that combination of mental discipline and focus it takes to get through on top of the physical tasks that have to be accomplished. That's why the guys don't have to brag.

We don't do Rambo in the Teams. The guy who does Rambo doesn't make it through training. To the guy who comes in and says he's going to do what's in the movies, kill 4,000 enemy single-handed, save the girl, and fly off in the helicopter, we tell him that that's the movies, that's entertainment. It's wonderful entertainment, and I'll go to see that movie again, but that's not real life, and that's not what the SEALs do. We don't want a Rambo.

We have SEAL Teams. There's no "i" in Team, and that's what it's all about. We operate as a Team, always. When the three guys in my squad were wounded—two guys shot through the chest, one in the legs— there was never the thought in their minds that anybody was going to

Never is a Teammate, wounded or dead, left behind. It has never happened, and it never will. During training, these BUD/S students have that lesson brought home as they carry one of their classmates along to simulate a wounded man.

U.S. Navy

leave them behind just because they couldn't move. That's not part of what we are. Those men knew that they could depend on their Teammates out there in the rice paddy with them. That's what it's about. It isn't Rambo.

If I suddenly had the mission to win the Super Bowl of football with a group of Navy SEALs, that's probably a do-able mission. That is, if I can pick and choose my SEALs.

I was at SEAL Team Two once with Mike Thornton. There was a guy there by the name of Jack Ford, who had been a wide receiver at the Naval Academy. I hadn't played organized football, but I was just big enough that I could keep anyone out of anyone else's way. So we had an interesting crew put together for a football game.

What happened exactly during that game, I don't quite remember. Mike Thornton had his arm in a splint and I was limping. Unfortunately, Jack Ford had his knee dislocated to a degree that it resulted in his ultimately leaving the Navy. But we won the game, that was the important part. You play the game to win, and you find a way. If we had to play the Super Bowl, we could do that.

SEALs have tenacity. It gets real easy, because it goes back to focus, focus and mission accomplishment. And that's what Naval Special Warfare brings to the equation. We thrive on challenges. What is the mission? What is it we need to do? What is the objective, and what are the obstacles in our way?

We take a look at whatever that mission might be, and we break it down into parts. We examine the parts to see just what could go wrong here or there. We do that so that if something does go wrong, we have an SOP, a standard operating procedure, to deal with that.

Everyone in that platoon is known to everyone else, and their skills and abilities are augmented by their Teammates. There was an event in Southeast Asia I remember. It was in a coconut grove at night. There was no moon, and it was so dark that you couldn't see your hand as you held it in front of your face. But there was a faint outline in front of me. I knew that outline was Jim Roland. I knew that just because of the way that outline carried itself, how he moved. My squad was that well known to me.

Tenacity is, give us this mission, and we will accomplish it. There's no question. That's why we exist. What else is there?

We teach the new SEALs our history. You have to know what your roots are. You have to know what the organization is built on, what it's based on. The SEALs of today came from the Underwater Demolition Teams and the Naval Combat Demolition Units of World War II. We are the water side of Special Operations. The Navy talks about our cornerstone capability of coming from the sea. And that's exactly what we do in Naval Special Warfare—we do special operations from the sea.

Up along the coast of New England, there are beautiful mansions here and there, facing the sea. On the third or fourth story of the mansions, they have a cupola or doorway leading out onto what's called the widow's walk. Back in the days of sailing ships, the families would go up on that widow's walk, and they would look out to sea. They would look out to see if there was any sign of the ships that would be bringing their family members back. Not only when, but if. The sea is a very unforgiving environment. It always has been. And that's the environment that we live and operate in.

The SEALs don't consider an ocean, river, or bay an obstacle. That's what we live and work in. That's the environment we've mastered. And that is why it is so important that the young SEALs of today understand where that mastery came from.

Barry Enoch won his Navy Cross doing operations up and down the rivers of Southeast Asia. Mike Thornton received his Medal of Honor by swimming out to sea, carrying Tom Norris. Special operations from the sea are what we do, so we had to master that very unforgiving environment.

SEALs are human beings. We're not loners, and we certainly aren't Rambos. We come from the family next door, just like anyone else. I'm not a whole lot different from anyone else who was born in Brightwaters, Long Island. We're part of society, and we're no different from anyone else in that society.

We have something we call "SEAL Pups." We bring together the kids of the SEALs and the Navy Special Warfare Combatant Crewmembers who are assigned to work with us, and we have a sports day for these kids.

During one of these days, I was standing and talking to the mayor of Coronado, who is a former Navy aviator. Standing there, we looked at all the people who were known to the public at large as these hard cases, loners, or whatever. And here was this 220-pound SEAL, on his hands and knees, a target for the water balloons being launched at him by these three four-year-olds. We're just like anyone else.

One thing I could promise that you would find in a SEAL Team is yourself. When you go through training, you have to dig deep, concentrate, and focus to master those challenges. What you learn about yourself is just what challenges you can master.

Anybody knows that you can't just stay up three days, run X number of miles, swim X number of miles, paddle a rubber boat, and do all these other things. Mind over matter. If you are going to do it, you're going to have to pay attention and focus. What you will learn about yourself is that you can do that. And that's what you get out of being a SEAL. You learn what you can do.

And we're a family, we're all accepted. If somebody from Class 54, or Class 55, the class I graduated with, were to call me up and ask me anything, I would stop what I was doing and meet that request. That's an absolute given.

Barry Enoch and I were not in a platoon together, we didn't go through Training together, but we were assigned to SEAL Team One at the same time years ago. But if Barry or Mike Thornton, or any one of my Teammates was to give me a call, I would stop what I was doing to do whatever they need me to do.

A nineteen-year-old BUD/S trainee is probably about as connected to the original Naked Warrior of World War II as you can get. That youngster is about as naked as he can be. He's standing there, freezing his butt off, wearing nothing but a pair of UDT shorts and a coating of water. And he's hoping like hell that he has the guts to stick it out and graduate from training. That's the same person, he has the same core as the first NCDU during World War II. He has the drive, the discipline, and the risk-taking mentality that makes that individual meet whatever challenge you give him.

Joe Maguire, Captain

When this interview was taken in 1998, I'd been in the Teams for twenty-two years. For the first two years of my Navy career, I'd been a surface warfare officer, a rather undistinguished surface warfare officer. After scraping enough paint off the ship, I decided to change and come into the Teams.

Brooklyn, New York, was where I first heard about the Teams. It was while I watched the recovery of the astronauts from the Mercury, Gemini, and Apollo space capsules that I saw the men who jumped from *the helicopters and were the first to reach the capsules after splash-down.*

When I was young, a lot of my friends who were watching the shows with me wanted to grow up to be astronauts. But I wanted to be one of those guys in the water who were recovering the space capsule. The news shows always had some human-interest stories about the guys who were recovering the capsules, men from UDT 21. Some of these guys were Olympic swimmers and really impressive men. So I just said to myself that it looked like something I would like to do when I grew up—and here I am.

To get to the Teams, I first had to go through training just like everyone else. To get to Basic Underwater Demolition/SEAL training (BUD/S) was pretty interesting and rewarding. During my first two years in the Navy, I had applied to BUD/S a number of times. When I finally arrived at BUD/S, it had already seemed like an accomplishment just to have gotten here.

I really enjoyed the training. It was twenty-five weeks of very demanding training and hard work. But if being in the Teams is something you want to do, and something you've had to work hard at just to be there, the work is good.

Instead of being aboard ship, I was outside most of the time. There were three meals a day and I was told what to wear, where I had to be, and when I had to be there. There was never a question about what I had to do, and I had no trouble sleeping at night for twenty-five weeks.

As an officer at BUD/S, I had a different experience than enlisted students. It wasn't that the instructors were really any harder on the officers than the enlisted men. Because there were so few officers in comparison to the number of enlisted men in a class, the instructors provided them with a lot more chances to excel than the rest of the guys in a class.

My class, Class 93, had 4 officers and 20 enlisted men graduate in August 1977 from a starting group of 145. So those of us who finished had been scrutinized pretty closely by the time we were done. We offi-

cers wore a khaki belt and a stripe on our helmet liner to identify us as the officers in a class. That made us visible to our classmates, as well as the instructors, as we went through training.

What is attempted at BUD/S is to give the officer students leadership opportunities. They clearly have to be just as good operators as the enlisted men, but they also have to be more than that—they have to be leaders. So the instructors give the student officers a lot more of a leadership challenge during their training. We're such as small community in Naval Special Warfare that the officers who go though training one day will very possibly have those same instructors working for them some time down the road, so the instructors are pretty careful about who makes it through BUD/S.

The role between officers and enlisted in the Surface Navy is more formalized than it is in Naval Special Warfare. The relationship between officers and enlisted, in training and what I could see among the instructors, was a lot less formal. There was still a tremendous level of respect between the officers and the enlisted, but the bar that separated the two groups so much in the regular Navy had very much been lowered.

To me, one of the big differences between Naval Special Warfare, the SEAL Teams, the rest of the Navy, and the Department of Defense was the quality of the enlisted people who make up the ranks of the community. Right now, as the commanding officer of the Naval Special Warfare Center, I can say that 35 percent of the enlisted men who graduate from BUD/S have their Bachelor of Science degrees. These are some very high-quality individuals. The rest of the Navy, and the rest of the military, is really not as fortunate to have such a high-caliber enlisted community.

As far as the relationship between the officers and enlisted men in the Special Warfare community goes, it starts at BUD/S. As an officer in training, your swim buddy will most likely be a junior enlisted man. Then, when you get into the SEAL Team, the guy who is swimming alongside of you—the person whose hands you're placing your life in—

he's an enlisted guy, too. That gives us a much more fraternal relationship than just a professional one between the officers and the enlisted in the Teams.

The training I underwent at BUD/S was wonderful. It was everything I had hoped it would be, and then some. The initial part trying to get used to life as a trainee was a little bit difficult, but once you finished Hell Week and went on to the diving phase and the land warfare phase, training was wonderful. The thing that really struck me was the image of what the instructors were like, and what SEALs were like when you were a trainee. Comparing them to what the men are actually like in reality is vastly different.

When I went through training in 1977, I would say that 99 percent of my instructors were fairly recently out of Vietnam. The vast majority of them either had the Bronze Star or the Silver Star. I even had the good fortune to have Mike Thornton, a Medal of Honor recipient, as one of my instructors. These were men who had ably demonstrated that they knew what they were doing and had brought the lessons home and were passing them on to us.

The thing that struck me about the instructors I had was their willingness to work with somebody and to be kind to someone who needed it. During my third phase of training, a situation came up for me when I had a stress fracture in my right leg. I really didn't know that I had a stress fracture, but I was running about ten minutes behind the class on most runs when I had earlier been right up there with the pack. The swims and obstacle course were things I could still compete in pretty well, but the pain was getting bad.

One day, I was going to go across the street to the Amphibious base to get my leg x-rayed to find out just what was going on. One of my third-phase instructors was Johnny Johnson, a SEAL corpsman. Chief Johnson came up to me and said, "If you go across the street, you're going to come back with a cast. You've got a broken leg. But if you're willing to stick it out and work with us—I'm not making any promises—but we'll see what we can do for you."

So I continued to fall behind in class in a lot of ways, but they remained my class. But I was able to work through that stress fracture and keep going. It finally did heal. But the point that stuck out to me was that the instructors cared enough that I made it through training. It had been shown over time that the longer you stayed at BUD/S, if you had been rolled back from an earlier class due to an injury or whatever, the less your chances of successfully completing training were.

If you got rolled back, to recuperate from an injury or to work on an academic problem, statistically, you had a lower chance of completing the program than someone who had never been rolled back. You have to be up all the time during training. Every single day during basic Underwater Demolition/SEAL training is game day. For the twenty-seven weeks you are there, you have to put out the maximum you have every day. After a certain period of time, your battery just runs out. You just lose some of that self-motivation and enthusiasm you need to get through the program. And you can't just fake it through BUD/S; you have to be "up" every day.

So if you're at BUD/S just a little too long, you can really get too tired and things can seem to be too much for you. And that can be a terrible waste, because you had to accomplish so much in just getting through the first parts of BUD/S. Once you've completed Hell Week, you've demonstrated that you have the personal drive to get through the program.

I really don't recall much details about Hell Week when I went through it. One thing I do remember was that you really couldn't tell just who would be able to get through it—you still can't even today. We started off with about 145 students. By the time Class 93 had gotten to Hell Week, we were down to around 60 students.

The first guy who quit during Hell Week was somebody who I never would have thought would quit. He had been first in the runs and first in the obstacle course, and he had a tremendous amount of leadership. But he quit on Monday afternoon of Hell Week. When that individual quit, there were about ten men who went with him.

That individual might as well have had a big red "S" on his chest for "Superman" from what the rest of us saw during the first five weeks of training. I think when he quit, a lot of the guys figured that if he couldn't make it, they never would be able to make it through. Even though I was just a trainee going through the same misery myself, I felt that this guy quitting was a bad thing. I went up to him and tried to tell him to hang in there with the rest of us, that things would be fine. But he had just had it, he was done. The fact that when he quit, he took ten guys with him, was very significant to me.

I never really thought about quitting during Hell Week. There was one moment when I was down in the sloughs, the mud flats, near Tijuana, probably about Wednesday night, that things got tight for me. We had set up Camp Swampy, a collection of tents and so forth, near the mud flats. We had been in the mud for seven or eight hours when for some reason I found myself just standing alone in the mud. The cold and exhaustion got to me and I just started shaking uncontrollably. The shakes happen to every student during Hell Week and you usually get through them together. But while I was standing there, I started to think. What I thought about was just how miserable things were and that my situation really stank.

At that point in time, one of the instructors came by, grabbed my life jacket, and threw me back into the mud. Once I was back into the mud, I was back into the game and I was just fine. But that was about as close as I came to considering quitting during my Hell Week.

I was also impressed by the camaraderie the instructors showed. Almost every one of those men had been through Vietnam either as platoon mates or as Teammates in SEAL Team One or Two. They were focused on conducting our training. They knew what was required to get through training, and they kept it demanding and forced us to meet a high standard. That made things hard for those of us who made up the class, but it also made the final result very rewarding. And we had an awful lot of laughs along the way.

Graduation from BUD/S was an interesting day. The thing about graduation was that we were ready to leave BUD/S and go on to the SEAL Teams, and yet we still felt like students. Even on the day of graduation, we still weren't really convinced that we had made it through the program. Up to the morning of graduation day, the instructors were still the instructors, they were still on us, challenging us, and being very demanding on our performance.

I remember being there at graduation when they went up to announce the honor man award for the class. I just assumed that the award would go to one of my classmates. When the commanding officer read my name as the class honor man, I just sat there for a little while. Part of me was still not convinced that I was going to graduate, let alone be the honor man of Class 93. I had thought that there were a lot more men in the class who should have been the honor man rather than me, and no one was more surprised than I was when the announcement was made. Graduation was quite a defining moment for me.

Once you've gone through BUD/S and successfully completed a six-month probationary time with a Team, you are awarded the Naval Special Warfare Breast Device. That symbol you wear on your uniform tells the world that you are a Naval Special Warfare officer or enlisted man.

The thing that is remarkable about the device we wear is that it is the only warfighting insignia in the U.S. Navy that the officers and the enlisted alike wear. That's to signify that we go through training right alongside each other. The officers and enlisted men share the same mud, cold, and wet of BUD/S. In some of the other warfare specialties, there are distinct qualifications as well as training pipelines for officers and enlisted. But as far as the SEALs are concerned, whether you are Admiral Tom Richards, Admiral Tom Steffins, Admiral Ray Smith, or one of the youngest petty officers in a SEAL Team, you all wear the same device.

To me, the Trident doesn't necessarily signify the warfare specialty of the wearer as much as it says the man is a member of a very close fraternity. When I work with somebody who has worn the Trident, they don't even have to have it on. They can be in civilian clothes, but I still know we have a tremendous number of things in common. And what I especially know is that I can count on that individual—if we were in the face of adversity, that individual would not call "time out," no matter what.

The Naval Special Warfare device, the Trident, is made up of several different parts assembled into a single whole. SEAL stands for SEa, Air, and Land, the three environments a SEAL can insert from. The device identifies those three areas of insertion.

The eagle is the largest single part of the device, signifying strength, but also showing that we come from the air. The vertical anchor and horizontal Trident show our heritage and membership as part of the U.S. Navy and the water it operates in. In the right talon of the eagle is a flintlock pistol, cocked and ready to go. That pistol also symbolizes the land warfare side of the SEAL Teams.

Once I had graduated from BUD/S, I had the good fortune of reporting to Underwater Demolition Team 21 on the east coast at Little Creek, Virginia. It was quite a remarkable group of men at UDT 21, both officer and enlisted. There were about thirty officers who were assigned to UDT 21, twenty of whom had been former enlisted men who had served in Vietnam. The men had taken their commissions and become "mustangs," the term we had for prior enlisted officers.

As far as the enlisted men in the Team were concerned, most of them had rotated from SEAL Team Two into UDT 21. With this mixing of personnel, there were a tremendous number of people in UDT 21 who were true warriors with a great deal of combat experience. They were also people who liked to work hard, play hard, and have a lot of fun getting the job done. I can't think of a better place to have broken in to Naval Special Warfare than UDT 21.

It could have gone either way for me, having all those people around me who had seen so much combat and were so highly decorated. They could have ostracized me as someone who had never faced the challenges of combat. But I really feel that those men took me under their wing, put their arm around me—especially the senior

The sign for the NCDU training base at Fort Pierce during WWII. The octopus is holding a sledgehammer over his head, has a case of TNT in one of the other tentacles, and has secured himself to a horned sculley obstacle under the water.

enlisted at UDT 21—and taught me a lot about how to be a Special Warfare operator.

You only get one chance to make a first impression, and the impression I received in UDT 21 was that this was a community. And being a part of that community was something I thought I would like to be for a long, long time.

A little more than the first two years of my career in Naval Special Warfare were spent at UDT 21. Then I left the UDT and went to the Amphibious Force, Seventh Fleet, over in Okinawa for a couple years. Once I came back to Little Creek, I was in SEAL Team Two as a Platoon Commander. While I was at SEAL Team Two, UDT 21 became SEAL Team Four.

The ending of the history of the UDTs, and the continuation of the SEAL history, was something that came up among us. You always have to remember where you came from and just what your origins are. In the SEAL Teams, we certainly have a history, a distinguished history, of the Teams in Vietnam. But the people who were involved in the Underwater Demolition Teams, and the Naval Combat Demolition Units who came before them in World War II, had a long and respectable history themselves.

The UDTs performed heroically during the Korean War and earlier, and they did a number of pioneering actions over the years. It was the guys from the World War II Teams and from Korea, their history and capabilities, that got us the SEALs Teams today. When we changed over from the UDTs to just the SEAL Teams, there was a tremendous sense that we were losing something. I agree with the decision to make the change; it was something we needed to do. And yet it was very difficult to say good-bye to that past. To this day, those of us who were in the UDTs, still pretty much refer to ourselves as Frogmen as opposed to SEALs.

As the Commanding Officer of the Naval Special Warfare Center, I have a number of courses that are conducted under my watch. BUD/S is really the most important course taught at the Center; without BUD/S, we would have no community. At the time of this interview (1998), I have Class 223 getting ready to class up. In a couple days, Captain Bob Gormly will be the guest speaker at the graduation of Class 220.

The changes over time at the Center and at BUD/S have been for the better, in my opinion. We try to train a little smarter and do things a little better than we did in the past. But in essence, BUD/S is the same training that Class 123 received and that Class 23 received.

I graduated in 1977. Since then, there have been tremendous technological advances in weapons systems and communications just in our boats. But BUD/S training has not changed very much over those same years. We've incorporated new weapons systems and have different dive gear today, but for the twenty-seven weeks that the student goes through training, we test their spirit just as hard now as we did in the past.

When a student graduates from BUD/S, they have only finished Basic Underwater Demolition/SEAL training. What we know about them is that their spirit has been tested and proven. When called upon to use the wonderful technological weapons available for the defense of freedom, these guys will do the same fine job today as the SEALs have done in the past.

It is our philosophy, our ethos, in Naval Special Warfare, that it is the spirit of the men who lead and the spirit of the men who follow, not the weapons that achieve victory on the field of battle. So we're still working on the spirit at BUD/S.

To me, the most important factor for a man to become a SEAL, to pass though BUD/S, is clearly his mind. BUD/S is, without a doubt, the most demanding physical program in the Department of Defense. But every single day is game day at BUD/S. You could be a tremendous athlete, but you have to be up and psychologically prepared for this program that will humble anybody.

We have all-Americans, national champions, and other people of extremely high physical caliber who don't make it through the program. The man who does make it through is someone who has made up his mind that being a SEAL is what he wants. That's what it takes, that goal to say, this is where I want to be to be able to make it through. That's what makes it clear to me that the psychological part of BUD/S is much more demanding than the physical part—although they do get their money's worth physically.

The student who starts, and completes, Basic Underwater Demolition/SEAL training is, in many ways, similar to Mike Thornton, Moki Martin, Bob Gormly, and all the other people who have come before them. And in a lot of ways, those same students are vastly different today than their forefathers. Of the enlisted students who complete the program, 35 percent have their Bachelor of Science degrees from major universities. A large number of them have also been accepted into Officer Candidate School, but the wait for OCS ranges from two to two-and-a-half years. These men make the decision that, although they would like to be commissioned officers, they would really rather be SEALs. They forego their commission in order to go through training.

I think we have always had a very high caliber of enlisted man in Naval Special Warfare. Years ago, if a lot of the men in the Teams had been afforded the economic advantages some of the men have now, I think we probably would have had just as many enlisted men with their college degrees as opposed to their high school degrees. But in essence, all the men from then and now still have the same spirit, and that's what we're looking for at BUD/S.

It isn't your academic achievements, or your physical ones, that will get you through BUD/S. It is whether or not you have the spirit, the intelligence, and the wherewithal to not only complete the basic program, but to be highly effective and sophisticated, in challenging missions of national importance. Right now, as in the past, I feel that the student of today is every bit as good as his forefathers were.

So if you want to be a Navy SEAL, there are two ways to go—officer and enlisted. For the officers, the number-one source of commissioning is the Naval Academy. Along with the Naval Academy, officers can receive their commissions from the Naval Reserve Officer Training Corps (NROTC), Officer Candidate School (OCS), and some other smaller programs.

This year (1998) we will bring fifty-eight officers into our BUD/S program, but we will receive hundreds of qualified applications for those fifty-eight officer slots. It is much more demanding for an officer to get accepted into the program than it is for an officer to complete the course of training. Accepted officer applicants have to have succeeded in many different things, be at the very top of their graduation class, and just be well above the average.

A large percentage of the enlisted men have completed advanced education. When I went through training in 1977, the average age for an enlisted man at BUD/S was nineteen years of age. Now, the average graduate from BUD/S is almost twenty-five years of age because so many of them have completed college.

Each man, officer or enlisted, has to be able to swim five-hundred meters in a certain period of time. They all have to be able to run a mile and a half in a certain period of time wearing long pants and boots. Push-ups, pull-ups, and sit-ups are all basic and part of the physical standards that have to be met in order to qualify for BUD/S.

The enlisted men have to be able to pass the same physical standards the officers do. And they also have to meet the highest scholastic aptitude scores that the Navy requires for any training. When a young man walks into a Navy recruiter's office and says he wants to be a SEAL, he will take a battery of tests. Scholastically, if he passed the tests and qualifies, he is also a candidate to become a nuclear propulsion technician, and filling those slots is a higher priority for the Navy.

So the individual who comes into the SEAL Team could compete in any category he wants in the whole of the U.S. Navy. We are very fortunate to have that caliber of individual coming to us.

When a man goes through training, he first has two weeks of pretraining and then he has seven weeks of First Phase. The fifth week of First Phase is Hell Week. During that week, we start off on Sunday evening and keep the students up continuously until Friday evening. On the average, the class will receive an hour-and-a-half of sleep on Wednesday and another ninety minutes of sleep on Thursday.

What we do is stress the students during that week. We give them as close as we can to real combat conditions. The reason we give them the rest we do is that our sleep studies have shown that's the minimum amount of rest they need in order to make it through to Friday.

Hell Week is also our highest attrition week. We lose more students during that week than during any other evolution in the training.

Once they've completed the basic phase, First Phase, they go on to Second Phase, the diving phase, for an additional seven weeks. Second Phase is where the students will learn to be basic scuba divers. They will also be exposed to the LAR-V, a closed-circuit pure oxygen breathing rig, and they'll start to become combat swimmers.

When the students are finished with Second Phase, they'll move on to Third Phase, the the land warfare phase, and the final phase of the BUD/S program. During the ten weeks of Third Phase, we conduct a lot of training in the local San Diego country area. Four weeks are spent out on one of the Channel Islands, San Clemente Island, where students are put through rigorous training and are exposed to high explo-

A swimmer pair of BUD/S students. They are wearing the Draeger LAR-V rebreather systems on their chests. With the Draeger system, swimmers have their backs clear to be able to transport additional materials, such as pack-boards carrying limpet mines.

Kevin Dockery

sives and their use. On the island, the students will also put together everything they have learned for a final exercise.

During the course of their training at BUD/S, every week the students have to compete in a two-mile ocean swim, a four-mile timed run, and the obstacle course. When they finish First Phase and go on to Second Phase, the times the students have to complete those competitions decrease. The times decrease again when they go from Second to Third Phase.

A two-mile swim in Third Phase must be ten minutes faster than the two-mile swim in First Phase. We bring these young men to a very high level of physical condition during training. We have to keep raising the bar to keep challenging them, because these are men who need to be challenged.

Once the students have completed our program, they go on to basic airborne training at Fort Benning. From there, they go into their SEAL Teams, where they will conduct their advanced operator training, SEAL tactical training. After about nine months to a year from having come onboard at BUD/S, they will be designated Naval Special Warfare operators and receive their Tridents.

It takes about four years, two cruises, to get somebody who's really up on step. That's when they are a quite competent as a Naval Special Warfare operator.

When I came in to UDT 21 for the first time, two-thirds of the wardroom were mustang, or prior enlisted, officers. Now, it's rare to have mustangs in the community. We have a great number of very qualified enlisted men in the Teams who would make good officers, so we have tried to expand the commissioning opportunities in the community for the enlisted men.

We have increased the number of Officer Candidate School quotas for our SEAL enlisted operators. That lets them go on to OCS and come back to the Teams as commissioned officers. We also have the seaman-to-admiral program in the Navy, and last year (1997) we had two of our SEALs selected for that. So there's still upward mobility for the enlisted men.

We also have the warrant officer program and the limited duty officer program in the Teams. These are programs where senior enlisted SEALs can apply to be appointed as warrant officer or commissioned as limited duty officers. This is a program that has been highly successful in Naval Special Warfare during the last several years.

We've had a number of very successful enlisted SEALs become officers. One of these men is Michael Thornton, who I've known since 1977, when he was a first class petty officer and I was a trainee. I would say that Mike is like every other SEAL in that he's reserved, humble, intelligent, and extremely competent.

If you saw Mike, he would strike you as a very physically imposing person. There would be nothing about him that you could pick out from across the room that would cause you to say that he was a Medal of Honor winner, but when Mike was working as a SEAL, he was very competent and one of the most professional people I know.

BUD/S students on San Clemente Island carefully prepare live explosive charges as part of their training. All SEALs, no matter what their individual specialty training may be, know basic and advanced demolition techniques.

U.S. Navy

Other SEALs have been officers who went on to make a name for themselves outside the Teams. Bill Shepherd is a Naval Academy graduate who had extensive experience as a SEAL operator. He went to and received his graduate education from MIT. In the 1980s, Bill applied to become a mission specialist at NASA.

You have to be careful what you wish for. Bill had to leave the Teams when he was picked up by NASA to join the space shuttle program. He went into space on the mission following the Challenger disaster. I believe that after the successful completion of that mission, Bill received an automatic promotion from commander to captain. Bill has stayed with the space program and has done successful things for NASA and for our country.

It is a real source of pride for those of us in the SEAL community to have a member of the astronaut community among us.

At BUD/S, we really test the spirit of the students. It is a course that has the highest attrition rate of any in the Department of Defense. This is not something we're proud of, because the mission is to graduate men and send them on to the SEAL Teams. And 95 percent of the people who leave the program do so voluntarily; they drop on request (DOR).

We do stress these people, these men, and try to build their confidence and test their spirit. It is our feeling that "that which doesn't kill you, makes you stronger." After their twenty-seven weeks at BUD/S, these men are certainly a lot stronger.

Every day they have to be physically and psychologically up to the challenge. But BUD/S is also the type of thing that you can't do on your own. Getting though the course has to be done by a team effort.

No matter how good you are, one day just won't be your day. And you don't want to have to ask, "Hey, I need some help." When you start falling behind, you just want that hand extended to you, someone lowering the rope down to you and pulling you up without your asking.

So we work on teamwork, and the spirit, that really makes the Teams what they are. The testing of the spirit of the men tells us that when somebody completes Basic Underwater Demolition/SEAL training, they aren't going to call time out.

No matter how difficult the situation you are in, in the Teams, you know you can have confidence in the man to the left of you and the man to the right of you. They are going to be there for you, no matter what. And they can look over at you and realize that you're going to be there for them. That's why we work so hard to prove that the individual has the spirit within them at BUD/S.

I would never talk anyone into becoming a SEAL. This is just something that you have to want, and you have to want it a lot, in order to successfully complete the program. Only three out of every ten stu-

dents who show up at BUD/S finally graduate. With that high an attrition rate, I personally wouldn't want to be responsible for bringing somebody in and setting them up for a program like this. I would have to be absolutely, thoroughly convinced that they were the right person for the program. As I have said, we've had all-Americans and national champions in BUD/S who just don't make it through the program. You just never know what a man has inside of himself.

On the other hand, the mission of the Naval Special Warfare Center includes the recruiting of students for BUD/S, so I've got to get out there and try to bring them in the door. But on a personal level, it's difficult to bring somebody in, knowing what they're going to be put up against.

But if someone wants to come in on their own, we're glad to have them. The Russians have a saying, "you can't tell a man who is warm what it's like to be cold." And our students at Basic Underwater Demolition have a realistic appreciation for what it's like to be cold.

After a couple decades in this business—I've been UDT 21, SEAL Team Two, SEAL Delivery Vehicle Team, Naval Special Warfare Development Group, Special Operations Command Pacific, and Naval Special Warfare Group Two—I've had a lot of experience in a lot of different areas. That experience has shown me that you can pretty much tell who doesn't have the spirit for the Teams. So if I met an individual who had all the tools physically and who qualified academically, but just didn't have what it takes to come in here and make a contribution, to be a part of the Team, he would be someone I would actively discourage from coming to BUD/S. Because SEAL Teams are a Team and the work we do is a team effort, he would be getting himself into the wrong business. The individual who cannot work as part of a team and make a contribution for the common good of everyone really has no business in our community.

Out of all those people who quit the course, the vast majority of them quit because they couldn't come to terms with the cold, and it's best that they realize that now. When you're out there operating in the

Teams, you're cold and you're wet—that's the environment we work in, that's the environment we thrive in. So when the cold drives most of them out during training, it's really for the best.

Last year (1997) we brought in close to 800 students—712 enlisted men and about 65 officers. Out of that group we graduated 250 people. There is no way we can predict who will successfully complete the program. An individual might have all the tools necessary to do the job, but if they become weak psychologically, they could quit.

Or an individual might just get a bad break. People break their legs, stress fractures of the lower leg are not uncommon at BUD/S, and we have stress fractures of the femur as well. The femur is a pretty large bone. For that bone to be stressed, it shows we're conducting some pretty demanding training here.

As far as who makes it through, right now we are conducting studies to determine predictability on just who would successfully complete the program. We should be able to identify the people who were studied and compare them to the predictions.

I've been the commanding officer of the Naval Special Warfare Training Center for a little more than sixteen months now, and I wouldn't want to place a bet on who would or wouldn't make it through the program. We keep the standards high—lives and the success or failure of our missions depend on those standards.

As far as describing the Teams, I think the term elite is overused. To me, just SEAL is enough. That says it all for me. I don't consider myself to be elite; I consider myself to be a person who works very hard, who loves what he's doing, and who enjoys his work. I would say that's pretty much the same for everyone I know.

We're fathers, we're sons, we're brothers. We work in the community, and we go to church on Sunday. But when we have to go to work, we do it to the best of our ability. We have tremendous talent in the Teams, and the people of America have given us the best technology and the best equipment available in the world.

With the raw talent and the marvelous technology we have, we can really do the job. To me, the job is wonderful. Blowing things up, shooting machine guns, jumping out of airplanes, locking out of nuclear submarines, driving in the SEAL delivery vehicles—it's all quite interesting. But after twenty-two years, even that can get old.

The thing I find wonderful and highly rewarding in the Teams is the people I get to work with. That's why I get up every morning and put my feet on the floor, and look forward to coming to work. I know there are a lot of people out there in the civilian sector making a lot more money than I am, but I don't think there are many people in our country who enjoy their work as much as I do, and that's because of the people I have the opportunity to work with—it's pretty wonderful.

If you become a SEAL, you'll be exposed to the best people in the world. We are a family; we are a fraternity. You will be challenged every single day—not just during your basic training, but in your job. You'll be challenged with people who enjoy challenging other people.

If you are an officer, you will be given tremendous leadership challenges at a very, very junior position. Even in the platoon, if there was a power vacuum, the caliber of our enlisted people is such that they would fill that vacuum in a nanosecond. It is a rewarding job. But most important, it is working with the most wonderful people in the world that's kept me around and made my career rewarding for twenty-two years.

You might get the impression that, in my opinion, the best part of being a SEAL is the people you have to work with. And that doesn't necessarily mean just the SEALs, because our job is really a team effort. In Basic Underwater Demolition/SEAL training, we conduct 7,500 high-risk evolutions a year. What I have, and what the Naval Special Warfare community has given me, are the best people to go out there and conduct training and look after these young men. These students are quite literally putting their lives on the line every day to go through this basic training.

Those people working here include the physicians. We had a case during a recent Hell Week, where on Thursday night during the evening meal, one of the students came up and told the corpsman that he was having difficulty with his arm. The student could no longer move his fingers, and there was a lot of tenderness and swelling in his arm.

We were fortunate that the student went and talked to the corpsman when he did. He had already invested more than three days in Hell Week, and I'm sure he didn't want to come and point out a problem to the corpsman that might get him rolled out of Hell Week and forced to complete it again with a later class. The nature of the kind of trainee we have, and of SEALs in general, is that they really don't complain about aches and pains. They're always fine.

The corpsman took a look at the student's arm and wasn't quite sure what the problem was. He went to one of our doctors, Dr. Mark Gould, who was one of the physicians with the Hell Week class that evening. Mark took a look at the arm and recognized it as necrotizing fasciatitis, a flesh-eating disease.

These young men are torn down so much during Hell Week, that they are exposed to a lot of different bugs that can take hold where they normally couldn't. Dr. Gould immediately called the hospital, had the student admitted, and operated on him within the hour to attack the bacteria and clear out the site.

Necrotizing fasciatitis was a very fast-moving disease. I asked the people involved to walk me through the timeline of events. Somewhere around 11 to 1 o'clock that day, the student was exposed to the bug. By 5 o'clock in the evening, it started to bother him. About 5:15, the student reported his problem to the corpsman. Several minutes later, Dr. Gould identified the problem as the flesh-eating disease.

We admitted the student to Balboa Hospital within the hour. By 7 o'clock that evening, the operation was ongoing. If the student had not identified and announced the problem when he did, if he had just waited two hours more, he would have lost most of the muscle tissue in his arm. If he had waited a few hours longer, there was a likelihood that he would have lost his arm to the disease.

It's to the credit of somebody like Dr. Mark Gould, who is intelligent enough, experienced enough, and caring enough, to be able to identify something like that and make the immediate decision to get the young man admitted into a hospital.

We will look out for the students to the very best of our ability, but we will also stress them and challenge them every day they are here.

Right now, I'm twenty-two years older than when I went through training. Although I'm a captain, I look on these students a lot like a father would. These young men going through training are somebody's sons. We owe it to the individuals going through training, to their families, and to ourselves, to make sure that we maintain control of the situation at all times. If there's a problem, we identify it. We put these people through tremendous challenges and they excel, but we must maintain control of the program. And it is people like Dr. Gould, as well as all the other instructors, who every single day walk out there and push these young men, who make sure that no harm comes to them.

We control the situation, we're the experts, and we know what's needed to become a SEAL. It's the caring attitude and professionalism of all the instructors on staff that makes my job possible. Whether you're a SEAL, a physician, a special warfare combat crewman, or a data processor, the program is a team effort. In Naval Special Warfare, we really don't judge ourselves as far as how important you are or by how close you get to the target. It's a Team effort.

Joseph Hawes, Quartermaster First Class, USN (Ret.)

Within a few months of now, it will have been twenty-two years since I first came in to the service. The Navy wasn't my first choice of the service; originally I wanted to be in the Marine Corps because I wanted to be a Frogman. One of the recruiters told me, "Hey, we have Frogmen. We could get you here . . . there. . . ." It was just one of those little ploys to get me to enlist so they could fill their quota of recruits.

Later on, the recruiter for the Navy saw that I was disgruntled with the Marine Corps recruiter and he said, "Hey, we have Frogmen. They're called UDT/SEALs, and you would love it."

I said in return that the reason I wanted to be a Frogman was that I wanted to go on the astronaut recovery program. The Navy recruiter told me that they had that, so I decided to go for it. The recruiter did warn me that it would be hard, but I replied, "Whatever it takes."

I did all my enlistment things and finally arrived at BUD/S. Later on, I found out that the astronaut recovery program had gone out the window because of the space shuttle program coming online. But I have never had any regrets about going into the Teams, though, because it's been great.

At BUD/S, I started out originally with Class 104 and graduated with Class 105. This was on the West Coast and the classes were a combination of a summer class and a winter class. It felt like winter every time we went out because the water was cold. Whether it was in the pool or in the ocean, the water was cold. And the things they have you doing—it's always cold for the students.

The cold wasn't the hardest part of training for me. I can deal with cold; I've always dealt with cold; I'm from Connecticut. One time my brother and a few friends carried on a little tradition of ours of breaking the ice at the lake and going swimming. That finally got to me as a kid when I came down with pneumonia, which turned into whooping cough. My brother got a beating because of that.

"Why'd you get sick?" I was asked.

"Well," I said, "Benji and some guys made me jump into the water. . . ."

But we really only wanted to swim. It was just one of those stupid things kids do.

The main thing that bothered me during BUD/S was the mind games. You would look at your classmates and go, Well, they're cold and I'm cold. Are they any better than me? Do I have any special privilege because I'm cold? Do I get a time out?

No, the main thing was that we were together, and we were all cold. If you let the mind games bother you, that's when you start to get weak. You needed to stay strong.

My Hell Week wasn't fun. In those days, it seemed like a free-for-all, with the instructors doing whatever they pleased. What I remember is finding friends in boat crews or in class, clinging to them for strength, praying, and saying that this can't last forever.

Once Hell Week was over, we cried, knowing that we had made it past a big one. Because Hell Week was the main thing, the big stumbling block, we all saw we were on the way to becoming SEALs. First Phase was Hell Week. Second Phase was diving, drownproofing. Third Phase was gun theory, land warfare, and demolitions.

In getting through Hell Week, we knew we had passed the part that causes most people to drop out of training. I really can't pinpoint anything that was particularly hard during the long week. It was something that you can't really describe, but you will never forget.

You get a lot of wannabes that say, "Hey, I was a SEAL." I run into them every day. We sell "I'm a SEAL" T-shirts at the exchange that people buy and wear. Wearing a shirt does not make you a SEAL. It comes from your mind and from your heart. If you don't have the heart of a fighting man who went through BUD/S, you shouldn't claim you're a SEAL.

There are things you'll forget about training. You'll forget those who quit before you. You'll never remember their names. You will remember the classmates who graduated with you. You will remember instructors who put you through all the stuff you had to endure. You won't forget your class numbers, and you won't forget what you had to do. Going through BUD/S is the only way to get to the Teams.

Training is hard, and yes, I did think of quitting during Hell Week, because I had good friends who fell by the wayside. But I kept going. It's just like any other athlete running a marathon, or anybody who goes through a maximum sport. They find their mind telling their body to shut down, they shouldn't have to go through this, there's a better life on the other side. All you have to do is quit.

We had a little saying that the instructors would put out to us when we were in the water. "You guys can get out of the water," an instructor would holler at us. "All we need is a few quitters."

"Quit, shit!" we would yell out. And that was all we would shout.

In life, we all sometimes want to quit. I don't feel like working here anymore. I don't feel like doing the same old job. It's just human nature to want the change. But I didn't quit. And I didn't because of the embarrassment.

That's just one of the things that go through your mind. The embarrassment of guys in your class seeing you walk away. It's the embarrassment of telling your family that you gave up. It's letting yourself fall short of something you really want to do. And I said there were people in that class who were no better than I was, and if they could keep going, so could I.

We had this thing we did involving holding our breath in the water. Some guys could hold their breath for three minutes, some for two minutes. No one wanted to be the first one to say, "I can't do it," so we all tried and kept going. Being a Team guy means you are competitive, with others and with yourself. So I didn't lose to myself. I didn't quit.

The words "secure from Hell Week" are unbelievable to hear. Tears come to your eyes as you look around you. I think we started out with 126 people; after Hell Week, there were only 30-something left. And the mind games had continued right up to the end.

Before we actually heard the order to secure from Hell Week, we had been told that we were going into Saturday, that there had been a lot of things we hadn't done right. We were marching across the street, over to the base, to go into that water and stay there. Why? Because we had messed up.

We thought the others had secured by now and our Hell Week was going to continue. We were stopped in front of the main building of the base, because the commander of the base had wanted to see us secure. So the instructors stopped us, we faced the building, and we were told that we were secured from Hell Week.

Under the careful eyes of their instructors, BUD/S students practice free-diving and tying knots at the bottom of the training pool. They will do this evolution, a simulation of the UDTs tying demolition charges together during World War II, until the actions become automatic.

U.S. Navy

I hugged my friends, I cried, and I was overcome with a feeling I can't describe. Even though I was beat down and tore up, I called my mom and told her I had made it. It was great.

I did have problems in training, drownproofing particularly, because I'm negatively buoyant. There are few minorities in the Teams and people always ask, "You're black, how did you get to swim?" or whatever. Kids coming up from the inner cities often don't know how to swim, and neither did their parents. So the parents tend to tell their kids not to go in the water because they'll drown.

I have eight brothers and four sisters. My father's from Jamaica, and we have always swum. It never bothered me to get into the water, and I've been swimming since I was big enough to walk. When I arrived at BUD/S training, I figured I had the swimming part down. I also knew I could run, and I'd played football and other sports. But when the instructors told me we were going to do drownproofing, all I could say was, "What's drownproofing?"

Drownproofing is where the instructors tie your hands and feet together and you have to relax and function in the water. I still didn't have in my mind that this was a secure thing. There are instructors all around the pool, there were safety divers, and all the people conducting the training are skilled in what they wanted us to do. In spite of all of that, the evolution still didn't sit well with me.

They tied my hands and feet and put me in the water. I was so scared that I broke the ropes. So they tied me up again, and I broke the ropes again. We did that three times, my being tied and breaking the ropes, until the instructors came up with some line that could hold me.

Chief Knepper, now retired Master Chief Knepper, instilled in me the absolute knowledge that nothing was going to be allowed to happen to me. The environment was safe at all times, and there were instructors around who were highly skilled and experienced in running that particular evolution. There was no way they were going to allow anything to happen to me, but I had to get that fear out of my system.

That was before the test came for drownproofing. On the test day, I passed with flying colors. That was another hurdle I had to get through, the fear of the unknown, that the Teams helped me get by. I knew what was happening; I knew what was expected of me. And I accomplished the task.

It was great to stand there on the grinder that last day and graduate from BUD/S. Looking around, I could see all my friends who I had started with. And I gave some thought to the people who fell by the wayside. Not all of my family was there, although I wish I could have had the whole herd there to see me graduate. My brother-in-law came down to see me graduate. He was really impressed about what went on. It was kind of upsetting that my mom and dad couldn't be there, but it was good to have one representative of the clan there.

Graduation from BUD/S felt like being on top of the world, and I've stayed on top of the world since I've graduated and gone on to the

Teams. There's the respect that we have in being a Team guy, that all the other warriors laid down the roots to before us. I look back at those men who came before me and know that if it wasn't for their courage, skill, and sacrifice, there wouldn't be any of us. That made me feel great about being a a part of such an elite group.

Six months after training, your probationary period is over. If you completed it successfully, you are awarded your Trident. The Trident is a symbol of respect to me. It is also the symbol of great warriors who came before me in the Teams. These men were tasked with jobs that no one else could do—and they accomplished those jobs. Wearing it also means that I'm part of an elite group of people. And most of all, it symbolizes the camaraderie and the brotherhood of the Teams. I'm with a fraternity.

I have a twelve-year-old son, and he loves wearing Teams shirts. He goes to school and says that his dad's a Team guy. They ask him if he's a Team guy, and he says no. But I tell him, "Yes you are. You're my blood, and that makes you a Team guy." But if he wants to wear a Trident as an adult, he had better go through training. And God knows, that if I'm still around, I'm going to tell the guys to make it hard on him.

After I graduated BUD/S, I went to Jump School and then checked in to UDT Twelve. Here I was, a new guy, who didn't know what was going on. All I knew was that I was in the Teams now, and I had no idea what to expect. I hear "Drop" bellowed out from across the grinder, so I immediately dropped to the deck and pushed them out [push-ups] and shouted "Hooyah!"

"Hooyah what?" comes back to me.

"I don't know your names," I said.

It was two guys, one a Master Chief, the man who became my sea daddy. He showed me a lot of how to be an operator in the Teams, and he did a lot for me.

The Master Chief came up to me and said, "I'm Herschel Davis, Master Chief, and this is Roy Dean Matthews. You know what? Recover."

I scrambled up from the ground as Master Chief Davis continued. "You don't have to drop for us," he said.

"I don't know anything that's going on," I said. "All I know is that I don't want to cause any waves, so I'll do whatever you guys tell me."

Davis started calling me Black Beauty, and that became his and my private joke. That was my introduction to life in the Teams and UDT Twelve. Before too long, I was pulled aside and asked if I would like to be in a platoon. Immediately I agreed, even after they told me that we would be deploying overseas in about a month. I didn't care, and it sounded good to me.

Then I was asked if I would mind carrying a 60 (an M60 machine gun). That was easy enough to answer: I told them that I carried a 60 in BUD/S and that the weapon was fine with me. So I was picked up for that platoon.

It was Lieutenant McTighe, now Captain McTighe, who was the officer in charge of my first platoon. I remember all my guys to this day, and I was on top of the world to be able to deploy with them. All my other friends who had graduated BUD/S with me were still sitting around and going through training. Here I was, the new guy in a platoon, hanging out with the older guys. It was great.

Deploying was so good that I started doing back-to-backs, deploying with the next platoon to get ready to leave as soon as I had come back with another. During my career now, I've had fourteen platoons and thirteen deployments. I'm sorry to see the deployments go, but I'm getting older now and it's time to shut it off.

The "Hooyah" I shouted out for Master Chief Davis is a saying we have in BUD/S and in the Teams in general. It means, "okay," or "right on," or "you got it." It's just one of those things that is said to help build enthusiasm and camaraderie among the trainees. When I was an instructor, hooyah could mean other things, like "Don't get wet, the water's cold," or "You're going to stay out there and sit."

Hooyah can also mean things that can help you feel a little bit warmer, such as "I never liked you and I hate your mother." I hooyah all

Navy SEALs

the time. If you get pulled over by a cop and he wants to give you a ticket, you just go "Hooyah." You know what it means, but he'll probably thinks it means something else.

My first combat deployment was when our first platoon went over during the Iranian Hostage Crisis in the late 1970s. That was really my first look at preparing for war where a hot engagement looked like a really possible thing. My first actual conflict was Desert Storm.

In my first combat platoon, we were called to do ops and practice for ops, because the U.S. Embassy had been taken over in Tehran. We were the platoon on station and got the pep talk about how we might be the guys who were going in. Preparing ourselves for what-ever might come up was something we always did. We trained on the ships, shooting outboard, swimming in and swimming out, and sharpening our skills. So it was during the Iranian Hostage Crisis that I had my first taste of getting ready for war. Then there was DESERT STORM.

Between those two events, something took place in the Teams. The UDTs were decommissioned and ended their direct history in 1983. The men went directly into the new SEAL and SEAL Delivery Vehicle Teams that were created at the same time. I never really understood the history of the UDT. When we were broken down into the classes at the end of BUD/S, we were told who would be going to SEAL Team One, who would be assigned to SEAL Team Two, and who would be going to UDT 12, 11, or East Coast Teams.

You kind of felt disappointed if you didn't get picked for a SEAL Team. I hadn't understood the whole aspect of being UDT. The UDTs were the first Naked Warriors to go across the beach and blow open the way for the landing troops during World War II. Before there was a SEAL Team, there were the UDTs.

There's a lot of history that goes along with being UDT that I just didn't understand. Because I hadn't been picked for a SEAL Team, I must be a dirtbag. Then you were teased by guys in your class who said things like, "Aren't you Joe, the Navy SEAL? Naw, you're just UDT."

After a while, I learned just what our history was in the UDTs, and I was very proud to be a member of the real Frogmen and happy that I was a UDT operator.

It was kind of a sad moment when the UDTs went away. But it was more of a misconception when people thought that there were UDTs and SEALs and that they weren't the same. We were the same. The UDTs' primary job was in the water, and their secondary job was on the land. The SEAL Teams' primary mission was on the land, and their secondary job was in the water.

It was a great thing when we all became SEAL Teams, but there was a small feeling of loss when the UDTs were gone. That feeling was relieved when a lot of my friends in the SEAL Teams had to do the recons and the water work that the UDTs had done and hated it. That just made me laugh. Now, I feel privileged that I was part of UDT and SEAL Team.

I was a SEAL Platoon LPO, leading petty officer, the lower senior enlisted in charge of the rest of the guys during DESERT STORM. We went out to the Persian Gulf and trained for missions that the higher-ups had on the planning boards. We also performed our normal duties of keeping in shape, doing physical training, and swimming each and every day on the ship.

On some of the swims, the ship would drop us off three or six miles and then continue on. We would swim back to the ship, escorted by our safety boats. The safety boats were important because the Gulf waters were very warm and you could get overheated easily. The fact that the waters were infested with sharks wasn't lost on us either.

We also worked hand-in-hand with the Marine Reconnaissance Platoons, Marine Recon, who are the Marine equivalent to SEALs just like the Army's Special Forces (Green Berets). We trained with Recon doing ship-boarding and other various joint operations training.

A couple times, when an Iraqi ship or other cargo ship was observed going through our ship's area of responsibility, they were told to stop and prepare to be boarded. The boarding was to see if they were carrying any contraband for Iraq. When they didn't stop, we would do a VBSS (Visit, Board, Search, and Seizure) op.

For a VBSS, we would load into a helicopter equipped with a fast rope system. Then we would fast rope down on the ship while it was moving. There, either the Marines or we would set up security—whoever got to the ship first.

Whoever boarded the ship first would take down the deck and hold security there. The next helicopter would drop off the guys who would take down the engine room and other priority compartments. During all of this, we would

The point man in a SEAL formation prepares to open an interior hatch during VBSS training. The breacher behind him stands ready to open the door with his shotgun if necessary.

U.S. Navy

have sniper helos circling overhead, off on the side, to make sure that no one was able to come up on us. These operations were done to make sure that the local shipping was in compliance with the UN Resolution 665—enforcing trade sanctions against Iraq.

In spite of the concerns we had about the shark infestation in the Persian Gulf waters, nothing ever happened. In my twenty-two years of swimming out there in the open ocean and looking out for things, I have never had an encounter that bothered me. Yes, there were sharks, but they must have had plenty of natural food, or else they didn't like dark meat and weren't even going to bite me.

But guess what the instructors showed us before we went out and did the five-point, five-mile swim at San Clemente Island—the movie

---

Jaws. Most of us had never seen the movie before, so of course we had to see it the day we had our longest swim. I think I was doing more looking out for sharks than swimming that day, and we were doing a lot of swimming.

Later in my career, I became an instructor at BUD/S. Being a BUD/S instructor was something of a privilege for me. Now I had a first hand on the raw talent we had coming in, questioned what we could make from this raw material, helped make the decision as to whether an individual was salvageable or if he wasn't cut out to be a Frogman. Basically, someone had given me the power to become God, to choose Team guys and add their talent to the SEALs.

There was no way I could have picked out the ones who would make it and those who would quit along the way as they came through the door at BUD/S. Whether he's skinny, fat, tall, or short, there just isn't any physical guideline for picking out anyone who will make it. It's what they have in their heart that counts the most.

There are a lot of people who I had seen come into training who I just didn't think had what it took. But they can surprise you. In some way, they bring out from inside themselves something they might not have known they even had. They just decide to prove me wrong.

Time and time again, there were guys who we would tell to stop trying to impress the girls by telling them they were going to be a SEAL or that they were the toughest guy around. Those were the guys who we would tell to stop fooling her, and themselves, and just quit.

One time, I had a 5 A.M. PT. There were more than one hundred students around, and it was dark. You just can't keep your eyes on everyone all the time. I would go in every day at 4:30 to do the 5 o'clock PT. Once I was done PT'ing them for an hour, I would go into the gym for about two hours to work out myself.

One of the talks I gave the guys was to tell them that there were some guys among them who knew they didn't belong here. Now they were hiding in the bunch, but as soon as we weed out the class, they would pop up to the top and we would get rid of them. I told them to stop wasting my time during our 5 o'clock PT, because I already had my Trident, and I was going to get my workout in spite of them. But if they didn't get their workout, they would just fall farther and farther behind and end up getting booted out anyway.

Command Master Chief Chalker came in then to add his part to the talk. He would say that he saw everyone out there on the grinder, and that he wanted to see each one of them standing there on graduation day. They didn't have to do anything to impress him. They just had to be able to look at themselves and say that they had given it everything they had and that would be fine.

Then I told the class officer to move them out and take the class to chow. As they were leaving, one student was already heading over to the bell.

"Hey, bonehead," I said, "come over here. Where are you going?"

"I'm going to quit," he said.

"Why? Because of what Master Chief Chalker or I said?"

"No, Instructor Hawes. I'm just not a morning person."

That floored me. "What?" I practically shouted.

"I'm not a morning person," he repeated.

"I can't believe that you came here and now you want to quit. Didn't you know that we do ops in the morning?"

"Yes."

"Did you know that we do them late at night?"

"Yes, but I just thought you guys could change me."

"Go to chow and think about it," I said. "Then come back and see me."

He came back, and he ended up quitting. But I take my hat off to that guy. The thing he wrote down on his DOR (drop on request) sheet was that he quit because he wasn't a morning person and couldn't take getting up early in the morning. So I give it to him on that. He wasn't fooling himself at all. Besides, taking him in to see Master Chief Chalker and telling him the reason he was quitting was a lot of fun. That must have been a full mouthful of coffee Chalker was drinking when that student told him his reason—at least it looked like a whole mouthful when he sprayed it out of his mouth in surprise.

Because I was assigned as an instructor, I've only missed one Hell Week. My normal shift was from midnight to 8 in the morning. We would take normal eight-hour shifts doing whatever to the students during Hell Week. If I wasn't out there being a bad guy to the students, I was in the truck taking a little nap.

Sometimes, what I did to the students was mean, and it certainly looked thoughtless at times. But it was all part of making them dig down deep to give me, and the Teams, all they've got.

As far as being an instructor, things could be somewhat hard on you during Hell Week. Typically, a shift was made up by the number of instructors who were needed to manage the class. Because the class size changed so much—always getting smaller—the number of instructors on a shift could change. No matter how many instructors were on a shift, you had to stay sharp all the time. Some of the kids in training were so worried about passing that they disregarded safety, especially as the week went on and they became tired and disoriented.

You could tell a student to get wet, to go dunk his head. He might say to himself that he wanted to impress the instructor by holding his head underwater until he passed out. That's where the instructor had to keep a heads up. And you wouldn't want to push the guys too far, and there might be one or two you would want to keep a particular eye on—not because they weren't putting out, but because they were getting a little wobbly.

Judgment took part in a call on a student as well. One might not look like he was putting his head underneath the boat enough, not carrying his share of the boat. Why? Because a patch of his hair is gone where his hat and the sand rubbed the top of his head raw. You just don't want to be the instructor then. I don't know anyone in the Teams who wants to be an instructor just to go to BUD/S and hurt anybody. Each and every instructor I have ever known wants the same thing—to get the best-quality people for the Teams and get them in a safe manner.

As to list the priorities of what would get a person through training from the heart, mind, or body, for me, it was one—I had to do it from the heart. I had to really want, deep down in my heart, to be a Frogman. After having it in your heart, your heart can tell your mind, that you have everything you need to make it through this training. Then, your mind can tell your body to get in shape.

When you twist an ankle, your ankle hurts, and it sends that signal to your mind. Then your mind says whether it shuts down, gives in to the pain, or keeps going. The heart is the one that says to keep going, because it wants to be where it is. Those are my priorities. And I'm sure if you ask anybody, those are somewhat their priorities, too.

There's an expression at BUD/S, the "fire in the gut." What the expression means is that you set out with that burning desire in your gut to do a job and finish the training, and you did. That fire was never put out. It didn't matter when people talked about your mother, when you were cold, when your wife was home alone, or when your kid was sick and you had duty and couldn't leave the base, or it was Hell Week. That personal fire never went out. That's fire in the gut. And every Team guy who went through training has that same fire. You ask some of the old-timers, and they'll say they still have it.

I never won the fire in the gut award. That's an award they give out at the end of BUD/S, but I don't think it should be given to just one individual. Everybody that's up there grabbing a diploma has earned that award. I still have that fire today, and I'm getting ready to retire. It's one of those things that make you wish you could stay young forever and still do the things we do with each other.

When I was a kid, I played with Army men. I grew up doing the Army man thing, jumping out of planes and swimming in the ocean. But I can't really say I'm doing the Army man now that I did when I was a kid. Actually, I'm not an Army man, I'm better than that. I'm a Frogman. I'm a SEAL. That has made my life more interesting.

That's why you have the guys who pretend. They go into the bars and say, "Hey baby, I'm a SEAL." They know what goes along with that name—the honor, the awareness of people who know what a SEAL is, and what that name stands for. And that's also why we make life very miserable for those phonies when we find one.

Anyone can be hard to the students as an instructor. But you have to have some kind of compassion, you have to put yourself in their place sometimes. I don't try to play the "Billy Bad-Ass" instructor. What I do instead, when I want someone to do something, is to let them know that I did it and that the other instructors and Team guys around all did it as well, and that we aren't trying to make the students do anything different from what we all had to do.

Normally, when I swim, for some reason I don't get very cold in the water. I swim with a hood, fins, and my Speedos on. One day, I was out with the class and we had already swum out through the surf zone. One of the students asked me if I wasn't cold. I told him that was his problem—he worried about being cold. If he worried about doing his job and getting the job accomplished, then good things would come after that.

Finish the swim, complete the job, and a hot shower and meal are waiting for me. Everything from the swim is over, then we start the rest of the day. Nothing can last forever, no matter how bad it is.

So when I was an instructor, I didn't stay down on somebody all the time. Instead, what worked for me was to let up, reward the students, and tell them to hang in there. There were a couple times that I made threats to people while I was an instructor. I told them that if they quit, I was going to look for them and they wouldn't like it. And I said they could tell the skipper, the captain, and I would admit to what I had said, then I would beat them twice as hard for telling on me.

Sometimes, that gave the guys who needed it that extra push. They could see that I would yell at them as if I didn't want them there, but then they could see that I was trying to help them.

When I went through training, the guys in other classes followed a tradition that I never understood. It really made me feel bad that the class ahead of us made more problems for us than the instructors did. But while we were going through Hell Week, those same students would shout to us to hang in there. They would even leave candy bars underneath our pillows. Those actions touched me, and I never forgot them.

When I became an instructor, if I saw a guy who was doing good, and if I had an extra lunch available, I'd ask him if he wanted more to eat. And I brought candy bars for the students myself. Then one group of guys I gave some candy bars to messed it up for everyone. They had stuffed the Snickers bars in their faces at the wrong time. The senior chief on the shift asked them to turn around and saw that chocolate mess all on their faces.

So when the senior chief roared out that he wanted to know where they had gotten the candy bars, one of the students just flat out told him that Instructor Hawes had given them the candy.

That dime-dropper.

It was just one of those things. Later on, after they had graduated, those students came up to talk to me. They said that they knew I had acted like a real person, and that even though I was just as hard on the class as anyone else when I needed to be, I wasn't like some of the other instructors. I believed that you could be compassionate and still do the job. We don't have to beat anyone into the ground to get them to do what we want them to. You beat them to a point, then let off. I was sometimes known as "Mr. Softy," though.

It was my responsibility to see that there was a level of pain in the training, and I did that just as hard as every other instructor. You push the students until they feel that they can't go on any farther, then you keep pushing them. The ones who can shut it off and keep going are the ones who learn that they can do more than they ever thought they could. The others just fall away.

Everybody has their limitations as to how much pain they can stand, and there are all kinds of pain. When you look at some divorces, or even just breakups between girlfriends and boyfriends, the people

---

involved will say that the other put them through a lot of pain. But if asked if they were beaten, they usually have to say no. It isn't the physical pain, it's the mental and emotional pain they feel. Pain can be mental, or it can be physical. I don't really have a way to describe it. But you can learn to force yourself through the pain and come out the other side.

A good example of pain that can be dealt with happens during the students' 5.5-mile swim. The student swimmer pairs know that it's their last big swim and that the water is icy cold. A pair of swimmers might start off in third place. As they go along, turning over their strokes, all of a sudden, one of the pair starts to fall behind. The swim buddy is starting to become incoherent and can't speak. So the safety boat is called over and they find out that he's going into hypothermia.

So the swim buddy is pulled into the safety boat, and the other swimmer has to stay there in the water and wait for the next swimmer pair to come up so he can swim with them. Trying to just hold position in the water, the swimmer will cup his hands together, but his hands are so cold that he can't lace his fingers together. But he continues to wait and gut out the cold until he can continue the swim.

Three hours later, the swim would finally be over. Only now the student's knees and joints lock up from the cold. He would fall to the ground and not be able to move. A grown man would be forced to ask for help. He couldn't walk by himself, he couldn't even get up off the ground without help. That's pain, not only physical, but mental. That man's dignity and pride are gone, flushed away with the cold that racked his body. That hurts like hell.

But the help he needs is there from his classmates. That's one of the other lessons of BUD/S—no one is ever left behind. That student's classmates, suffering from the cold themselves, would help him get up and move. The ones who can move the best help the ones who can't.

In spite of the fun we have between the services, there's a lot of respect that goes along with the jokes and ribbing. Yeah, we kid each other, make up songs, or whatever, but underlying that is the respect of warriors. The same thing we had to go through to earn our Trident—a very hard course of training—Marine Recon had to go through their own version, as did the Army Rangers and Green Berets. The one thing that stands out is that all our main jobs are different. We SEALs take the jobs that nobody else wants and that nobody else can do.

When you're telling a guy to swim from 4 in the morning until some-time in the afternoon, then get lunch, put on wet rubber, and do some more swimming, a beach recon, or a dive, you can only be talking to a SEAL. There were times I had to do those things in cold water. We were diving for bombs or live shells that were dropped over the side of a ship, or looking for a camera that someone was dumb enough to drop into the water. Things like that happen, and the only people the higher-ups think to get to solve those problems are the SEALs.

That used to bother me, but now it makes me proud. If there's a problem, they think first to give it to the SEALs. It's like we have some kind of big "S" on our chests. I know not to believe that, but it does make me feel good that we're thought of so highly. It makes me proud, and it makes my family proud.

Even saying that, you can't take anything away from the Green Berets, the Rangers, the Air Force PJs, or the Marine Recon. In their communities, they are the top dogs, and their families are just as proud of what they went through and what their accomplishments are. So we have a rivalry amongst ourselves, but it isn't really a rivalry. It's more just something that's traditional and fun.

Twenty-two years in the military and although I didn't make the rank I wanted to, I am still very proud of what I did. I'm proud that I didn't avoid any conflict, that I didn't avoid coming into the military. I'm proud of the guys who I work with and the people who laid down the founda-tion of the Teams before I actually got there, did the history, and left it for men like me to carry on the story. I'm proud that my family has pride in me.

These things are easy to say after my time in the Teams. Sure, I could have been a high school drop-out, or I could have decided that the military wasn't for me. If I'd have wanted to, I could have been a gang-banger, or even have turned into a statistic in prison. But I had enough pride in myself, instilled by my mom and dad and by my brothers, to make what were the right decisions.

It doesn't matter that time has passed. I might be a great big SEAL, but that doesn't mean I can ever go home and tell my mom that she can't tell me what to do because I'm a grown man. She'll still slap me, and Dad will be right there to knock the hell out of me. And if they didn't do it, I have brothers bigger than me who would show me that disrespect is not to be tolerated.

Wearing the Trident separates me from everybody else. When I go on the base, to the exchange or to take care of business at the personnel office, and I have my cammies (camouflage uniform) or dress uniform on with that Trident on my chest, that tells everyone that I'm someone special. But I can't say I'm someone special just because I wear the Trident; it comes from the whole mannerism that comes from being in the Teams. Your dress uniform is always squared away. In cammies, I always make sure that my boots and pants are properly bloused, my boots are shined, everything is sharp and clean. That tells other people that I'm special.

When they see that Trident, they know I'm a SEAL. And they see a squared-away uniform that tells them the pride I hold in being one. That's always been in my heart, and I try to instill that in the new guys I help train.

Some guys today who get their Tridents have smiles on their faces and tears in their eyes as they receive that symbol of the Teams. Then they'll say they are buying a keg for all their buddies, because they are now one of us, and we'll have a couple drinks at McP's or Danny's in celebration. And that touches you, because you remember being there yourself.

It was twenty-two years ago that I was a young pup like these new guys. And I remember just how good it feels to get that Trident. But the test is not over once you pin it on. You are constantly training, and you have to instill in the new guys how a SEAL has to constantly keep up. Passing the boards and qualifying is just one step. You have to keep on being better and better. That's what separates us from the other guys.

Once I became a SEAL, I cried. I have no problem saying that. People seem to fail to realize that we're people who are SEALs. If you cut me, I bleed. If you kick me, it hurts. We are human and we have emotions just like anyone else. But being a SEAL is a job, and I worked hard to get that job. Having gone through the phases of training does not close off my emotions. Going through BUD/S does not say that now I am a walking, talking machine, that I have no feelings. That is not a SEAL.

A SEAL has feelings. When we go to war and are asked to do things it's not like we can't wait to do those things. We aren't excited about taking lives, we can't wait to do whatever. We look at our job with compassion. Those people who we're going up against have families, too. But that doesn't get in the way of our completing our missions.

We also look at our jobs from another point of view. If we happen to have a mishap with explosives, on a jump, while shooting, or when we go to war, there is every possibility that we're going to die. So those emotions we have inside do have to be kept under solid control. I know I check out everything prior to a jump or any other operation. And I also say, "Please God, let my chute open."

I go through all the planning for a jump. Each action that I'm going to take, I go through step by step in my mind, and once that chute opens, I say, "Thank you, God." When I steer down to the ground and land, I say, "Thank you God, for another successful jump."

If anyone tells you that they were never scared, they are probably lying. Team guys are human, and we get just as scared as the next guy. We just don't let it stop us, or even slow us down. Whether I say it or not, being scared doesn't make me any more, or less, of a man. Most Team guys are secure in themselves. And when you are secure in yourself, you can let your emotions go, and you can let your feelings go. So that's why it doesn't bother me to say that I cried when I first received my Trident.

The first words that come to my mind when I think about the Teams are "camaraderie" and "brotherhood." We are the most elite fighting unit in the world. The camaraderie comes from knowing that you are a Team guy, and that you are with your Teammates. If you are having problems at home, you can always go out with a Team guy, and he will bring up your morale.

During the holiday season, there are a lot of guys who are away from home—some for the first time, some just like every year. They might not have any family to go home to and have to live in the barracks. They don't have to spend the time alone. There's always someone asking them to come over to their house, watch the games on TV while the wife is cooking dinner, and hang out with the kids and watch them open their presents. The Teams are a family unit, and because I have been in the Teams, that's how it has always been.

That's the thing I'm going to miss the most when I retire—the family of the Teams. I grew up in a big family, and leaving the military is like leaving another family. But it doesn't stop there. You can always visit with the Team guys. You can always sit there and partake of a beer, some food, and have some conversation. They will always be there.

In front of the UDT-SEAL Museum down in Fort Pierce, Florida, there is a statue of Bronze Bruce, the Naked Warrior, a UDT operator equipped with little more than swim fins, bathing trunks, a face mask, and a knife. I look at that statue and I see a guy who will ask for only the bare minimum, and he will get the job done. He has enough heart and ability, that even given less than the minimum, he will get the job done. If he has to go it alone, he will get the job done. Whatever it takes, the job gets done.

You don't have to have the best equipment. When I first came into

UDT, we didn't have all the high-tech stuff we work with today. We had Ingram MAC-10 and M76 submachine guns and .38 revolvers. We really thought we were high-speed then. We didn't even always get a holster; we would put a gun down into our UDT shorts. How roguish is that? But it was what we had and we dealt with it.

Now, the Teams are in an age of different weapons and tools. Now we have MP5 submachine guns, sniper rifles, this, and that. But what we are teaching the students is that you can give a SEAL whatever, and he will survive and get the job done.

Dennis Chalker, Command Master Chief Boatswain's Mate, USN (Ret.)

My career in the Teams spanned about twenty-three years. I finished my tour as the Command Master Chief at the Naval Special Warfare Center. That's where we run BUD/S, SEAL trainers and people who want to be SEALs through training. We run advanced SEAL programs there as well.

My military career started at the age of seventeen when I enlisted in the Army. I served a little over three years with the 82nd Airborne Division. Afterward, I took a break in my service time to try to go to school, because I wanted to be a game warden. Moving to Colorado, I found that I couldn't meet the residency requirements, so I couldn't afford to go to school.

Back during my Jump School days at Fort Benning, I had heard about the Navy SEALs. I even met a few of them there. When I went up to talk to the director of the forestry department in Colorado, he told me that there was a waiting list to be a game warden. When I told him that I was thinking about going into the Navy and try to go through the SEAL program, he told me that if I had my degree and completed that training, it would help jack me to the top of the list for a possible job as a game warden.

The thumbs-up sign is given by a fully equipped SEAL from SEAL Team Eight during VBSS training aboard the *Joshua Humphries* during Desert Storm. His primary weapon is an MP-5N submachine gun, this one fitted with a removable flash hider and loaded with a doubled set of 30-round magazines. The empty magazine can be removed and the loaded magazine quickly slipped into place with such an arrangement.

U.S. Navy

Boot camp was nothing. I only had to go through it because I had been out of the Army so long. The boatswain's mate rating was the quickest school to go through and get into BUD/S as fast as possible. Soon enough, I was at BUD/S and joining up with Class 101, graduating March 1979—a winter class—big time.

Training was challenging, which was one of the reasons I went into the program, as I love things that are a challenge. One thing I learned about in training was what it meant to work together and be a member of a Team. I learned in the program that there's no room in the Special Warfare community for an individual, what we call an "I." That's the lesson we relate to the students today.

What I learned in training first of all, was that the challenge was not exaggerated. I will admit that there is a time during your training that a little man does come up on your shoulder and works on your head. He asks you if you've had enough, and if you're sure that the program's for you. I know a lot of people say that they never had anything like that happen. Well, I don't think so. I'm not going to call anyone a liar, but I don't think so. The entire time I was at BUD/S, I was wet, cold, and sandy. That's one thing I'll never forget. There were times that were different, but that was only because you were wetter, colder, and covered in more sand.

Hell Week was very challenging, especially the first couple nights, because you're up with no sleep. Now I understand more about Hell Week. It's there for a very specific purpose. It's the most stressful situation you can put an individual through, short of dropping them onto a battlefield.

We use that stress on the students today, just as it was used on me then, to make sure they have what it takes to get through a stressful situation. The instructors try to make it as confusing, physically demanding, and stressful as a combat situation. That's where the fatigue comes in. No sleep.

By the time you hit Wednesday of Hell Week, things become a blur. I don't remember much after that day of my own training. After being Command Master Chief at BUD/S, and seeing the students after Wednesday, you realize you can't hurt them anymore. They just kind of go numb. But those first few nights, those are the ones you can make the most stressful on the students, physically and mentally, because they're entirely cold, wet, and sandy.

Can I describe the cold? All I can say is that it's something that starts from your head and goes through the core of your body. You can feel it through your bones. You shake, shivering to a point where it exhausts you. That's about all I can remember about being cold.

I think what got me through Hell Week was that first, I put my mind someplace else when I was sitting in the surf zone. Instead of being on that cold, dark, beach, I was on a Caribbean island. Looking up at the moon, I thought about the sun beating down on that island. Then I started humming. That helped out.

What else helped me through Hell Week was working with the other individuals as a Team. At BUD/S, there's that one time that one individual going to sit there and say, "I think I've had enough." His partner is going to look at him and say, "Take one evolution at a time. Hang in there until tomorrow." When tomorrow comes around, the roles have switched. Now the other individual thinks he's had enough and his buddy talks him up.

So the two things that really got me through Hell Week was, first, myself. You go into your mind and decide that you can take it, that you can keep going and push through the limits. The other was my classmates, my future Teammates.

A SEAL will always remember his class number, and he will also remember the Teams he was in. The number is not classified, but it isn't widely known, either. If someone says they were a SEAL and they don't remember their class number—if they haven't had a brain injury—they were never there. The only way into the Teams is through BUD/S. There are no shortcuts, special classes, or transfers in from other services. For a very short time, corpsmen had to go through special training to get into the SEALs, but that has changed now and they all go through BUD/S. It's the only way to become a Teammate.

Graduation day from BUD/S was probably one of the greatest feelings of my life. I had just completed twenty-six weeks of hell, and I felt good about myself. I was physically in the best shape of my life. I went from 200 pounds down to about 175 or 180, but it was hard weight.

But just the feeling of being able to join the ranks of the Teams, to become one of the elite after twenty-six weeks of not torture but really strenuous mental and physical training, was one of the real high points of my life.

After graduating BUD/S, I went straight to SEAL Team One. Like any new meat in the Teams, I was assigned to the Master-at-Arms shack and quickly put to work painting. Gary "Chambo" Chamberlin, who was my sea daddy, picked me up for Kilo Platoon and made me his point man. So my first year and a half in the community was spent at SEAL Team One on the West Coast.

A sea daddy is someone who takes you like a child and puts you under his wing. Pretty much what he does is groom you for the community. He's helping show you the way to be a good operator without stepping on you. Once you get to the community, you need someone like that. Usually, a sea daddy will pick you up and show you the ways of the command and what's expected of you, then let you carry on from there.

A swim buddy is, first of all, somebody you rely on whenever you're doing any type of water work. You swim as a team, you work as a team, and you watch each other. Deep down in your heart, a swim buddy is a brother. Like in training, you and your swim buddy and become close. I talked about being in training and how you have to pick up each other's morale. That's what you and your swim buddy do. You pick each other up, and pull or push as necessary.

The single most important thing about being a good operator and Teammate is teamwork. No one has ever been left behind. That fact is part of the Teams, a reflection of the heart and soul of the brotherhood that is first forged at BUD/S. Years in the Teams only makes that bond stronger.

When you first get to the Teams from training, you're on probation. I was fortunate when I got to Team One that a majority of Kilo Platoon was made up of classmates, or Class 100 guys who had graduated only a few months in front of me. So we had a young platoon. It was only after I had been at the command in Coronado for about six months that the platoon formed up and we deployed. That's deploying fairly early in your career. Back then we did a six-month workup to train and prepare the platoon for deployment.

You hold up to the standards, and you got to pin on the Trident after your probationary period was over, usually six months after graduating BUD/S. That was determined by a board who reviewed your record and talked to those SEALs who worked with you. We were in a platoon, so our board was run by the platoon officer in charge (OIC) and the platoon chief. The administration part of the command back in Coronado also had a say in how an individual's probation was going to turn out.

What the Trident meant was that I had finally earned something that I had been waiting to receive for about a year and a half, since I had joined the Navy. It meant a lot to me, and it brought back to me what I had gone through to earn the Trident. It also made me feel very proud to actually be one of the SEAL community.

Even today, I hold that symbol in high regard. I look at the people who have given their lives while wearing that symbol, or the people who have been with me, or fought alongside me, during my career. Then there are the future guys who are going through training today, and tomorrow, who will earn that same symbol. It all means a great deal to me and every SEAL I've ever known.

We have a connection with those who have gone before us, all the way back to the Naked Warriors of World War II. We're the next generation. There's a connection that goes back to the past through the UDTs, the Naval Combat Demolition Units, and even the Scouts and Raiders before them. I happened to be in the West Coast area when UDT Eleven and UDT Twenty-One converted to SEAL Teams. Then a couple more SEAL Teams were added to each coast. That's a constant history and a direct lineage to the Naked Warrior.

In the late 1970s, there was a new enemy rising up against the United States and the free world—terrorism. When a new SEAL Team was commissioned to fight that new enemy, I was one of the privileged ones to be chosen to be a plankowner for the new Team.

Being a plankowner means that you helped establish a new Team and that you were one of the first people in that new Team. The term comes from the old days, when the Navy used wooden ships. A member of the first crew of a new ship was said to own a plank from the deck.

When I first got a chance to meet Dick Marcinko, he struck me as a man who, once given a task, is going to complete that task whatever it takes. Yes, he has been known to burn a few bridges over the years while getting the job done, but that's to be expected. Dick was tasked with some very hard missions in Navy Special Warfare, and he rubbed some very influential people the wrong way. But he did what he had to do to get the mission completed, and you either like him or you don't like him. That's the type of person he is. I like the man because he took care of me just as he took care of all the guys in the enlisted community under him. That's the biggie right there.

The 1980s started a new era of operating. Dick Marcinko was tasked with the mission given to him by the CNO (Chief of Naval Operations—the boss of the Navy) to combat the new terrorism threat in the world. Before that Team was created, I had gotten out of Kilo Platoon and was in Echo Platoon at SEAL Team One. A lot of people have heard about MOB-Six at SEAL Team Two. On the West Coast, Team One's version of MOB-Six was Echo Platoon.

When Dick Marcinko started collecting the men he wanted for the new SEAL Team, he came out to the West Coast and conducted interviews. He combined men from both coasts in SEAL Team Six on the East Coast. When people ask why it was put on the East Coast, I think it was because it was closer to Washington, D.C., and the commander-in-chief's (CinCs) in that area. A CinC is a commander in charge of a certain area, such as CinCPac—Commander-in-Chief, Pacific.

The guys at SEAL Team Six were top-notch individuals. That's who Dick had to pick in order to get this thing off the ground. He had two years to accomplish what the Army took six years to do. The guys were all tight, and that first year we packed thirty hours of work into twenty-four-hour days. As a result, the bond between us developed into a very close brotherhood.

In the early 1960s, before my time, President Kennedy needed an elite group to work in the riverine environment, and the Army had a hard time filling that requirement. So to meet that need, they went to the UDTs and created the SEAL Teams. In 1972, when I graduated high school, terrorism was starting to affect the country a lot more than it ever had before. So in the 1970s, the planners in the military were taking a hard look at how to combat terrorism.

In the later part of the 1970s, both coasts had to have a Team to *answer to terrorist threats or maritime crisis situations. That is a major mission in and of itself. Instead of a whole SEAL Team being assigned that mission, a platoon in SEAL Team One and a platoon in SEAL Team Two were tasked for counterterrorism. That was how SEAL Team Six evolved, from those two platoons combining to a single new Team with the same mission. And when SEAL Team Six was first manned, I would say we had about sixty guys onboard—the same number of men as were in the first SEAL Teams.*

What did it mean to me to be chosen for the new Team? I had to answer this question even in the community. I remember my sea daddies talking about when they formed the first SEAL Teams out of the UDTs. They told me that I would enjoy the new Team and that it would be something different. But one thing that was going to come along with that new challenge would be the factor of getting to do something a different from the rest of the community, which could cause some friction with the operators in the rest of the Community.

But when I was selected for Team Six, I was honored, very honored. I feel that there were a lot of other people who could have been selected for SEAL Team Six. I think that when Dick started the new Team, he was looking for single people because there was going to be a lot of time involved with training. That counted out a lot of married people from the personnel pool.

And to call it like it is, I was in the right place at the right time. I happened to be in Echo Platoon at the time, and we were at the top of the list for the new Team. I was very honored for the opportunity to go there.

Team Six was commissioned in 1980, and our first active combat operation was in October 1983. The kind of unit we had meant that we had the funding to dedicate more time to training to bring us up to speed to face terrorism throughout the world. So for those three years, we trained almost constantly. Dick Marcinko said once that he was going to buy us new toys and buy us new gear—and to believe him that we would be using it. And we certainly did.

A Blackhawk helicopter flying in support of a ground operation. In the open doorway is the door gunner aiming a .50 caliber M3 aircraft machine gun. This weapon can be easily interchanged with either a minigun or M60D machine gun, depending on the mission requirements.

My first year at Team Six, I got a half-day off for Thanksgiving and the same for Christmas. Anyone who says there are 365 days a year didn't spend any time at Team Six. On Marcinko's training schedule, there were 465 days in a year. But things got a lot easier the second year, when I got a day off for Thanksgiving and a half-day off for Christmas.

Our first combat operation at Team Six was in Grenada under Captain Robert Gormly. Because it was my first actual combat mission, I will never forget one thing about getting ready to go in. When we were getting our intelligence dump on the operation, Gormly held up a blank sheet of paper and said that was our Intel on the island.

The mission I was involved with was down at the governor-general's mansion where we were going to recover Governor-General Scoon. We were a little bit late going in on the op. Our helicopters were supposed to have inserted us right at sunrise, but instead we ended up arriving in broad daylight. Whether the Grenadians were tipped off on the operation or not, I don't know, but we took antiaircraft fire coming in across the island.

In the helo, I remember looking across at all the people we had stuffed onboard. We had three more people onboard the Blackhawk helicopter than we were supposed to have. As the number one, I was going to kick the rope out the doorway when we were over the target. My partner, Rich, was with me, and he had his hand and elbow on the rail that extended out to hold the fast rope clear of the bird.

Looking over at the Vietnam vets we had in the Teams, they were all smiling at us. Then one of them said, "How's it feel to be shot at?"

Hey, not too bad, but we couldn't do anything back. Our M60 gunner had decided to test-fire his weapon across the ocean on our way in. He lifted the aluminum feed tray cover on the gun as we were moving at the helicopter's top speed. The slip stream just ripped the feed cover from the weapon, tearing it away and wrecking the gun for the insertion. So we had no M60 on our side of the bird.

Coming up to the governor-general's mansion, the situation was a little different than our limited intelligence had told us was the case. Most SEALs on the East Coast have spent time down in Puerto Rico and we know the Caribbean. Grenada was the first Caribbean island I saw that had Ponderosa pines, fir trees. And I'm not talking ten-foot trees. These things were forty or fifty feet tall. The gradient at the front of the governor-general's house was greater than a forty-five-degree angle in places.

As the helo came to a hover over the target, I kicked out the rope as the bird was taking fire. Going down the rope with Rich practically on my shoulders and Duke Leonard right above him, I was breaking every branch on one of those big pine trees on the way to the ground. Hitting the ground in a flurry of pine branches, we picked each other up as we stopped rolling down the hill. Now we had to get established and get up to do what we were supposed to do at the mansion.

We had a little trouble with some of the gear because of that fast rope insertion. There came a time when some armored personnel carriers came up to the mansion. They were coming to the gate, and Duke or Bill called down to where I was, saying to get the LAW (Light Antitank Weapon) ready in case we needed it. I looked over at my partner, Foster, and he had this M-72 LAW rocket launcher that looked like a banana. When he fast roped down, he kind of landed on the launcher as he rolled down the hill.

"Denny," Foster said, "you've been in the Army and have fired more of these than I have." And he handed off to me this bent, nasty, rocket launcher.

I actually got the launcher extended properly into its firing configuration, but the back of the weapon, where the rocket was, was bent around a bit. I thought that if I had to use this thing, it worked. Fortunately, I never had to fire it. Once the vehicles backed off, I just folded it back down.

We were supposed to have a bigger punch available to us in Grenada than just the weapons in our hands. There were gunships, AC-130 aircraft, that were supposed to be orbiting overhead and rotate off with each other so one was always there. As it got close to evening, both gunships started being on station at the same time. Sometime in the early hours of the morning of our second day at the mansion, we got the word that more than thirty individuals were coming up to our position. Because our radio's batteries were down, we were very short on radio communications.

Two of the older vets, Johnny Johnson and Tim Prusak, put Rich and me out forward about 50 meters, had us lie down, and told us to wait until they were almost on top of us. Then we were supposed to open up on full automatic and keep our heads down, because they would be behind us with M60 machine guns.

Rich had been wounded in the elbow just before the insertion by some antiaircraft fire. He told me that he didn't think he would be able to reload easily. I told him that I didn't think we would have the time to reload anyway.

While all that was going on with us out on the yard, Ma Bell was taking a hand with the SEALs. Some years later, I remember watching the movie Heartbreak Ridge, and I think they got the idea for a bit in that movie from what happened to us at Grenada.

One of the guys in the mansion used a calling card and got on the phone to Hurbert Field back in Florida and to the operations office there. Over the phone, he ordered a gun run. Both birds overhead were running low on fuel, so only one was able to make one gun run before it had to turn back. That gunship might have saved our butts, even with only one run.

From our "headquarters" inside the mansion, they called in the gunfire and walked in the 40mm gunfire close to our position to eliminate the threat facing us. We were okay as they walked the gunfire in to where we were laying. I remember the area looking like triple-canopy jungle, because the trees were so thick when we came in. The next morning, the area was pretty much open ground. The close explosions of the 40mm cannon shells from that gunship probably contributed more than a little to my losing a bunch of my hearing. But our mission at Grenada, for what we had to do, was a success.

Grenada wasn't the only combat operation I went on while in SEAL Team Six. Most of what we did is still highly classified, but the public does know that we were involved in some very high-profile operations. One of these took place just at the end of the 1980s.

Panama was a joint service, a joint command operation. Everyone knows that we went down there to pull Noriega out of power. As part of SEAL Team Six, our mission was to go and look in different areas, to search out Noriega, and prevent his escape from the country.

For my last assignment of my Navy career, I returned to where it had all started. I received the assignment to be the Command Master Chief at the Schoolhouse, the Training Center Command where all BUD/S training was run. That was a honor for me. I looked at my whole military career, and saw that the Teams have been good to me. What I wanted to do was give something back to the community, and the opportunity to be the Command Master Chief at the center, gave me the opportunity to do that.

I got to take all I had learned from all the veterans before me and all my own experiences to the center and use it to help make sure that we kept up the quality of training. It also helped me make sure that the individuals I was responsible for training would learn the new ways of being a SEAL. It was an honor to go there and have that responsibility. And I finally left, feeling that I did give something back to the community.

My job as Command Master Chief, in my view, was to motivate the individuals going through BUD/S. I used to go in as the new recruits arrived at the command, give my first talk on motivation, then give them a brief history of the Teams themselves. That history alone can motivate people to try to become a part of it.

What I would try to bring out in the individual is to work as part of a team. I would stress to them that teamwork was what it would take for them to get through the program. If they thought they were an individual, they might just have a problem successfully finishing BUD/S.

You cannot tell just by looking at a trainee, whether or not he's going to complete training. Anyone who tells you you can is wrong. The years I was at BUD/S, I would look at certain individuals and try to "see" if they would be among the graduates of a class. The trouble was, often as not, that was the first person to decide that the program wasn't for him. And I looked at other individuals and thought that they might have a problem getting through, but they ended up being the strongest in a class and helped motivate their classmates. Sometimes, a guy I thought wouldn't even make it, ended up as honor man for his class.

It was so funny to see who would and wouldn't make it. There was no standard. Most people think you have to be a football player or athletic star to be a SEAL. SEALs come in all sizes. To be honest with you, football player-types, which is nothing to say against that kind of person, I've played football myself, are usually the first persons to leave the program.

I've even had swimmers and marathon runners come through, but even that one field of expertise in their favor wasn't enough and they

Mud, mud, and more mud. Such is the life of a BUD/S student during Hell Week, as the face of this student well illustrates.

U.S. Navy

dropped. It's that individual who has a basic running pace and maybe a good swimming pace—the ability to pass the screening tests makes sure of that—are the ones who tend to make it through the program.

As the Command Master Chief, I had the opportunity to run a couple shifts during training and look at the students from the instructors' standpoint. During Hell Week there were times I would look in an individual's eye and you could see his desire to become a SEAL waver. This particularly happened during the first two nights, because that's when the students are still shaky about what they've let themselves in for.

Tuesday night, when they go into the chow hall (they get four meals a day, mid-rats are at midnight) they've been cold. Now, you've just put them into a warm environment. You know exactly what's going through their heads, because you can see it in their eyes. The motivation goes down.

So you try to pick them up. I used to walk around and add a few jokes to the atmosphere, to try to bring their motivation back up and not let them just sit there and clam up. I also used to explain to the individuals how there was this little man who would show up your shoulder and tell you that you'd had enough. What I used to tell them was to take their fork and just stab the little sucker, to get him off their shoulder.

Sometimes, especially on Tuesday night, I would be walking around and see guys stabbing at their shoulders when they saw me looking. They would smile and I would know that they had won the fight for at least that moment.

You might see a student next to the mud just shaking from the cold. And as an instructor, you could see that he was wavering but was otherwise a good prospect, so you'd toss him back into the mud. People who would see that might not understand. But it's a little bit warmer in that mud than it is standing there in the outside air.

Tuesday night was probably the worst night in Hell Week while I was Command Master Chief, as far as DORs (drop on request) go. If we took that warm chow hall out of the equation and had them eating out in the cold, I don't think we would have quite as many drop-outs. But that's all part of the program.

In spite of all of the testing they've tried, the physical and mental screening, no one has been able to come up with a guide to say who would or would not make it through training. It's the heart, what the guy has inside himself, that counts the most toward graduation and the Teams. You just can't tell by looking at them or talking to them. Who makes it is not determined until the day they graduate.

The purpose of Hell Week, and something I tried to stress when I took over as Command Master Chief, was to prepare the students for a combat situation. Hell Week is the most stressful situation that we get to put the students through to see if they have what it takes. They have to still be able to function in that situation and be productive, and the only way to know that is to put them through it.

I used to compare the students' paddle to a weapon. Their IBS (inflatable boat, small) was their way of insertion and extraction, so they had to take care of it. Their kapoks, or lifejackets, for flotation were their web gear. So if a student was coming through the surf and lost his paddle, he had lost his weapon, and he couldn't be productive to the team without it.

That kind of thing was how I handled Hell Week when I held the position. It was, and still is, a necessary test. There hasn't been anything better than Hell Week to weed out the ones who can't meet the challenge. And the concept of Hell Week has proven itself over time—since the very first days of training back in World War II.

The phrase I used to use in training was: "There is no 'I' in SEAL Team." That phrase means there is no room for individuals. That's not what the Teams are about. It isn't about an individual. You hear stories about certain outstanding people in the Teams, SEALs who have committed incredible acts of bravery. But guess who made that individual? It wasn't just the individual, it was his Teammates.

Sure, everybody gets and deserves personal recognition. One of the biggest things I ever heard one of these outstanding individuals say came from Mikey Thornton regarding his Medal of Honor. We had a discussion about it once, and I don't think he would mind me repeating what he told me. He said that it wasn't his Medal of Honor; it was the Teams', that the Teams earned it. I highly respect him for that opinion. That's what it's about. That's why there is no room for the individual in the Teams.

To complete BUD/S takes three things: the mind, the heart, and the body. The most important thing from those three factors to successfully get you through BUD/S is, first of all, to have the will inside you. You've got to have the heart, because it will take a lot of heart just to get to BUD/S and it takes heart to adjust to the situations you will face every day and take what's going to be dished out to you. The heart will drive you on when you think you can't take another step. When the cold gets to you and you can't face the icy ocean, the heart will move you into the surf.

The second thing in order of importance is the mind. You have to be able to sit there and mentally take each evolution as it comes. You have to not anticipate, not worry, and block out what you're facing and the misery you're in. And your mind has to be able to tell your body to keep going and how to get the job done, even when it says it can't.

The third thing you need is your body, but that's almost the least of the requirements. Because guess what we're doing at BUD/S? I don't care what you are when you get there or what you did in the past. We're going to physically and mentally break you down. Then, we're going to rebuild you to meet the needs of the Teams as we know them.

So the most important thing you can bring with you to BUD/S is your heart, the desire to be in the Teams more than anything. You will have to have the discipline, your mind, to keep going and to drive yourself forward. Last, you have to prepare your body to complete the screening tests and be able to do what's expected of you. But the instructors will see to it that you get enough exercise to meet that last requirement. We'll take care of that for you.

I wouldn't exactly use the terminology "made intentionally hard" when describing BUD/S. What would be a better question is why do the standards that we hold the students to seem so high? The standards at BUD/S are high because we are trying to get a good-quality person through the program and on to the Teams. Any person who volunteers for the program and steps through that door at the training center can be one of those quality people. It's up to the individual. I think because of the ratio of a graduating class compared to those who started, around 25 percent just for a round number, a lot of people think that it's just a too difficult program.

Don't get me wrong, it is difficult. But it's that way for a reason. It's the only way to test the heart and mind of someone who wishes to be a SEAL. The training has proven itself time and time again. And if it was to fail, Teammates would die in combat.

The money handlers, the bean-counters in the Navy, would see benefits if the standards at BUD/S were lowered. A higher percentage of students graduating would mean less money being wasted on the students who drop out. But the Teams would pay for those lowered standards in the long run. The thing that we get from BUD/S as a final product is a quality student. As Command Master Chief, I didn't like the idea of sacrificing quality to get the quantity. As an operator in the Teams, I couldn't stand that idea.

Making training easier by lowering the standards would save the Navy money in the short run, but it wouldn't benefit the Teams. You would be balancing quality against quantity.

As an operator, I would rather take two quality individuals to the field rather than thirty who met a lower standard. The standards have been set from the earliest days of the UDTs. The demands of BUD/S have not lessened since those days. If anything, they've gotten harder. Being Command Master Chief, I can say that the standards have to stay where they are.

We've gotten smarter since the days I went through training. Medically, we take better care of the students as we've learned more over the years. Some of the older Frogmen, myself included, still have scars from the old gear we wore in the sand. But that's been changed today. We still want an individual to make it through the program, but only if he's good enough. Anything less would hurt the Teams badly, and it would lower their mission profiles.

Who are SEALs? Most people have heard how they use SEALs bare hands as weapons, or that they're all martial artists. Or the SEALs are all weapons experts, spies, or supermen. The term I like to use to describe a SEAL is jack-of-all-trades. I didn't say expert-of-all-trades. What you have to do is be aware, be knowledgeable, and be competent in different fields, because SEALs do work in the sea, air, and land.

Once a man gets into the SEAL community, he might become an expert in demolitions or work in the communications field. Over time, a man might become the guru of Air Ops for his Team. And we do have our own program for close-in fighting skills. But the point I'm trying to make is that the better SEALs are not specific experts in any one field or even in several fields. What makes a very good operator is some skills in a lot of fields.

To any young man who would want to be a SEAL, I would tell to start being more active in your running and swimming. Start working out under proper guidance. Today, education plays a major factor in a person's career in the Navy, or anywhere, so study hard and learn. Keep your grades up, keep your motivation up, and keep driving forward. Whatever is telling you right now that you want to be a SEAL, keep that in mind. Don't get carried away by the books and movies you see—those are entertainment. There's no way to test yourself until you get the opportunity to step though the doors at Coronado and get to BUD/S.

Erick Peterson, Ensign

It had been a long haul to make it to the end of BUD/S training. Training was supposed to have been a six-month stretch, but because of an injury, I had turned six months into nine months. But in spite of a medical rollback, I had completed the course. A lot of the men I had been in charge of had been in the same boat as me, and I was as proud of their accomplishments as I was of my own. Completing BUD/S had been hard; the course was trying and difficult. But I had made it.

At the end of my BUD/S training, I had only been in the service for about fourteen months. In October, I had started to attend Officer Candidate School (OCS). By January, I had been commissioned as a ensign. Officially, I had only been in the active Navy for eleven months, and the bulk of that had been spent as a trainee at BUD/S.

It was well before joining the Navy that I had learned about the SEALs and the UDTs from reading books and magazine articles about them. I was thirteen or fourteen years old when I decided that being in the Teams was what I wanted to do. My father had been a fighter pilot and had flown F8s over Vietnam during that war, so I had grown up with the mind-set of being a fighter pilot. We even had a private aircraft when I was growing up and my dad had taught me how to fly. My focus had been on attending the Naval Academy and becoming a pilot after graduation, but when I discovered the SEALs, that all changed.

Swimming was always something I had been inclined to. Water polo was a sport I enjoyed, and spending time at the beach always had appeal to me. Camping and trail running were also some things I had done a lot of. So as strange as it sounds, being down and dirty, wet, and miserable sounded more enjoyable to me than flying some hunk of steel at mach one and passing over the countryside without ever really seeing it.

I sadly disappointed my father because of that but I had made the right decision for myself, and at a young age I focused all my attention and energy on making it to where I am now.

The Navy and my training at OCS hadn't been all that hard. When I first showed up at the BUD/S training center that first day, it was quite a shock. My ideas of incredible professionalism, rigidity, and regimentation pretty much went out the door with my first look at the inside of the training center. When I showed up, there were men running around on crutches while other men were all wet and sandy and doing jumping jacks. Still other guys, in the same wet and sandy condition, were doing push-ups. Some men were running about in camouflage uniforms while still others were wearing greens. And among all this chaos were the instructors yelling orders.

From my point of view, the whole place had a circuslike atmosphere. Later, I learned what was going on and how everything came together in that high level of professionalism I had expected. But my first impression of the BUD/S compound was one of controlled chaos, directed with a lot of yelling and shouting.

All in all, my first impression was that it was going to be a long, hard six months. And I was right, but not for the reasons I had first thought.

The hardest part of my six months of training was during First Phase. That is the initial physical training phase. During the first four weeks of training, we did small boat handling. We were introduced to the IBS, or inflatable boats, small, and we used those inflatable boats to conduct surf passage. It sounded simple—we were going to learn how to row a boat through the surf. It wasn't simple.

When I went through First Phase, it was in February with Class 218. The surf conditions in Southern California were dictated by the El Niño

A SEAL Boat crew penetrates the surf zone with their rubber boat during a demonstration.

U.S. Navy

effect, so an average day had four-to-six-foot waves crunching down on the shore, with the occasional eight-footer roaring in as well.

Going though that surf was a nightmare. A lot of my classmates just weren't used to the ocean and quit the course right there because of the surf conditions.

But there were a lot of other activities in First Phase to help weed out the trainees who didn't really want to be there. We had log PT, which was eight guys carrying around a telephone pole. With our poles held overhead, we ran races up and down the sand berms. And there were conditioning runs over long distances in that same sand, only without the telephone poles. Two-mile swims, the obstacle course, and lots of general PT kept us very busy.

The obstacle course was actually kind of fun once you figured it out. But the initial stages of figuring out the course and how to get through

---

the obstacles involves a lot of pain and more than a little heartache. During First Phase, we would be constantly doing physical evolutions, five or six of them a day.

That much exercise and effort breaks down your body. Your body doesn't get a chance to relax, heal, and grow stronger. Instead, you just continually have to force yourself along. It's just a matter of hanging on and staying strong inside yourself. Then there's the fifth week.

The fifth week of First Phase is Hell Week—and it lives up to the hype it receives. That week is just as miserable as it sounds. Somewhere along the way during that week-long period of maximum output and minimum rest, your brain just turns off. The misery stops and you just kind of go into overdrive. Then, things become just a matter of finishing the evolution.

Getting acclimated to being physical from 5 in the morning until 6 or 7 o'clock at night was what made the first four weeks of training so hard for me. As I was an officer, the instructors gave me more attention, but only in that I had to act as a leader to the men under my command. It's unavoidable at BUD/S, that as an officer, you are going to be spotlighted by the instructors from time to time.

As an officer at BUD/S, you are in charge of your boat crew, so whatever the boat crew does, it is a reflection of your leadership. The instructors understand that during First Phase, the officers are learning how to go through training just as the enlisted men are. They don't expect you to be the great leader right from the start, so they don't come down on you more than you can handle—but you do get spotlighted for that extra attention that points out that they will expect a lot from you down the line.

During Second Phase, which was the diving portion of BUD/S for my class, an officer would be put in charge of certain departments. The department I was put in charge of was communications, so whenever we needed radios, or anything to do with communications, if what was needed wasn't there, it was directly my fault. The same situation existed for the other class officers with their departments of diving equipment

A boat crew of students at BUD/S learns the value of teamwork as they struggle to do sit-ups during log PT. The helpful instructor behind them stands ready to shovel on more sand with his boat paddle to help get the students used to working in a sandy environment.

U.S. Navy

and such. If the gear wasn't there, it would be some student officer's fault, not the class's fault, and not some enlisted man's fault. The blame would fall squarely on the officer, because he hadn't checked up on it.

In Third Phase, leaders would really get spotlighted. This was the time that the instructors really brought officers forward and expected more of them. In Third Phase, the class was now broken up into squads instead of the boat crews that we had been in for the first two phases.

The same situation extended to the men's uniforms and equipment. It was the duty of the officers in Third Phase to check their men over every day. You had to be sure everyone's boots were polished perfectly, that their uniforms and equipment were all in order, and that knives sharp and clear of any spots of rust. If one of the men in my squad hadn't shaved correctly or had missed a spot—well, that would be my fault because I hadn't checked him correctly.

That situation introduced the junior officers to the level of responsibility that we would encounter when we finally got to the Teams. In a SEAL Team, we would be responsible for men's lives. In training, we would just be responsible for seeing to it that everyone's knives were sharpened. But if you couldn't handle that, it was a lot better to learn it in training rather than later when lives would be on the line. In was a very good introductory phase on just what responsibility actually was.

The attention to detail that was driven into us, from the very first day when we showed up at training, to the very last day, was constant. Even three days before our class graduated, I was yelled at in regards to attention to a detail. That attention would be what would keep you alive in the Teams. If part of your equipment wasn't right during an operation, if you hadn't paid attention to it, you had a chance of not only killing yourself, but also the men who looked to you for leadership. When you cleaned your weapon, every piece had to be perfect. The attention to detail had to be there, otherwise things couldn't be expected to work when you needed them to. The point that was ground home from day one was that someone could die because you missed a detail.

It was out on San Clemente Island where the final training for Third Phase is held, that they really drove home the need to pay attention to the details. For the twenty-nine days we spent on San Clemente, we studied and trained with small arms and demolitions.

During that time, the instructors made sure that we all knew just what the attention to detail was for. Making sure the small points were all covered and that everything was ready to go when you had the time to pay attention to it was the bread-and-butter of what we were there to do. It was the little things that could get you killed.

That was the important point brought home during training, but it was only one of the points. The really detailed training didn't come until after you had passed Hell Week. A lot of people never got through that evolution. I went into Hell Week with an injury, and a lot of people thought I wouldn't be able to get through it. The tendon in my left knee was torn and I had a hard time walking. But you didn't do much walking in Hell Week—mostly running.

One of the things that got me through the week was the fact that so many of the instructors and others didn't think I could make it. That helped give me the sheer determination to prove them wrong, that I could make it. At least that was half the reason I wanted so badly to stick it out.

The other half was that I really didn't want to go back to day one of training. There was no way I would go back to week one, day one of First Phase training and do log PT, IBS training, and the four-mile timed runs again. In part, it was the fear of having to go back and do all those things that I just didn't enjoy the first time that helped keep me going.

FIRE IN THE HOLE! A UDT operator uses a ten-cap electrical blasting machine or "Hell Box" to fire an explosive shot out in the water. A 500-foot reel of firing wire is lying on the sand next to his knee. This training and the live firing of explosives is experienced by BUD/S students for the first time on San Clemente Island off the shores of California.

U.S. Navy

Of course, there was another way out instead of just getting through that week. To be quite honest, I think most of the guys in my class thought about quitting at one time or another. You thought about it, especially when you would sit down for a meal. That was when the situation would sneak up on you.

At a meal, you would finally be allowed to just sit. You were exhausted, more tired than at any other time in your life, and all you wanted to do was close your eyes. That was when the specter would loom over you, that you could take the easy way out and just quit. We all knew quitting was an option, but most of us never seriously contemplated it. It was an option, but not a viable one. Quitting just wasn't what we were there to do. I didn't go through all it had taken me just to get to BUD/S only to quit.

It was kind of a catch-22 situation. We all thought about quitting at one time or another, but we really didn't acknowledge it as an option.

It was down in the demo pits, about half a mile from the training center, that we heard the phrase that only really means something to a person who has gone through BUD/S. It was next to that stinking pond of muddy water on a Friday that our Command Master Chief secured us from Hell Week.

The instructors were scolding and yelling at us for something we had supposedly done wrong. At that stage of the game, it just becomes accepted that everything we do, no matter what it is, will be wrong.

We were wet, we were sandy, and we were cold—pretty much the standard condition for students during Hell Week. We had been in the surf for a while and then moved back into the sand. Now the instructors had us put our life jackets back on. That meant that we would be getting back in the water and paddle the boats some more.

The instructors told us that we still had a number of hours to go during Hell Week. The morale level plummeted at that point. We stood by in our life jackets and listened to the Command Master Chief scold us, then his words turned around. He started to commend us and congratulate us. Finally, he said that it was his honor and that he was very proud to say that Class 218 was secured from Hell Week.

Men all around me were jumping and screaming, just overwhelmed with joy. I was just pleased it was over with. At that point, my leg was pretty torn up and I was going to be very happy just to get off it for a while. But it was a tremendous feeling of relief and no small amount of pride in myself, that I had eventually accomplished what I had set out to do.

Hell Week is really just a very small portion of the training at BUD/S. But it's what is considered by many to be one of the bigger milestones of the program. And it was a great feeling of relief to have that week behind you. It was another stepping stone toward graduation and the Teams.

There was an expression we learned early on during training, "There is no 'I' in SEAL Team." That meant exactly what it said, that everything you did was for the betterment of the Team and not for yourself. At the end of the day, when you cleaned your equipment, you first cleaned the class's equipment, then the squad's equipment, your swim buddy's equipment, then your own. You, the individual, always came last, and the Team was first. You looked after each other.

The benefit of this philosophy would come up when you were down and hurting, tired, and miserable. The natural thought process would be just to close up, to think about yourself, and to just survive. The idea in the Teams was to think about your buddy. If you were spending all your energy thinking about if your swim buddy was doing well, or if a man in your squad was making it, then it took your mind off your own pain. That helped you; it made your own pain a bit less. And it motivated your buddy to do better. Then he, in turn, motivated you.

If you just sat there thinking about yourself, wrapped in your own misery, then you would miss a detail. If you just worried about your own equipment, you wouldn't get everything ready. But with two, three, four, or eight pairs of eyes on everyone's equipment, everything gets done, and everyone is the better for it. All the equipment gets cleaned and prepared faster, better, and more efficiently. And with that many people paying attention to the details, not much has a chance of being missed. That makes it better for the whole operation as well.

An individual, a person just concentrating on his own situation, could get through a certain part of the training at BUD/S. A number of individuals made it through First Phase, and they even got through Hell Week. But once you got to Second Phase, that's when you had to rely on a swim buddy to get through the evolutions. There was a lot of diving and you could only work with your swim buddy, that other person who was with you on a swim. You had to operate as a team, or you couldn't get the job done.

There are certain aspects of BUD/S that an individual can get through. But the overall aspects of the training prevent that individual from graduating. There just isn't any way to get through training without learning the value of teamwork and just what it means to be in a Team.

During Second Phase, you relied on just one other person. Underwater, your life would literally be in their hands. There's no way to call for help when you get in trouble underwater. In Third Phase, you were relying on seven other individuals. You had to work as a squad. As a group, you had to patrol and do the mission together.

For one individual to do what he wants to do, what he felt was best for himself, that would jeopardize the lot. That kind of behavior is unacceptable in the Teams, and it is gotten rid of in training. The instructors would see it, and the class officer in charge would see it. If that person wanted to be an individual, if he didn't want to become part of the team, he would be singled out and reprimanded accordingly. Or he would just go away.

We were told in training that no SEAL has ever been left behind in the field of combat. That is bred into us from the first day of training. Out at San Clemente Island, my squad went through a fire and movement exercise where we were broken up into two fire teams of four men each. One fire team would give supporting fire to the other fire team as it moved back. The orders somehow got mixed up and one of our fire teams ended up getting "killed," according to the instructors.

That was a simulation, of course; we didn't have students killed just for a training point. But because of that situation, the fire team I was in charge of had to recover the others. We had to run in, under fire, and recover our Teammates and their weapons. Rushing forward, we grabbed up the bodies and the gear, threw them over our shoulders, and carried them out for about a klick and a half or two klicks.

That situation was conducted under training conditions, in a very controlled atmosphere. As soon as we picked up the men and had them on our shoulders, the aggressor squad backed off on their firing and we were allowed to carry our simulated dead away.

That wasn't enjoyable. I didn't like it at all. It hurt to even move, and the area was very hilly and full of potholes. But it gave you the feeling that men's lives depended on you. You would have to carry a man out on your back if anything happened to him. That really drove home the point that you wanted to stay alive—and that there was no way you would ever leave anyone behind. You would bring them back with you.

The BUD/S student of today learns the traditions of the Teams as he goes through training. All the military looks on their traditions, those things that made us what we are today, with pride. In the Teams, the first men who conducted operations against the enemy were the Frogmen of World War II. From what I understand, they've called these ancestors of ours the "Naked Warrior." They went in and conducted their missions on enemy beaches wearing a pair of swim trunks and fins, and very little else. They did their work basically naked, with limited or no weapons and little in the way of even clothing.

These were our ancestors, they were where we came from, and we wanted to hold on to that somehow. Today, we run around in jungle boots and cammies, with thirty pounds of gear on us, but we still have that connection with the Naked Warrior. That UDT man in World War II, in just a pair of shorts, isn't that different from us today.

Often times, our job is to go in "slick," with minimal equipment and as little weapons as possible. What you are carrying with you is what you have, and you aren't going to get any more once you go in. With that, we're doing a job that nobody else can do, that nobody else wants to do. And we're in an environment that few are familiar with—the water.

The SEALs are the best there is in the water. That's our environment. When something has to be done in the ocean, river, or riverine environment, that's when the commands call on us. We look back on those men in a pair of shorts, with maybe a dagger strapped to their leg, and that was all they had to work with. They got the job done, they were our ancestors—could we do any less?

Those are who we look up to, who we want to remember when we go in on an operation. Whether we're loaded for bear or stripped down to our shorts for a basic reconnaissance, we keep the image of the men who have done it before us.

Even though BUD/S training is just about behind us, we still have a way to go before were are really in the Teams. For six months, we'll be watched and tested. Only after our probationary time is completed will we be awarded the Naval Special Warfare Insignia—the Trident.

The Trident means acceptance to me. It is the symbol that you've made it, that your initiation into the brotherhood of the warrior is behind you. To join the Teams, you have to pay your dues, and BUD/S and probation are those dues. The Trident shows that you've earned your right to wear it. It isn't like other military training. You don't just pass classes, do your flights, and boom, there's your pin. You don't just spend time onboard a ship, take a test, and wear a badge. You have to earn the right to wear the Trident.

BUD/S training is considered the hardest military training course in the world. And it's only the basic selection course. All BUD/S does is weed out the men who don't have the heart to do what it takes; it's from there that you go on to advanced training. It's only after you have completed your advanced training that you go on to your probationary period with a Team.

They evaluate you during probation to see if you have learned just what it takes to be in the Teams, and not just that you can do the job, but that you have the heart and mind to continue.

In the Teams, it's a never-ending process of training and evaluation. At the point that it is decided that you have actually proven yourself— and that's a year down the road from when you started in BUD/S— then you receive your Trident. It's a well-earned symbol. It's the Holy Grail for BUD/S students.

Then, once you've received your Trident, the training starts all over again. Now, you're expected to step up to an even higher standard of performance, do even better, keep training, and keep performing. You have to work to stay the best.

Jacob Woroniecki, Operational Specialist Third Class

I've been in the Navy approximately a year and a half, and approximately seven months of that have been at BUD/S. It's a straight-through class for me, no rollbacks. I only want to do this once.

I heard about the Teams from a friend of mine who was a martial arts instructor and an ex-SEAL. I just learned about his lifestyle and was interested for about four or five years. Now, I've gone on from there.

BUD/S was a lot different than I expected when I arrived here. It was a little more regimented than I thought it would be, and it was definitely a stress-shock at first. But you acclimate to the situation very quickly with the rest of the students and hear all the different stories about what you need to do and what you need to not do. You get the scoop on the situation and soon get used to it.

The physical end of BUD/S during First Phase definitely is a stress test. It wears you down both physically and mentally. But if you come in as a regular athlete or someone who has done any kind of physical activity beforehand, it's not as bad. But it doesn't matter what kind of athlete you are or what kind of physical level you are, it definitely will be draining. That is for sure.

The most draining part is the cold water. Cold water takes the most from you simply because it taps as much as it possibly can out of you. The push-ups and the sit-ups and all of that take it from you as well, but nothing like the cold water does. It takes more out of you than anything else.

You remember about the first two and a half days of Hell Week. After that, it starts to become like a daydream. It was stressful, but you just do it. You just keep on going through it. You forget a lot. Even *though you're going through it, and your legs are moving one in front of the other, you start to forget. Then it becomes basically like a dream.*

I just had to keep going. You don't quit, not because everybody else is, you just keep going because you don't stop. That's part of the training, too, I guess. You just don't stop because you have to keep going, you have to do it.

What got me through it? Well, I have a family, and I knew they were behind me 100 percent of the way. That's always good to have in the back of your mind when it's dark and cold. Even though you have a lot of friends around you, you have to have something inside you. For me, it was my family. The friends I was with helped, too, but it was definitely my family who pulled me through the most.

Every day when my alarm went off, I thought of quitting. If the bell would have been close to my alarm, I'm afraid that would have been ringing just about as much. But the walk to the bell was too far, and much too far in the morning. Everybody who says they don't think about quitting is a liar; they always do, but you just don't—that's the real difference.

The most enjoyable part of training for me probably was Third Phase, where you learn tactics, demolitions, and weapons. The parts you don't like stand out slightly, but they're a good majority of BUD/S. The things you enjoyed and the things you learned that you can use later on, you definitely remember. Those are the things that stand out in my memory the most I think.

Hearing the phrase "secure from Hell Week" is incredible. At first, you don't believe it. The entire week is stress games and more than a little bit of mind games. The first time you hear that phrase, what goes through you is of course doubt and disbelief. Then, when you look around and you see that it's really happening, it's just such a relief. You can finally let down some of that guard you had during Hell Week. You can finally consider sleeping and actually getting some good food. It's just an awesome relief.

I helped a few of my Teammates get through Hell Week. A few of them you can't help. Some guys just want to quit. You can restrain them as much as possible, but when they want to really quit, you can just see it in their eyes and you have to let them go. That's really hard.

But the friends you know can make it just need a little push, a little shove, or a little nudge—mentally or physically. Those are the ones who you definitely remember. And we have a lot of them in our class at this point, guys who didn't want to do it, but they did, and they're so happy that they did.

Everyone helps everybody in BUD/S. Everyone is going to have a lull, a low time and you help them past it. I've been helped before. Just a nudge can do it when you're slightly depressed because the last few days have been really hard, really difficult, and you're mentally and physically drained. That's when someone kind of gives you a mental push, just says "let's go," and you go.

There's an expression, "There is no 'I' in SEAL Team." That expression comes from the fact that you're not necessarily a robot, just going along like everyone else. But it's everything together, everybody together all at once. If one guy gets wet, everybody's going to get wet. If one guy suffers, everyone will suffer. If one guy's behind, everybody's going to be behind. That's true, it goes throughout BUD/S. And I don't know yet, but I'm sure it goes throughout the Teams as well.

We never leave anybody behind. It doesn't matter if it's in training, in PT, on a run, or anywhere. We wait for everybody. Everyone starts and stops together.

Having a swim buddy is something that's drilled into us from the beginning of BUD/S. It's the buddy who watches your back. When you're tired, he's the one watching. When he's tired, you're the one watching. A swim buddy is from the first day of BUD/S until, as I understand it, the last day you're a Frogman. A swim buddy is important. He's covering your back, watching your six behind you and you're watching the front. It's just the most important thing.

The Trident, to me, means accomplishment. Everyone goes into BUD/S, or goes into the SEAL program, for one individual thing, and I'm *sure that thing is self-accomplishment, to prove something to themselves. To me, the Trident means accomplishment. It means I've gone through some of the hardest training in the world—and I have more to go—and that I've taken it by the neck and accomplished it.*

I've been climbing that hill, but I'm not near the top yet. It's a long road. But after six or seven months of training, you start to realize that patience is so important. I have a feeling getting that bird is going to be better than graduating from BUD/S.

The Naked Warrior is a reference that basically means you don't need all those breathing tanks and all that different armament, you just need yourself. It's the thinking warrior.

There are a lot of different parts of the military that suggest you need a lot of weapons, a lot of equipment, a lot of this and that. But the Naked Warrior, to a lot of us, means that you are a thinking warrior. You don't need all that, you just need yourself and your brain, and you can get through so much more than the average.

Who are the men who've been in the Teams before me? Wow, there are so many, so many people who I look up to. All the chiefs, the stories we've heard from our different instructors, you just look up to them for all they've been through, all the training they've done, all the different platoons they've been a part of, and all the deployments they've done. It's amazing just to meet these men.

Why do I want to be a SEAL? Interesting question. Self-accomplishment. It's just another rung on the ladder to being a better person, and being one of the best. That's about it, being the best. Everybody wants to be good, not many get to be the best. Being a SEAL in the military today, you can't do much better than that.

■ Chapter 17

THE NEW TEAMS AND THE FUTURE

Since 2002, the organization, deployment, and even the number of SEAL Teams have undergone substantial changes. As it was when the UDTs became SEAL and SDV Teams in 1983, the new changes should significantly enhance the operational capabilities of the SEAL Teams and the Naval Special Warfare Groups. The Teams shall remain a force multiplier, with an effect far greater than their size would dictate, well into the foreseeable future.

Odd-numbered Teams—SEAL Teams One, Three, and Five as well as SDVT-One—are still on the West Coast under the overall command of Special Warfare Group One. Even-numbered Teams— SEAL Teams Two, Four, and Eight as well as SDVT-Two—are on the East Coast at Little Creek, Virginia, and are under the command of Special Warfare Group Two. As of 2002, two new SEAL Teams have been added to the roster, SEAL Teams Seven and Ten.

SEAL Team Seven, part of SpecWarGru-One, was commissioned on 17 March 2002. On the East Coast, SEAL Team Ten was also commissioned on 19 April 2002. Although the newest SEAL Teams add to the overall number of Teams, they do not add significantly to the overall number of active SEALs, which currently stands at about 2,200.

The lack of increase in the number of SEALs is due to the change of size of the Teams themselves. Instead of being made up of eight operational platoons of sixteen men each, SEAL Teams were reduced in size to six platoons. The concept of the smaller Teams fits in with the new idea of deploying SEAL Teams as a whole unit, a squadron, complete with a special boat team and necessary support personnel.

The idea of geographical areas of responsibility for each separate Team has changed with the new deployment procedures. Now, a SEAL squadron will deploy for six months as a unit. Each SEAL Team will have an eighteen-month period at their home base between deployments. This allows the SEALs of a particular Team to train for at least six months prior to a deployment with the support people, especially the special boat personnel, who they will be operating with.

New equipment and technology is being adopted by the Teams to meet new challenges. The newest big-ticket item for the Teams, especially the SDV Teams, is the Advanced SEAL Delivery System (ASDS). Instead of being the wet-type of underwater craft that the Teams have been using since the 1950s, exposing the men to the cold of the water, cramped conditions, and the need for breathing equipment, the ASDS is a true mini-submarine.

The inside of the ASDS is dry. SEALs will be able to operate in a shirt-sleeve environment, traveling to their target until it becomes time for them to lock out of the ASDS and continue with their mission. The ASDS is transportable by air, and the new classes of nuclear submarines being developed today are designed with the means to attach the ASDS to their hulls. The nuclear submarines of just a short time from now will have the ability to transport and deploy SEALs, dry deck shelters, or the ASDS from the moment of their launch.

■ ■ ■

THE SEALs have met every challenge given to them over the years. They have adapted to meet the requirements of their job or of a

A nuclear submarine moves out on an exercise with the Navy SEALs. Secured to the deck of the submarine, and accessible through a loading hatch, is a Dry Deck Shelter (DDS) capable of transporting an SDV or rubber boat and launching or recovering the same while remaining submerged.

U.S. Navy

changing world environment. With the joining of a SEAL to NASA and the space program, they have even gone beyond what they themselves thought possible only a few decades ago. Thanks to Captain William Shepherd, the first commander of *Space Station Alpha,* the SEALs may now be able to change their famous name. Instead of being SEa, Air, and Land, SEALS can now stand for SEa, Air, Land, and Space.

Dave Maynard, Corpsman Second Class

My mother used to read us stories out of Reader's Digests, *and one day she picked this story about the Navy SEALs. That was where I first heard about them and was really fascinated. I think I was a freshman* or so in high school, and the first time I heard the story about the SEALs, I wanted to be one. It was instant, that's what I wanted to be. All the way through high school, I knew I was going to join the Navy and become a SEAL.

When I was a kid in school, I was a total John Wayne, Audie Murphy wannabe warrior. I wanted to join the military. I probably was going to be a Marine, I just wanted to do that. I felt a calling that I should spend my time serving my country, and that's what I was going to do out of high school. What I specifically was going to go into, I didn't know. But ever since I was a small boy, I knew I was going to be in the military. I just knew it.

My enlistment into the Navy came right out of high school. On the delayed entry program I had six months to report, and the time counted toward my reserve time. That was cool, I thought. The reserve time wouldn't take effect until after I got out. That would be time I wouldn't have to spend in the reserves after I left active duty. It wasn't really much of a deal anyway, but as a high schooler it looked pretty good to me. That was 1971, the year I actually enlisted, but I didn't have to go on to active duty until January 1972.

Believe it or not, I had a Navy recruiter who actually told me the truth. And I got into a special BUD/S guarantee program, which meant I would go straight from boot camp to BUD/S. While in boot camp, I was in a special company for prospective SEALs. So I went through four weeks of regular boot camp, then I was already into a regular SEAL boot camp company. We did special training, our regular boot camp stuff, and trips to Coronado, where we ran on the beaches. We did all kinds of things to make us more prepared for BUD/S.

As long as I stayed qualified, everything would go according to the paperwork. So I did everything my recruiter said, because as far as I was concerned, he was the bible on the subject of my getting to the Teams. That guy told me everything I needed to do, and I went by the book and got there. I went straight from boot camp to BUD/S training.

Class 68 was the BUD/S class I started with, but I broke my arm *during about the eighth week of training and finished with Class 69. I didn't have to go through Hell Week twice, but after I broke my arm, I was really afraid that I would be dropped from training. In those days, a rollback was a rare thing. If you got hurt in training, you were usually gone until you could rehabilitate and come back maybe a year or two later. That's what really frightened me, the idea of going to the Fleet. To me, that was worse than dying.*

Fortunately, I had managed to impress Scotty Lyon, the officer who was in charge of our phase at the time, along with Chief Kenny Estok. At least I think they thought a lot of me because I was a really motivated trainee. So they rolled me back to the following class and I didn't have to leave while I recuperated. The medical department put a fiberglass cast on my arm, and I continued BUD/S training with this lightweight cast in place.

When you're nineteen years old, it's great to have a mentor, somebody you really look up to. Scotty Lyon had that professional look, he was the consummate professional, and he had a way of motivating me like I've never been motivated in my life. I had some great instructors, but Scotty Lyon really stood out.

It didn't matter what physical condition I was in or how cold or how miserable I was; when Scotty Lyon walked into an evolution, I felt no pain. In his presence, I was unstoppable. If he was to tell me to jump off a tower on my head, I would jump from the tower. I knew he wouldn't want me hurt and would only tell me to do things I needed to do. I had that much trust and faith in him that I wouldn't question any direction of his. It was because that was the kind of people I idolized that meant I could never quit BUD/S. How could you quit BUD/S when you would give your life for this guy? That's the kind of person he emulated to me.

Overall, the cold, the shivering until you felt like you couldn't move anymore, was the hardest part of training for me. It wasn't just the cold, it was being literally fatigued from shivering so much. Parts of my body would ache from the shivering, and there would be the pins-and-

---

needles pain from the cold and the shaking. I would have preferred to be numb from the cold, anything but that complete pain of just shivering. I became so tired of it. My jaw, and my neck muscles would all convulse and twitch. That drove me nuts.

As far as the running and the swimming, I loved running—they couldn't hurt me with running. The swimming I loved because we were moving and I could stay warm. The obstacle course was something I loved. Obstacle course day was something I could look forward to, especially in comparison to some of the other things we could have been doing. The physical part, the physical challenge of BUD/S, was something I loved. When they were trying to make us do things, I was having fun. But it was the cold that really got to me. That was the biggest thing about that training that got to me.

I was so driven that the thought of quitting never even came to my mind during Hell Week. I was going to be a Navy SEAL. Period. End of story. There was never any question of my quitting; it wasn't an option. I was going to make it through. They would have to physically get rid of me or I would have to break something (which I managed to do) or die—but I wasn't going to quit.

The swim buddy concept is basically the two-man rule. Never do anything without your swim buddy. My swim buddy's name was Mike Faketty. I had torn a cartilage in my knee right before Hell Week and when we did the fourteen-mile run, I literally limped the fourteen miles. When I got done with the run, I could barely walk. And we went right from the run, ate chow quickly, and went into a couple-mile swim. As soon as I hit the water, my whole body turned into one giant cramp, and I could not move my legs. The only way I could swim was to crawl along with my arms. Mike hooked into me and started towing me. He towed me for two miles.

The instructors came over in the boat, told me to get out of the water, and told me to quit. I told them to go fly a kite—in gentle terms. They told Mike to stop towing me or he was going to get thrown out of training. He told them to pack sand. And he got me to where I had to be, in spite of my being physically screwed up. I was a handicap, and he towed me anyway, even at the threat of being thrown out of BUD/S. That's a swim buddy.

Maybe I'm twisted, but Hell Week for me was a proving thing. It helped me define myself, to see myself measured against other guys who went through Hell Week, guys who I really looked up to. I was with these guys the whole way; went through what they did. The ending of Hell Week wasn't so much a relief. I could have gone more days, it wouldn't have mattered to me. The bottom line was that it told me I had accomplished something here. And I was damned proud to be next to those guys who I finished Hell Week with.

To be honest with you, graduation from BUD/S wasn't a big up for me. I just didn't want to get out of there. I wanted to get into the Teams. Vietnam was still going on, and I was so motivated that I wanted to go to the jungles and operate. I was dying to operate. I wanted to get graduation over with, get the pins and diploma, and head out of the door. Just let me get to Jump School; I already had my orders for the trip to Fort Benning.

So for me, graduation was a nice thing, but I had my objectives down the road. Graduation had been a long time coming. I had rolled back a class with that broken arm of mine, so I was there a long time— from May to December. Now I was very impatient and glad to be out of there. All I wanted was to be a SEAL, not a BUD/S trainee.

Fort Benning and Jump School were a blast. I have tremendous respect for the Army. They put up with us, and we were a bunch of jerks. We just had to break all the rules, and we pissed them off all the time. On the runs, we would have to have cigars in our mouths just to piss them off. We would do thing to make them drop us for extra push-ups. Because I had broken my arm, I became very proficient at one-armed push-ups. Even though I had a broken arm at BUD/S, I still had to do push-ups.

When they dropped me down once, I had my hand in my pocket, so I banged out ten one-armed push-ups. The Army only dropped for ten push-ups at a time. I'd just gotten out of SEAL training. When we were dropped for push-ups at BUD/S, it was for fifty at a time. I was going to drop for ten push-ups? Oh, hurt me please.

We had to piss off those Army instructors so they would drop us for push-ups a lot, because we needed the workout. It wasn't like they were going to work us out; what they were doing looked like a joke to us. One sergeant would just get pissed at us. When I was doing my push-ups one-handed, he would run up to me and get in my face shouting. It didn't affect me any, because I had been shouted at by BUD/S instructors.

We did have another sergeant who had been to Vietnam, and he loved SEALs. All the other sergeants hated us, but this one thought the world of SEALs. He called me over and told me to drop down and "Do that again." More one-handed push-ups.

"Now do it with the other arm," he said.

No problem. I banged out ten with the other arm.

"Now do twenty."

I just kept banging out push-ups. It didn't matter which arm I used, and he just stood there amazed as the number of push-ups I was doing kept getting higher and higher. I dug it because I was working out.

Later on, that same sergeant called me into his office and told me that he had the world of respect for SEALs. But he had a job to do and just wanted to know if I would play the game. He knew we were the best and he respected us, and just asked me to play by the rules.

When he said that, just by treating me with that respect, I snapped in and played the Army game. I became an Army, squared-away airborne trooper at that point. He gave me respect, and I had a lot of appreciation for that, so I certainly had to give the same respect back.

To be honest about it, while I was going through jump school I was still pretty motivated. Yeah, this was great. I was sitting there with my buddies through two weeks of ground school and jumped from towers, little buildings, and everything. This was going to be great.

As soon as they opened the doors to the plane and I saw Mother

Earth and realized I was going to be stepping out into that big wind tunnel outside the plane, I literally freaked. This was a new fear, and I'd never had fear like that before. It blew me away. We were ordered to hook up, and I eventually hooked my static line to the overhead cable. I was shaking just a bit.

Then we checked equipment, and everything was okay. I hoped to God that it was all okay, because I didn't want to meet him right now. I was actually going to do this thing. Motivation wasn't what was on my mind right then—the great big step out that door and down was on my mind. All of a sudden, there was the shout for us all to go, and I see these guys going out the door.

They would jump out the door and—woomp! They would be snatched away by the wind. Everybody was going out the door and the line was getting shorter, and I could swear I heard guys bouncing off the outside of the aircraft. Then it was my turn at the door.

Supposedly, you have this airborne position you're supposed to take as you stand in the door. You jump out and count to four. I went out the door and had my eyes closed tight. My scream was snatched away by the wind, just like I was. I knew I was going to die or get sucked up in the engine or something. As it was, I did end up banging off the side of the aircraft.

Supposed to count to four? Yeah, right. I had my eyes closed and just felt the wind go by. The parachute opened and so did my eyes. Looking up, I had a good, full canopy. I had no idea what the count was when that canopy opened, but it was open and I wasn't going to splat into the ground or gum up the inside of an aircraft engine.

Now, I was right back to being Joe controlled SEAL again. Yeah, this is great. Okay, the landing didn't go badly and I'm alive. No problems. It scared the crap out of me. It took two or three jumps for me to finally get squared away on doing that. But it was good, because it made me face my fear. That was the thing about overcoming fear: it wasn't about not having it; it was about getting past it and doing the job. But it did scare the crap out of me.

Finally, I got to a SEAL Team, and I loved it. I was over there with legends like Mike Thornton and Leon Rauch. Leon Rauch looked like James Coburn, only this guy was for real. James Coburn is an actor who does movie parts; Leon Rauch walked it for real life. And he was just one of many. I got in a platoon where my leading petty officer (LPO) was a SEAL named Wade Puckett. He had six or seven trips to Vietnam or some crazy thing like that and I didn't know it. He didn't even look like a SEAL. He was the quietest, mellowest guy in the world, until we started operating and he was training us.

The first time I saw Wade Puckett tactically move and patrol, I was in awe. I'd never seen a human being move like that. What he taught me was invaluable. He took a liking to me and was training me to become a point man, so I got a lot of personal attention from him.

Another guy in the platoon was Kirby Horrell, a crazy and funny guy. Other guys—Frank Sale, Terry Davis, and more—were just funny. Every evolution we would do was like spending the day with a bunch of Richard Pryors because they were so funny. Until they started operating or serious training that is. Everything would click. All of a sudden they were all these serious, dedicated, knew-what-they-were-doing professionals. Total professionals. But in between, they were the Keystone Cops, and I was very happy to be there.

One thing that really stood out, and this was probably a major event for me, was a training op we did with Wade Puckett when I was all of maybe twenty years old. After a training op, the standard thing is to do a debrief of the op. We were all just standing there, and I was surrounded by these guys who just impressed the hell out of me. I felt lucky that they trusted me enough to let me have a gun, let alone be out there working with them.

Then Wade just floors me during the debrief. He looks at me and asks, "Well, Dave, what did you think?"

He was asking me, airhead of the north, what I thought. And I started putting out what I thought. He took what I thought under consideration, and he listened to what I said. I actually helped developed an

SOP for an upcoming event, because Wade developed the SOP from my recommendations right there on the spot. All I could think was, Wow.

That pulled me into the Teams. That took a twenty-year-old kid standing next to these decorated combat veterans and made him an accepted person. I had gone from being a kid in high school, and after a year's training, and was now standing next to men I considered some of the best fighters in the world. Here I am, I thought, I'm home.

After six months of very intense work went by, I had completed my probationary period in the Teams, although I hadn't noticed the time going by. I was called in to the air loft for something. I think I was getting ready to head out to Free Fall school, so I figured they were going to give me another briefing on something.

When I got to the air loft, there were a bunch of the guys from the platoon in there. One of the guys had a Trident in his hand. He said something like, "Hey, we want to give you this award. Here's your Trident." And he stuck it on my chest.

There were three metal prongs, about a quarter-inch long, on the back of the Trident so it could be secured to the uniform. I had no idea what was coming; I was too new to the Teams. After he put it on my chest, he hauled back and slammed his hand down hard onto it. Boom. He stuck it right into my chest.

It actually felt kind of good, after the shock wore off. I looked down and saw that big, gaudy, metal badge on my chest and just said, "Hooyah."

That was a good day. I had to buy the beer, but I was a very proud young man, and I felt very fortunate to be standing there with these men, and to be accepted as one of them. Very fortunate indeed.

For me, the Trident is an emblem of honor. That I could wear something that has represented so much to so many men is humbling. Here I was, just this average Joe Blow guy, and I'm wearing something that represents to me these heroes who have done all these wonderful things through their history. I was just one of the guys who came along through the flow of time, and I got to wear that. Honor, that's what it means.

One thing that all the guys do is tell Hell Week stories. Joe DiMartino went through kind of a different Hell Week. His Hell Week was actually landing on the beaches in Normandy during the D-Day invasion. He didn't do the five-or six-day no-sleep deal, but going through that qualifies him I think.

In BUD/S, you go through Hell Week to simulate the exhaustion and stress of a battlefield. The mental toughness of that guy and the guys with him to do that landing without being properly prepared, that tells you a lot about that gentleman. That requires a lot of respect.

Some of the operations I did with the Teams included training to go to Vietnam. My platoon was the next one in order to rotate to Vietnam, but we never went. Command shut down deployments to Vietnam just as my platoon was trained up to go.

For me, that was a big let-down. To spend a year and a half to train to go do a job, and then be told no, you can't go do what you were trained to do. That was a tough thing to hear.

At that point, I worked up with two more platoons, going overseas on several different occasions. They were just your typical platoon workup, go overseas, and train foreign troops. There was no combat; all the wars were over and there was no combat left. America's position at that point was definitely no more fighting.

However, I did get recalled for the Gulf War. That was a good opportunity for me to see what the Teams were doing, see the new guys, and watch how they operated. They're still the same as they've always been. Watching the platoon work up, you see the same characters today as were in the Teams back then.

What I do see is a difference between the peacetime platoons and the wartime platoons. With my first platoon I worked up with, I felt honored when they finally came up to you and asked you to be a part of the platoon. That was no small honor that they would trust you to operate with them. The older SEALs would kick guys out of a platoon in a heartbeat if they didn't want to operate with them. There were guys who graduated BUD/S and went over to the SEAL Team who nobody wanted to work with. Boom, they were out in the Fleet.

As time has gone on, things have changed. Without war, you don't get to test the true mettle of the men. So some of the platoons are just made up of a lot of green guys. There is a lack of combat experience today. The newer platoons I was working with during the Gulf War were good, but they just didn't have that combat experience that gives you a greater edge.

That doesn't mean to say that once those new guys got their taste of combat, that they wouldn't be ass-kicking SEALs. You could easily see that they wanted that opportunity. They were eager, and they wanted to go into harm's way very badly.

I had a chance to train some of the platoon for the Gulf War, and it was a great opportunity to work and train with them. Other than that, I wasn't in any special operations that are worth even mentioning.

Is there anything a SEAL can't do? That's one of the biggest issues with SEALs, because you learn what your limitations are. You understand what you can't do. That's why you have to cheat a little. You know if you can't do something, so you figure out what you have to do to get around it and still get the job done.

When you can't do something is the most important lesson to learn, and that's probably what gets more SEALs killed than anything else. There are idiots out there who think that SEALs can do all these weird things like jump at night into high seas with high winds, not prepared for that kind of jump. There's a guy who thinks you can do that— and you can't. Other guys will plan ops where the SEALs have to swim fifteen miles to get to the beach, then patrol for another twenty miles. There is a plain reality about what a SEAL actually can and cannot do. What your limitations are is the first thing you have to realize and it can be a very hard lesson to accept.

When you put a platoon of SEALs together, and they put all their heads together to attack a problem, it will absolutely amaze you what they can come up with. When everybody starts throwing their ideas in, you can come up with some incredibly unique and innovative ways to accomplish the objective.

Say the platoon was ordered to go in and hit these Marines. We did this mission as a reserve unit. Going in, we found that there were some three hundred Marines guarding one target. They had night vision, heat sensors, thermal imagers—all the hi-tech gadgets to try to catch us. We sat and figured out what we were going to do by putting our heads together as a team. In most cases, the officers stood by but just kind of shut up and let the enlisted men figure things out.

With out plan roughed out, we told the officers what we wanted to do and we all worked it out together. The officer did the big planning thing and we prepared to do the op. Going in, we had four different squads hit that target from four different directions. The Marines never knew we were in and out.

When you see stuff like that done by a group of men, it's impressive to watch. Some of the operations we did were sudden actions that took a fast response. When the Mayaguez incident went down and the Khmer Rouge captured the Mayaguez off Cambodia, I happened to be overseas at the time. We were called on to go in and take back the ship. We were supposed to go in unarmed to the beach where the ship was being held, hold up a white flag, and ask for our sailors back. Obviously, we told them to go fly a kite.

We did have one SEAL platoon, Bravo Platoon, that was going to go in and hit the target, recapture the ship, and take back the hostages. My platoon was a backup platoon to support the first one in. We were all locked and loaded and ready to do it. Then Command backed down from sending us in. Instead, a bunch of Marines were sent in, got shot up, and generally didn't have a very good time of it.

We weren't going to go walk in on the beach, like the Marines were directed to do. We would have done it the smart way—sneak in and kill them before they could kill us or the hostages. Command just didn't want us to go.

A result of the incident was that the SEALs received a directive to develop a way to get onboard a ship. So we figured out a way to get onboard a ship from the water. That platoon started the ship-boarding procedure, working from the water where a group of swimmers can get on deck to take back a ship.

That's evolved into quite a large evolution now for ship-boarding and ship takedowns. It's kind of interesting to see how it's grown. That just shows you how people adding their ideas to one idea keeps it growing and growing. We literally used to use a slingshot to shoot a little lead ball up and over a boom that was sticking out over the side of a ship. That lead ball would carry a fishing line up and over the boom that would let us pull a heavier line up after it. Then we could pull up a rope and finally a ladder.

Another way we used to board a ship was by going in with swimmer delivery vehicles, up to a ship underwater, work the ship, get all the way up on deck, and continue on. That worked great. Now they are a lot more scientific about coming up with these ideas.

SEALs spend a lot of time in water. Ocean critters have not been something I've ever had much trouble with, although some of the encounters I had while I went though BUD/S training were interesting. Because I worked as a point man, I was always selected as the swimmer scout, the first man in, on insertions.

My swim buddy and I were swimming in to the beach during training when some sea lions decided they wanted to play with us. The problem is, at night, when big things swim through the water, they make this phosphorescent glow. All you see is this big missile-looking thing swimming around your legs, and you don't know if it's a sea lion or a shark.

I was not having a good time on that insertion. All I was doing was waiting for the crunch of teeth into bone. I didn't know what these things in the water around me were, and I was freaking out. I didn't know they were sea lions until one of them popped up and looked at us. It was just kind of a "Hey, what's happening?" kind of thing on his part, then he was gone.

I was trying to be quiet, but when you see something come up and look at you, and it looks like some kind of sea monster in the dark, you tend to swallow a bit of sea water. I think I put down about three gallons. That was hairy, and swimming at night was not my forte—especially not after seeing that stupid movie Jaws.

Watching Jaws and then doing a night swimmer recon was a dumb thing to do. Real smart. Your imagination tends to run a little wild, and any deep string music from the background would have gotten a very bad reaction from me. So of course my swim buddy starts singing the soundtrack to Jaws. He could see that I was really strung out. To this day, I still think he's an asshole for that.

Other than that problem with my imagination, I never had much in the way of shark encounters. Mostly, I had problems with sea snakes—the most poisonous snakes on earth. We would be out doing operations in the water and I would have some wrap around my feet. Sea snakes aren't aggressive, so if you're careful and play the game with them, they don't give you much trouble. They have really small mouths so it's hard for them to bite, but don't piss them off.

There was another critter encounter several of us had underwater, but this one was done on purpose. We were one of the first groups to be tested for the dolphin program, which was the counterswimmer program where the Navy would use dolphins to locate swimmers around ships.

The testers, a bunch of idiots as it turned out, told us to go and swim in to a designated ship. They told us that there were going to be dolphins in the area and when they tapped us or butted us with their nose, we should swim to the surface. In effect, we were told to surrender to a fish.

I thought this was kind of cool and not much work, so my swim buddy and I were swimming in to the target ship, really hugging the bottom and staying low. We figured that the lower we were, the harder it would be for the dolphin to figure out just what and where we were. Wrong.

The next thing I knew, my swim buddy was knocked into me. This wasn't a tap—his whole body slammed into me from the side. We were *just swimming along and then—boom! He was freaked out and pretty close to panic. When I looked at him, all I could see were these two gigantic staring eyeballs filling his face mask. I wondered was just what the hell his problem was. Then I found out.*

Tuffy, one of the first porpoises trained by the Navy as part of their Marine Mammals program.

U.S. Navy

*The dolphin came back around and stopped right between us. That critter looked at us and we could see the meaning in his eyes—*You want some more? *My swim buddy and I just looked at each other for a moment. We didn't know what to do, and both of us were frozen in place. We were so scared and didn't know what the hell this thing was going to do to us. We didn't know if he was horny, playful, or just mean.*

Freaked out is a pretty good description of how my swim buddy and I felt right about then. The dolphin took off and we both knew that he was coming around to hit us again, so we headed to the surface fast— real fast.

Our original plan was to cheat, to just ignore the dolphin when he tapped us and just keep going. Well, it wasn't a tap and we didn't ignore him. After we were hit like that, we were on the surface quick. No more of that, no more of those big fish under the water. That's their ocean.

Fortunately for me, when I left the active service, I stayed in the Department of Defense training programs, where I've been able to continuously train with the SEALs, either as a reservist or as a DoD employee. Over the course of the last thirteen or fourteen years, I've had the opportunity to train SEALs in a variety of areas. What I've seen in the younger SEALs is that they are very hungry for knowledge. They want to be SEALs as much as I did, and they have the skills and the physical capabilities to do it all.

I see these guys, and it's really great to watch them as we train them. We do some radical training with these guys today. You watch them at first struggle with the training, then all of a sudden they pick up what's going on and kick in and just blow you away with their capability. I get a chance now to train with S.W.A.T. teams and other special forces and law enforcement units—a lot of different training groups. The SEALs compared to these other people is just night and day.

With working with the history project, and having the opportunity to interview the guys from the World War II Teams and way back when, has solidified the connection I feel with the Naked Warrior of days gone past. When you go through BUD/S, a big part of it is UDT training. You're doing the drop and pickup (cast and recovery), the recons, the swims—you are a Frogman. You're still the Naked Warrior. Even today, the students are still doing BUD/S training as a Naked Warrior. It's a good portion of the curriculum.

And you totally identify with those older Frogs. If you could change time, you could take that guy from 1943 and put him into today's platoon of SEALs, you would have a group of all the same men. I really believe that. Listening to those vets, how they look at life, how they respond—that's the same guy as in the Teams today. I feel totally attached to them, and I feel blessed that those guys learned all those lessons in the past, some at a terrible cost, they were able to pass down to us. They give us all this history to look back on and live up to.

Working with these men on this project, saving their history, their own personal stories, it's just undescribable. Sometimes, you listen to these guys give an interview about say, landing at Normandy. These aren't actors, this isn't a movie, these men did it—they were there on those sands, hearing those explosions, feeling the bullets snapping past, and they did their jobs. Sometimes I have to go outside and take a half-hour walk just to get emotionally back for the next guy.

And you have to be ready for the next guy. You must show that respect. These guys have done so many phenomenal things, and the humility they show about what they did comes across. They give their Teammates credit for the job getting done—not what they did themselves but what they feel they all did. It puts you in your place. It humbles you to a point where you have a hard time accepting the fact that you are privileged to receive the honor of hearing their stories, let alone record them.

It's a high honor just to be able to sit next to these men and listen. We're very lucky.

I want that older generation to be known for what they did, and I want to see the younger generation accept the older. I want them all together to see that they are all uniquely one. They are all the Teams, all the way back. If it wasn't for those guys in World War II, doing what they did, these guys coming out now wouldn't have it. They would have a bunch of good gear and hard training, but they wouldn't have that soul inside. It wouldn't be there.

That training that was created way back in those dark days in World War II has followed through all these years. It's still finding the right guys to come out of the test of training. All the gear, all the high tech doesn't mean a thing without the right guys. And by doing this project, we're going to bring all the guys together.

When these new guys coming out of training go to reunions, they'll see the old guys sitting there, gray hair and not a lot of it, some hardly able to walk. Now they'll realize that those men are legends, that those people built the story of the Teams. They made the legend real with their blood, sweat, and sacrifice. I don't want to see the legends die, and this project will bring the legends to the forefront.

One subject I have studied for years is the mind-set of being prepared for combat. Because I trained to go to Vietnam, I went to sleep every night expecting to go into combat. I was prepared to go into combat, and I wanted to go. When I didn't get that opportunity, I missed out, and that desire to go never left me. The mystery of what combat is like, and how I would react to it, has never left me, either. I've been a student of it ever since.

I do a lot of force-on-force training—that's man-to-man fighting with hands or weapons, or shooting nonlethal projectiles at each other—for years and try to really understand the mind-set, and what's going on inside the heads of the guys who do this work.

What I see with the SEALs is an initial breakdown in their technique. They will make mistakes. But what you constantly see with the SEALs is their commitment to each other. Once you get them focused on their commitment to each other, past the nuts and bolts of what they are trying to learn, that's when they start doing incredible things so that they don't let their buddy down. They are more worried about their buddy getting shot than they are about themselves.

Of everything I've seen from this project, it is these people talking about their combat experiences and how they're bonded with the men they had those experiences with that stands out the most. They were in these hellacious gunfights, where they didn't know whether they would come out alive or not. When the fight was over, they looked to their left and right and saw their buddies still standing there. They fought right alongside each other.

That sends a message. They don't say it out loud. You're not going to hear the words come out of a SEAL's mouth. But there's a message in their actions, a knowledge that each and every SEAL lives with every day. That message is, "I love you so much that I'm willing to die with you. I'll die for you. There's no way I'll leave you in the field, dead or alive. I cannot leave you there." That's a powerful message.

How many people do you know in life that will give his or her life for you? Here you have a whole platoon of these guys working with each other on a day-to-day basis. That's why these guys cannot leave the Teams, because they'll never be with a group of people that care that much about them, that will sacrifice that much with them and for them.

Your Teammate is your brother, somebody you come to care so much about and know so well that you would do anything for—and you know he would do anything for you. You can abuse him physically, get in fights with him, argue with him, and cut him down, but it all actually brings you closer together. Being in the Teams is like having an extended family. When you get into a platoon, you have fourteen new Teammates, and you get very close to those new Teammates. That platoon goes away and you get another platoon, and now you have fourteen new family members. You get very tight with them as well.

The Teammate concept extends even beyond the platoon level. Maybe you'll work with another platoon and perhaps one of the guys you were in BUD/S with, or were in an earlier platoon together with, is there. You ask him what he thinks of another operator, and he tells you he thinks he's a good operator, that he would operate with him. That's probably the ultimate compliment you can get in the Teams: "I'd operate with that guy."

That's saying a lot. That's not just saying that you'd go and work with somebody. Operating with someone means that you trust them, that you can trust them with your life, that you'll risk your life for someone, that you'll go into combat with them. That's what makes it a tremendous compliment.

When you hear that no SEAL has ever been left in the field, a lot of people wonder why, if the guy is dead, would you risk everything to go back for a body? To put it in a more understandable frame, think about yourself as a parent and then think about your kid being hit by a car or something. Would you just leave him there, just laying at the side of the road? You couldn't leave your kid. And because you love your kid so much, whether he was dead or alive, you couldn't ever leave him behind. You'd risk your life for your child. The thought of walking away just couldn't enter your mind. That's loving your brother, your Teammate, so much that you wouldn't ever leave him behind.

That tenacity is what brings the Teams together. That's why they fight so well together, because they will die together. You'll have to kill every one of these guys if you're going to beat them—that's the only way.

Bill Shepherd, Captain, USN (Ret.)

First I was an ensign in UDT Eleven, a lieutenant, junior grade in SEAL Team One, then lieutenant and lieutenant commander in SEAL Team Two. Presently (1997), I'm assigned to NASA on a military detail as an active duty Navy captain. I've been working here at the Houston Space Center for fourteen years and have been on three shuttle flights. Fairly soon, my title is going to be Expedition Commander as I take my position as the first commander of the space station.

In the early 1960s, when the war in Vietnam was fairly active, I heard about the SEALs exploits in the Mekong Delta. Shortly after that, I went to the Naval Academy and there was a lot of insight at the Academy about what the SEALs were doing. We had several presentations at the Naval Academy during the course of my four years there that made me very interested in the Naval Special Warfare program and got me headed that way.

To be honest, I was kind of torn between being a pilot and being a Frogman. It turned out that I couldn't see quite well enough to do the kind of flying I wanted to do so I went to Coronado and became a Frogman.

There's an interesting question about what Hell Week was like for me. There were several classes, from about Class 59 through Class 67 that didn't have a Hell Week. As a member of Class 64, I'm in one of the few groups of Frogs and SEALs to go through BUD/S and never have a Hell Week. An observer from Class 68, the first class to resume Hell Week, watched Classes 66 and 67 and noticed that the instructors well made up for the classes not having a Hell Week. The expression was that they had Hell Month instead.

It's probably something that few SEALs will ever admit, that they never had a Hell Week, but there were very few SEALs who would even have had to admit it. It was a political thing for the most part. They tried to lower the number of people who dropped out of the course, but the numbers stayed the same pretty much throughout all the classes. The instructors just made up for the lack of that traditional week by harassing the students for a couple weeks instead of just one solid week.

One observer from Class 68 remembered watching Class 66 be up all the time. The instructors worked the class hard to be certain that the quality of the graduating students was up to their own exacting standards. Not having a Hell Week actually made training harder for us. We were under the gun until the day we graduated. That would have been different if we had gone through the Hell Week rite of passage.

Some family friends worked with the SEALs and I knew a lot about their activities before I made my decision to volunteer for training. I thought the Teams would be a real challenge. When I got to Coronado and became involved with the kind of work that Frogmen and SEALs were doing, I found that my original idea of it was very true. I think it's a very individual and very challenging part of the Navy.

I think our training as SEALs is important in a whole range of activities, including being an astronaut. The training teaches you to be responsible, to never underestimate yourself, and to always be a good Teammate. These are things that apply to almost any walk of life. It's helped me a great deal here at NASA with my being an astronaut, and I think the Teams would be a great experience for people in general.

It's kind of hard to say as a student just where you sit in the ranking of the class. I tried to be good at all things, not bad at any of them, and not really a standout. Part of being a good SEALs is being able to do everything at least well, which is what I've tried to do.

Comparing BUD/S training and astronaut training is difficult because you have two completely different groups of people. The difference between BUD/S and astronaut training is that the people who come to NASA to be astronauts have already been really accomplished people in their own careers, either operationally or academically. So you don't need a lot of sorting out or filtering of the people in order to get a good product. That kind of thing is done up front well before they ever reach training.

At BUD/S, it's a very stressful environment because you want to mold people into a certain way of thinking and acting. I think BUD/S is a lot more stressful to the students who attempt it, but I also think it is so stressful for good reason. Only those who can overcome the stress and still achieve the necessary requirements of BUD/S can complete the course. It filters out those people who are not motivated enough or who are just incapable of pushing themselves past their perceived limits.

In 1975, after having been in the Teams for five years, I went through part of the Navy's post-graduate program, which happened to be in Boston at MIT. It was just one of those career moves you don't often get the chance to make, so I jumped on it and did that for a couple years, then went right back to the SEAL community, except now on the East Coast.

I think BUD/S training is great from almost any aspect. There, you learn to accept huge challenges and learn not to limit yourself. We didn't have a lot of cold weather–specific training at BUD/S, but we were certainly made to stay out all night, wet and cold the entire time. That just shows you that your body and your mind can take a lot more than you think they can. That sort of knowledge is very useful in any kind of survival situation.

To me, the most notable guys in the SEAL community were some of the folks I worked with: Bill Foran, who we called fearless, was an incredible personality; Don Crawford, who's still out in Coronado as a schoolteacher; Mike Fitzgerald, a lieutenant who worked with me a couple times. Mostly the guys who I remember and respect are some of the enlisted and senior enlisted I worked with, even the instructors at BUD/S.

My flight suit is part of my military uniform, and I wear my Trident on it every time I go flying. The outfits you wear here at NASA, either in the training aircraft or the space shuttle, are like a military uniform. The Air Force and the Navy pilots wear their wings, and people who have other military insignia wear them on their flight suits. I wear the Trident. Hopefully, when we're up on the station and doing something that gets televised back to earth, you'll be able to see the Trident up there.

It's kind of interesting what the Trident means, and what it means to me. I'm not sure who designed the Navy Special Warfare Insignia, but I think it's very appropriate for the kind of work we do. I also think it's significant that of all the military insignia on the planet, it's one of the few that's actually a complete animal, as the whole eagle is there.

In the heraldry and business of emblems in the United States, Federal Eagles with their heads erect and up are a sign of peace. When the head of the eagle is looking down, that means you're ready for war. I think that makes it a very fitting insignia for Team guys.

Working with the Russians today really is the last chapter in the Cold War. It's absolutely incredible. When I was an ensign of a junior grade in the Teams, being here and working with these guys was the last thing I thought I would ever be doing. And here we are, not only working together, but having a situation where we fly together in very tight, confined, hazardous environments where we've got to depend on each other. It's a complete turnaround from the roles we all had as military people two decades ago.

Just to give you an example, I've been training in Russia for the better part of two years. All the folks I work with were on the military base outside of Moscow that was set up in the 1960s specifically to provide the Russian military with their corps of cosmonauts. I was there for a long time and people were very curious about what kind of aircraft I flew in my service days before I got to this place called Star City.

"Well, I'm not a pilot. I don't fly airplanes," I said.

"Well, what did you do?" I was asked.

"I was a SEAL," I said. "It's like your special commandos that go underwater and attack things."

The Russians all thought this was absolutely incredible, that in front of them was a guy who, ten years ago, was facing them as their counterpart underwater, somewhere else on the planet. The Russians were very surprised that we were in that situation.

In Russia, I've been in their equivalent of the huge swimming pool we train in for weightless simulation. They had their Navy divers in there. They all support the submarine program and are kind of like a ship's company on a submarine. They're not dedicated diving units separately attached to the cosmonaut program.

The divers knew who and what SEALs are, and they knew the SEAL equivalent in Russia. It took a while for me to establish with them that that was my background, but after they came to know what I had been, we really hit it off well. Those guys thought it was absolutely incredible that a Russian Naval Spetsnaz equivalent from the United States was diving in a pool over there. It took them a while to believe it—it was just such a psychological disconnect that such a situation would be how our two countries would be relating.

Two winters ago, before I started my Russian training at Star City, I went over to do some leg work, some ground work, to see what I was getting in to. I had the privilege to go to Kazakhstan, which is the launch site for the Russian space hardware.

The site is about a thousand miles southeast of Moscow. I went in February, and it was about twenty degrees and blowing snow. I was a guest of the base general, and we went into the compound where their active space crews are isolated the day before their launch takes place. There, I attended a pretty good buffet and party.

As I was leaving, the general took me and another American astronaut aside and we went to the general's apartment and had some vodka. One thing led to another, and we all decided that we had to get up the next morning and go shooting.

It was 7 o'clock the following morning when a bus pulled up and this other astronaut and I got on board and went down to the local police station. There, they had an indoor pistol range set up with about seven firing positions and these 9mm Makarov automatic pistols, a little like an American .380 automatic.

There was a pistol at each position, so we started shooting. Blasting away off-hand, I was at the far end of the firing line. We would shoot a magazine, then put the weapons down and go check our targets.

The first target was the general's. Out of eight rounds in the magazine, he had eight of them in the body. The same thing stood for just about everybody as you went go down the line. There were a pretty good set of holes in the target. Then the general looked at my silhouette target down at the end.

The body of the target was clean—there wasn't a mark on it. Right up on the forehead of the target, there was a cluster of holes about the size of a fifty-cent piece. The general looked at that, then he looked at me, then he looked back at the target.

"I see you've done this before." he said.

It was just one of those things. It took a while for the Russians to figure out just where I was coming from.

Back in the Teams, my sea daddy were a couple of guys really. I think my first sea daddy was Tom Lawson, who was the XO of SEAL Team One, when I went from UDT to SEAL Team. He was a great guy, and one of the things I remember most was that on Friday afternoons, we would have a junior officer bull session. There, we would discuss what was going right and what was going wrong with the Team. That was very productive and one of the few opportunities in my military career that we could really air out what was on our minds.

Another sea daddy I had was Chester Stevens, who was an E6 who got out of the Navy and went to work for the government as a civilian. He did a lot of different special activities, and I had a lot of interaction with him. He was a really good guy, and I would certainly rank him as one of my sea daddies who brought me up in the Teams.

There are people I wouldn't put in the sea daddy category, but who were more than a little impressive. Tom Richards is a legend in the Teams and a great guy as well as a tremendous athlete. He's a very level-headed person. I think the Navy did very well to put him in the position he currently holds. We need more people like him. And people such as Ray Smith, who has been one of the standouts in the Teams' officer corps for a long time. I think the Navy is really well served by having him as a flag officer and doing the things he's doing at SOCOM.

Where's the space program going? I'm not sure anybody has a good answer to that question. One of the things we're trying to decide what this space station is about is the place and the role for humans. Are we destined to live only on this planet, or are we going to go somewhere else? We're going to do research and try to solve the problems that will come up, with the space station.

So hopefully, the space station is a way to allow us to go a long distance from planet Earth and view places we haven't seen yet. This is just a first step in that direction. I wish I could tell you how we're going to do that, what's going to happen, and what steps are needed to make that a reality, but that's all yet to be defined. That's really what the space program is about—learning what we have to learn.

What I would like to bring to the space station and the space program is pretty much the kinds of things I did in SEAL Team or in the UDT platoon as a platoon junior officer. I want to have a good team, to have people do their jobs well and know what they are doing. I want to be able to be given a nice, clear mission and get it done.

Being an astronaut was something I thought about as a kid. When the space program really got going in the Mercury days in the late 1950s and early 1960s, it was clear that you had to be an aviator in order to be an astronaut. It wasn't until I was in grad school that it I realized I could be an engineer or some other type of technical person and get into the astronaut program.

For a period of about nine or ten years, between thinking about flying and getting through grad school, I didn't even think about being an astronaut. One day, it just kind of occurred to me to compare scuba diving and space walking. Some of the things we do in space as astronauts and in the water as SEALs are pretty similar. So I decided to see if I could get in to the space program.

When I was told I would be the first commander of the space station, I felt it was a big challenge—I still think that. Being in charge of an expedition that has this multinational character to it is a huge deal. We're under the control of two control centers, one in Moscow and one in Houston. Most of the hardware is Russian. There's a language issue; we have to be able to think and act in Russian as well as in English. It's something way beyond the types of jobs I've been faced with before in the space program. I think I like that it's such a big challenge.

I'm honored and really kind of humbled that other SEALs look up to me as an example of the lack of limits on what a SEAL can do. Their outlook on me is something I think about it a lot. It's very visible here, being an astronaut and being a Team person. A lot of new guys who I never worked with or never even met probably know a lot about what's going on here and what I'm doing. I think that it's very important that I bring a Team outlook to some of the challenges here at the space center.

The kinds of training and the things that SEALs are prepared to do are very appropriate to some of the demands of space and what the crews are going to be faced with on the day-to-day operations as well

Men from Underwater Demolition Team Eleven make ready an inflatable boat next to a mock-up of the Apollo 14 Command Module during recovery training.

as the hard times in orbit—the bad situations and emergencies. Even though not every SEAL is going to get the chance to fly in space, the average SEAL needs to realize that the training and the things they've been through are very unique.

One of the things I think is really interesting about the SEAL community goes back to one of our best-known symbols, the Frogmen and frogs. Why should frogs even be a mascot? You've got this little animal that jumps in and out of the water all the time. Well, above all else, frogs are very adaptable. One of the virtues of our communities, SEALs and frogs, is that you can put a SEAL in a strange place, like here at the space center, and he'll adapt. That's the way people in our community are trained, and to have people ready to go and adapt to whatever comes along is a very powerful attribute.

Jumping out of the SEAL community and getting into NASA was really kind of strange for me. You apply and go through a lot of screening and selection. You show up at the Houston Space Center and go through interviews, spend an hour before a board made up of a lot of NASA managers, then, you're kind of in the dark for months about whether you made the cut or not.

The first time around, I didn't get in. I waited four years after that and reapplied. This time I was selected. I don't think there's any obvious correlation between being a SEAL and being an astronaut, although a lot of the good things SEALs do and know how to do certainly apply to the job here. I think that was a major factor in my being fortunate enough to begin here.

The Teams: they are always ready, always capable, and always willing.

USSOCOM PAO

In the earliest parts of the space program, we lost a Mercury capsule in 1961 when Gus Grissom was recovered after his flight. After that, NASA decided we needed Frogmen to jump out and put flotation collars around the spacecraft. All the way through the Apollo mission to the moon, UDT people were jumping in and meeting the capsule in the water. But those guys were always on the outside of the hatch. One of the things about the space program now is that we have SEALs on both sides of the hatch. It's kind of an interesting turn of events.

The reason why a SEAL is going into space, probably the first of many, is that space is a unique place. There is no horizon, no limit, no *boundary, to what you can do or what you can think about doing. It's very much the same way SEALs are trained to think when they go through BUD/S. There are no limits to what SEALs can do. There's no place that's too far or too high, and no water that's too cold. That's just the way SEALs are, and that's probably why SEALs will have a place in space for some time in the future.*

Index

Page numbers in *italic* indicate photographs.

USS *Tripoli*, 276
USS *Wisconsin*, 222

KEVIN DOCKERY has been a soldier in the President's Guard under Presidents Nixon and Ford, a grade-school teacher, radio broadcaster, gunsmith, and historian. He even spent time in Iraq and Kuwait during Desert Storm as what he refers to as a "corporate mercenary." As a noted military historian, he has written a number of books detailing the history of the Navy SEALs and the lives of the men who lived that history, including *Navy SEALs: A History of the Early Years*. He has also written a number of firearms reference books, some of which are considered unique in the field. Presently living in southeastern Michigan, Mr. Dockery follows his hobbies of raising Rottweilers, blacksmithing, and knife and sword making.